Social Theory and African

Tribal Organization

Social Theory and African Tribal Organization

THE DEVELOPMENT OF SOCIO-LEGAL THEORY

by

Kenneth S. Carlston

University of Illinois Press
Urbana, Chicago, and London 1968

To My Son

Peter

Contents

Part 5

Part 6

Part 7

Part 8

Introduction

MAN settles upon the land. He is a hunter, a tiller of the soil, a pastoralist. He is a tribal man. A tribal society and a culture come into being. The study of the life of such a people is the concern of the anthropologist, who is found in modern society. The study of the life of the people of modern society is the concern of the other social sciences. No longer is there the anthropological overview of the life of man in a society and a culture. Man becomes segmented into psychological man, sociological man, economic man, and the man of politics and law. Anthropology, the one social science which is capable of growing into a unified body of social theory, remains preoccupied with, although not limited to, tribal man. It is largely a technique of observation and description. The anthropologist is, in essence, a trained observer, living with a people, listening to his informants, making notes, and eventually describing their ways of life. Yet the anthropologist, no less than the psychologist, the sociologist, the political scientist, and the legal theorist, is turning to other social sciences than his own for enriching his discipline. The boundaries of the social sciences are blurring. Those which were laggard in the use of the scientific method are resorting to it in increasing degree. The social sciences are becoming what is known as the behavioral sciences. The behavioral sciences, in turn, may one day converge into a unified body of social theory. To state such a possibility is to create it as an actuality. For it has been the history of western man that, whatever he has dreamed, he has created.

Law is another vantage point from which all the action of a society in a culture comes into view. Law protects the valued expectations of a people. As man performs his host of roles in a society and a culture, repetitive or institutionalized sequences of action appear. They are valued because they enable the realization of values and the attainment of valued goals. Departure from them or interference with them leads to frustration, but aggression must be curbed, if the group is to hold together and continue in its familiar paths. Law emerges as the way in which a society regularly imposes sanctions upon those who depart from or interfere with the performance of valued social norms. Legal norms are but the obverse of the conduct embodied in the ideal norms of conduct with which they are linked and which they protect. Thus legal norms pervade all social action and reveal its structure and functioning as they support its performance.[1] He who would understand law and its place in a society must know and understand that society as a unique whole. Yet his perspective cannot stop at the boundaries of the society. His concept of law and his vision of society must be broad enough to encompass all societies and cultures, if legal theory and legal science are to attain full maturity. It is possible that the legal scientist and the anthropologist will join hands as each pursues his way in the decades to come.

The prodigiousness of the anthropologist's task of describing the total life of a tribal society, revealing all its aspects and their interdependency, meant that much of the literature of anthropology presents slices of life of a people. From the total output of a Fortes or Evans-Pritchard a fairly complete representation of a life of a people may emerge. But he who would seek to re-create from the literature the whole life of a people must, for the most part, search for it in diverse sources. The result is often a patchwork, ragged coat and not a garment of unity of design and intricacy of detail.

Again, the literature sometimes seems to present tribal society in a series of still-life photographs rather than a moving picture. It is social action in arrested motion. The reader finds that at this instant in time, this is the way the society behaved. Forces of integration and disintegration, tensions, hostilities, ideals, values, the ebb and flow of life, are largely hidden.

As a study in social and legal theory, it was felt necessary to investigate a considerable number of tribal societies in order to develop a wide range and variety of data. Each tribal society also had

---

1. For, if in the words of Plato, law is "the leading string, golden and holy," which binds a society together, then the pattern of its golden skeins reveals the structure of the society itself. As it is the scientist's faith that there is an ultimate symmetry, order, and truth in nature, so it is the lawyer's faith that the body of law will express the full image of the society which it unites. K. S. Carlston, *Law and Organization in World Society.* (Urbana, Ill., 1962), xi.

to be seen as a whole, with the law as a product of its life and culture. The author was drawn to Africa as an area for investigation because of the variety of its ecologies and cultures. It is also an area the understanding of which will be enormously important to the world. The tribal past persists in the facade of the modern state. Tribal structures of social action and values clash with modern organizational structures of social action and values. A successful integration of the two is yet to be achieved by the newly emerged African states.

As a study in social and legal theory, the author viewed the science of anthropology as a means and not an end. That is to say, the statement of theory was not to be solely determined by the tribal data and integrated with the tribal data and nothing more. The study was not to be solely a study in anthropology and customary law. It was instead another facet of a search for an understanding of law and society to which the author has long been committed. The first two volumes in this search were of a somewhat macrocosmic nature. They were entitled *Law and Structures of Social Action* and *Law and Organization in World Society*. They adopted the concept of the organization as the principal means for ordering the data. This study has the triple perspective of seeing *man* acting in a *society* and a *culture*. A new and larger domain was thereby opened for integrating social and legal theory.

Kenneth S. Carlston

Ocean Shores,
Washington

Part One

Theory of
the Organization
of Action

Chapter I

The Organization
of Action

The Ordering of Action

THE PSYCHOLOGICAL ORDERING OF ACTION

SOME 2,000 centuries ago the australopithecenes or "ape men" of Southern and Eastern Africa appeared as hunters and the makers of tools. Some 200 centuries ago *homo sapiens* appeared, endowed with the human brain and employing the brain to develop and use a culture in societal groups. Aristotle hypothesized that man was by nature a political animal. The anthropologist hypothesizes that man is by nature a social animal. He is also a psychological animal, an organism endowed with a central nervous system, manifested particularly in the neo-cortex, which becomes meaningful because it is used to learn the inherited culture of his society for guiding his action.[1]

A person goes through a number of phases of psychological action as his objective behavior assumes an order of adaptation to his environment. His life in his culture provides him with the symbols whereby he gives meaning to the sensory impressions he receives. These symbols are, among other things, expressed in the language of his culture and are used to express referents or meanings as found

---

1. C. Geertz, "The Impact of the Concept of Culture on the Concept of Man," *Bulletin of the Atomic Scientists,* XXII (1966), No. 4, 2.

in that culture. Through the learning processes, a person acquires a storehouse of experience, which he draws upon for his cognitive processes. They enable him to identify his environment and adapt thereto. Thinking, planning, and decision making represent the means whereby a person consciously orders his future action. Values or preferences determine the content of his action. A person seeks to realize his values both in affective action, which satisfies immediate, activity needs, and instrumental action, which is directed toward the attainment of goals or future states of affairs. He evaluates past action as he shapes his future action.

Just as culture is the grand design of action of a society, so personality is the grand design of action of a person as a result of his experience in his culture. Just as a society assumes a constituted order in the broad patterns of coherence and interaction of its constituent groups (see pages 20 to 22 below), so a person assumes an order in his personality. A personality consists of the characteristic ways in which a person organizes his psychophysical systems and acts in order to realize self, express ideas, attain goals, and satisfy needs. It is the consistent patterns or tendencies evidenced by a person in integrating himself with situations. The order which it exhibits is subject to conflict, and control is exercised over such conflict so as to maintain the order.

The concept of personality enables the observer to understand, evaluate, and predict individual behavior as a composite structure of the individual's physical and psychological makeup, coupled with his experience or knowledge of self and culture. It postulates that individual behavior can helpfully be understood to be a product of a basic order and dynamism of the mind, emotions, and experience, which all individuals share but in a structure that is peculiar to each. It provides an integrating, dynamic view of the organism as a whole. Such ideas as the notion of self, the ranking of the needs of the self from the standpoint of self realization, the view of individual action as ordered over time, the characterization of behavior as of an instrumental nature or as satisfying activity needs, which are concepts derived from personality, are most fruitful methods for analyzing individual behavior.

Freud's terms, the id, the ego, and superego, have passed into our language as terms of fairly general usage, as distinguished from technical psychological concepts. The view of the personality as essentially a flow of energy, which is given expression by the ego and controlled by the superego, possessed simplicity of structure and congruence with empirical fact. In the interplay between id, ego, and superego, it was possible to consider questions of value as they influenced action. There was the subjective, unconscious world and there was also the world of reality. The individual lived in both worlds. To understand him, it was necessary to understand his drives and tensions in his unconscious world and their relation to the world of reality in which he expressed himself in action.

Freud's concept of the personality provided a basic conceptual framework for viewing the broad contours of action of the individual as he participated in the life of the society. The id could be said to represent the psychological endowment of man and impulse to action, the ego directed action by coordinating the drives of the id and the repressions of the superego, while the superego and represented the introjection of social control. The ego could be called "the executive department of the personality . . . impelled by the basic needs and heedful of the strictures of conscience, it is the function of the ego to remain in touch with reality, to take note of changing conditions, to seize opportunities for gratification and security, and to initiate change in order to facilitate gratification and security." The superego could be called the "judicial department of the personality. . . . Its dictum to the ego is, 'What is good enough for your forefathers is good enough for you.' The ego is the agency of change and adaptation; the superego is the carrier of tradition and the defender of mores."[2] In Freud's later lectures, the superego included "the holding up of ideals" or "the impulse toward perfection."[3]

The concept of the self is closely linked with the concept of the personality. It has been said that it may refer to the "self-as-object," consisting of "the person's attitudes, feelings, perceptions, and evaluations of himself as an object." In another sense, it may refer to the "self-as-process," that is, the self acting through cognitive and other mental processes.[4] The self may be said to be a person's ideal image of his personality or his personality goal. It is "the content of con-

2. A. Wheelis, *The Quest for Identity* (New York, 1958), 98-99.

3. S. Freud, *New Introductory Lectures on Psycho-Analysis* (New York, 1933), 94-95, see also S. Freud, *The Ego and the Id* (London, 1927), 30. For works on personality and culture, see A. Kardiner, *The Psychological Frontiers of Society* (New York, 1945); C. Kluckhohm, H. A. Murray, and D. M. Schneider (eds.), *Personality in Nature, Society, and Culture* (2nd ed.; New York, 1953); R. Linton; *The Cultural Background of Personality* (New York, 1945); S. S. Sargent and M. W. Smith (eds.), *Culture and Personality* (New York, 1949); A. F. C. Wallace, *Culture and Personality* (New York, 1961).

4. C. C. Hall and G. Lindzey, *Theories of Personality* (New York, 1957), 468.

sciousness at all times when one is thoroughly comfortable about one's self-respect, the prestige that one enjoys among one's fellows, and the respect and deference they pay one."[5]

Maslow's concept of priorities among basic needs as a key to the unfoldment, or the enlargment and deepening, of the personality is most significant. It could be said with some validity that the empirical school of psychology has tended to place motivation in terms of such concepts as release of tension, movement toward equilibrium, attainment of quiescence, and the like. Maslow, on the other hand, affirmed the positive aspects of personality and developed a theory of motivation based on the realization and expression of the healthy personality.

Maslow held that an organism possessed a group of basic needs. These were the physiological, safety, belongingness, esteem needs and the need for self-actualization. These needs were, in the organism, arranged in a hierarchy on the basis of the principle of relative potency. The physiological needs took precedence over the safety needs. The latter were stronger than the love needs, which, however, took priority over the esteem needs. When the esteem needs were satisfied, attention could be given to the need for self-actualization. Maslow affirmed that as the organism was able to gratify these needs in an order of moving from the lower to the higher needs, it achieved a greater and stronger individualism and one which adhered more closely to truth. It should be appreciated, however, that the above hierarchy or priority of needs varies among different individuals and also over time as a consequence of individual experience.[6]

A brief and elegant statement of the above theory later appeared in a paper published in 1958.[7] Maslow there stated that an organism has at least five sets of goals, which may be called basic needs. These were physiological, safety, love, and esteem needs, and the need for self-actualization. The first four of these largely indicate their meaning without further explanation. The last referred to "the desire for self-fulfillment, for full flowering of the capacities and potentialities of the person, to the tendency for him to become actualized in what he is potentially. This might be phrased as the desire to

---

5. H. S. Sullivan, *Fusion of Psychiatry and Social Science* (New York, 1964), 217.

6. A. H. Maslow, *Motivation and Personality* (New York, 1954), Chaps. 5-8.

7. A. H. Maslow, "A Dynamic Theory of Human Motivation," *Understanding Human Motivation*, eds. C. L. Stacey and M. F. de Martino (Cleveland, 1958), 26, quotations at 38, 39, 40-41, 43, 47. See also Kurt Goldstein's view of self-actualization as the creative development of the organism in Hall and Lindzey, *Theories of Personality*, 304.

become more and more what one is, to become everything that one is capable of becoming."

There were also certain "prerequisites for the basic need satisfactions." These included "freedom to speak, freedom to do what one wishes so long as no harm is done to others, freedom to express one's self, freedom to investigate and seek for information, justice, fairness, honesty, orderliness in the group."

The cognitive capacities of perception, learning, and thinking were to be considered as purposive in the sense that they were a "set of adjustive tools" used for the satisfaction of basic needs. The motivation of behavior was to be understood as a matter of multiple causation or as being a product of a number of determinants. "Within the sphere of motivational determinants any behavior tends to be determined by several or *all* the needs simultaneously rather than by only one of them."

The pathology of human conduct was characterized as a departure from the ideal pattern thus described: "Any thwarting or possibility of thwarting of these basic human goals, or danger to the defenses which protect them, or to the conditions upon which they rest are considered to be psychological threats. With a few exceptions, all psychopathology may be partially traced to such threats. A basically thwarted man may actually be defined as a 'sick' man."

The views of man as an open instead of a closed system, as a unique entity capable of growth and unfoldment in patterns of ever greater complexity, beauty, and order, as a unique configuration of potentialities for the expression of the self, and as a personality which is constantly "becoming" a richer and higher being, are some of the contributions of existential psychology.[8] Existential philosophy, starting with Soren Kierkegaard and Friedrich Nietzsche and continuing with such writings as Karl Jaspers, Martin Heidegger, and Jean-Paul Sartre, denied that man could ever be brought within any closed system. Man is open to the future, he is free, he is a creature who can exercise choice, and, as a consequence, he is a being whose growth does not reflect wholly predictable patterns. He is a person who must, with courage, choose and act so that he transcends himself. Life is not bounded by science and rationalism. Life is as we live it— individual, personal, concrete. Life is also a product of time in that it reflects the design of the past and continues to repeat the concrete patterns of the past, while it looks to the future as a region for achievement of potentialities and transformation of the present.

---

8. R. May, *Existential Psychology* (New York, 1961); H. M. Ruitenbeek (ed.), *Psychoanalysis and Existential Philosophy* (New York, 1962).

RELIGION AND THE SYMBOLIC ORDERING OF ACTION

Religion satisfies the private needs of each member of society for a cognitive map that will express the world in ideal terms, define his place in it, and give him an ethical system of norms to be prized, on the one hand, and norms to be abhorred, on the other hand, together with rewards for behavior adhering to the ideal of the good and penalties for behavior departing from the good.

Each individual creates his own private fantasies and beliefs that help him to adapt to the world of reality, such as myths of past communion with his mother and family or myths of success in his manner of relating himself to the world. As each individual participates in common patterns of social interaction and finds his place in the structures of social action, he discovers that he shares experiences with others. At these points his personal myths converge into those of his fellows and overlap them. Collective myth supplants and performs the function of personal myth. Dominant myths and themes emerge in the society. Religion develops as a system of beliefs which symbolically interprets existence, taps its deepest meanings, holds out the holiness, beauty, and virtue of the desirable, and condemns the undesirable as evil and profane. Through such a system of beliefs, man is given guidance and support in the realms of cognitive action as he moves through life. He is helped to find his way in life and to pursue it, notwithstanding the trials, tribulations, and temptations of existence. As he participates in ritual, he lives in the ideal world of religious beliefs and experiences the deepest and most profound of emotions.

Religious symbols fall into the class of symbols which have been referred to as condensation symbols. They are not simply referential symbols. Both classes of symbols share the distinguishing quality of symbols as signs pointing or referring to meanings. They are things which stand for something else. A referential symbol, however, simply refers to objective events and behavior and is essentially a perceptual response unaccompanied by important emotional reactions. Oral speech, writing, and the telegraph code represent systems of referential symbols whose referents or meanings enable economical, effective cognition and communication to take place. However, some symbols add to their referential significance an ability to evoke psychological behavior which is substitutive behavior for direct expression and enables the release of emotional tension in conscious or unconscious form. The words, murder, incest, and god, have referential significance, but the first two also create emotions of horror and repugnance, while the third creates awe and reverence. The richness of meaning of a condensation symbol grows in the degree it is dissociated from its referential meaning. Condensation symbolism grows as it strikes deeper into the unconscious and spreads to tap wider and wider sources of emotional experience. A referential symbol, on the other hand, grows with the formal elaboration of definitions in the realm of the conscious.[9]

Religion may be defined to consist of a traditional system of beliefs concerning the nature of the supernatural world, its interaction with the temporal world, and man's linkage with the supernatural world. Religion describes in spiritual symbols man's ideal and valued order, as exemplified in man himself, his society, and his natural environment. It states the ethical norms of this ideal order and the circumstances in which supernatural means may reward or punish behavior in the light of these norms.

Religion represents a body of supernatural beliefs and practices which is a part of the cultural heritage of society and satisfies private needs of a universal character. The belief systems of religion are products of human fantasy. They come into being and endure because the private fantasies of the members of the culture functionally correspond to the culturally constituted fantasies and may be projected into them. They may accordingly be classed as projective systems.[10]

Religion symbolically reflects the social order and endows with sacredness and virtue its modes of action and its basic values. Religion symbolically delineates man functioning through the universal structures of action of his culture to express those virtues and realize those values whereby he integrates self with society.

Religious symbols fall into category of master symbols. Master symbols identify the central ideas by which a society characterizes and justifies its order, action, and major values. In modern society, the religious belief of the ability of the individual directly to worship and to have communion with God corresponds to the value of the freedom of the individual to participate in the institutions of the society in order to express the good life. The belief in the omnipotence of God reflects the value of authority in a society ordered so

---

9. E. Sapir, "Symbolism," *Encyclopedia of the Social Sciences* (New York, 1934), XIV, 492. For a more complete structure for the analysis of symbolic behavior, based on the above distinction, see V. W. Turner, "Symbols in Ndembu Ritual," *Closed Systems and Open Minds: The Limits of Naivety in Social Anthropology*, ed. M. Gluckman (Chicago, 1964), 20.

10. M. E. Spiro and R. G. D'Andrade, "A Cross-Cultural Study of Some Supernatural Beliefs," *American Anthropologist*, LX (1958), 456.

largely by the authority of the organization, including the state as the greatest of organizations. Other master symbols in the political and economic spheres are "freedom," "liberty," "dignity and worth of the individual," and "free enterprise society." Master symbols serve to legitimate the social order by identifying its central values as expressed in social action. They are viable in the degree to which they lend meaning, importance, and even sacredness to the roles men pursue and the institutions which embrace them. They are effective in the degree to which they represent the common values of a people. When the master symbols of a society or of a particular institutional order are unquestioned, they are likely to be deeply internalized in its members. On the other hand, when role performances and institutional orders change more rapidly than the master symbols which describe and justify them, the members of the group become alienated from the master symbols and question them. They then search for and move toward the acceptance of a competing set of master symbols.[11]

The religious symbols of tribal societies assume an order corresponding to the structures of action and relationships of the societies. They may be said to provide a cognitive map whereby man finds his different positions in his society.[12] The dominant aspects of the landscape, such as the earth, the sky, a massive mountain, a river, or a large tree in a savanna county, become symbols representing important forces or values in the society. The earth is seen to represent the fertility of the land in yielding crops and the fertility of wives in yielding offspring. The earth or the sky becomes the residence of powerful ancestral spirits.

It has been said that "ritual action and belief are alike to be understood as forms of symbolic statement about the social order." Ritual expresses symbolically "the system of socially approved 'proper' relations between individuals and groups." Ritual and myth define the ideal society and duplicate in the supernatural world the relations between persons and groups in the real world. "Ritual

11. H. Gerth and C. W. Mills, *Character and Social Structure: The Psychology of Social Institutions* (New York, 1953, edition of 1964), 29, 276-277; compare the concept of "themes," M. Opler, "Themes as Dynamic Forces in Culture," *American Journal of Sociology*, LI (1945), 198. A pioneering and valuable study on the symbolic aspects of political action will be found in M. Edelman, *The Symbolic Uses of Politics* (Urbana, 1964).

12. *Cf.* G. Swanson, *The Birth of the Gods: The Origin of Primitive Beliefs* (Ann Arbor, 1960), 28-29, 100-104, a comparative analysis of fifty primitive peoples based on Human Relations Area Files.

and mythology 'represents' an ideal version of the social structure. It is a model of how people suppose their society to be organized, but it is *not* necessarily the goal toward which they strive. It is a simplified description of what is, not a fantasy of what might be." Ritual " 'serves to express the individual's status as a social person in the structural system in which he finds himself for the time being.' "[13]

In Durkheim's view, religion was a system of ideas enabling man to relate himself to society. Religion was a symbolic representation of society and its parts and in this manner was linked with the real world. Society was the source of religion. Religion both expressed the ideal society to the real society and was a part of the real society. Man attached himself to society through his religious beliefs. Religious sentiments strengthened social sentiments. In its supreme god, the tribe expressed its tribal unity. Ritual was the means whereby the social group periodically reaffirmed itself.[14]

Max Weber further elaborated the social aspects and functions of religion. In tribal groups, the ancestral gods performed the function of unifying the group, endowed it with legitimacy, and punished violation of norms. Misfortune came to a group not because its god was weak but rather because man himself was weak. The sins of the group brought the punishment of god. Religious behavior was not worship of the god by man but rather the god's coercion of man. Invocation was not prayer but rather the performance of magical formulas. Man attributed to god the human behavior patterns of a powerful temporal king, whose favor could be won by entreaty and gifts, as well as faithful service in conformity with divine will. The rationalization of taboos led to a system of norms, violations of which were sanctioned by the power of the taboo to bring misfortune. Totemism not only regulated sexual relations between groups but also placed fraternal groups under magical sanctions. The sacrifice of an animal and its eating in the ceremony of a communal meal produced a fraternity between those who sacrificed and their god. Commensality was a means of producing religious fellowship, which could lead to political and ethnic alliances. A basic concept was that

---

13. E. R. Leach, *Political Systems of Highland Burma* (London, 1954), 14, 15, 182, 286, 11.

14. E. Durkheim, *The Elementary Forms of the Religious Life: A Study in Religious Sociology* (New York, 1954 [?]), 225-231, 296, 387, 418-424. For early classical contributions to the theory of religion, see E. B. Tyler, *Primitive Culture* (2nd ed.; London, 1873); J. G. Frazer, *The Golden Bough: A Study in Magic and Religion* (3rd ed.; London, 1911-1915).

of charisma, which referred to the ability of an individual to produce extraordinary effects, either as a result of his natural endowment or by some unique means.[15]

The social functions of ritual were emphasized by a number of other writers. Ritual and magic were the means whereby man sought to manage the unmanageable or the unpredictable as he carried out his various pursuits. They were used "to master accident and ensnare luck."[16] Magic was a ritual enactment of a desired goal and was performed in order to enable man to overcome unanticipated failures in reaching his goal. It was viewed as a practical means to overcome danger and risk in important pursuits or critical situations. It enabled man to meet confidently and with poise the important crises of his life and to overcome despair and anxiety. For example, food was an all-important aspect of primitive life. The sacrificial sharing of food with the spirits was a means to bring their blessing to the obtaining of food.[17] Ritual served to instill in the individual an awareness of the social value of the situation which the ritual symbolically represented and the action appropriate to the situation. Ritual created a common concern of the members of a society in a situation which was of importance to the society and supported the performance of the social norms which the situation indicated.[18] The performance of ritual expressed "social relationships so as to secure general blessing, purification, protection, and prosperity for the persons involved in some mystical manner which is out of sensory control." Ritual invoked the supernatural world to favor the desired outcome of a situation. On the other hand, reliance upon ritual to deal with social conflict simply by affirming the traditional ideal order cloaked the bases of disruptive conflict and failed to deal realistically with them. Ritualistic reconciliation between conflicting groups led only to a temporary truce, since it provided no effective catharsis for the conflict.

To understand ritual, as it depicted idealized versions of important role relationships in a society, "the anthropologist has to trace its symbolic actions and apparatus through a major range of social

15. M. Weber, *The Sociology of Religion*, trans. T. Parsons (Boston, 1963), 2-43; see also T. Parsons, "The Theoretical Development of the Sociology of Religion," *Essays in Sociological Theory Pure and Applied* (Glencoe, 1949), 52.

16. B. Malinowski, "Culture," *Encyclopedia of the Social Sciences* (New York, 1931), IV, 635-640.

17. B. Malinowski, *Magic, Science and Religion* (Glencoe, 1948; reprint New York, n.d.), 42-43, 71-72, 90.

18. A. R. Radcliffe-Brown, *Taboo* (Cambridge, England, 1939); see G. C. Homans, *The Human Group* (New York, 1950), 323-330.

activities and other customs and complexes of symbols."[19] Religious prescriptions symbolize and focus the personal moral commitment which a person must have to carry out the requirements of an office or post which he occupies. Religion serves to commit a person to "all the legitimate offices, statuses, and roles a person can have in a society."[20] Religion is a major part of the "moral order," which includes "the binding sentiments of rightness that attend religion, the social solidarity that accompanies religious ritual, the sense of religious seriousness and obligation that strengthens men, and the effects of a belief in invisible beings that embody goodness."[21]

Religion is used to define in spiritual terms and to link with the spiritual world the charters of social groups, including peoples, tribes, and lineage groups. A social group will establish its position and claim to legitimacy of that position on the basis of its historical origin or genealogy. The symbols, myths, and rituals of religion reinforce such claims by linking them with the spiritual world. Religion provides a system of beliefs and practices for validating the transmission of occupancy of office and post and legitimating such occupancy, as well as a sanctioning process for supporting the exercise of authority in the performance of office and post.[22] This system of beliefs and practices extends into such matters as the capacity to assume the rightful use of land and to transmit its use to others. Unless one is a legitimate member of the community having the capacity to exercise such rights in accordance with the received scheme of the social order of the community, including its spiritual reinforcement, then one simply has no place in the order of things.

The fear, anxiety, and physical shock which the organism experiences in rituals associated with the passage of the individual from the status of boy to man and warrior and the status of girl to woman, wife, and mother[23] create a psychological state in which the organism is transformed to internalize the set of perceptions and cognitions of rights, duties, and privileges involved in the new status.[24]

---

19. M. Gluckman, "*Les Rites de Passage,*" *Essays on the Ritual of Social Relations,* ed. M. Gluckman (Manchester, 1962), 24-25, 42, 46-47.

20. M. Fortes, "Ritual and Office in Tribal Society," *Essays on the Ritual of Social Relations,* ed. M. Gluckman (Manchester, 1962), 83-87, quotation at 87.

21. R. Redfield, *The Primitive World and its Transformations* (Ithaca, 1953), 21.

22. *Cf.* A. I. Richards, "Social Mechanisms for the Transfer of Political Rights in Some African Tribes," *Journal of the Royal Anthropological Institute,* XCI (1961), 175.

23. A. van Gennep, *The Rites of Passage,* trans. M. B. Vizedom and C. L. Caffee (London, 1960).

24. P. Spencer, *The Samburu: A Study of Gerontocracy in a Nomadic Tribe* (Berkeley, Los Angeles, 1965), 246-247, 258.

Religion holds up to the world of tribal man the ideal society, its central values, and its ethical system of norms. Modern man, as compared with tribal man, relies less on religion and more on ideology and politics to give him his image of the ideal society. Religion provided tribal man with a supernatural system of sanctions to punish wrongs. Modern man relies upon the legal apparatus and laws of the modern state to regulate conduct and provide means of retribution and reparation.

A system of religion also incorporates beliefs concerning the modes of intervention of the supernatural world in the temporal world. Among these are beliefs concerning the manner in which the supernatural world may be influenced by living actors in the society to support existing patterns of goal attainment and attendant value realization and to bring about preferred outcomes of particular situations or activities.

Religious behavior is symbolic behavior and may be affective or instrumental in character or both. Viewed as affective behavior expressed in ritual communion with the spiritual world, the resultant experiencing of awe, exhaltation, mystery, and excitement satisfy basic activity needs of the individual. The invocation of spiritual power through ritual, including the use of magic and fetishes, frequently represents activity of an instrumental character. Such uses vary in accordance with the structure of the society.[25] The forces of nature are personified in the form of gods. Tribal man then appeals to his gods to protect him from the terrors and cruelties which nature inflicts. Religion alleviates anxiety in the fact of fear, fills the demands of justice, and, in general, provides a means of wish fulfillment.[26]

The resort to religion as a means to desired ends rests upon the belief in the reality and efficacy of the spiritual world and the ceremonies and objects which are used to invoke its action to bring about desired outcomes. The latter include good crops, the fertility of women, the avoidance and dispelling of catastrophe and misfortune, and the projection of hatred and displacement of hostility upon others. Belief in the omnipotence of the spiritual world also carries with it the conviction that the gods intervene in their own inscrutable way in the affairs of man without invocation or in spite of the pleas of believers.[27]

---

25. E. E. Evans-Pritchard, *Nuer Religion* (Oxford, 1956), 315-316, and "The Morphology and Function of Magic: A Comparative Study of the Trobriand and Zande Ritual and Spells," *American Anthropologist*, XXXI (1929), 641.

26. S. Freud, *The Future of an Illusion* (New York, 1957).

27. *Cf.* R. Horton, "A Definition of Religion and its Uses," *Journal of the Royal Anthropological Institute*, XC (1960), 201.

THE ORDERING OF ACTION IN SOCIETY

In tribal societies, kinship relationships are predominantly the means for creating structures of social action. However, pluralistic societies also appear characterized by a variety of types of social structures based on other criteria than kinship relations, such as age and the performance of specific functions. Modern societies are characterized by the movement of individuals to attain valued goals through the instrumentality of the organization. The course of human history has been a movement from kinship to organizational structures of social action. It has been a movement from acceptance of the father or the father-figure, as the respository of authority, to the acceptance of the official or executive, as the holder of authority. It has been a movement from role performance in institutions to role performance in organizations.

Man has always effectuated cooperation through the nuclear family of parents and their children. As such families expand and live and work closely together, they become identified as the extended family. The extended family is composed of more than two living generations descended from a common living ancestor. It may also include the families of consanguinal descendants of a common living ancestor. Cooperation, notably in the resolution of conflict and the prosecution of war, may require still larger structures of social action. Kinship becomes the basis for creating lineage groups, which are perceived to consist of persons unified by sharing increasingly remote ancestors. All such groups are perceived "as if" they were a family.[28] The family group was tribal man's existing conceptual frame of reference which he employed to identify larger cooperative groups. The principal successive larger extensions of lineage groups are known as minimal, medial, and maximal lineage groups. Beyond these groups, common descent, including fictional or mythical common descent, become the basis for creating the still larger groups of the clan and the tribe.

Other groupings of tribal man were on the basis of age or territory. Still others were made on the basis of the exercise of authority in political, economic, military, and religious spheres. Authority was, of course, present in tribal society. Chiefs, headmen, councils of elders, grandfathers, and fathers made decisions affecting in various ways the lives of tribal man. The settlement of conflict, the allocation of land, the direction of action in an unpredictable situation, were matters demanding the exercise of authority. Tribal society, however, frequently denied its figures of authority the ability to use

---

28. *Cf.* H. Vaihinger, *The Philosophy of "As If"* (London, New York, 1924).

physical force to constrain adherence to their commands. The linkage of posts of authority with the power of the supernatural world often became a support for the exercise of authority.

THE ORGANIZATION IN TRIBAL SOCIETY

In tribal society, the father was manager of the family as a corporate group. He allocated its resources among his sons, provided bridewealth for their marriages, organized action in the fields, and acted as its representative in larger groups, such as more inclusive lineage groups and the village. Action was also organized in the extended family and larger kinship structures.

Authority appeared in the supernatural world in the offices of custodians of shrines, diviners, priests, and chiefs, who were intermediaries with that world and were perceived to be able to manage its intervention, favorably or unfavorably, in the temporal world.

As the society learned the ways of war and sought its prizes of land, slaves, and booty, authority in those who acted as leaders in war appeared, and action was organized for aggressive or defensive war.

As contacts between family groups took place in the village, tribal society learned rudimentary organization of action through the headman, the council of elders, or age groups. As concentration of settlement developed in wider territorial settings than the village, new and larger structures of social action developed in the form of the tribe and the kingdom. Authority in the tribe was important for war, ritual, and conflict resolution. The authority of the king became felt throughout his land in the levy of tribute, the waging of war, and the brutal exercise of power to support authority, as well as the provision of justice through his court and the courts of his ministers and chiefs.

THE CONCEPT OF THE ORGANIZATION

When a society has learned to use impersonal authority in the form of the office in order to coordinate action and to control conflict, it has created the social structure known as the organization.

While authority is a constant in all societies, tribal as well as modern, the kinship structures and institutionalized patterns of action of tribal society were adequate for adaptation to a fairly stable environment. Impersonalized authority found in the organization, however, is an imperative means of cooperation for modern society in order to enable it to adapt to its highly complex and changing environment. The movement of tribal to modern society is a movement from kin relationship, as a unifying and coordinating principle of action, to impersonalized authority in the form of the organization. It is a movement from the kinship group to the organization as the basic structure of social action. Authority, in this study, should be understood to mean simply the ability of a decision maker, occupying a post or office, to effectuate action in accordance with communicated directions or commands and without reasoned persuasion. Authority is thus to be distinguished from the forces which support it, such as legitimacy, power, or force.

Authority arises from and is supported by its performance of function. There must be some one or some organ to determine with authority who gets what, when, and how. There must be some one or some organ to lead a group with experience, wisdom, and judgment as it encounters new situations of unpredictable content which fixed, stable patterns of behavior cannot effectively handle. Basically, authority arises and is accepted because it is able to bring about performance of desired function or attainment of valued goals.

It is from the performance of function that there arise the fundamental notions of the jurisdiction or competence of a post of authority, on the one hand, and abuse of authority, on the other hand. In most societies, it would be unthinkable or outside the sphere of authority of a father to sell or pledge one of his children. Yet in some societies this is permissible. Even in such societies, it would likely raise an issue of abuse of authority if he should do so for purposes of personal gratification instead of family need. The jurisdiction or competence of a post of authority is derived from the perception of what is appropriate for the exercise of authority by the occupant of the post. The concept of abuse of authority, however, is concerned with the manner of exercise of authority. Arbitrariness, tyranny, undue severity or cruelty are aspects of abuse of authority.

Authority in organization cannot act without the communication to it of information upon which decision and action may be based. Authority in organization cannot act without communication of decisions and commands to the members of the organization for the purpose of action. Communication, and integrity in communication, accordingly represents an imperative in organizational action. Without empirical truth in the information flow of the organization, it cannot successfully adapt to its environment, solve its problems, attain its goals, and realize the values of its members and participants.

Organization is a system of action in which persons occupying posts of authority make decisions, which allocate and utilize resources and coordinate action in order to attain the goals and realize the values of those who act in the system. The boundaries of such system of action are reached where action ceases to be influenced by the exercise of authority. The selection and priority of goals and the character of action involved in their attainment enables a surplus of gratification to be achieved over the psychic costs of participation in the system. Decision making is characterized by the need for the system to maintain itself, integrate, adapt to its environment, and achieve goal gratification.

Organization, in its mature stage of development, may be defined as a system of action which is coordinated in a structure of hierarchically-ordered role-relationships through the exercise of authority inhering in offices with a view to the attainment of goals and attendant value realization by the actors participating in it. Such actors are members when their action is a consequence of their acceptance of the authority of the organization within its sphere of competence. Such actors are participants when they take part in the system of action without necessarily accepting for this purpose the exercise of authority over them. The repetitive sequences of action of actors in the system of action become institutionalized and coalesce into valued norms. Conflict arises over the allocation of the resources of the organization and the manner of performance of roles and norms. Modes of authoritative control of such conflict exist. Control of conflict in all the organizations created by and acting under the legal system of the modern state takes place by the operation of such legal system, although posts of authority in the organization also resolve conflict among the members of the organization arising out of their relation to it and their relationships with one another.

THE ORGANIZATION AS AN INSTRUMENT FOR COORDINATION OF ACTION

To arrive at an understanding of the organization as a means for the coordination of action, its action must be viewed as taking place in the realms of (1) idea and form, (2) value, and (3) time. Each of these realms of action has in turn three perspectives from which action may be viewed. Action taking place in the realm of idea and form implies (1) the creation of the idea, (2) the objective expression of the idea as physical action in the world of reality, and (3) the appraisal of the fidelity of the physical action to its idea. Action taking place in the realm of value implies (1) the perception and choice of value, (2) the realization of value in the world of reality, and (3) the appraisal of the selection and realization of value. Action taking place in the realm of time implies a view of action in (1) the future, (2) the present, and (3) the past.

To state these thoughts somewhat more fully, first of all, action must have form or substance as an embodiment of an idea. The organism searches for and creates ideas of action whereby it may realize its values, selects and performs certain of those ideas, and examines the form which past action has taken to the end that future action may be improved as much as possible. For example, a tennis player tries continually to be a better tennis player or reach that point where the energy which he expends returns the highest degree of personal satisfaction in the display of skill. In the organization, personnel must be selected and given specific responsibilities for insuring that the organization, as a system or entity, performs corresponding functions.

In the realm of time, an organism must exercise temporal foresight and plan future action, perform action in the present, and reflect upon past action in order better to control the future performance of action from the standpoint of fidelity to idea. The organization must institutionalize such types of action in executive conduct concerned with long-term and short-term planning, the carrying out of plans in organizational performance, and the control of organizational action in order to perfect the expression of idea.

In the realm of value, the business organization is the meeting place of many individuals and a means for the realization of their values. Diverse groups contribute to its functioning and make claims upon it, namely, stockholders, management, labor, consumers, and the public. The order of the organization is an order in part achieved by managing the tensions arising from conflict among groups and individuals. This is accomplished through the allocation of values to groups and the recognition of the values of individuals. The order of the state is similarly achieved through the political process as a means of allocating values to groups and the judicial process as a means of resolving interpersonal value conflict.

The modern organization, with its flow of information to and from its authoritative decisive makers, who engage in coordinating the activities of its members at all levels, has aptly been called an environment for decision making.

LEADERSHIP AND CONSTITUTIVE ACTION

A global view of organizational action in the long-run perspective of time was developed by Selznick,[29] when he called attention to the need for and the function of leadership in organization. Executives

---

29. P. Selznick, *Leadership in Administration: A Sociological Interpretation* (Evanston, Ill., and White Plains, New York, 1957).

exercised leadership when their decisions dealt with critical rather than day-to-day problems in the life of the organization. Such problems had to do with the organization's mission and fundamental aims. Leadership was concerned with: (1) the definition of institutional mission and role, (2) the institutional embodiment of purpose, (3) the defense of institutional integrity, and (4) the ordering of internal conflict.

Leadership performs the function of peak coordination as it surveys the entire domain of organizational action and allocates energy of the organization in macrotime to attain the goals and realize the values of its members. Leadership performs the constitutive action of the organization. It insures that the mission of the organization continues to embody a viable social system in a world of changing technology and values. Leadership endows the organization with its properties or essential characteristics. It draws upon the human and physical resources of the organization to perform action viewed in an abstract way over the long term to reach broad goals. It creates, performs, and controls organizational action in a global manner over the long perspective of time and in the perspective of the total system of action of the organization.

Leadership performs the creative function in organization in its boldest aspects. Leadership creates the grand design of action; administration brings that design into reality. Leadership defines the basic structure of the organization; administration operates within the limits of that structure. Leadership faces the crucial issues of organizational life and makes its most critical decisions; administration faces the day-to-day issues and brings to concrete reality the broad commands of leadership.

Leadership is concerned with the maintenance of the fundamental bases of order. In the state, the legislature and executive branches of government perform the leadership function. In the administrative agency and the economic organization, it inheres in the sphere of administration or management. The kind of order which it is the function of leadership to establish and maintain will be call the constituted order. The type of action in a social system with which leadership is concerned will be called constitutive action.

The introduction of a new symbol in social theory should take place only when significant data appear as its referent and demand it for purpose of conceptualization. The term constitutive action is a symbol which is appropriate for the referent which it signifies. It does not misuse the ordinary meaning inhering in the phrase. Yet V. W. Turner, when confronted with describing conflict concerning the constitution of order among the Ndembu, could only symbolize it by the phrase "social drama."[30] His work will be summarized in Appendix A. The terms constitutive action, it is felt, evokes more readily the meaning with which it is linked than the term social drama.

In terms of political theory, constitutive action is not merely the political organization of a society, namely, the manner in which a government constitutes itself or has a set of working rules, which may or may not be embodied in a written document, termed the constitution. It is the basic order of the society as found in its central values, the institutions which embody those values, and the long-term ranking and power of its member groups. The term political action has, upon occasion, been used to refer to constitutive action in the state. Political action also has been used to refer to the type of action termed politics, in which groups struggle in the short-term for ascendancy and power within a given political system and men seek offices of leadership and authority. It is so used in this study. Politics has to do with settling short-term issues in the struggle for power within a polity; constitutive action has to do with long-term issues. The constituted order may be said to embody the "personality" of the body politic.

One helpful way of arriving at an understanding of the meaning of a constituted order is by defining it in terms of the structural rules of a social system. The structural rules of a social system may be said to define the bonds which hold a society together, its authoritative or other important offices or roles, the manner in which they are filled or vacated, their respective functions and sphere of authority or influence, and the propriety of the incumbency to office or role of its holder. Behavioral rules are to be distinguished from structural rules in that they refer merely to institutionalized or fixed patterns of action, the performance of which is expected by particular actors from other actors in certain typical situations. Structural rules possess formal legitimacy when they reflect the shared belief that they embody traditional propriety or that they eventuated from some symbolic constitutive act, which may be passed on to succeeding generations by written or oral means. Structural rules reflect substantive or social legitimacy when they emanate from the shared conviction of the members of the social system that they ought to exist and reflect the true state of affairs within the system. Substantive or social legitimacy exists when there is a consensus that the holders of the important offices or roles and the working of the system in accordance with the structural rules bring about a satisfactory realization of the dominant values of the group.

---

30. V. W. Turner, *Schism and Continuity in African Society* (Manchester, 1957).

The establishment of the structural rules of a society and the order which thereby results, viewed from the standpoint of the attainment of substantive or social legitimacy, may be said to represent constitutive action. Constitutive action involves the emergence and definition of authoritative roles in a society and the allocation of the energy of the society over the long term to the realization of its common values in accordance with their priorities. In briefest compass, it is action which determines the characteristic properties of a society as a means of value realization.

ADMINISTRATION

Administration brings the broad decisions of leadership down to earth in the form of concrete action. Administration takes place in the sphere of tactics as it performs the decisions of strategy. Administration must be faithful to leadership's defined goals.

Administration deals with the hard, practical questions of what the organization shall do specifically to satisfy the *existing* demands of the groups making claims upon it. In the economic organization, these claimant groups are management, stockholders, labor, and consumers. In the organization which is the governmental department, the claimant group is the clientele of the agency. Demands of interest groups that are the subject of politics in the state are resolved by political institutions and the political process. Demands of the constituent interest groups of an economic organization are resolved by the decision-making process of management. Demands of the clientele of a governmental agency are satisfied by the decision-making process of administration. Administration deals with the short-term aspects of organizational action. It answers the question of what concrete form of action the organization shall carry out today.

Leadership in the large scale business organization is lodged in a small group of corporate managers and directors, sometimes vaguely referred to as "top management." Administration is the concern of management generally. In the state, the performance of the leadership function is somewhat diffusely shared by the legislative and executive branches while the governmental departments of the cabinet or the presidency perform the administrative function. The state viewed as an organization will be a later topic in this chapter.

POLITICAL ACTION

The use of the term "political" in this study does not have the restrictive connotation of association with the constraint of force, which is often ascribed to it. For example, Radcliffe-Brown in the classic study, *African Political Systems*, gives it the meaning of "the maintenance of establishment of social order, within a territorial framework, by the organized exercise of coercive authority through the use, or possibility of use, of physical force."[31] It is believed that for the purposes of comparative study of primitive social systems that which is political should not be determined by the *mode of control* used by a society to maintain order and handle conflict. The fact that government in modern western societies is universally associated with the use of force does not affect the validity of the more universal proposition that all societies, modern as well as tribal, are concerned with problems of a political nature, which they deal with in different ways. States handle such problems in part through the institutions of politics, such as the legislature and political parties. The ultimate sanction for legitimate authority is the application of measures of force in an institutionalized manner. Other types of social order handle such problems by other means, including decision making by heads of kinship social structures or by intervention of the spiritual world (ritual). If one is interested in comparative political or social systems, parsimony and accuracy of conceptualization demand that the universal, rather than the particular or incidental, be taken as the basis for categorization of data. In other words, what is the *content* of political action as distinguished from the sanction for its authority?

Political action includes the determination of the goals to which common action shall be directed as of the moment and the allocation of group energy to the attainment of such goals, all viewed from the standpoint of effective value realization by the social system. Political action is to be distinguished from constitutive action. The resolution of political conflict may entail deliberation and decision, among others, by diviners, chiefs, councils of elders, kings, kings in their councils, parliaments, or legislatures. Such decisions may be supported by force or supernatural power or other means. That which is political in nature, however, should not solely be determined by the fact that it is action controlled by a decision-making process, that is, "the formulation and execution of binding or authoritative decisions for a social system."[32] It is conceded that con-

---

31. A. R. Radcliffe-Brown, "Preface," *African Political Systems*, eds. M. Fortes and E. E. Evans-Pritchard (London, New York, Toronto, 1940), xiv. Such a meaning for the term political is admittedly widespread, e.g., M. Weber, *The Theory of Social and Economic Organization*, trans. A. M. Henderson and T. Parsons (New York, 1947), 155; P. Bohanr.an, *Social Anthropology* (New York and others, 1963), 266.

32. D. Easton, "Political Anthropology," *Biennial Review of Anthropology, 1959*, ed. B. J. Siegel (Stanford, Calif., 1959), 226.

flict concerning political problems may, among other things, be handled by "binding decisions for the direction of the affairs of a society."[33] The essence of political action is that it refers to how a society or group orders itself *at a particular time,* as distinguished from the long term, in order to realize its values. If the term political were taken to mean the making of authoritative decisions for a social system, then it would be so broad as to include the making of legal or judicial decisions. That which is political is to be distinguished from that which is legal by virtue of the fact that the latter refers to the making of authoritative decisions to resolve past interpersonal conflict on the basis of the application of those ideal and valued norms of the society or group whose violation is sanctioned by repressive, retributive, or restitutive measures. Political conflict refers to intergroup conflict, as groups seek to have their respective values prevail over those of other groups in the action of the society. It is to be noted that such conflict may be present in legal conflict. The segregation cases before the Supreme Court entail intergroup conflict of the highest degree, yet they still involve the application of legal norms. The author has elsewhere put the matter as follows: "As the priority of, and intensity of attachment to, competing values by actors in a conflict situation increases and the number of such actors in the society also increases, the likelihood that categorization of the situation as one of a political, rather than a legal nature will increase."[34]

Fallers[35] prefers to define the concept of that which is political in terms of "political institutions." These are simply "the rules governing the legitimate use of power." They are *not* "the social units to which such rules apply." Such an approach avoids a great many pitfalls and makes it possible to classify data of comparative social behavior in a more universal manner than Radcliffe-Brown's approach, based on what is perhaps a more classical notion of the concept of that which is political. Fallers' definition, however, does not point to the milieu or type of situation in which "rules governing the legitimate use of power" appear; it does not make clear what is "legitimate" and what is "power," and it does not enable comparative analysis of such a society as the Tallensi unless "power" is given quite a comprehensive meaning, such as the ability to exert authority or in-

33. M. Shepardson, "Navajo Ways in Government," Memoir 96, *American Anthropological Association,* LXV (June, 1963), No. 3, Part 2, p. 44.

34. K. S. Carlston, *Law and Organization in World Society* (Urbana, 1962), 239.

35. L. A. Fallers, *Bantu Bureaucracy* (Cambridge, England, 1956), 5, 7, 3.

fluence. Faller's example of power, given in connection with his definition, has not such a broad meaning and is limited to an ability to
apply a sanction. Moreover, "institutions," in Fallers' view, means
"patterning, rules and sanctions."

Whereas Malinowski's concept of institution refers to a universal
form of social structure or type of corporate body, Fallers' notion of
institution means "a pattern of behavior which a group of persons
consider 'right' or 'correct'—a norm of conduct. For a pattern of
behavior to be institutionalized means that persons approve of its
being followed and disapprove of its not being followed." Others
might prefer simply to use the term institutionalized behavior in
such circumstances. It has been said the institutionalization of behavior exists "when each actor in the situation does, and believes
he should do, what the other actors whom he confronts believes he
should do."[36] The author has described the institutionalization of
behavior as follows: "when (1) a sequence of action in a typical situation encountered in the functioning of a social system becomes a
repetitive and fixed pattern of action, and (2) an actor in such
a situation has embedded or 'internalized' in his mind that such a
pattern of action is expected to be performed by him, an institutionalized pattern of action may be said to have appeared. It may be
termed a behavioral rule."[37]

Fallers correctly terms such behavior as also implying a role. He
defines a role as "that behavior which is imposed on an individual
both by the expectations of others and his own desire to conform,
and which he is expected to display under certain circumstances."[38]
The concept of role was discussed in the opening pages of this chapter. The author has defined the term as follows:

> When the patterns of interaction of an actor and those with whom he
> interacts become so fixed as to establish a set of expectations of conduct
> for those involved and when, in addition, the actor is perceived to occupy
> a post or a position in a social system, he is said to possess a role. More
> briefly stated, a role is "a way of behaving associated with a defined posi-
> tion in a social system."[39]

It may well be that the notion of post, position, or status is implicit
in the concept of role, that the idea of position is but a different way
of describing performance, and that the concept of post or position

36. T. Parsons and E. A. Shils, *Toward a General Theory of Action* (Cambridge, Mass., 1951), 194.
37. Carlston, *op cit.*, p. 129.
38. Fallers, *op. cit.*, p. 3.
39. Carlston, *op. cit.*, p. 94, citing Selznick, *Leadership in Administration*, 82
and Parsons and Shils, *Toward a General Theory of Action*, 23.

is therefore an unnecessary concept.[40] Nevertheless, the above statement reflects a fairly well accepted view of the concept. It is believed that the concept of post is a useful one for the characterization of the type of performance expected of an actor in performing a role and for otherwise identifying types of action in a social system.

The principal virtue of Fallers' approach is that it points to how "the legitimate use of power" is allocated in a society and does not constrain the investigator to search for something like "governmental" bodies, as they are known in western society, before he may conclude that anything "political" appears to exist in a society. It is believed that the concept of "legitimate" would be more useful in comparative social studies if it were equated with conduct which a society perceives to be right and proper because it is in accordance with traditional social norms associated with the use of authority. The term social or substantive legitimacy could usefully identify such a concept of legitimacy. The idea of "power" should not be limited to the ability to apply sanctions but should be more comprehensive and should refer instead to the ability to exert dominance or, alternatively, "the ability to produce intended effects, on oneself, on other human beings, and on things."[41]

Schapera's concept of political organization is most comprehensive and would appear to extend to substantially the entire range of action of a society, including action designed to control deviance as well as action of a cooperative nature to achieve valued goals. He defined political organization as "that aspect of the total organization which is concerned with the establishment and maintenance of internal cooperation and external independence." It implies "the whole system of communal leadership and all the functions (as well as the powers) of the leaders." It concerns "the mechanisms making for orderly life in any community," such as "the organization of religious ceremonies or collective hunts, or the concentration and distribution of wealth." The performance of such functions "are as relevant as the administration of justice and are similarly significant for comparative purposes."[42]

In Smith's view, political action involves the determination of policy, which in turn consists of a "course of action, i.e., a particular organizational process, adopted or proposed for adoption by a government, ruler, individual, party, or other group. Action is thus po-

---

40. S. F. Nadel, *The Theory of Social Structure* (Glencoe, Ill., 1957), 29-31.
41. Bohannan, *Social Anthropology* (New York, 1963), 268.
42. I. Schapera, *Government and Politics in Tribal Societies* (London, 1956), 217-219.

litical when it focuses on the adoption, pursuit, or reversal of policy." The writer would make the clarifying remark with respect to this statement that a "course of action . . . by a[n] . . . individual" would not ordinarily be thought of as being political. Doubtless Smith had the idea, in his use of the term "individual," that an individual might propose policy for a group. Otherwise, Smith's concept of the nature of political action appears to be most useful. It differs from the definition advanced above in that the writer would have it refer to the manner in which a group as a whole organizes itself at a particular time in order to realize its values. Coincidence in the two viewpoints may lie in the fact that Smith appears to share this writer's view that the political process implies the adjustment of conflicting demands or the compromise of conflicting values in a group. Smith makes the statement in this connection that political action characteristically invokes "a competition for power over the policy-making process."[43]

Schapera's concept of political organization emphasizes, but is not limited to, the meaning of the symbol of constitutive action as above defined. Smith's concept of the term political, on the other hand, is close to that of the writer. The difference between constitutive and political action lies in the perspective of time. Constitutive action concerns problems of social order as they are viewed over the long term; political action views them in the short term. Placing one's perspective of the world as one of change, viewed both in the long run and the short run, constitutive action consists of a long-term order, while political action consists of a short-term order.

THE STATE AS ORGANIZATION

The organization of a society into an enduring order requires that it shall establish means for allocating its resources to competing group and individual demands for their use, coordinate action to attain the valued goals of its groups and individual members, and resolve conflict on the basis of a common system of values and value priorities. Procedures for the resolution of constitutive, political, and interpersonal conflict must exist. Ideal and valued norms for conduct must be perceived and accepted as guides for conduct, applied to determine deviant conduct, and such deviant conduct must be subjected to retribution or its injurious consequences repaired.

---

43. M. G. Smith, *Government in Zazzau 1800-1950* (London, New York, Toronto, 1960), 17; M. G. Smith, "On Segmentary Lineage Systems," *Journal of the Royal Anthropological Institute*, XCVI[2] (1956), 48; see L. Mair, *Primitive Government* (Baltimore, 1962).

The growth of organization in society has been a movement from the use of authority in kinship structures, supported by the gods and the ancestors, to authority in office, supported by force. The organizational development of society into a state implies the constitution of a political and social order, the impersonalization and secularization of authority into office and the development of authoritative bodies endowed with legitimacy, the establishment and maintenance of a political consensus, and the resolution of interpersonal conflict by judicial bodies on the basis of legal norms. Functions that were performed in a diffuse manner in primitive society are now institutionalized in the organs of government. As stated by the writer elsewhere:

> The "State" accordingly comprises (1) all those persons who are habitually influenced in their conduct by belief in the legitimacy of relevant decisions and commands emanating from (2) other persons in carrying out the requirements of their respective roles as members of a territorially identified government, including decisions as to sanctions to be applied in case of behavior determined to be deviant. . . . Thus the state is the ultimate organization of the national society, since it is characterized by a common acceptance of a certain authority and by the fact that its members identify themselves with it. The national society moves to attain its purposes sometimes through governmental organizations and sometimes through private organizations.[44]

SOCIETY AS A FRAMEWORK FOR LIVING

It is believed that there is a need for a new symbol which will refer a certain type of order or structure which a culture assumes. It is suggested that the term "framework for living" be adopted and be deemed to the grand design of man's relationship to his society as embodied in concrete patterns of action.

The concept of framework for living views society as an order to be appreciated and evaluated on the basis of the provision which it makes for the development of the personality of its individual members. In this sense, the concept should also be applied to the individual viewed as a member of an organization. Each of these types of order should be judged on the basis of the same normative criterion.

Tribal society's framework for living made man a part of a constricted whole. Tribal man had meaning as self in a perspective in which he was a part of his kinship groups. He attained his goals and realized his values simply as a consequence of the central fact that he was a part of his kinship groups.

---

44. K. S. Carlston, *Law and Structures of Social Action* (London, New York, 1956), 60-61, 65-66, see also discussion at 99-109.

Modern man's framework for living makes each man an island into himself—free, yes, but also isolated. Modern man lives in a society which is a constellation of interdependent groups, mostly organizations, except for his family. He is separate from these groups, even as he participates in them. He never gives up his self completely to them. As he participates in their action, he has his own space of free movement. It represents the permeability of his society to his participation in its group and organizational life. In that participation, he never perceives himself as indissolubly a part of a group which is central to his life in the same manner as tribal man perceived his membership in his kinship groups. The self of modern man does not assume meaning only as a result of his membership in a group, as in tribal man. Groups are mostly instruments for value realization in the view of modern man. Thus tribal society and modern societies are at polar extremes as frameworks for living. Nevertheless their worthwhileness is to be judged from the same normative criterion: to what extent do they provide the opportunity for the full, healthy growth of the personality?

It may be observed that modern man's framework for living increasingly fails to provide him with the opportunity to pursue the good life. He is becoming the organizational man and the ideological man and less the man of the family and the neighborly community. The family and the community are disintegrating in modern, urban culture. The environment of natural order and beauty, which once characterized the world in which man lived, is being eroded by the harsh, mechanistic environment of megalopolis. The isolation of modern man and the increasing psychological pressures and tensions which he encounters lead to a proliferation of personality disorders and warped personalities. The cool, detached, and even alienated personality is supplanting among youth the warm, committed personality. The consequences for future political and social order are forebidding and will require the exercise of leadership of the highest quality.

Conflict

PSYCHOLOGICAL CONFLICT

The pursuit of goals and the realization of values create conflict within an individual as well as between individuals and social groups. An individual may experience conflict in a number of ways. He may find existing needs or ways of satisfying needs to be incompatible. Conflict may occur in choosing means to satisfy a need.[45] Actual response to a situation may conflict with or be inappropriate to the perceived character of the situation. For example, a situation of risk and danger may be met with foolhardy action.[46] An individual may find himself torn by conflicting pulls as he approaches a situation promising reward but also entailing anticipated deprivations.[47] Carrying out a particular activity may bring both rewards and deprivations. When conscious commitment or decision to perform the activity is made, the individual will fail to recognize or will diminish the importance of information pointing to the deprivations involved in the activity and will select or enhance the significance of information which is consistent with and justifies the activity.[48] Opposing tendencies within an individual may influence the way in which alternative possible responses to it are formulated, the consistency and intensity with which a given alternative is chosen, and the degree to which the chosen course of action is carried out.[49] Of these various aspects of inner conflict of an individual, the concept of the organism being exposed to opposing pulls of reward and deprivation and moving toward reward and away from deprivation is most fruitful for general analytical purposes. Lewin categorized such pulls as positive and negative valences.[50]

A statement of the value aspects of the cognitive action of a person reaching a decision to violate a legal norm will help to illuminate the foregoing concepts, as well as to provide an understanding of the interaction of the legal process and psychological action. It may be hypothesized that a person will be likely to reach a decision to violate a legal norm, and will be inhibited from doing so only by his personality characteristics, when he is in a situation where he appreciates the possibility of attaining a highly important goal by action violating a legal norm and realizes that such goal attainment is near at hand and is drawn to it by virtue of that fact. On the other hand, the future operation of the legal process and its applications of depri-

45. E. B. McNeil, "Psychology and Aggression," *Journal of Conflict Resolution*, III (1959), 201.

46. C. E. Osgood, "Cognitive Dynamics in the Conduct of Human Affairs," *Public Opinion Quarterly*, XXIV (1960), 341.

47. K. Lewin, *A Dynamic Theory of Personality: Selected Papers* (New York, London, 1935), 123-153; M. B. Arnold, *Emotion and Personality* (New York, 1960), II, 272-273; N. E. Miller, "Experimental Studies on Conflict," *Personality and the Behavioral Disorders*, ed. J. McV. Hunt (New York, 1944), 431.

48. L. Festinger, *A Theory of Cognitive Dissonance* (Evanston, Ill., and White Plains, New York, 1957).

49. I. L. Janis, "Motivational Factors in the Resolution of Decisional Conflicts," *Nebraska Symposium on Motivation, 1959,* ed. M. R. Jones (Lincoln, 1959), 198.

50. Lewin, *A Dynamic Theory of Personality,* 123-153.

vations or sanctions will be perceived as remote in time, their occurrence, subject to chance, and their outcome, in any event, uncertain. Unless his personality characteristics inhibit him, he will resolve the conflict between grasping the rewards near at hand and avoiding the remote and uncertain deprivations by a decision to perform the prohibited action.

Types of situations exist which are highly promotive of law violation. They include the familiar one of a person of visible affluence walking down a dark deserted street in a slum neighborhood. The cognitive conflict in reaching a decision to rob is decreased by the perception of the heightened ease and safety from apprehension by the police. In white-collar crime, they include the situation of a business executive attracted to the values incident to the performance of his post, such as wealth, esteem, and personal gratifications, but subject to the threat of future deprivations in loss of employment if he does not meet competition. The present certitude of loss of employment and the loss of value realization which it implies, unless he decides to violate the antitrust laws in order to retain his post, overcome the conflicting elements of remoteness and uncertainty of the sanctions involved in the application of the antitrust laws, resulting in a decision to commit a violation of such laws so as to handle the problem of meeting competition in a manner which will enable retention of his post.

Two aspects of psychological conflict will next be discussed. The sequence of frustration and aggression is believed to be the psychological basis for legal behavior in society. The phenomenon of witchcraft is directly related to the concept of projection.

FRUSTRATION AND AGGRESSION

The frustration and aggression sequence received its first full statement in the work of Dollard and others at Yale.[51] Frustration, in their view, was an interference with an ongoing activity. Aggression was defined to be the primary and characteristic reaction to frustration. It was manifested in an act having the goal of an injury to an organism or a substitute for an organism. An actor would be impelled to aggressive action in direct relation to the strength of his motivation to perform the activity, the degree of interference with the activity, and the number of frustrations experienced. The expression of an act of aggression was a catharsis which reduced the instigation to aggressive action.

Frustration can be more broadly defined as interference with the

51. J. Dollard, *et al., Frustration and Aggression* (New Haven, 1939), Chaps. 1-3.

realization of a value or with the gratification of some motive, need, or drive. Frustration may also be said to arise from privation, deprivation, or obstruction.[52] Frustration is held to create anxiety, that is, a state of mental distress, and anger or hostility.[53] A critical element is the emotional state which the thwarting of the drive creates. The intensity of the frustrated drive determines the emotional reaction to the obstruction of the expression of the drive. The strength of the instigation to aggression is directly dependent on this factor. While the venting of anger or hostility in aggressive action reduces subsequent aggression, this proposition must be handled with caution. If the cause of frustration continues, there will be no lessening of aggression. Also, when frustration is perceived to be arbitrary, the instigation to aggression is increased. On the other hand, when frustration is perceived to be reasonable, there is a lessening of the tendency to aggression.[54]

Aggression can be expressed by directing it to the object of hatred or hostility, or it can be expressed by the mechanism of displacement, that is, directing the hostility to a substitute object. Displacement may be said to be an aspect of the ability of the organism to perceive and act in a symbolic world or a world of fantasy. An organism indulges in fantasy when it delays a response to a situation and substitutes for it transformed behavior created through the imagination. The strongest aggressive response is that directed against the frustrating object. The tendency of aggressive responses to be directed to other substitute objects diminishes as their similarity to the frustrating object diminishes. When aggressive tendencies generated by frustration cannot be directed to the person responsible for the thwarting, aggression will be directed to another person in direct proportion to the degree of dislike for such other person. If another group is to receive displaced hostility, it will become the object of aggression to the degree it is disliked for its differences.[55]

A recent writer questions the hypothesis that aggression is always a product of frustration and asserts that the frustration-aggression

52. *Cf.* E. B. McNeil, *op. cit.*, pp. 201, 203.

53. *Ibid.*, p. 201; L. Berkowitz, *Aggression: A Social Psychological Analysis* (New York, 1962), 32.

54. *Ibid.*, p. 40, citing N. Pastore, "The Role of Arbitrariness in the Frustration-Aggression Hypothesis," *Journal of Abnormal and Social Psychology*, XLVII (1952), 728; E. B. McNeil, *op. cit.*, pp. 204-208; S. Feshbach, "The Stimulating versus Cathartic Effects of Vicarious Aggression Activity," *Journal of Abnormal and Social Psychology*, LXIII (1961), 381; Arnold, *op. cit.*, I, 255-256.

55. Berkowitz, *op. cit.*, pp. 107-108, 152; L. Berkowitz and J. A. Green, "The Stimulus Qualities of the Scapegoat," *Journal of Abnormal and Social Psychology*, LXIV (1962), 293; E. B. McNeil, *op. cit.*, pp. 252-253.

hypothesis has limited utility today. If aggression is defined as an attacking response in which noxious stimuli are inflicted upon another organism, he points out that it may occur simply because such a type of conduct has led to reward in the past and not as a result of interference with goal-gratification.[56]

The relation of the frustration-aggression sequence to the legal process may be illustrated in the following situations. A role performer intentionally failed to carry out conduct which his role partner justifiably expected to be forthcoming. A custodian of a fishing canoe in the Trobriand archipelago carelessly moored it, and it was lost, to the injury of other members of the crew. A father who had control of the family herd of cattle arbitrarily used part of the herd of cattle for some personal purpose to the injury of his son, who was relying on it for bridewealth in an anticipated marriage. A father of a daughter was denied anticipated bridewealth from her marriage as a result of her seduction. A head of a family was murdered by a member of another family. In each instance, there is a frustration of an ongoing activity which was highly valued. The expression of aggression against the person who was the source of the frustration, which would otherwise take place, is inhibited. A conditioning process takes place whereby persons in such a situation permit a societal sanctioning process vicariously to inflict deprivations upon persons responsible for such frustrations.

A society cannot tolerate the social expression of aggression in violent action. It demands the application of a sanctioning process to the wrongdoers. Legal norms accordingly appear. They embody statements of conduct which will lead to the application of an institutionalized sanctioning process. Such a process is found either in the spiritual world, in the form of the wrath of the gods or the ancestral spirits, or in the temporal world, in the form of physical punishment or death. The individual learns to inhibit his aggressive responses and to accept in their place the sanctioning process of his group. He becomes, in course of time, the law-abiding citizen of modern culture.

It must be realized, however, that the psychological explanation of the growth of law and the legal process does not lie merely in the perceived need to provide a social control of the frustration and aggression sequence of action. In the realm of emotion, interpersonal conflict is disturbing and a source of tension. The inhibition of aggression which membership in a social group demands is only part of the psychological processes involved. The failure by another to

---

56. A. H. Buss, *The Psychology of Aggression* (New York, London, 1961).

perform a valued norm is a deprivation of valued social cooperation. Expectations of realizing the values and attaining the goals upon which the performance of the norm depends are thereby denied. The ideal of harmony in interpersonal relations is broken. Disappointment ensues. The member of one's group who does not perform a valued norm is perceived as opposed to one's interests, or as an enemy. Such conduct is perceived as selfish and culturally irrational. Inability to control departures from valued norms in a group is perceived to interfere with locomotion of the group toward desired goals, to disrupt its solidarity, and to promote its disintegration. The imposition of deprivations through the sanctioning process thus becomes a part of a learning process. Members of a group who fail to adhere to a valued group norm must be taught to conform. Punishment for such misconduct strengthens inhibition against its future performance.

The resolution of conflict within the group becomes a social imperative. It is no longer simply a matter of developing a sanctioning process in society to supplant the disruptive response of aggression in interpersonal relations. It is a matter of turning to the head of the family or lineage group, the elder, the council of elders, the chief, the king, and the courts of the king for the solution of conflict through the process of rendering decisions for resolving conflict. The legal process of defining norms and applying them to the solution of interpersonal conflict begins. The sage, wise elder, learned in the ways, norms, and past situations of conflicts of the society, becomes a valued figure in conflict resolution and the prototype of the judge. The man skilled in the arts of persuasion, cool in situations charged with tension and conflict, possessed of judgment, and respected by others becomes a valued member of the group and the prototype of the advocate. The resolution of conflict by courts is so valued by society that it becomes a support for their exercise of authority. Chiefs and kings find that man will even pay fees for access to their courts. Thus man has constantly pressed forward over the thousands of years of growth of culture to develop law and the legal process.

PROJECTION

In the view of Freud, the social practice of taboo was a product of internal conflict and ambivalence in primitive man. The two basic precepts of totemism were prohibition of killing the totem animal and the avoidance of sexual relations with members of the opposite sex of the same totem clan. The savage, however, had a primeval desire to carry out the prohibited conduct, which led to an ambivalent attitude on his part toward the prohibited activity. An ambivalent attitude is one in which the desire to perform an act, which may be in the realm of the unconscious as well as the conscious, struggled for paramountcy over the realization that it must not be performed. Primitive man, no less than modern man, often hated those who were close to him and whom he was supposed to love. Yet expression of his hostility was socially prohibited or taboo. When the person whom he hated died, the survivor projected to the dead the characteristics of a demon in order to express the hatred he had previously held either consciously or unconsciously.

Man's resort to magic was simply a product of his belief in the power of his wishes. He resorted to magic in order to accomplish his wishes. His culture had grown to the point where he could engage in abstract ways of thinking. He created spirits in the world of fantasy because he was subject to the moral barriers of taboo. He projected outwards his internal perceptions and created demons who symbolically represented those he hated.[57]

In short, projection attributes to Alter the hatred and hostility Ego feels toward Alter and assumes that Alter hates and is hostile to Ego. Gluckman called attention to an episode demonstrating that African diviners were not unaware of the phenomenon of projection. A wife had died, and the widower accused the governor of hatred toward him and expressing that hatred by killing the wife through sorcery. The diviner said: "Obviously the accusation is absurd. Why should the governor hate the cousin [the widower]? The governor possesses political power and has inherited the main family herd. The cousin thinks the governor hates him, because he hates the governor."[58]

The Freudian hypothesis of ambivalence and projection of hostile attitudes was adopted by Opler in his study of the Apache. Fear of the power of living and dead relatives was held to arise from the ambivalence of the dislike and antagonism felt toward them accompanied by the societal affirmation that they should be respected figures. The ghosts of dead relatives were believed to become an owl, which could then be killed, driven away, and reviled with good conscience.[59] Spiro's study of the Ifaluk described a small island society of about 250 members located in the South Pacific in which aggression toward fellow members of the group was displaced outward upon figures conceived of as evil ghosts.[60]

57. S. Freud, *Totem and Taboo: Some Points of Agreement between the Mental Lives of Savages and Neurotics* (New York, 1952), 29-32, 60-64, 83, 92-93.
58. M. Gluckman, *Custom and Conflict in Africa* (Glencoe, Ill., 1955), 90.
59. M. E. Opler, "An Interpretation of Ambivalence in Two American Indian Tribes," *Journal of Social Psychology*, VII (1936), 82.
60. M. E. Spiro, "Ghosts, Ifaluk, and Teleological Functionalism," *American Anthropologist*, LIV (1952), 497.

Social Conflict

All interaction among individuals creates friction and conflict. Competition, rivalry, interference, and disappointment are ever a part of social life. The institutionalized patterns of action implicit in role relationships become norms which are valued by the role partners and others involved in such relationships. Departure from them leads to conflict. Demands which are made of authority for the allocation of resources which authority controls, struggles by persons and groups for ascendancy and power, are continuing sources of conflict. The organization within the modern state looks to the state to handle conflict arising from the violation of legal norms by its members to the injury of others, but it must also handle its own conflict situations if it is to survive and prosper. Authority in the organization is accordingly used not only to coordinate action but also to resolve conflict concerning the allocation of its resources as well as conflict arising out of its own organizational norms. Authority in the organization becomes valued by its members for its ability to control conflict.

In tribal society, as well as in modern society, conflict was experienced at the three levels of cooperation consisting of constitutive action, politics, and interpersonal relations. Its techniques for the social control of such conflict were, however, much more imperfectly developed. Reliance on symbolic means of control, on the other hand, were much more highly developed. The structural rules of the tribal society were reinforced by their linkage with the spiritual world. Offenses which struck at the foundations of the social system, as legitimate in the supernatural world, were the most serious of offenses. The spiritual world operated to punish violation of norms. The practice of ritual was an instrument for effectuating social cohesion as well as goal attainment.

Release of tension periodically took place in rituals of rebellion or rituals of conflict. When a lineage group grew to the point where its formal status in a segmentary society did not correspond to its actual status, fission instead of civil strife took place. Mystical, symbolic, sanctioning processes handled situations of interpersonal conflict. Ritual reaffirmed and repaired social relations damaged by conflict, although some societies developed procedures for compensation by the transfer of economic goods to repair such relations.

In general, conflict in society appears in one of two basic types of situations. In the first, the actors challenge the validity of the constituted order itself, including the status of groups within it, and seek to change the basic character of the constituted order itself. This may be termed constitutive conflict. In the second, the actors accept the constituted order but experience dissatisfaction in particular situations with the manner in which it allocates its energy and resources or the realization of values takes place. For example, conflict exists among groups for preferred status in the social system, as well as over the allocation of resources and for posts of leadership or authority. This may be termed political conflict, but political conflict, as the term is ordinarily used, also includes constitutive conflict. Conflict also arises in interpersonal relations, including conflict arising from the failure to perform rules in accordance with ideal and valued norms implicit in such relationships.

The nature of constitutive and interpersonal conflict in society may be clarified by pointing to the fact that the Supreme Court of the United States is a specialist in the management of tensions arising from constitutive conflict in the national society. Thus, when a case comes before the Supreme Court involving some concrete, interpersonal conflict situation, which also raises issues which are or may become issues of profound public importance and conflict over values, the Court does not permit the judicial ideal of fidelity in the application of existing legal norms (*stare decisis*) to prevent it from dealing directly with such issues. On the other hand, it is the function of courts, including the Supreme Court, to handle interpersonal conflict situations involving the application of legal norms.

Although the literature does not use the term constitutive conflict, the concept is, of course, a familiar one. Such conflict arises when existing structures of social action fail to give recognition to the ideals and values of important groups. As a consequence, they challenge the validity of the constituted order itself and the status which the order accords them, seeking to change the constituted order.[61]

Otherwise social conflict is seen to arise in situations in which the actors accept the constituted order but experience dissatisfaction with the manner in which it is allocating its resources and energy among the competing demands made upon it by various groups, the occupancy of important posts, and the performance of important roles. This is herein called the sphere of politics.

Conflict may also arise when the actors accept the constituted order

---

61. L. Coser, *The Functions of Social Conflict*, 74-75, citing J. Ortega y Gassett, *Concord and Liberty* (New York, 1946), 15, J. S. Mill, *On Bentham and Coleridge* (New York, 1951), 123, and G. Simpson, *Conflict and Community* (New York, 1937), 4, the last-named making the distinction between communal conflict, which presupposes a common acceptance of basic ends, and non-communal conflict, which manifests no common acceptance of basic ends.

but experience frustration in interpersonal relations. Such conflict typically takes place when expectations of role performance have been denied through deviant performance of valued norms inherent in roles. Alter does not perform the conduct which Ego has learned through repetitive action to expect from him and Ego experiences deprivations as a result of Alter's deviant performance of his role. In modern society, the control of such conflict is principally the concern of law. When organizational action fails to conform to legal norms, the judicial system controls the deviant behavior.

To be distinguished from conflict over the form of a social order or within a social order is that form of aggression in which noxious stimuli, such as killing in the form of warfare, are inflicted by an in-group upon an out-group as a means to the attainment of such rewards or goals as the acquisition of land, booty, and slaves.

Participation in primary groups, such as the family, is more likely to generate attitudes of both love and hate with respect to others than participation in secondary groups, such as a business association. The total personality of the individual is more likely to be involved in interaction within primary groups. The closeness or intimacy of relationships and the high degree of involvement by the members of a group correlate positively with the intensity of conflict in the group. Yet the warm, personal nature of such relationships may be so idealized that avoidance and suppression of overt expression of the conflict takes place. When direct expression of hostility against the objects of hatred is denied, symbolic or unrealistic conflict will appear through such psychological mechanisms as displacement or projection. However, the release of tension through abreaction is but momentary in its effect and represents no real solution for the conflict the organism is experiencing. Indeed, such a solution creates the potentiality for a disruptive explosion in the social system.

Conflict which tends to create a cleavage of a society into two opposing groups which question its basic consensual agreement or order is likely to lead to a disruption of the society. On the other hand, a society organized into multiple groups and attachments or loyalties to such groups is one in which conflict is likely to cut across the society in many different ways without affecting the basic stability of the society, provided that the society has a strong consensus on basic values and their priorities.

When a group is lacking in a basic consensus over its order, and its members have a low degree of attachment to the group, then external threats or outside conflict will lead to general apathy and disintegration of the group rather than cohesion. On the other hand, the small, close group will tend to preserve rigidly its ideological purity. With-drawal of members from the group is perceived to be a threat to its unity, and it is likely to create a violent reaction. Such a group will tend to exhibit "scapegoating" reactions as a means of release of internal tensions. It will even search for enemies to strengthen its internal solidarity.

When a group has a common sharing of goals and values and oper-ates within a common universe of norms and rules, then conflict creates new situations to which the group adapts by creating new norms and rules. This rule-creating process extends and modifies the existing body of norms and rules and thus creates a new framework within which conflict takes place.[62]

WAR

When *homo sapiens* appeared on earth, he shared certain qualities of his biological predecessors. He, too, was a hunter and killer and lived in groups with his kind. *Homo sapiens,* however, was unique in his possession of the human brain. He could communicate in symbols and employ symbols in thinking. When faced with prob-lems, he could think creatively. His mind could bring forth new combinations of elements. He could adapt more successfully to his environment than his predecessors. His innovations enriched his culture and, identified in symbols, enriched his language. The in-vention of writing enabled his knowledge of his culture to be pre-served by means other than memory and oral communication. He became what each century in turn looks upon as its modern man.

Today's modern man retains the biological and cultural endow-ments of his past. He remains a thinking and social animal. He loves those who are his kind, and he kills those who are not. When he kills one of his kind, he experiences guilt. His culture calls it murder and views it with abhorrence. Those who were his kind were his family, kin, and tribe. They now include his countrymen. The closer they are in relationship, the greater is his sense of guilt for their killing. But the stranger is outside the group. He is a non-person. Tribal man killed him for the sport of it and enslaved and despoiled him for the profit of it. Modern man kills members of stranger groups because it is noble and necessary. He is trained to kill stranger groups in orga-nizations called armies. He assumes a uniform, and, in the capacity

---

62. Coser, *op. cit.,* pp. 48-49, 62-80, 93, 102-110, 123-128, citing E. A. Ross, *The Principles of Sociology* (New York, 1920), 164-165, on disruptive social conflict and M. Rheinstein (ed.), *Max Weber on Law in Economy and Society* (Cam-bridge, 1964), 68, on the development of customary law.

of another "self," kills without experiencing guilt. His opponent in another army wears a different uniform and is not merely a stranger. He is also a symbolic menace, a "Hun," a "Nazi," or a "Red," on the one hand, or an "imperialist," or a "capitalist," on the other hand.

In tribal society, man found gratifications in the activity of war in experiencing excitement, thrill, and danger and employing bodily skills in the sword and the spear. Skill and success by a warrior was a way to achieve honor, esteem, and rise in status. War operated to release tensions created by frustration and disappointment. It was a way of revenge and sometimes took the form of obtaining through force compensation for injury. Tribal war, in general, fell into two patterns. First, it was the use of force upon another group for the purpose of acquiring land, booty, or slaves. Second, it was retributive action visited by one group upon another for offenses committed upon its members, such as murder, rape, abduction, seduction, and theft. When uncontrolled in its violence, as a result of the perception that the opposing groups shared no common identity in a larger social order, it was war in the pure sense of the term. When it took the form of *lex talionis* and was subject to social controls which regulated the expression of violence, it became a sanctioning process and an emerging form of legal behavior.

It is possible that at the deeper level of consciousness of both tribal and modern man, war can be viewed to be a product of the projection to stranger peoples of the hatreds and hostilities which arise within the group. It may be a displacement upon other groups of aggression which arises from the frustrations of life experienced within the group. It is frequently said that, when a dictator finds his position of power slipping, he will resort to war and seek to maintain his power by inculcating hatred of the enemy. It may also be a direct expression of aggression upon other groups which arises from frustration experienced at their hands.

In any event, war served a number of social functions in the life of groups. Internal tensions build up which cannot be released against the holders of authority or by leaving the group. War operated, at least momentarily, to release those tensions. War against others helped to hold the group together. It served to maintain group identity and group boundaries.

War became an integral part of the rhythm and process of the relations of states. It was simply a part of the international system of action viewed in its long-run perspective. It enabled a discharge of the tensions which the system accumulated. It brought about a restructuring of the system to accommodate political, social, and economic change. The order of peace which ensued simply represented a new order of things. The new order in turn became increasingly unstable as a consequence of change and the process repeated itself.

The foreign policies of one state were viewed as inimical to those of another. Communication of information concerning the political character of the other state and its acts was inadequate. Moreover, such information was perceived in a distorted way because the other state held a different ideology. An armaments race began. A local conflict, a small disturbance, was magnified in its significance. War was viewed as imminent. Decisions were made under pressure. War broke out and continued until the actors became fatigued. The peace treaty acknowledged victory, defined the new international order which was its outcome, and the new order was accepted by the actors until once again a new crisis arose.

These, then, were the classic contours of the war system. In this light, war was instrumental rather than suicidal. It had its psychological, sociological, and political functions. It was part of the struggle of states to secure and expand their bases of power, their wealth, and their influence. It represented the use of force to maintain a balance-of-power system. It was, in short, an instrument of national policy.

Our globe is now organized into states. Colonial outposts of other states have almost entirely disappeared. Yet the emerging states of Africa and Asia have populations which largely remain at earlier stages of cultural development. Their peoples are at the village level still organized for the practical affairs of life in kinship structures. The central government intrudes in their life in the form of taxation. It provides roads to markets but not education, sanitation, and protection against catastrophe. The old way of life, the traditional perceptions of the social and supernatural order, persist. Such states have a thin layer of élite who perform the functions of government, management, and direction of the army. The élite train their young in the schools but the submerged agricultural group and what little industrial group there is remain substantially uneducated. These states, composed of a thin veneer of élite and a submerged mass of agricultural and industrial proletariat, could well be called veneer states. The Latin American states have not progressed much beyond this stage, and they may also be called veneer states. Thus the globe can be seen to be peopled by the advanced, industrially-organized, modern welfare states mostly found in the Atlantic basin, by veneer states, and by states of an intermediate stage, such as China and India.

In this light, the pattern of the wars of the two decades after World War II suddenly assumes significance. These wars were the wars of Asia, the Middle East, and Africa. India and Indonesia have been the scene of mass genocide on the scale of hundreds of thousands killed. The wars of the emerging states were, from the standpoint of the protagonists, mostly civil wars. They were struggles to determine what groups should possess legitimate authority and power in a territory. There is a striking parallelism in this regard between the war of North and South Korea and the war of North and South Viet Nam. The Chinese-Indian border war and the forceful absorption of Goa by India, on the other hand, fall into the pattern of war as an instrument of national policy.

States in the stage of cultural development of the veneer state are oriented to the local scene. For most of them, the western world is the home of the former colonial powers. The world they perceive, the values they share, and the goals they seek to attain have a local or national frame of reference. War is for them a familiar way of life and a rational means to ends. They have little perception of themselves as actors in a world scene and of their wars as a form of national suicide.

War for the technological industrially-organized, modern state of the Atlantic basin and certain other parts of the globe still retains in some circumstances its classic character of an instrument of national policy. The threatened use of force by the United States against Russia in the Cuban missile crisis possessed credibility because it was a rational means to carry out national policy of the highest magnitude of importance. The Russian goal of establishing missiles in Cuba did not possess equal value importance to it, either as a state or as an exporter of Communist ideology, and was accordingly relinquished. To understand fully the nature of twentieth-century war, however, we have to perceive the nature of the new world in which we live. We may now characterize the cultural developments which are significant for this purpose.

First, there is the emergence of a continuum of science, technology, the arts, manufacture, trade, travel, and communication, which knows no boundaries of states. One may describe this growth as the appearance of world society. Yet politically and, to a considerable extent, perceptually, the world remains compartmentalized in states. Moreover, states have proliferated in number. The interdependence of world society clashes with the autarchy of states.

Second, a symbolic way of life has superseded man's direct contact with reality. Not long ago man saw what he did. He used his hands and his physical strength to deal with his environment. He was still one with his biological predecessors in that he employed essentially simple tools. He once found his identity in kinship terms. He now finds it in an IBM card. He now perceives and manipulates symbols to attain his goals—symbols of the printed word, numbers, mathematical formulas, signs, signals, graphs, dials, and buttons. He works with computer language to make decisions. Mass media of communication tell him about the world through symbols. He finds his entertainment in the symbolic, conventionalized performances of westerns and spy dramas on television and movie screens. In their killings and inflictions of violence, he vents vicariously the impulses to aggression which the frustrations of the day create. Television, movies, drama, and the novel are increasingly expressing pure fantasy and symbolism instead of objective reality. Man finds a symbolic release from the pressure and friction of his work environment.

Third, thus accustomed to the symbolic way of life, man turns to ideologies and ideologues and to the master symbols of mass movements to interpret and give meaning to his life and to provide him with new goals. Politicians, mass leaders, writers, and speakers communicate in symbols that have referential significance, that is, symbols intended to refer to reality. They also employ symbols which have significance as condensation symbols, that is, symbols which embody a great deal of emotion. The primitive symbols of the earth, the sky, the gods, the spirits, and the ancestors were condensation symbols. Today we are moved by such words and phrases as "freedom," "liberty," "free enterprise," "the individual," "the rights of the individual," "civil rights," and "black power." Whereas religion once depicted and justified a societal order in supernatural symbols, it has now become to a considerable extent an ethical system for appraising and evaluating life in terms of moral norms. The former legitimizing function of religion is now performed by the master symbols and precepts of political ideologies. This is why, among other things, modern wars are all-or-nothing affairs. There can be no compromise with the moral rightness of the political positions of the warring parties.

Fourth, the interdependence of the states of the Atlantic basin and of their linkages with the rest of the world, which is part and parcel of the development noted in the first point above, takes organizational form in regional arrangements, such as NATO and the Common Market. It still lacks, however, a new ideology or set of master symbols to depict and justify it.

Classic master symbols of the "national interest," "human freedom," and "grandeur" persist. The collective interest in peaceful relations, stability, and order is symbolized in such legalistic phrases as "aggression cannot be permitted" and such moralistic phrases as a state must "not molest its neighbors." The participation of Russia, China, and the Communist states in the world society is viewed by such states as part of a historical mission to achieve the world-wide revolution and dictatorship of the proletariat. The participation of the emerging states of Africa and Asia in the world society is depicted in such master symbols as "freedom from neo-colonialists," "African unity," and "nègritude." The United Nations, as a universal set of master symbols and structure of world order, is not yet adopted by the peoples of the world as a way for perceiving world order or as embodying their important values.

Fifth, when local wars appear, either as conflicts between incompatible national policies or as civil conflicts, the ramifications of world society and the precariousness of the equilibrium of peace among states are such that local wars tend to spread quickly and become world wars. World wars are wars which involve constitutive conflict. They present to the warring parties the question of what type of international order and its accompanying ideology shall become the paramount and universal form of world order.

Control

The concept of control appears in a number of behavioral contexts. The viewpoint which the control of action implies was poignantly expressed by Beethoven when, overtaken by deafness, he said; "No more to hear my music and know that it is as I meant it to be." The universality of the concept of control was described by Sinnott:

> That the insistent tendency among living things for bodily development to reach and maintain, as a norm or goal, an organized living system of a definite kind, and the equally persistent directiveness or goal-seeking that is the essential feature of behavior, and thus finally the basis of all mental activity, are *fundamentally the same thing*, merely two aspects of the basic regulatory character all living stuff displays. Regulation implies something to regulate *to,* a norm or goal. The goal in embryonic life may be regarded as the series of stages that lead to a mature and properly functioning individual; and the goal in psychic life as a purpose or series of purposes, simple and unconscious in primitive instinct, but rising in the mind of man to far higher levels. Mental activity is the most complex form and culmination of that universal regulatory behavior in life which we have been discussing. . . .

The goal of the organism, implanted first in the genetic constitution of the egg, unfolds itself in structure and activity as development progresses. In every cell of the body, so it seems, are to be found the same genes, derived from those first present in the egg. These cells gradually become different as growth proceeds, until the great diversity of structures present in tissues and organs of the mature individual is reached. This goal is not a static one, gained once for all, for genetic control does not cease when growth is ended but extends to the behavior of the mature organism. At all levels the organism is held to a straight course by constant regulation, which brings it back whenever it deviates from the norm. The pattern of development and activity that works itself out in this way is not the result of a mere collection of independent genes, like beads on a string or marbles in a bag or separate chemical substances, but of a precisely integrated and continuing *relationship* between them. It has well been said that the organism is not an aggregate but an integrate. The nature of this relationship is the basic and still unsolved problem of biology.[63]

The organism exercises control in perception as it matches sensory impressions against mental categories until a workable, acceptable image and category for purposes of further action is created. Control in the cognitive processes takes place in order to eliminate incongruity, unify, and create a workable, acceptable order. Control is exercised over physical action to bring it closer to ideal form.

From the standpoint of the mechanics of action, control brings action into conformity with intention. It operates as a feedback mechanism to regulate behavior. From the standpoint of value, control evaluates the contentment following the realization of a value in action and decides upon the worth of action. It weighs such contentment as against other values which press for realization, as the actor moves into its next phase of action. The questions are asked: Could the action which took place have been bettered in its physical expression and also as an expression of values? Did the action represent the best allocation of energy to realize values?

The organization which is the state has its rules of law which pervade all forms of social action, including that of individual organizational structures operating within the state. Such lesser organizations have their own structural and behavioral rules supported by the inducements of promotion and wage increase and sanctioned by demotion or discharge.

The description of the process of control which was made by the author in an earlier volume may usefully be recalled at this point:

Control, it has been said, is the appraisal and regulative phase of action. It is that aspect of action in which the individual (1) reflects upon

63. E. W. Sinnott, *Biology of the Spirit* (New York, 1955), 52-53, 57.

specific past action, (2) verifies whether the action had in fact carried out the decision to act to which the individual had committed himself, and (3) appraises past action from the standpoint of (a) economy of effort or efficiency of the means selected as against alternative available means and (b) goal gratification, that is, weighing of contentment following the attainment of the goal from the standpoint of whether it justifies further commitment to the goal as against the values embodied in competing goals. It is also that aspect of action in which the individual reflects upon the design of the totality of his past action and, as a consequence, re-shapes his values and value priorities so that he commits himself to a different design of action.

In the organization, three levels or aspects of control are perceived. There is, first, that type of control to verify whether or not specific authoritative decisions or rules for behavior were performed and, if not, the respects in which there was a departure of behavior from command or rule. This leads to regulation designed to restore behavior to its de-sired pattern. There is, second, that type of control to resolve interper-sonal conflict arising in an organization, typically as a consequence of behavior departing from specific commands or expected standards or norms of behavior. There is, third, that type of control concerned with appraising the adequacy of the total design of the action of the organiza-tion, as a means for realizing the values of the participants and reflecting the relevant goals, values, and standards of the society and culture in which the organization finds itself. This last phrase of control refers directly to the leadership function and provides it with information which is essential for the effective performance of its task.

Thus control is not to be perceived as operating in an unchanging system. It is not to be viewed as having the sole function of mechanically regulating deviant behavior and thereby restoring equilibrium to the system. Control has a creative function as it regulates conduct. Control is exercised to appraise and evaluate a deviation in conduct and to decide whether some other alternative mode of action might be more appropriate than the previous institutionalized or established action, which was the standard for determining the deviance. Appraisal and regulation are not to be confined to deviant action; they are to be ap-plied to the entire action of the social system in the light of experience, cultural standards, and cultural change.[64]

CONTROL IN PSYCHOLOGICAL ACTION

The term control seems to be very little used in psychology, though some of the referents for it, which will be mentioned below, are familiar. Control involves the processes of reflection, appraisal, evaluation, comparison, matching, feedback of information, and the like, together with the responses engendered as a consequence of such cognitive activity. It imports the existence of ideals, ideal

---

64. Carlston, *Law and Organization,* 92-93.

standards, and norms, coupled with the evaluation of past performance in the light of such factors with a view to its control so that future performance will more accurately embody the ideal image of action. In cybernetics, it is the control of an operation by the "feedback" of information, when it departs from some fixed standard of performance. Control examines the results of action. It verifies whether goals have been reached and whether desired, planned, or directed performance has taken place. Control steps in after action has been completed and evaluates past action with a view to its possible or necessary reshaping. It looks to the past and decides how its lessons shall influence action in the present and the future. In the domain of value, control constantly weighs and determines the value significance of past action as a factor in decision making as to the content of future action.

Control involves the verification of action as a matter of form and substance and making sure that intention was accomplished and style of performance was satisfactory. It further involves appraisal of the value significance of action, whether value realization experienced in past action measured up to anticipation, and how experience in value realization shall influence priorities among values in determining future action.

The view of behavior as made up of approach and avoidance, action and inhibition, may be said to place inhibition in a control role.[65] The evaluative aspect of control was pointed out by Lewis:

> Knowledge, action, and evaluation are essentially connected. The primary and pervasive significance of knowledge lies in its guidance of action: knowing for the sake of doing. And action, obviously, is rooted in evaluation. For a being which did not assign comparative values, deliberate action would be pointless; and for one which did not know, it would be impossible. Conversely, only an active being could have knowledge, and only such a being could assign values to anything beyond his own feelings. A creature which did not enter into the process of reality to alter in some part the future content of it could apprehend a world only in the sense of intuitive or esthetic contemplation; and such contemplation would not possess the significance of knowledge but only that of suffering and enjoying.[66]

The concept of control postulates the evaluation and appraisal of action as a central phase of action. The view of psychological functions as circular, looped, process, or involving feedback is im-

---

65. O. H. Mowrer, *Learning Theory and the Symbolic Processes* (New York, 1960), 414.

66. C. I. Lewis, *An Analysis of Knowledge and Valuation* (LaSalle, Ill., 1947), 1.

plicit in a number of theories. Allport's cyclical theory of perception;[67] Bruner's confirmation check in perception;[68] Thorndike's law of effect, in which rewards and punishments were seen in a trial and error continuum of exploratory acts operating selectively to determine successful adaptive behavior;[69] Freud's concept of the superego;[70] the concept of reinforcement of responses, either positively or negatively, as a result of experience; the notion of the development of habit as the repetition of responses perceived to be successful among non-successful responses, including Hull's concept of the "pure stimulus act," whose function it is to serve as stimuli for other acts;[71] Goss and Wischner's concept of "vicarious trial and error";[72] Miller, Galanter, and Pribram's basic TOTE unit of test-operate-test-exit, which was conceived as a feedback loop in which a sequence of action took place testing the congruity and incongruity of action with an ideal image, sequence, or plan;[73] Wiener's suggestion of the possibilities for psychology of applications of automatic control in cybernetics;[74] Ashby's attempt to construct a learning mechanism relying upon feedback to create conditions of stability and ultrastability;[75] Sinnott's brilliantly stated view of the basic regulatory character of life, in all its forms, and mind;[76] and the notion of evaluation represent some of the applications of the concept of control in the literature.

For the purposes of this study, there would be little value in developing the above references to the literature or psychology in further detail. They are alluded to in order to illustrate how the broad concept of control manifests itself in many directions. Control may helpfully be visualized as operating after action is completed. Its principal function is to verify the quality of performance and to appraise the value significance of such performance. Judgments

67. F. H. Allport, *Theories of Perception and the Concept of Structure* (New York, London, 1955).

68. J. S. Bruner, "On Perceptual Readiness," *Readings in Perception,* eds. D. C. Beardslee and M. Wertheimer (Princeton, 1968), 686.

69. E. I. Thorndike, "The Law of Effect," *American Journal of Psychology,* XXXIX (1927), 212.

70. *Supra,* p. 5.

71. See C. E. Osgood, *Method and Theory in Experimental Psychology* (New York, 1953), 395-396.

72. A. E. Goss and G. J. Wischner, "Vicarious Trial and Error and Related Behavior," *Psychological Bulletin,* LIII (1956), 35.

73. G. A. Miller, E. Galanter, and K. H. Pribram, *Plans and the Structure of Behavior* (New York, 1960), 25-31.

74. N. Wiener, *Cybernetics* (New York, 1948), 14-15.

75. W. R. Ashby, *Design for a Brain* (New York, 1952).

76. Sinnott, *op. cit.,* pp. 52-65. See the quotation from Sinnott *supra* at p. 44.

reached on both of these aspects of prior behavior are considered in the planning and performance of later behavior. Control thus becomes a part of the continuing adaptive behavior of the organism, flowing into the organization of thought concerning the form which such later behavior shall take.

RELIGION AS A MODE OF SOCIAL CONTROL

Ideal and valued norms of conduct develop in a society as a consequence of the performance of repetitive sequences of behavior in role relationships. When the actors of such roles depart from such institutionalized patterns of behavior, they deprive others with whom they are interacting of valued expectations of behavior. If no third-party decision process exists to handle such situations of interpersonal conflict in a society characterized by multiple role relationships, then ritual may be relied upon to handle such conflict.[77] Religion provides a symbolic system of supernatural rewards to reinforce adherence to approved norms of social behavior and punishments for violations of such norms, including invocation of supernatural means to discover offenders.[78] The use of the ordeal to point to those guilty of the violation of approved norms of conduct, coupled with their punishment, may be said to represent a process of adjudication and a sanctioning process. The use of diviners to discover offenders, together with the subsequent punishment of such offenders, similarly represents an adjudicative and sanctioning process.

Commands of the religious and ethical systems of tribal societies to display love, esteem, and respect to family heads and elders, when their actual conduct is not perceived to justify it and when their exercise of authority is held to be selfish and arbitrary, create tensions within kinship structures, family relations, relations between the sexes, and relations between the elders and others. Gluckman called attention to rituals of rebellion, in which socially approved and organized expressions of hostility against rulers took place, as well as expressions of hostility based on grievances and expressions of hostility between social groupings, such as between the old and the young or between clans and tribes. These rituals of license and hatred operated to release accumulated tensions in the social relations in question. Even though the release may be only momentary

---

77. M. Gluckman, "Les Rites de Passage," *op. cit.,* 26, 34, 40.

78. E. Norbeck, *Religion in Primitive Society* (New York, 1961), 170-176; D. Forde, "The Context of Belief: A Consideration of Fetishim among the Yako," *Frazer Lecture* (Liverpool, 1958), 21; see *supra* at pages 11 to 14.

in its effect and does nothing to alleviate the basic causes of the tensions, nevertheless the occasions are ones of great joy and make it possible for the social system to continue its operation.[79] The fact remains, however, that as conflict moves from surface levels to deeper levels and from conflict over values which are of slight importance to those which are intensely held, it becomes increasingly difficult for ritual to deal effectively with such constitutive conflict.[80]

On the other hand, tribal man, notably in kinship-structured societies, developed a belief in supernatural power operating as a sanctioning process to punish those who violated valued norms. Those who showed disrespect to their elders, those who wronged others or who committed offenses, might not receive physical punishment for their misbehavior. A father or a grandfather found it difficult to beat his strapping male offspring. Such societies had not developed the legal system and the sanctioning process characteristic of more maturely developed societies. In this situation, the head of the kinship group frequently held the post of acting as an intermediary with the supernature world and was deemed to be supported by its power in the performance of his role. The supernatural power of the ancestors and the gods performed the function of sanctioning disrespect of his authority. The commission of wrongs and offenses was punished by the ancestors by visiting illness, misfortune, and even death upon those guilty of such misconduct.

WITCHCRAFT AS A SYMBOLIC EXPRESSION AND CONTROL OF CONFLICT

While the phenomenon of witchcraft has disappeared in modern society, its prevalence in tribal society demands that it be briefly explained. There is considerable evidence to support the hypothesis that witchcraft represents a means for handling symbolically a very wide variety of situations involving ambivalence and frustration experienced by an actor. It can be considered to be a form of projection of hostility or of displacement of hostility onto substitute objects. Since the persons who are frequently charged with witchcraft are frequently those who exhibit generally disliked traits, witchcraft may also serve a useful purpose of social control of culturally disapproved behavior.

79. M. Gluckman, "Rituals of Rebellion in South-East Africa," *Frazer Lecture, 1952* (Manchester, 1952); Gluckman, *Custom and Conflict;* M. Gluckman, *Order and Rebellion in Tribal Africa* (New York, 1963); E. Norbeck, "African Rituals of Conflict," *American Anthropologist,* LXV (1963), p. 1254.

80. *Cf.* M. Gluckman, *Politics, Law, and Ritual in Tribal Society* (Chicago, 1965), 247.

Witchcraft has been seen as a form of projection, "a means of expression and control of repressed desires, anxiety, and hostility." It serves the function of relieving the impact of external catastrophe or internal tension. Integration of a group is promoted as a result of expressing feelings of hostility or frustration against an out-group composed of witches.[81] Witchcraft is positively correlated with social structures in which interaction takes place in importantly valued aspects of life and which do not possess public and legitimate procedures for dispute settlement.[82]

Kluckhohn investigated witchcraft among the Navahoes as a psychological phenomenon. He pointed out that hostility developed in interpersonal relations in a kinship-structured society but that social pressures made it difficult to express directly hostility against kin. In such a situation, witches and ghosts provided personal targets against which hostile feelings could be directed. They personalized threats and deprivations. When other means failed for handling hostility, such as withdrawal, sublimation, and conciliation, witches became scapegoats. He listed a number of social functions served by witchcraft beliefs:

1. In-group aggression was displaced upon Navahoes who were socially and territorially distant to the Navahoes but never upon whites.

2. Witchcraft also provided a means for direct aggression. Guarded imputations of witchcraft were made against close objects of hatred.

3. Witchcraft provided a means for the release of special tensions arising in personal relationships, such as hostilities between siblings and hatred of the rich.

4. Witchcraft provided a socially approved, institutionalized means for relieving anxiety.

5. Witchcraft sanctioned anti-social conduct, such a lack of generosity or meanness.

The first three of these were means of handling aggression within the group, the fourth was a means for handling anxiety, and the fifth was an instrument of social control.[83]

Evans-Pritchard made a detailed study of witchcraft among the Azande. His findings empirically validate the above hypotheses to an extraordinary degree.

He noted that the Azande were ridden with malice, hatred, and

---

81. Norbeck, *Religion in Primitive Society*, 192-194.

82. Swanson, *op. cit.*, pp. 146-152.

83. C. Kluckhohn, "Navaho Witchcraft," *Papers of the Peabody Museum of Archaeology and Ethnology* (Harvard University, 1944), XXII, No. 2, 51-64. On point 5, see Gluckman, *Custom and Conflict*, 93-95.

envy. Jealousy was rife among close relations. Children feared and often hated their fathers. If a man failed in his affairs, it was held to be due to the witchcraft of a jealous neighbor. The Azande were a highly sensitive people and viewed casual remarks by others as veiled attacks on themselves. Ill will, slander, envy, and jealousy were everywhere manifest and were the source of imputations of witchcraft. Tension often broke out into physical conflict.

Witchcraft appeared to be a product of frustrations experienced in the normal, every-day aspects of life. It was commonplace. If an untoward event, failure, or misfortune of any kind occured, it was attributed to witchcraft. When a normal activity miscarried and created an injury or misfortune, witchcraft was held to be responsible. The natural cause of some misfortunes was acknowledged, but the occurrence of the natural cause was perceived to have been brought about by witchcraft. If a man was killed by an elephant, the Azande said that the elephant was the "first spear" and that witchcraft was the "second spear" and that "together they killed the man."

Witchcraft accompanied misfortunes. When a person was ill or his actions met with failure, it was said that "his condition is bad." This meant that he was exposed to witchcraft and that it was causing him injury. "In such a state, a man is vexed. Someone among his neighbors wishes him ill and has bewitched him." Witchcraft was believed to be an intentional harm inflicted by magical power by a person on another whom he hated. It was said that "malice, hatred, jealousy, envy, backbiting, slander, and the like first appeared and that witchcraft then followed." The emotional reaction in a situation in which the response of witchcraft appeared ranged from "annoyance to anger rather than from fear to terror." Witchcraft was a response to situations of value deprivation. "Zande notions of witchcraft express a dynamic relationship of persons to other persons in inauspicious occasions. Their meaning is so dependent on passing situations that a man is scarcely regarded as a witch when the situation that evoked an accusation against him has disappeared."

Charges of witchcraft were made between persons of substantially equal status who were not kin. They arose between persons who had close, intimate relations with one another. Witches attacked only people in the vicinity. The more intimate the social interaction and the closer the witches were territorially to their victims, the more serious were their attacks.

Persons who failed to meet community standards of desirable, approved conduct or moral standards were those who were most frequently charged with witchcraft. Persons who were mean, spiteful, glum, ill-tempered, ill-mannered, or greedy were those who were most frequently charged with witchcraft. Yet, since everyone was disliked by someone, no one was free from the possibility of being called a witch. Accordingly, no one could believe that when he was charged with witchcraft that this could possibly have occurred. The person accused would be astonished, plead his innocence, and yet return his belief that all witches committed intentional acts of hatred.

Witch doctors who acted as diviners of witches were always well informed of local scandal. When they were asked to name a witch, they would select a person who had ill will against the questioner or whom the questioner thought to bear him ill will. They thus performed a third-party decision process in cases of interpersonal conflict.[84]

SOCIAL CONTROL: LAW

Of the wide variety of measures of social control, such as custom and convention, fad and fashion, honor and ostracism, mores and morals, and reward and ridicule, this study will center its attention upon law.

In his admirable study of the linguistic and conceptual problems incident to the study of law and legal institutions in African tribal society, Gluckman[85] raised a number of basic questions concerning the approach to be adopted in the investigation of law in African tribal society. Should law be equated with the rules for behavior which a society considers to be obligatory or should it refer to rules subject to sanctions? The conclusion was reached that the term "legal" should be used "to cover the various kinds of sanctions." What are courts for purposes of anthropological investigation? It was held that they are bodies which examine and weigh evidence in reaching their decisions. They are not to be restricted to bodies which are backed by means for enforcing their judgments. Is it possible, in his view, accurately and faithfully to characterize the nature of the adjudicatory process and legal concepts, as viewed in one cul-

---

84. E. E. Evans-Pritchard, *Witches, Oracles and Magic among the Azande* (Oxford, 1937, reprint 1950), 32, 63-119, 176, quotations at pp. 74, 84, 100, 107. The hypothesis that beliefs in witches and witchcraft are correlated with the appearance of frustration and resultant tendencies to aggression is also borne out in S. F. Nadel, "Witchcraft in Four African Societies: An Essay in Comparison," *American Anthropologist*, LIV (1962), p. 18. Less insightful studies of witchcraft appear in G. W. Wilson and M. Wilson, *The Analysis of Social Change* (Cambridge, 1945), 89-104; M. H. Wilson, "Witch Beliefs and Social Structure," *American Journal of Sociology*, LVI (1951), 307. See Gluckman, *Custom and Conflict*, 93-95.

85. M. Gluckman, "African Jurisprudence," *Advancement of Science*, XVIII (1962), 439.

ture and expressed in its language, from the standpoint of another culture and its language? Bohannan denied this, insisting on the uniqueness of each "folk system."[86] Gluckman affirmed that with the resources of the English language and the jural concepts developed in the English legal system, it is possible to compare English legal concepts with analogous concepts of Roman law and tribal law as well. On the other hand, the distinctions apparent to the English jurist and capable of elaboration by him in his language could not be expressed by the Tiv jurist, because he "lacks the necessary words." Finally, Gluckman pointed out that one must distinguish the study of the mechanisms of social control, such as African beliefs in witchcraft and ancestral spirits, from judicial procedures.

Schapera[87] noted that a number of anthropologists, such as Hoebel,[88] had defined law to consist of social norms sanctioned by the legitimate use of force. He then pointed out that if one applied the concept of law, as known today, to the behavior of primitive societies, it would follow that many do not have law, or that their law is different from law in advanced societies, or that the definition of law drawn from advanced societies is inadequate and must be expanded. In his study of Tswana law, he stated that in many primitive societies "rules of conduct" developed "which specify the rights of one person and the duties of another," apart from the existence of courts.[89]

To identify law broadly as obligatory rules, or rules which specify rights and duties, is to move to a degree of abstraction which would embrace a plethora of social norms and a most expanded area of social control. This is the difficulty of Malinowski's often-quoted definition of law.[90] What marks the expectation of the institutional-

---

86. P. Bohannan, *Justice and Judgment among the Tiv* (London, New York, Toronto, 1957), 4-5, 69. See the analysis of the approaches to law of these two authors *infra* at pp. 229 to 233.

87. I. Schapera, "Malinowski's Theories of Law," *Man and Culture*, ed. R. Firth (London, 1957), 139.

88. *E.g.*, A. R. Radcliffe-Brown, *Structure and Function in Primitive Society* (London, 1952), 208, 212; S. F. Nadel, *The Nuba: An Anthropological Study of the Hill Tribes in Kordofan* (Oxford, 1947), 500; M. J. Herskovits, *Man and His Works: The Science of Cultural Anthropology* (New York, 1948), 345; E. A. Hoebel, *The Law of Primitive Man* (Cambridge, Mass., 1954), 28; R. H. Lowie, *Social Organization* (New York, 1948), 156.

89. I. Schapera, *A Handbook of Tswana Law and Custom* (2d ed.; London, New York, Cape Town, 1955), 37.

90. B. Malinowski, *Crime and Custom in Savage Society* (London, 1926), 55, 58:
   The rules of law stand out from the rest in that they are felt and regarded as the obligations of one person and the rightful claims of another. . . .
   'Civil law,' the positive law governing all the phases of tribal life, consists

ized performance of a sequence of behavior as obligatory or a duty, on the one hand, and a right, on the other hand? What modes of social control reinforce the performance of such behavior? The identification of behavior as law is derived from a number of sources and consists of a number of elements.

The roots of law probably lie in the need for social control of the frustration-aggression pattern of behavior. An organism is moving toward an important goal or is engaged in the realization of an important value in an ongoing activity. It finds its path unexpectedly obstructed or interfered with by the action of another. For example, a useful article under one's control is borrowed and not returned or is stolen. The expectation of exclusive enjoyment of a sex partner is denied as a result of adultery. A person is injured because of another's heedless act. In all of these situations, aggressive action against the person responsible for the frustration that would normally be expected to occur. When such aggression is prohibited and a sanctioning process is substituted for it in the society, it may be said that law has appeared. One may go beyond this and simply say that a legal norm appears whenever a social norm becomes a corrective point of reference,[91] that is, whenever departure from the norm is marked by the regularized imposition of sanctions upon the deviant performer. In other words, a legal rule is a rule departure from which is subject to a sanctioning process or the perceived consistent imposition of deprivation or retribution.

In such a view of law, the sanctioning process may be self-help carried out in accordance with custom, as in the appeal of felony in early English society.[92] It may be institutionalized in a military society, as among the Plains Indians[93] or in an age group of African tribal society. It may even be extended to the perceived intervention of ancestor spirits by way of punishment.

---

then of a body of binding obligations, regarded as a right by one party and acknowledged as a duty by the other, *kept in force by a specific mechanism of reciprocity and publicity inherent in the structure of their society.* (Italics supplied).

91. J. Fried, "The Relation of Ideal Norms to Actual Behavior in Tarahumara Society," *Southwestern Journal of Anthropology,* IX (1953), 286.

92. J. Goebel, Jr., *Cases and Materials on the Development of Legal Institutions* (Brattleboro, Vermont, 1946), 67-69.

93. J. H. Provinse, "The Underlying Sanctions of Plains Indian Culture," Social Anthropology of North American Tribes, ed. F. Eggan (2d ed.; Chicago, 1955), 341; R. H. Lowie, "Military Societies of the Crow Indians," and "Hidatsa Men's Societies," *Anthropological Papers of the American Museum of Natural History,* XI (1916), 147, 225; K. Llewellyn and E. A. Hoebel, *The Cheyenne Way: Conflict and Case Law in Primitive Jurisprudence* (Norman, Okla., 1941), Chap. 5.

When a society accumulates measurable wealth, such as livestock or fowl, it then has the cultural foundation on which a new type of sanction can be provided for the infraction of a legal rule, namely, the requirement of reparation or payment of compensation to the injured party. The psychological basis of the desire to make reparation for damage wrought as a consequence of breaking a rule for conduct is said to lie in "an urge to make reparation out of a sense of guilt for damage caused."[94] The injured party accepts a substitute restoration of the situation prior to the injury in the form of the transfer of wealth by the wrongdoer, measured somewhat proportionately to the nature of the wrong and the damage experienced.

Not until a society reaches the stage of cultural development when a violator of a valued norm is subjected to a sanctioning process of a retributive or reparational character can it be said to begin to travel the long road that ends in the law and legal institutions of modern society.[95] The next step on that road is the creation of a third-party decision-making agent for the purpose of determining the breach of norms and the linking of norm violations with a sanctioning process.[96]

The norms out of which interpersonal conflict in a society arise are sometimes broad and abstract in their behavioral content and are, at other times, of a highly specific content, referring to narrow sequences of behavior. Examples of norms of a vague content are those commanding the display of certain kinds of attitudes in role relationships.

A father's concern for the welfare of his son, a son's respect to his father, a young man's respect to his elders, an age-mate's generosity to his fellow age-mates are all valued norms of conduct but are of diffuse content. For example, the rule among the Cheyenne that one must generously share one's goods with others encountered conduct consisting of the borrowing of horses by one warrior from another

---

94. R. Bienenfeld, "Prolegemena to a Psychoanalysis of Law and Justice, Part II—Analysis," *California Law Review*, LIII (1965), 1329.

95. Compare Bohannan's definition of law as consisting of (1) a breach of a norm, (2) counteraction, comprising institutionalized procedures for controlling breaches of norms, and (3) correction, comprising the correct performance of the original norm by the violator thereof brought about as a result of the measures of counteraction. *Social Anthropology*, 284-285. For a more complete statement of Bohannan's approach, see *infra* pages 226 to 227.

96. It will be observed that this statement carefully avoids limiting the control of the application of the sanctioning process to the third party decision-making agent. This enables the statement to comprehend situations in which a supernatural sanctioning process is perceived to be applied by the gods or the spirits to norm violators.

at times when they were needed by the owner for the hunt in order to feed his family. It may have been that the rule of generosity resting on the owner conflicted with a rule resting on the borrower that one should show concern for the needs of another. The solution, however, was not found in selecting one rule over another on the basis that it possessed a higher value importance which the society shared. Such an approach is basic to the legal process, namely, the selection of one of two competing rules of behavior in a conflict situation on the basis that it embodies a value which the society would acknowledge to be of higher importance. An equally fundamental approach of the legal process was instead adopted. A third-party decision-making body formulated a new rule. It was that there should "be no more borrowing of horses without asking."[97] The established rule was one of a more abstract quality. The new rule was consistent with it and its consistency was made possible because of the specific type of behavior which it commanded.

As the anthropologist approaches his study of tribal societies, he must work with the concepts and bases of perception and cognition which his culture gives him. The learning which he has derived from his culture directs his search for data in another culture. The data which he finds there, in turn, have their own impact upon the concepts with which he approaches them. He learns that the data have an obdurate meaning and order of their own that places the heaviest of burdens upon his ability to employ the symbols of his language to describe them faithfully. A principal source of his difficulty is that their reference is different, to use the semantic system of Ogden and Richards. He learns that behavior bearing a resemblance to what he calls law in his culture cannot be placed in the pigeon hole of Holmes' famous dictum that law is the prediction of what courts will in fact do. Nor will a broader concept of law as the action of an adjudicatory body engaged in formulating and applying norms and subjecting their violators to sanctions suffice to enable the classification and comparison of the wealth of variety of procedures and institutions of conflict settlement which are found in tribal cultures. One must instead search for the elements of legal behavior, as described above, and indicate the extent to which and the manner in which they have developed in a particular society.

Classification of legal rules may be made on the basis of structural rules and behavioral rules, as defined elsewhere herein.[98]

There is another category of norms which are classed with legal

97. Llewellyn and Hoebel, *op. cit.*, pp. 127-129.
98. *Supra* p. 21 and *infra* p. 59.

norms but do not involve prohibited conduct, the performance of which leads to the application of a sanctioning process. Norms of this category define the creation, nature, and termination of interests in or statuses which individuals have with respect to objects in the form of land, things, and persons. Such norms are necessary because individuals develop a high degree of attachment to the realization of values arising from the land which they farm, the things which they use, and the persons with whom they have important emotional ties, as in the marriage relationship. Thus property law and marriage law arise.

In the author's first book on social theory and law, law is described in terms of social norms as follows:

> Thus we have two different types of norms for conduct, one of which *must* be performed and, when performed, leads to no reaction by the group, other than approval, and the second of which *must not* be performed, and, if performed, leads to the application of group sanctions. The latter is a product of the former in that the *must* conduct is the standard used to determine the *must not* conduct. The sanctions applied are designed to eliminate the *must not* conduct so that the *must* conduct will take its place. The stimulus to the application of such conduct lies in the "expectancies" of conduct of others which become imbedded or "internalized" in the consciousness of each member of the group. It became expected that each member of the group would perform his role in the established or expected way. Each member felt that he owed the rest such a performance.[99]

In his next book, the essential nature of law and the legal process was described as follows:

> *Law is an entity of an ideal and valued norm of action coupled with regulatory behavior designed to restore to the ideal norm action deviating from it.*
>
> When the culture establishes an ideal and valued norm of action, that norm then becomes the standard for, or the determinant of, the regulatory action of law which subjects deviant behavior to control. . . .
>
> The creative idea of a goal as an end of action of the individual organism becomes the concern of leadership in the social system and the

---

99. Carlston, *Law and Structures of Social Action,* 5. Compare Bohannan's later notion of law as the "double institutionalization of norms and therefore of legal rights," that is, law as "custom which has been restated in order to make it amenable to the activities of the legal institutions," P. Bohannan, "The Differing Realms of Law," *American Anthropologist,* LXVII[2] (1965), No. 6, 36, and Malinowski's later definition of one type of law as "the specific mechanism which is brought into existence when a conflict of claims arises or a rule of social conduct is broken," that is, *"retributive and restitutive social action."* B. Malinowski, "A New Instrument for the Interpretation of Law—Especially Primitive," *Yale Law Journal* LI (1942), 1243, 1244.

province of the political institutions of the state and the directors of the economic organization. The performance of action by the organism becomes the concern of administration in the state and management in the economic organization. The regulatory behavior of the organism becomes the concern of law and the legal process in the state, and of authoritative roles in the organization itself, coupled with resort by the organization to law and the legal process. As the culture develops ideal and valued norms of action, regulatory patterns of behavior appear designed to inhibit departures from these norms. When such regulatory behavior assumes the discrete form of the sanction of force applied pursuant to decisions made by occupants of authoritative roles termed judicial, then regulation or control reaches its full institutionalization in a social system. . . .

The regulatory process of law identifies those institutionalized rules of behavior within a social system which embody shared values of the members of the system to the degree that control of deviation, designed to inhibit its further occurrence and to restore the equilibrium of the system, is essential for self-maintenance, goal gratification, integration, and adaptation.

To identify law solely in those patterns or norms of behavior which are sanctioned by the imposition of force in a social system is to observe the outward manifestations of conduct apart from the inner perceptions and motivations of the actor which give meaning to action. To identify law with its institutionalization in the courts and to say that law is simply the predictable behavior of courts is to remove law still one step farther from its meaning in action. It is the value inherent in the norm that is identified as a legal norm and that brings into being the regulatory behavior we call law and the legal process.

When (1) a sequence of action in a typical situation encountered in the functioning of a social system becomes a repetitive and fixed pattern of action, and (2) an actor in such a situation has embedded or "internalized" in his mind that such a pattern of action is expected to be performed by him an *institutionalized* pattern of action may be said to have appeared. It may be termed a behavioral rule.

When behavioral rules embody shared values of such importance in the social system that interference with or departures from their performance create conflict and tension, it may be said that at such departure point the members of the system will regard such rules to indicate behavior which ought to be performed. The expectation of the performance of the rules is so emotionally reinforced by the values which they embody that the actors involved feel they have a *right* to their performance and, conversely, that their performance is *obligatory*.

Obligation is involved in the performance of a behavioral rule when the conduct embodied is perceived to be important to the attainment of goals whose gratification involves strongly held values. It is true that a necessary condition for the involvement of obligation is that the rule shall reflect mechanical rationality, that is, a rationality of appropriateness of means to end. The norm of conduct described in the rule must be viewed as essential to the expression of the idea of the action as developed by the culture. The departure from the norm thus becomes erratic, irrational behavior, which destroys the ideal image of appropriate action in the situation. Behavioral rules become rules of law when the values they embody are so critical to the social system that the rules not only reflect a standard for the determination of deviant behavior but they are also a stimulus to the diversion of some of the energy of the social system to the control of such deviance.

The foregoing may be summarized in terms of group theory by stating that, as norms for conduct emerge within a group, deviational conduct will also from time to time appear. No group exhibits a neat, invariable adherence to its rules for conduct. When rules for conduct have become so established in a group that it is expected that roles will be performed in consistence with their appropriate rules, unexpected conduct departing markedly from these rules is perceived to interfere with cooperation. The performer of a complementary role is no longer able to mesh his action successfully with that of the deviant actor.

The deviant behavior may reflect a desired innovation. If recognized as such and accepted, then no problem or conflict arises. If, however, it is perceived as behavior tending both to frustrate effective cooperation within the group and to reduce its efficiency in reaching a valued goal, the need for control is seen. Some group energy must be used to repress the deviant conduct and keep the group on its accustomed track to its desired goal. In the primitive group, a whole range of pressures may be applied, ranging from the informal and diffuse, such as loss of respect and prestige, ridicule and denial of reciprocity, to the formal, such as ritualistic purification and punishment, and finally to the institutionalized office of control, such as the police function of the military societies of the Plains tribes.

The regulatory phase of law, therefore, is found when repressive group action takes place in situations where there has been a departure from a valued behavioral rule of the group. Law as control imports a determination of deviant behavior, using a valued behavioral rule as the point of reference for such determination, and in addition, a determination that such deviance shall become the point of reference for the application of corrective measures.

The rules of law thus become those behavioral rules of a social system which are so valued as to lead to the regulatory action of the legal process in the event of deviance. The regulatory process in primitive society is institutionalized in a variety of behavioral patterns, applying sanctions of differing degrees of constraint, ending, of course, in the application of force. In the state, it is institutionalized in the judicial organ.

The rules of law can be said to be an index or basis of prediction of the appearance of the regulatory action of the legal process. To fix upon the behavior of the judicial organ apart from its organic context or its post and function in the social system, however, is to create a partial and distorted image of law and the legal process. Law and the legal process are an entity. Law comprises those norms for conduct which embody valued expectations in the functioning of a social system, deviation from which leads to measures of control, which may or may not be institutionalized in a judicial organ but which are designed to prevent the further occurrence of such deviance and to repair the resultant injuries. . . .

Law and the legal process reflect, consider, and evaluate past action, and require that future action shall adhere to those patterns which embody the ideal and valued image of action in situations which the culture has come to recognize as typical. Law and the legal process are concerned with insuring the appropriateness of means to end in action and demand that action shall reflect *mechanical* rationality. Most important, they penetrate beneath the objective reality of mechanical rationality into the subjective realm of *value* rationality, and insist that action shall also reflect that fidelity to the realization of important and shared values of the social system which is necessary for self-maintenance, goal gratification, integration, and adaptation, including provision for the realization of significant values of other social systems to which the system must adapt itself. The legal process orders action in an authoritative way to restore the disturbed equilibrium of the system resulting from conflict and tension. It also influences the future course of action in the system by its continued clarification of required forms of action, as it affirms positive legal rules for action in situations of interpersonal conflict.[100]

For those interested in further investigation of the literature of anthropology on law, reference is made to the careful and thoughtful study of Nader.[101] A theoretical contribution which has been largely overlooked is that of Pospisil.[102] He conceived law to be "rules or modes of conduct made obligatory by some sanction which is imposed and enfoced for their violation by a controlling authority." He affirmed that cross-cultural research reveals that law had a number of "attributes," rather than "one sweeping characteristic." These were (1) authority, that is, a person or sub-group which can influence a majority of the members of a social group to accept its decisions, (2) the universality of application of decisions made by such authority, (3) the imposition of obligation as a result of such decisions, and (4) the imposition of sanction as a result of such decisions. The author shares the view that any definition of law adopted for comparative anthropological study must be sufficiently broad and abstract to comprehend the cultures under investigation and must be

---

100. Carlston, *Law and Organization*, 129-132.
101. L. Nader, "The Anthropological Study of Law," *American Anthropologist*, LXVII[2] (1965), No. 6, 3.
102. L. Pospisil, "Kapauku Papuans and Their Law," *Yale University Publications in Anthropology* (1958), No. 54, 248-272.

conceived as consisting of attributes or, as the author would put it, elements. From the author's standpoint, law at its minimum comprises valued social norms the violation of which are subject to sanctions. It consists of (1) "must not" behavior, which is set in opposition to, and stated in terms of the violation of, "must" behavior, (2) the obligatory quality of "must" behavior is derived from its value importance to the members of the social group, and (3) the performance of "must not" behavior consistently has the consequence of the imposition of sanctions upon the performer. The function of legal norms, as a statement of the circumstances in which the sanctioning process of a society will operate, is accordingly to support valued obligatory norms.

Law becomes more maturely developed in a social group when, in lieu of the injured person making a decision that "must not" behavior of another has occurred, an established third-party decision-making agent or body makes such a decision. The final step in the development of law occurs when such agent or body is authorized to determine norm violations and to impose sanctions upon persons who commit "must not" behavior. If law, as we know it, does not exist in some tribal societies, the anthropologist must, nevertheless, faithfully describe what takes place in such a society in subjecting violators of norms to sanctions and determining those who are guilty of the violation of norms. He must search for the elements of legal behavior and indicate the extent to which and the manner in which they have developed in a particular society. If a definition of law for such purposes must be had, it can be said simply to consist of those valued norms violation of which subjects their violators to a sanctioning process, together with those procedures which determine that violations of such norms have occurred in situations of interpersonal conflict.

Not merely for the purposes of anthropological study but also, and more importantly, for the purpose of understanding human behavior, law is to be seen as a progression from blind aggression to institutionalized or socially-regulated modes of self-help, in which the injured is both decision maker and the means of applying sanctions, together with such sanctioning instruments as the gods, the ancestors, the age groups, the military societies, and the police of the state, on the one hand, and the ordeal, the diviner, the village moot, the council of elders, the court of the king, and the court of the state, as decision-making instruments, on the other hand. Law is thus a particular type of instrument of social control marked by the fact that it controls social conflict resulting from the deviant performance of valued social norms by a sanctioning process.

Law as an instrument for the coordination of social action is to be equated with the appearance of posts of authority in a society. Authority is to be seen in a progression from the head of the household to headman, chief, king, and the command of the sovereign.

If law is not to be so conceived for purposes of anthropological study and instead limited to a notion of law derived from the institutions of our culture, then it would seem that the anthropologist should find some symbol to identify the above-described process of social control which is so basic and so universal. To limit law to Hoebel's conception of a social norm supported by the regularized application of force by an agent socially authorized so to act[103] or to adopt the notion of much of modern jurisprudence, stemming from Austin, that law is a command supported by the coercive power of the state,[104] is to lift a concept from our culture which is simply inappropriate for the study of tribal societies. The concept of law here advanced would seem not only to be more useful but also to possess some evidence, at least, to validate it as a universal concept of law for purposes of social theory.[105]

---

103. Hoebel, *The Law of Primitive Man*, 28.

104. E.g., Roscoe Pound's definition of law as "the systematized control through the orderly application of force of politically organized society." R. Pound and T. F. Plucknett, *Readings on the History and System of the Common Law* (3d ed.; Rochester, N.Y., 1927), 3.

105. For other discussions of the concept of law, see H. Kuper and L. Kuper, "Introduction" and M. G. Smith, "The Sociological Framework of Law," *African Law: Adaptation and Development*, eds. H. Kuper and L. Kuper (Berkeley and Los Angeles, 1965), 3 and 24. A useful discussion of the jurisprudential aspects of the problem of defining customary law will be found in T. O. Elias, *The Nature of African Customary Law* (Manchester, 1956), Chaps. 1-4. See also P. Bohannan (ed.), *Law and Warfare: Studies in the Anthropology of Conflict* (Garden City, N.Y., 1967), and M. Gluckman's concept of the "reasonable man" discussed *infra* pages 230 to 233.

Chapter 2

Elements of a Theory
of the Organization
# of Action

Explanatory Note

THIS chapter represents an attempt to move from the expository level to the level of propositions and principles in the description of social theory. It also includes a normative basis for prescribing and evaluating action resting on the concept of the good life as defined therein.

Basic Assumptions

A. The development of a unified body of social theory requires, as the development of any science requires, a statement of its field or area of concern. That is to say, the investigation requires a peak perspective with respect to the data which it is the function of the scientist to investigate and a statement of the basic order assumed by the data when it is perceived from such a perspective. The next statement represents a step in that direction.

B. *Man* performs *action,* which is both *symbolic action* and *social action,* in the dimension of *time* to create *order* for the purpose of realizing his *values.* He experiences *conflict* and performs *control* of action in so doing. (Each italicized term becomes a category of principles and propositions below.)

MAN

1. Selectivity in the evolution of living forms created man, possessing to a unique degree the quality of being a psychological and social organism.

2. Man is a genotype, reflecting his genetic constitution or hereditary endowment.

3. Man is a phenotype, reflecting the physical, objective order assumed by the interaction of organism and environment.

4. Man is a psychological animal performing symbolic action. The evolution of the design of the brain reflects this principle.

5. Man is a social animal performing social action. The predecessors of man in the selective process of evolution exhibited this type of action.

6. Symbolic action and social action are dyadic in man, not dichotomous. This perspective of action is essential for the development of a unified body of social theory comprising the behavioral sciences. (Note: Differentiation between symbolic and social action will be made below only where the context requires it. Usually the term action will be employed.)

7. The concept of the personality is an implicate of the concept of the phenotype (see statement 3 above). It refers to the order which an observer perceives to be manifested by a person's social action, which is a product of his history of social action. It is an integrate of social action, the conflict exhibited in such integrate, and the control manifested over such conflict for the purpose of maintaining or perfecting the integrate.

8. The concept of the self is a product of symbolic action and refers to (1) the ideal order which a person strives to attain in his social actions because it is the embodiment of his value system. (2) It is a perception by a person of the order assumed by his *own* social action as a result of his history of social action. (3) It is an ideal, valued order which a person (a) holds up as a goal, (b) seeks to express in social action, and (c) endeavors to control the conflict arising from the incongruence of the ideal subjective order and the objective order of the personality by modifying the order represented by the self or the order represented by the personality or both. (4) It is an order which changes in the course of a person's history. (5) It is a subjective, conative, normative order.

9. In the degree that man is unable to control conflict between self and personality, as he pursues the good life (as defined in state-

ment 55 below), he will tend to resort to symbolic action eventuating sometimes in personality disorders.

10. Through his learning processes, man in society developed a culture which represents the grand design of his adaptation to his environment as he performed social action. Cultures differ among peoples as a product of their history, and, in this respect, the concept of culture represents a perspective of the action of a society analogous to that which personality represents for a person.

11. When his environment is rapidly changing, man's personality, experience, learning, and culture are ill-suited for successful adaptation. Man's ability to think creatively is demanded for this purpose.

Action

12. All action takes place in a process of creating an idea or order of action, performing such idea, and controlling action.

13. All action takes place for the purpose of value realization. It may take the form of affective action, which is enjoyed for the effect which it produces in an actor, or instrumental action, which is directed to goal attainment and is enjoyed in anticipation of the realization of the values incident to goal attainment, as well as in the realization of the values attendant upon goal attainment.

14. Action taking place in the realm of values does so in a process of perception and choice of values, the realization of values in social action, and the appraisal of such realization of values in order to determine the content of future social action.

15. Action taking place in the dimension of time is action which assumes an order as a result of adopting a perspective or cognition of the past, the present, or the future, or all three perspectives in a single, comprehensive order.

16. All action is determined by its appropriateness and importance as a means of value realization.

Symbolic Action

17. Perception reflects the principle set forth in statement 12 above in that it is a search for order in the flow of sensory impressions, the tentative selection of an order in symbolic action, and the subjecting of such tentative selection to control by appraising the fidelity of the content of such order to the inflow of sensory impressions (i.e., reducing the conflict involved between symbolic and objective order) with a view to arriving at and selecting a final order of symbolic action for the purpose of future social action.

18. Cognitive action reflects the principle set forth in statement 12 above in that it is a search for order in the form of the appropriate frame of reference, construct, judgment, opinion, or the like and the control of the conflict encountered in such search by creating alternative forms of order and appraising such forms with a view to arriving at and selecting a final order for the purpose of future action.

19. When a society is undergoing rapid cultural change, the symbolic depiction of its order fails to keep pace with empirical reality. Since the perceptual and other cognitive processes of man, including his learning processes, are bounded by the symbolic structuring of his culture, the learning which man acquires in such a situation is accordingly insufficient to enable him to comprehend the newly emerged reality and to determine adequately his own action and the action of social orders, including the state, in adapting to the newly emerged reality.

20. When a person experiences value conflict in selecting action and selects action which appears to be irrational from the standpoint of value realization, he will seek to create rationality in such action by cognitive processes which recognize and enhance the importance of information which is consistent with such action and ignore and depreciate the importance of information inconsistent with such action, thereby creating a more rational cognitive order.

21. The maintenance of a social order requires the communication of its ideal form, norms, and values to man in the form of condensation symbols. Religion performs this function for man in society and ideology for man in the state.

22. Political action in the state employs condensation symbols or master symbols, which promote attachment to the constituted order of the state by asserting the ultimate characteristics and justification of such order. As such order changes, new master symbols must be created which identify and justify the new characteristics of the order. The failure to do so promotes constitutive conflict.

23. Religion creates and holds up to man an ideal supernatural order which mirrors his environment and social order and his place therein and expresses such ideal supernatural order in condensation symbols. It enables man to communicate with that order in condensation symbols and to invoke its action in support of goal attainment, value realization, and the control of conflict as he adapts to his environment and all its vicissitudes.

24. Religion serves to satisfy a number of basic needs for man in society and, as a consequence, to promote the maintenance of a so-

cial order. (1) It employs condensation symbols to create an ideal and importantly valued order in the form of a supernatural world, which unifies the cosmos, society, and man and gives meaning to the otherwise inscrutable forces of nature. (2) It gives man a position in that order and indicates the ideal role performance, or the good life, which he should strive to reflect and the norms of social action to which he ought to adhere and the immoral and sinful norms which he ought to avoid. (3) It gives man support as he encounters otherwise unmanageable conflict in adapting to the temporal world. (4) It provides him with means, in the form of ritual, to communicate with the supernatural world and to invoke the application of its power in goal attainment and control of conflict, such as success in war, overcoming catastrophe, reward of faithful observance of importantly valued norms, and punishment of violations of such norms. (6) Its ultimate end is to define the good life in condensation symbols and to give man support in its pursuit.

25. The church, as an organization, should provide man with a physical environment (church edifice and facilities), theology, and ritual, which express an ideal supernatural order, norms of behavior in that order, and ways of resolving and controlling conflict in that order, to the end that man can perceive in condensation symbols the nature of the good life and receive support in his pursuit of the good life.

26. When religion and the church significantly fail to perform their functions, as set forth in statements 23 to 25 above, notably in failing to take cognizance of social change and value change, then man will turn to other types of symbols for such purpose.

27. When control of constitutive conflict in a social order (e.g., society or state) fails to maintain a viable order, symbolic forms of order, action, and actors, will tend to appear. They provide a substitute or illusion of an ideal, valued reality which in fact does not exist for the members of the society which accept them. The underlying *malaise* is thereby cloaked.

28. It may be hypothesized that the frustrations which the United States will encounter in the coming years in integrating culturally deprived groups into a common culture, in providing opportunity to live the good life (as defined in statement 55 below), and in solving the problems of adapting a technological, industrial society to a rapidly changing national and world environment, will lead to a movement toward symbolic substitutes for the value realization and goal attainment which reality denies. This trend is already evident. A trend to symbolic substitutes for imperfect reality is also evident in other national societies.

SOCIAL ACTION

29. All social action takes place in a process of placing its content into an order of symbolic action, expressing that order in social action, and appraising such social action from the standpoint of its appropriateness and importance for value realization (mechanical and value rationality) with a view to determining the content of future social action.

30. Social action may be said to fall essentially into two categories: (1) cooperation in groups, including role performance, and (2) coordination in organizations, representing action directed by authority.

31. When his environment is rapidly changing, man's social action requires the exercise of authority to determine its content for the purpose of successful adaptation.

32. Organization is that form of social order in which the content of its action is determined by the exercise of authority.

33. Other forms of social order arise in (1) kinship structures of social action, dependent upon the perception of order in terms of kinship relations, (2) territorial structures of social action, dependent upon the perception of order in terms of territorial relations, (3) age structures of social action, dependent upon the perceptions of order in terms of age relations, and (4) associational structures of social action, dependent upon the perception of order in terms of group action for the purpose of value realization, without reliance upon authority for such purpose.

34. As a result of his action in groups, man (1) developed a genotype useful for the purpose of such action, (2) satisfied his basic personality needs, (3) realized his values, and (4) developed his ability to adapt to his environment by (5) developing, using, and transmitting a culture through (6) communication.

35. Action in small groups involves high-frequency interpersonal contacts and, mostly, affective action, while action in large groups involves low-frequency interpersonal contacts and, mostly, instrumental action.

36. The most significant influence in determining personality characteristics is man's experience in situations involving small groups.

37. Denial of the opportunity to pursue the good life (as defined in statement 55 below) in small groups promotes the appearance of personality disorders to a greater extent than denial of such opportunity in large groups, although the latter may importantly influence the former.

Time

38. Action in the dimension of time implies creating an idea for future action, which involves the use of memory to recall and create order out of the past in order to arrive at such an idea, expressing that idea in present action, and appraising past action with a view determining the content of future action.

39. Action over a period of time will exhibit maximum value rationality when the performance of affective and instrumental action enables the realization of the largest possible aggregate of values by the actor, weighted according to their importance to the actor.

40. Time influences instrumental action in that a person's value attachment to such action will increase as the goal to which it is directed nears in point of time. On the other hand, a person's motivation to avoid a situation embodying negative values increases as the situation nears in point of time.

41. The dimension of time determines the perspective of data which is adopted to differentiate the short-term span of data involved in such concepts as the situation, on the one hand, and the long-term span of data involved in such concepts as the personality, the self, and the constituted order of a social order, on the other hand.

42. The perfection of action for the purpose of successful adaptation to environment is a product of the ability of a person to bring order to his action in increasingly larger spans of time.

43. The cognitive ability of a person is in part a product of his ability to perform cognitive action in the dimension of time extending from the present into the future and the past. It is a function of his ability (1) to process information embracing the past, the present, and the future, (2) to think imaginatively and creatively, (3) to make plans, (4) to create and decide upon plans which reflect optimal mechanical and value rationality from the standpoint of allocating and using energy during the time period involved, (5) to direct action, (6) to appraise past action from the standpoint of the congruence of actual performance and value realization with anticipated performance and value realization, and (7) to determine the content of future action in the light of such appraisal with a view (8) to creating an order of equal or greater mechanical and value rationality. The total process is, in short, one of remembering and appraising past action as future action is determined and action takes place.

44. A person's cognitive ability to give order to his future action is a product of his ability to exercise foresight, that is to say, to give order to the increasing disorder of future action as it is extended in time through the imagination. The determinants of the quality of foresight are a person's hereditary endowment, his experience in a culture, and the learning thereby obtained, notably in the possession of frames of reference and constructs which enable him to plan action and define goals in an orderly, effective manner.

45. Organizational action in the dimension of time represents an orderly institutionalization of the planning and decision-making processes of the cognitive action described in statements 43 above and 48 and 49 below. Leadership in organization acts in the long-term perspective of time, administration acts in the short-term perspective of time, while control appraises past action with a view to shaping future action.

46. Planning future action requires the definition of a goal and the sequence of steps necessary to attain such goal, together with the allocation of future action in a given period of time, so that the order represented by the time allotments for each plan comprehended therein and the sequential order of the performance of the several plans comprehended therein exhibits the optimal mechanical and value rationality attainable.

47. Decision making is the exercise of choice. It acts in the dimension of time when it selects a plan for future action. It is a process consisting of a series of steps in which a person (1) searches for and organizes information concerning a situation with a view to determining the content of his future action in the form of the performance of a plan, (2) creates plans, (3) appraises the mechanical and value rationality of such plans, and (4) exercises choice among such plans so as (5) to attain an order of future action which reflects optimal mechanical and value rationality.

48. Decision making will tend to become precarious and hesitation in exercising choice will be exhibited by a person when decision leads to experiencing the realization of positive values (rewards) and negative values (deprivations) of approximately equal strength. When such a decision is made or a decision is irrational from the standpoint of value realization, a person will thereafter move to diminish the conflict in values and establish an order of value rationality by recognizing information which is consistent with the rationality of the choice made and enhancing the importance of such information and by ignoring and depreciating the importance of information which is inconsistent with the choice made.

49. The cognitive, value, and conflict aspects of psychological action terminating in a decision by a person to commit a violation of a legal norm may lie in (1) an appraisal of future actions ending in a judgment that a highly important goal may be attained by action violative of a legal norm, (2) the realization that such goal attainment is near at hand and feasible, while subjection to the legal process and its imposition of sanction is remote, subject to chance in its occurrence, and its outcome uncertain, and (3) resolving such cognitive conflict by grasping the rewards near at hand by a decision to perform the prohibited action. In such a situation, the personality characteristics of the person comprise the principal barrier to the making of such a decision.

50. Leadership in organization acts in the long-term perspective of organizational action, administration in the short-term perspective, while control appraises past action with a view to shaping future action.

51. Control, in the dimension of time, represents an appraisal of past action with a view to determining the content of future action.

ORDER

52. Social order is a product of the cognition of social action as exhibiting sequence, relationship, and interdependency in the perspectives of time, space, and value. A social order emerges through the action of man in society in the dimensions of time and space for the purpose of the realization of values.

53. The most inclusive or universal forms of social order are the group and the institution. They comprehend more sophisticated forms of action, such as the organization.

54. A social order will come into being when its numbers possess, among other things, a common experience in a culture, including a common language or other common means of communication, values, and priorities of values. They must also perceive and accept the social order as an appropriate means for value realization.

55. A social order provides an opportunity to live the good life to the extent that it enables each member to develop the self to its full potentialities for growth and unfoldment. An illustrative concept of growth of self for this purpose is the movement of a person towards an ordering of his relations with others in which he enjoys self respect, respect by others, and satisfies his physiological, safety, love, esteem, and self-actualization needs, in the priority of the listing of such needs.

56. A social order is viable in the degree that it exhibits mechan-

ical and value rationality and provides opportunity to pursue the good life (as defined in statement 55 above).

57. Mechanical rationality reflects the rationality of the appropriateness and economy of means to ends. It is that form of order which exhibits the greatest economy in the use of resources to accomplish ends.

58. Value rationality is defined in statement 39 above.

59. A social order will tend to disintegrate, and personality disorders will tend to appear therein, in the degree that it fails to provide its members with the opportunity to pursue the good life (as defined in statement 55 above).

60. A society assumes order as a result of (1) its movement through groups and structures of social action (2) to attain the goals and realize the values of its members (3) by allocating and using its resources of personnel, land, and equipment, (4) by employing communication in the form of reference and condensation symbols, (5) by exercising authority in the performance of post and office, (6) by role performance, (7) by adherence to norms, and (8) by subjecting conflict to process of social control.

61. Societal action represents a system which will operate to create healthy personalities by affording opportunity to pursue the good life (as defined in statement 55 above) or sick personalities by denying such opportunity. Variation in the characteristics of the elements of the system will influence the characteristics of personalities of members.

62. The normative criterion of all social orders is the degree of opportunity which they provide to pursue the good life (as defined in statement 55 above).

63. The progression of forms of social order is from the group to the orderly relationships of a structure of social action, which develops into an organization when its action is determined by the impersonal exercise of authority.

64. Order in tribal society assumed a variety of forms in structures of social action. Each type of structure of social action assumed its characteristic form by virtue of the manner in which its members arrived at a common basis for ordering their action. These were kinship relationships, territorial relationships, age relationships, relationships arising from the pursuit of common goals in association with one another, and relationships arising from the pursuit of common goals under the exercise of authority (organization).

65. Order in modern society is primarily a product of the action of organizations.

66. The historical progression from kinship-structured societies to organizationally-structured societies, with its intermediate stage of pluralistic societies embodying a number of types of structures of social action (see statement 2C of Chapter 17 below), suggests that the proliferation of international and regional organizations in the society of states, including supra-national organizations such as the European Common Market, may represent the stage of pluralistic society in the progression of an order of states to a future world order of organization. The emergence of such a world order is subject to the principles set forth in statement 54 above.

67. The concepts of personality, self, and constituted order of a group refer respectively to an order assumed as a result of the past history of the entity, the conflict exhibited therein, and the control exercised over such conflict.

68. The concept of the constituted order of an organization refers to both an objective order of social action (charter) in terms of leadership, administration, and control, and a subjective, normative order (ideal charter) in which leadership, administration, and control act in the realm of value realization of the persons who are members of and participants in the organization.

69. The order of an organization is a product of decisions by the occupants of posts or offices exercising authority in the performance of the functions of leadership, administration, and control.

70. Leadership foresees an ideal constituted order of an organization in the long-term span of time, makes decisions to bring that order into being, and controls its action by appraising its mechanical and value rationality with a view to the further performance of its function. Leadership is excercised in decisions of critical importance to the maintenance of the organization.

71. Administration determines the concrete action of an organization in the short-term span of time, makes decisions to bring that order into being, and controls its action by appraising its mechanical and value rationality with a view to the further performance of its function. Administrative decisions are primarily routine decisions which, if mistaken, do not significantly affect the maintenance of the organization unless such mistakes are frequent.

72. Control appraises the past action of an organization from the standpoint of its appropriateness and importance for value realization (mechanical and value rationality) with a view to determining the content of future action.

73. Each of the spheres of leadership, administration, and control requires the exercise of foresight, performance of action, and control in order to discharge their respective functions in the organization.

74. The action of an organization may be viewed as a system in which authority makes decisions which coordinate action and allocate and utilize resources in order to attain goals and realize the values of the members of and participants in the organization. Such persons should be perceived to be individuals possessing personalities and engaged in the pursuit of the good life (as defined in statement 55 above).

75. An organization, including the state, will expand its foundations of power in the degree communication brings to the occupants of its offices exercising authority information upon which decision making can effectively take place and such decision making is directed to creating an order which reflects mechanical and value rationality and provides its members and participants opportunity to live the good life (as defined in statement 55 above).

76. A most significant and enduring basis for the growth of an organization is the opportunity which it provides persons who are not members opportunity for value realization by participating in its system of action. The provision of such action may be said to be action directed to the improvement of the social base of the organization.

77. A state attains power in the degree to which it (1) possesses a creative, achieving society; (2) develops and employs science, technology, and organizational technique; (3) reflects mechanical and value rationality in its action; and (4) provides its members and participants opportunity to pursue the good life (as defined in statement 55 above).

78. The state is the largest and most sophistically developed form of organization so far created in world culture. The European Common Market represents the highest form of organization so far achieved in the progression of organization from the state to the international form of organization.

79. The action of the state in world society will develop its foundations of power on an enduring basis in the degree it provides opportunities for value realization by participants in its system of action pursuant to statement 76 above.

80. States have increased their foundations of power by resort to war. The principles and propositions relevant to the phenomenon of war are set forth in statements 105 to 107 below.

VALUE

81. The content of action is determined by its appropriateness and importance for the purpose of value realization (see statement 16 above).

82. Value realization is accomplished by affective action, which is enjoyed for its own sake or effect, and instrumental action, which is directed to goal attainment and is enjoyed in anticipation of the value realization incident to goal attainment, as well as in the realization of the values attendant upon goal attainment. The strength of the value attachment by an actor to instrumental action will increase as the actor moves nearer, in point of time, to the attainment of the goal of such action.

83. Value rationality represents the optimal amount of value realization which can be enjoyed in a given period of time. It is more precisely defined in statement 39 above.

84. Value conflict affects cognition as set forth in statement 20 above and decision making as set forth in statement 48 above.

85. The negative values of fear and deprivation are highly potent in influencing the content of action. This is a principle in the exercise of authority in organization, notably the state, as well as in the social action of a person. The reliance of authority upon means whose effectiveness lies in their embodiment of such values diminishes the opportunity to pursue the good life (as described in statement 55 above).

CONFLICT

86. The resolution of conflict engenders creativity in the search for a new form of order which will bring previously conflicting elements into an order embodying harmony and consistency.

87. Creativity implies a search for a new order. This new order may be either symbolic, in the realm of the cognitive processes, or temporal, in the realm of social action. It unifies and brings order to the conflicting elements of an existing order. Creativity is a product of conflict (as set forth in statement 86 above) and is a requisite for the maintenance of a social order undergoing change or experiencing change in its environment.

88. A society becomes creative through encountering conflict as it coheres and moves toward goal attainment and value realization. As unmanageable conflict spreads, a society will move toward symbolic, substitute forms of social action. (See statement 27 above.)

89. An achieving, energetic society will tend to arise as a result of the conflict encountered by a pluralistic society, comprised of many types of personalities, groups, and social structures, in its movement toward constituting and maintaining a viable order in a variety of environments.

90. An achieving society is one characterized by a high degree of

attachment by its members to the value of the possession of status and power, opportunities for realizing such value, and competition to grasp such opportunities.

91. Conflict in the self exists when there is incongruence between the ideal order of the self with its expression in the objective order of the personality. Control is exercised to reduce that conflict by changing the characteristics of the self or of the personality or both. (See statement 8 above.) Failure to control such conflict tends to create personality disorders. (See statement 9 above).

92. Interpersonal conflict is, among other things, a product of (1) frustration, hostility, hatred, fear, envy, and the like, (2) deviance in role performance, (3) failure to adhere to valued social norms, and (4) pursuit of incompatible goals, or (5) interference with value realization.

93. Constitutive conflict in a social order is a product of the incongruence of an ideal, valued social order and the actual social order, as perceived by the members of such order.

94. Constitutive conflict in a social order takes place in a process in which the conflict between the ideal, valued social order and the actual social order, as perceived by the members, proceeds to the point that disintegration may occur. Unless those who are the leaders or the occupants of posts or offices of authority in such social order are able to arrest the trend toward disintegration by controlling the conditions leading toward its occurrence, disintegration and the constitution of a new social order or new social orders will take place. An episode of interpersonal conflict may engender such a process of disintegration and reintegration.

95. Constitutive conflict or disintegration will tend to take place in an organization in the degree that (1) leadership fails (a) to foresee long-term trends in the character and importance of social values and goals and change in environment and (b) to plan and make decisions for organizational action to adapt to such trends and change, (2) administration fails to cause organizational action (a) to respond to currently shared values and (b) to reflect mechanical rationality, and (3) control fails to bring about a viable order of organizational action reflecting mechanical and value rationality.

96. Constitutive conflict in the state is the concern of leadership in the political process, group conflict in the short-term perspective of action is the primary concern of political parties and the legislative process, and interpersonal conflict is the concern of the judicial process.

97. Revolution, civil war, or peaceful change in constituted order

of a state takes place when the incongruence between the ideal, valued order and the actual constituted order reaches the point that a conflict situation will engender a chain of reactions throughout the state resulting in the creation of a new constituted order or, as a result of civil war, new constituted orders in separate states.

98. The appearance of constitutive conflict in a society will lead to symbolic forms of action therein, as set forth in statement 27 above.

99. Interpersonal conflict will lead to (1) inner conflict in the persons involved therein, which is manifested in stress, tension, hostility, frustration and aggression, and symbolic processes of control, such as projection and personality disorders, and (2) processes of social control, notably the legal process.

100. The failure of a society to provide adequate processes of social control, including a sanctioning process for the violation of valued norms, will lead to symbolic processes of control, as set forth in statement 99 above, and to symbolic forms of social action, as set forth in statement 27 above.

101. Value conflict influences cognition as set forth in statement 20 above.

102. One of the most important sources of social conflict, and particularly constitutive conflict, lies in the influence of value conflict upon the cognitive processes and their influence in turn upon the content of social action. Thus, when conflict in a society takes the form of conflict over the priorities of important values, as manifested in the diverse and conflicting claims of interest groups, associations, organizations, and even states themselves in international society, then a type of cognitive conflict may ensue which might be termed the conflict of organizational and empirical rationality. Members of the opposing social orders are incapable of the receipt and organization of information relating to the social conflict on a basis of empirical rationality for the purpose of determining their social action. Communication to them of an empirically rational content, which conflicts with their own particularistic, value-laden frames of reference, is ineffective to resolve such cognitive conflict. The task of bringing their conflicting orders of rationality into congruence with an order of emiprical rationality is extraordinarily difficult and at times insuperable. The irreconcilability of the opposing cognitive orders of rationality seems to be an application of the principle of cognitive action set forth in statement 20 above. When such cognitive conflict exists, a third-party decision-making body requires force to make its decision operable. Cognitive conflict of this nature

explains in part the manifestation of constitutive conflict in social action.

103. Conflict becomes a support for and strengthens value attachment to action when such action successfully resolves conflict. Thus the exercise of authority by the holders of posts and offices, including third-party decision-making bodies, is supported by their successful resolution of conflict.

104. Many of the problems of the transformation of kinship-structured tribal societies into organizationally-structured, modern societies arise from the conflict experienced by their members in their identification with and value attachment to kinship groups and their lack of identification with and value attachment to organizations, which is necessary for the modern state. Nepotism and corruption are often a product of this conflict.

105. War represents a conflict situation in the sense that it refers to a situation in which two groups are engaged in violent action designed to inflict death or physical injury upon each other. Its rationality diminishes with the course of history and the development of culture.

106. War, as rational social action, represented either (1) a sanctioning process, which a kinship group inflicted upon a structurally distant kinship group for serious offenses committed upon members of the former group by members of the latter group or (2) a process of goal attainment. Wars of the first category were subject to procedures designed to restrict the sanctions employed so that their severity was correlated with the degree of structural distance of the two kinship groups and the degree of seriousness of the offense. Wars in the second category among tribal groups were for land, booty, or slaves. Wars in the second category among states were for the enhancement of the foundations of state power. The rationality of wars in the second category was a means-ends rationality of loss of resources entailed in war compared with the acquisition of resources resulting from war. War, in the context of the conditions of international and world society today, is likely to possess little means-ends rationality, particularly among the industrially organized states of the Atlantic basin, and loses all rationality when it takes the form of nuclear warfare. It is a highly inappropriate means for the pursuit of the good life (as defined in statement 55 above).

107. Global war is to be understood as a form of constitutive conflict manifesting itself in a process of integration, disintegration, and reintegration of international order. The rationality of such a type of conflict lies in the fact that it is a conflict between two op-

posing groups of states for the kind of an international order which will yield a greater degree of value realization and goal attainment for the victors than for the losers.

CONTROL

108. Control consists of a process of appraising past action with a view to shaping the content of future action.

109. The functions of law in the control of interpersonal conflict are (1) to reduce tensions arising from such conflict, (2) to promote inhibition of agression and provide a substitute means for its expression, (3) to develop personalities which conform to valued social norms and avoid violation of their supporting legal norms, (4) to deter the making of decisions to depart from such valued social norms and violate their supporting legal norms, (5) to define the ideal, valued order of a society by stating the legal norms which support it, (6) to support the performance of valued social norms by (a) defining legal norms, which set forth the conditions in which a violation of such valued social norms will be subject to a sanctioning process, and (b) subjecting violators of such valued social norms to a sanctioning process, and (7) to control conflict arising from the incongruence of the existing body of legal norms and the needs of a new or changed social order by creating new legal norms which support emerging valued social norms.

110. The rational frame of reference which leads to the linking of a valued social norm with a legal norm includes cognitions that (1) the social norm is important for purposes of value realization and goal attainment in the social order and (2) its violation would interfere with the performance of valued role relationships or otherwise disrupt social order.

111. The third-party decision-making process in the domain of law comprises the following steps: (1) the authoritative determination of the facts of an interpersonal conflict situation, (2) the search for a legal norm to resolve such situation, which implies an appraisal of the conflict aspects of such situation to determine the valued social norm which should have been performed therein, giving consideration in so doing to the value priorities of the society, (3) the selection of the legal norm which supports such social norm and identifies a failure to perform it, (4) the imposition of sanctions upon the violator of such social norm, and (5) recognizing emerging valued social norms by creating new legal norms which support them.

112. The structural norms of a society also tend to be norms of

the supernatural order, the violation of which is perceived to be a sin or serious moral fault.

113. Pursuant to the principle set forth in statement 103 above, the resolution of interpersonal conflict by a third-party decision-making body becomes so valued by the members of a society that it supports the authority of that body.

Chapter 3

Theory and Data

THEORY is derived from data, validated by data, and gives meaning and order to data. The ensuing chapters provide the data of this study but the theory extends beyond the data. The theory represents a search for an empirical and normative order derived from the behavioral sciences in which law will be seen in its social setting and as part of the life of a society—or, as this study now puts it—as part of the life of man in a society and its culture, which is to be evaluated on the basis of the extent to which it enables him to live the good life of developing his personality.

There was an independent value in exploring the data. The new African states may well be to the world of the future what the Balkan states were to Europe of the nineteenth and early twentieth centuries. Violent, unpredictable, immature, these will be some of the adjectives which will be applied to them—as, indeed, they already have been. They will need to understand themselves in the light of their tribal past, which so largely persists in the political framework of the state. We will need so to understand them. The anthropological literature concerning their people is scattered and of varying quality and depth. It is important to put it in order and to re-create tribal life for Western readers.

The selection of the peoples to be investigated took into account ecological, linguistic, and cultural factors. It was important to have a fairly wide and representative sampling, within working limits. Peoples of the coast, the forest, and the savanna of West Africa and of the highlands, as well as the Nile, of East Africa were chosen for investigation. Twenty peoples were made the principal subjects of investigation. Thirteen of these are described in the following chapters, together with supplementary investigations of the Nupe, Tutsi, Hutu, and Twa. The remaining seven peoples are described in Appendix B. The data concerning the latter were important for the purpose of carrying out the research design. They were investigated and recorded in the same manner as the thirteen other peoples. It was not considered essential, however, to present the results of this part of the study with all the detail of the ensuing thirteen chapters. The life of an additional people, the Ndembu, was investigated as an example of constitutive conflict. It is contained in Appendix A. All the data were utilized for the purposes of the inductive method adopted in Chapter 17.

To the extent the data permitted, the life of each people was described from the standpoint of their geography and economy, personality traits, values, attitudes, religion, social and political organization, conflict, control, and law. The categories of description were not limited to those named but included others as well when revealed by the data. On the other hand, it often happened, in the light of the data, that a full-range report on these topics was impossible. At other times only a most bare-bones report could be made.

The design of the categories was pragmatic. The categories selected simply represented the most convenient form for organizing the data to give as full a description as possible of the societies investigated and, at the same time, insure that the data desired in the light of social theory would be reported so far as it was to be found in the literature.

The design may have the merit of being close to the current state of the art in the discipline of anthropology. Its categories are familiar. It directs the investigation to an orderly study of the life of a people which should enable them to be portrayed with considerable vitality and completeness. It enables the investigator to draw upon social theory as he proceeds with his investigation. If it, or some similar approach to describing the life of a people were employed, the task of comparative anthropology and the development of a science of anthropology would be considerably facilitated.

By way of illustration, suppose the design were employed to describe the life of the people of the United States. An impressionistic, brief outline of an outcome of such an approach follows:

> Geographical support for an achieving society was found in the variety and richness of the resources of the contiguous group of the first forty-eight states. The climate ranged from the sub-tropic of the south to the sub-arctic of the western high plateaus. Rainfall varied from the deserts to the west to the rain forest in the Olympic peninsula of the

northwest. The climate was otherwise mostly temperate and with adequate rainfall. Farmland and minerals provided a base for a viable, burgeoning, agricultural and industrial economy. The economy was not, however, self-sustaining and could not function without certain mineral and other imports, while foreign trade furnished much of its dynamism. As farming became mechanized, the people largely dwelled in cities and towns. Cities and towns, in turn, often merged into a substantially continuous flow of settlement extending over wide areas of land, as in the northeastern coastal region.

The problems which a pluralistic society encountered in organizing itself brought into being an achieving society. These included conquering and settling a continent, organizing its raw resources into the flow of an industrial economy, assimilating successive waves of immigrants with their diverse cultures, and creating an appropriate form of government and ideology. The culture of the society developed and used the organization to a degree beyond that of any other people in history. The authority, technology, and power embodied in the American corporation, the techniques of corporate management, the energy displayed in the development of the physical sciences, together with the rich resources of its lands and access to other needed resources throughout the world, brought into being the most prodigious concentration and extent of power in a single country that the world has seen.

The role of the stern Protestant ethic in the growth in the power of the United States was the counterpart of the disciplined stoic ethic in the growth of Roman power. The erosion of that ethic in the affluent society of today is the counterpart of the decline of the stoic, natural law ethic in imperial Rome.

The pluralistic, organizational society of the United States believed in a supreme god. The individual, who freely participated in the diverse activities of organizations and groups, was believed to have direct contact with God and the ability to invoke His power and blessing. But the ideology of the organizational way of life, which was the American way of life, subtly tended to supplant the Christion faith in interpreting and giving meaning to life. Conformity to the American way of life reigned while Christianity became the bland, comforting interpretations of appropriately vague phrases of Hebrew religious records, which fashionable, agreeable preachers delivered from their pulpits to dwindling congregations. Religion helped to make the harshness of the organization and megapolis tolerable but it did not chart and justify their order.

Conformity was maintained by social pressures and sanctions. Those who did not fall into the familiar, deeply-grooved patterns of daily life faced social disapproval or even social ostracism. Those who failed to conform to organizational norms faced organizational discipline, including the extreme sanction of discharge and all its harsh consequences.

The authoritarian society which might otherwise have resulted was forestalled by the values of freedom of the individual and respect for the individual. These were deeply held and provided a strong integrative force, highly important in maintaining the system. Tension created by the concentration and use of authority and dominance in the society was also lessened by the value of freedom of speech. There was a constant theme of ridicule of authority-figures and their exercise of authority. Another tempering influence was the survival of the egalitarianism of frontier, farm, and village, such as in the form and style of interpersonal relations. For example, the use of first names as appellations in organizational relations, including those between superiors and subordinates, reduced social distance between personnel.

Yet the meaning and content of the healthy personality were little studied by the psychologists, who were more interested in the pathology of the human personality. The nature of the good life was the province of philosophers, not the concern of politicians or business men.

Among the American values and traits were achievement, principally in the form of the attainment of wealth, status, and power, although other modes of achievement were valued, conformity, display of possessions, mastery of styles for the display of possessions and modes of consumption of goods and services, familiarity with current clichés and slogans, movies, and TV programs, and physical, sensual gratifications. There were a number of sub-cultures, each with its own value system. These were more intense and, in general, extended more deeply into the lives of their members than a surface mass culture engendered by fashion, fad, and the mass communication media, together with the educational system. Such sub-cultures included the joint culture of the middle-class organizational life of the city and the suburbs, the culture of poverty of the slums and isolated rural regions, the culture of farm communities, the culture of intermediate towns composed of absentee land owners, small industry, and service industries, and the culture of research industries and their accompanying communities. As the tensions and sterility of urban life grew, preoccupation with sex and violence heightened. Tension-release mechanisms in the family car, mass sports entertainment, movies, radio, and television appeared. Liquor and, to some extent, narcotics provided momentary refuge from reality. The search for a new culture and new values appropriate to urban and organizational life was strongest among the youth. There was a most extraordinary creativity in the arts.

A dominant value and cultural theme was the attainment and mastery of organizational power in industry and government through the occupancy of posts of authority at all levels of authority. Teaching and practice of the exercise of authority in corporate enterprise and public administration eliminated much of the abuse of authority and power in interpersonal relations which might otherwise have occurred. The white-collar worker, however, had no administrative procedure to protect him from abuse of authority by his superiors, such as the grievance procedures of labor established through collective bargaining agreements. The laborer, however, was subject to the almost uncontrolled power of the union. Nevertheless, the denial of advancement in salary and post and other organizational benefits and the whip of discharge were powerful sanctions for the energetic and faithful performance of organizational norms. Not even members of the executive group were free from the threat of discharge.

The dominant family structure was the nuclear family, although some larger lineage groups existed, notably those characterized by the possession of inherited wealth and power. The family was patrilineal in form but the inherited, ideal authority-figure of the father as the male head of the household was little manifested in the organizational life of the city and the suburb. The wife and mother occupied the dominant role in the family and was the repository of authority in most matters. Many children became alienated personalities, partly as a result of the shadow-role of the husband and father and the separation of husband and wife within the family circle. The departure of the actual form of the family from its ideal form created considerable stress in marriage and family relationships, as well as personality problems.

Federalism enabled regionalism and diverse economies and their subcultures to persist in a common market under a central government. A public education system, including low-cost public universities, enabled individuals drawn from a wide number of income levels to achieve social mobility and rise in status. It should be noted, however, that access to such universities was very difficult for the lowest income groups, including most of the labor group. Payment of the living costs of a university student was for them almost impossible. Nevertheless, the value of the freedom of the individual and the openness of office, whether industrial or governmental, on the basis of ability, lessened tension and insured efficiency in the operation of the system.

A political democracy and a free-market economy directed social action to the realization of currently-held values and thereby reduced tension. The deprivations which the exercise of leadership in politics and the economy might otherwise have imposed were put off until air pollution, water pollution, water shortage, traffic congestion, and dwindling natural resources created crisis situations which made control measures acceptable, even though they were far more costly than the early exercise of leadership would have imposed.

A two-party political system, in which the opposing parties agreed on the fundamentals of the political order but differed largely on the pace of political change in response to social and economic change, assured stability in government. Political figures and mass communication media interpreted the complexities of life in symbols, slogans, and simple statements easily grasped by the teen-age mind of the American voter. Resentment, hate, and fear were fostered as instruments of political power, while needed society building was ignored. Constitutive conflict arose from the demands of Negroes for equality of opportunity, civil rights, and rise in status.

Much of the dynamism and character of the society was a product of war. Directly and indirectly, war considerably fed the growth of its technology and industry. The authority system itself was considerably dependent upon war. War provided an integrating influence lessening the impact of constitutive conflict.

Interpersonal conflict was handled by the legal system. The Supreme Court was in part a body of last resort for dealing with problems of constitutive conflict neglected by the political forums. The judicial system was relatively free to recognize new legal norms as social change necessitated them. The legal system was factually open to the middle class on the basis of cost and nominally open to the labor class. The latter group handled its conflict problems arising in work relations through collective bargaining arguments and grievance procedures, together with workmens' compensation. Insurance helped to meet catastrophe. Installment buying enabled a culture centered on the possession and use of goods to develop and maintain itself. As reality became increasingly unbearable, the society resorted to symbolic modes of life and dress, and even elected symbolic figures to office. The photogenic, admired symbol of authority which President Kennedy became, may be the precursor of the synthetically-made political figure of appealing face, voice, and bearing, who is the puppet of his staff and financial supporters.

How can one summarize a summary, impressionistic portrayal of the people of the United States? It is a land of dwindling natural resources, of growing crowding, and of a people who mastered the organizational way of life. It is a land in which the neighborhood and small community is disappearing and the isolation and friction of urban life is growing. It is a land whose people still cling to such basic values as freedom of the individual and the rights of the individual but in which the individual increasingly ignores his obligations and responsbilities. It is a land whose society is precariously poised on the dynamism of organizational energy, making extraordinary and increasingly insupportable demands upon the human personality for maintenance of the society. It is a land of cultural drift. Yet among the peoples of the industrialized nations of the Atlantic basin, its people may well have gone the farthest distance in mastering the organizational way of life that is modern society. They may be more aware of its problems and doing more about them than others. They display an extraordinary creativity, energy, and discipline, as they create the most affluent and powerful of societies.

The author hastens to remark that there is nothing particularly novel in the above description, except for the contribution of social theory to its perspective. Indeed, this is the very point which was made above, namely that the method of organization of the data concerning the tribal societies is familiar and enables the inclusion of social theory with factual description.

While the author is not an anthropologist, he may perhaps be indulged in a few remarks concerning theory and method in anthropology beyond those stated in the introduction to this study. These concern the movement of anthropology from the study of aspects of life of particular peoples to comparative anthropology and to social theory.

The first issue is whether the comparative study of peoples is empirically valid. Bohannan vigorously supported the proposition that empirical truth in the study of a people rested on the fact that each society and its unique culture was a "folk system."[1] His proposition flowed from a view of the life of a people as one which was life as they saw it and interpreted it through the symbols of their language and the referents they gave them in the light of their own culture. At best, an observer from another culture could never fully or accurately describe their life. Bohannan may be said to view the empirical truth, which it is the role of the anthropologist to state, to be contextual. There would appear to be no room for comparative anthropology in such a view. On the other hand, Gluckman asserted the view of studying tribal peoples in the light of the concepts developed in the culture of Western civilization.[2]

Before coming to grips with this issue, it would be useful to point out some of the problems of the use of the comparative method in anthropology. First, the data about any one people is always a product of a particular observer. Its validity is subject to his limitations in training and personality, system of perception and cognition, values, biases, prejudices, and cultural background. Second, the data about any one people, in most cases, and about a number of peoples, in all cases, will be the product of the writing of a number of observers, thereby multiplying the distortion noted above. Third, the literature about a people which eventuates is spotty, episodic, and of uneven quality and depth. There is no standardized reporting system, as it were. Fourth, communication by informants to the observer is subject to the semantic difficulties noted in the preceding paragraph, as well as the personal biases and limitations of the informant.

P. H. Gulliver made some remarks about the current state of comparative and cross-cultural work on African peoples.[3] He said that it was "small both in quantity and significance," that the anthropologists prefer to work on "a particular socio-cultural system," and that it was "a most complex operation . . . adequately to compare data . . . from different societies." He pointed out that: "A field of comparative study which has been of much importance is the establishment of typologies, which serve to order particular classes

1. P. Bohannan, *Justice and Judgment among the Tiv* (London, New York, Toronto, 1957), 4-5, 69.

2. M. Gluckman, "African Jurisprudence," *Advancement of Science,* XVIII (1962), 439.

3. P. H. Gulliver, "Anthropology," *The African World: A Survey of Social Research,* ed. R. H. Lystad (New York, Washington, London, 1965), 57 ff.

of data and to clarify the major factors of differentiation on which, hopefully, more intensive studies can focus." He described the "ultimate ideal" as "the establishment of generally applicable statements about human behaviour and social relationships and the discovery of the range and operation of factors which, under varying conditions, affect the application of these generalizations to concrete situations."

The task of research into the comparative behavior of tribal societies is to perceive regularities and similarities and differences in behavior, institutions, and systems of behavior, and to develop therefrom correlations and principles of behavior. The process of search for order in the diversity of different societies and their cultures is one of search for images of realities, as expressed in a system of language communication built up in the researcher's culture, selecting and forming the content of such images, and testing them for their faithfulness to reality. For example, what was yesterday's categorization of operation of a social system in terms of, say, a movement toward an equilibrium need not be accepted after testing as today's description.[4]

Each social system is unique in its own terms but all social systems contain some common elements, other elements appear in high-frequency patterns, and still others appear in low-frequency patterns. The comparative method of anthropological study implies the careful comparison of forms of action by given peoples "to establish, by a process of generalization, one or more basic types into which the various forms can be classified."[5]

The search for truth necessarily leads to Bohannan's insistence on the uniqueness of meaning of a "folk system" but not to the exclu-

---

4. *Cf.* M. Gluckman, *Order and Rebellion in Tribal Africa* (New York, 1963), 23, in which he abandoned his earlier concept of "unifying civil war" in favor of the view that civil war is one of a

> number of discrepant and perhaps conflicting processes at work in an area of political action. . . . I think therefore much more in terms of series of social processes, operating within an ecological setting and the bio-physical framework of human life, as well as of the restriction and action of a technology and a culture . . . We have, as Fortes and Firth have stressed, to think of a field of social action in which we can delineate certain processes set in motion by a series of customary institutions, which do largely "hang together", but only largely, and not perfectly.

See M. Gluckman, *Custom, and Conflict in Africa* (Glencoe, Ill., 1955), 23, 38-39; M. Gluckman, "Rituals of Rebellion in South-East Africa," *Frazer Lecture* (Manchester, 1952).

5. I. Schapera, "Some Comments on Comparative Method in Social Anthropology," *American Anthropologist*, LV (1953), 359. Schapera's limitation of effective comparative research to peoples of a region was criticized by M. Singer, "Summary of Comments and Discussion," *ibid.*, p. 364.

sion of the comparative or analytical system. The cultural uniqueness of a folk or people must be described with the utmost fidelity,
notwithstanding the semantic difficulties of trying to transform symbols and their referents, together with their body of reference, from
one language and its culture into another language and its culture.
In so doing, the investigator must try to avoid as much as possible
distorting his descriptions of data in order to fit them into more or
less inappropriate symbols and their meanings drawn from other
languages and their respective cultures. When, however, the behavior
of a people have been described, with as much accuracy and completeness as possible, comparative analysis of their behavior with that
of other peoples in terms of the investigator's language, knowledge,
and culture is a valid scientific endeavor.

The comparative method implies the search for symbols and their
referents which will categorize faithfully and with dedication to
truth data of a diverse character. It implies that this search will go
forward on the basis of trying to find symbols and their referents
which will provide an analytical structure which will *not* distort the
accuracy of description of empirical observation but *will* enable a
comprehensive, ordered view of the data revealing insights, interrelationships, and correlations that would not otherwise be possible.
The use of such a methodology is the essence of the scientific method
and the basis for erecting an integrated, interdependent system of
postulates, propositions, and principles that is called a science.

Anthropology accordingly will employ comparative techniques as
it moves to develop theory. This is simply because our culture demands such theory in its own terms. Steadily, writer by writer, writing by writing, anthropology will move toward the comparative
method and the development of theory no less than any other social
science. It so happens that its perspective of its domain will make
enormous demands upon its workers, as a part of this movement.
But the history of science has so far been one in which there are always those who assume the burdens, exacting as they may be, of
carrying forward its growth.

Chapter 17 represents an attempt to employ the classic inductive
method for the organization of comparative data. It is a tabulation
of the principles of propositions resting on facts to be found in
Chapters 4 to 16 and the appendices.[6] This type of an approach is
seen to be subject to the following limitations.

---

6. See G. Swanson, *The Birth of the Gods: The Origin of Primitive Beliefs*
(Ann Arbor, Mich., 1960) for a computerized development of principles of social
behavior based on data concerning 50 societies throughout the world drawn
from the Human Relations Area Files.

First, the statements thereby developed have no validity beyond the data from which they are drawn. They are based on the data and limited by the data. If it is desired to extrapolate them into more universal propositions for the science of anthropology, then one must look to the validity of the sampling process for gathering the data as supporting the more inclusive inferences drawn from the data. Inasmuch as the research objective was solely to explore African tribal society and law, and certain Western and Eastern African peoples within that context, the statements only apply to the peoples studied.

Second, statements resting on trends in the data rather than universally distributed propositions have qualified validity.

Third, statements which exhibit a high degree of correlation among the data are usually of a broad, abstract character, mostly possessing relatively little novelty.

Fourth, statements of correlations among the data are frequently limited to only one society or to so few as to be without much significance. Moreover, a reading of such scattered statements generally fails to reveal a particular pattern or trend. They merely exist as facts.

Fifth, many useful facts which might exist in the societies in question may have been overlooked in the reporting of data by the various writers consulted simply because the observer was not looking for them or lacked the perceptual and cognitive equipment to see them.

Sixth, the infusion of extraneous data or interpretations into the data or the statements is prohibited by the methodology. One must state the cold, pure conclusions or correlations. This is, of course, an absolute essential of the scientific methodology and there is not the slightest intention to gainsay or deprecate it. The statement is made simply to point out that beyond the formulation of findings lies the task of drawing inferences, hypothesizing, and theorizing.

For example, statements 1.1.2 and 1.1.3 tell nothing new. Statements 1.1.6 to 1.1.18 are simply stringing beads of information together. Statement 1.1.4 concerning a correlation between an ancestor cult and kinship structures of social action, is not a universal principle of tribal behavior. Neither can statement 1.1.6 be said to be a universal proposition of anthropology. Indeed, it rather minimally appeared even among the peoples studied. On the other hand, statement 1.6.1 appears to the author to be quite a significant finding, for the reasons set forth in his discussion of law in Chapter 1. It reads as follows: "A belief may exist in supernatural power acting as a sanctioning process to punish those who violate valued

norms. Such a belief is particularly characteristic of kinship structures of social action, which typically lack a sanctioning process
of a temporal nature." This statement was strongly supported by the
data. It should also be noted that the fifth and sixth sections on
conflict and control seem to fall into an interesting pattern and to
contain a number of useful statements.

The six principal categories for organizing the data of tribal behavior simply represented the theoretical concepts into which the
data most readily fell in the light of social theory. The first three
of them primarily reflect aspects of order while the remainder concern conflict and control.

It is the author's conclusion that Chapter 17 demonstrates that the
classic inductive method as a methodology for comparative anthropology is necessary but not always rewarding. The behaviors of peoples are too diverse, man is too infinite in the inventiveness of his
adaptation to his environment, to exhibit the regularities of behavior observed by the scientist working in the domain of the natural
sciences. Statements which have a high degree of correlation in the
data frequently state the merely obvious. Yet from time to time a
statement will yield an important new insight and a series of statements will fall into a significant pattern. The use of the inductive
method is something in the nature of a scanning process which
searches for new perspectives and for validation of old perspectives.

The concept of the system will have considerable usefulness in the
development of theory in comparative anthropology. For example,
it is hypothesized that the concept of dyadic social systems may have
considerable potentialities in the analysis of kinship societies. Segmentary groupings become significant only in the social context of
comprising a means for goal attainment and value realization by
their members. Thus lineage groups in a segmentary society often
represent a dyadic, symmetrical structuring of a conflict situation so
that groups, which are at the same time unified and in opposition,
provide a system of dispute settlement. There was a most unique
development of a dyadic social system as a means of dispute settlement, in the form of a mediation process, among the Arusha. (See
Chapter 14.) A dyadic, asymmetrical structuring of lineage groups
among the Tiv was a system for releasing social tension by providing
new land for occupancy by groups ridden by fear, hostility, and
tyranny. The alignment of opposing groups on the basis of their
structural distance, i.e., remoteness of kinship affiliations, was designed to provide overwhelming force as a means for such land
acquisition. (See Chapter 9.) To be contrasted with the Tiv system

for the expansion of territory through the use of force was the Alur process of peaceful expansion of territory. (Appendix B5.) The comparative analysis of the behavior of tribal societies, in the light of social theory, can open up new vistas for understanding human relations. The findings of a comparative study of tribal peoples, from the standpoint of social theory, are also useful in the implications which they have for modern society and culture. (See Chapter 18.)

If anthropology is to move toward social theory, if the behavioral sciences are to move toward social theory, it would seem that such a flow will take place in the light of the symbols and their referents that the several social sciences have already developed and, of course, all the new symbols that research in the forefront of knowledge always develops. One should ask of every new symbol, or type of symbol, such as the expression of data in mathematical form, how useful it will be in the organized growth of knowledge, how it will fit in with other symbols, how all of them will fit into larger wholes, and how the total structure and its contents will significantly and usefully contribute to the understanding and prediction of social behavior in general.

Regularities in social behavior are a matter of social forces resting, directly or indirectly, on value realization. One interprets social behavior in the light of the psychology of man as an organism and a social being possessing a personality and a self, on the one hand, and the outcome of his motivations in the action of social groups, structures of social action, and social forces, on the other. One searches for forces of integration and disintegration, patterns of order, conflict, control, and configurations of change in social behavior. In short, the anthropologist, as a social theorist, moves from description of objective behavior, as it is perceived with the eye and the ear, to include description of subjective behavior as a matter of the joys, tensions, fears, and frustrations of life. For it must be remembered that whatever is a characteristic of society is in fact a characteristic of man in society.

Part Two

GHANA

Chapter 4

The Tallensi

Geography and Economy

WE ARE at the land of the peoples of West Africa. The long rollers of the Atlantic beat upon Cape Verde and the mouth of the Senegal River. The land continues in a giant curve to the south, past the Grain Coast, the Ivory Coast, the Gold Coast, and the Slave Coast to the mouth of the Niger River. Now the ocean waves roll in from the south to crash on a beach which from time to time contains a lagoon. An occasional rush of river water into the lagoon or an unusually high tide may break through the sand barrier and let the fish of the lagoon escape or the fish of the sea enter. The beach merges into a flat, often dry grassland. The land then rises in rolling hills to the plateau of a vast rain forest. In the distant north the land changes to open woodland, scrub brush, and a treeless savanna of grass. Finally, the steadily lessening rainfall shrinks to a point where the Western Sahara desert begins.

The peoples of the savanna and forest zones may be said to belong to a single great group of languages known as the Western Sudanic family. In the northeast region, between the Niger and Lake Chad, the Chadic group of languages of the Hamito-Semitic family are generally spoken. Although derivation from a common stock is thus indicated, peoples of the savanna and forest spheres were culturally differentiated early from one another. Certain peoples, with their distinctive linguistic differentiation, appear to have expanded more readily across the open savanna land. The savanna peoples tend to emphasize the growing of grain, as compared with the growing of fruit and root crops by the forest peoples. Pastoral tending of livestock is long established in the savanna, whereas livestock in the forest peoples is largely confined to small numbers of goats, pigs, and fowl associated with the household.

Social, political, and economic organization ranges from essentially autonomous local communities organized on a kinship basis, which may also be linked by ties of kinship with other groups, to a hierarchical, complex, social structure exhibiting the qualities of statehood. The latter will reflect more advanced agricultural systems, specialized crafts, and political and legal organs and processes.[1]

The first state to be selected for investigation is Ghana. In it, three peoples will be studied: The Tallensi of the former Northern Territories, the Ashanti of the former Ashanti Colony, who predominate in numbers, and the Gã of the former Gold Coast Colony (Appendix B1). They are found in the savanna, the rain forest, and the coast, respectively.

The Tallensi live in the savanna and are one of the peoples of the Voltaic family of tribes inhabiting the basin of the Volta rivers in the Northern Territories of what was formerly the Gold Coast and now is Ghana. The peoples of the Voltaic region exhibit an unusual degree of cultural uniformity.

The Tallensi are a farming people. They grow mostly cereals and employ the same methods and the same type of tools as their forebears. Theirs is a subsistence economy; they press closely upon the food supply and frequently experience hunger.

Social Organization

The Tallensi were a segmentary society.[2] They organized themselves into lineage units of larger and larger dimensions, each em-

---

1. D. Forde, "The Cultural Map of West Africa: Successive Adaptations to Tropical Forests and Grasslands," *Transactions of the New York Academy of Sciences*, Ser. II, XV (1952-1953), 206.

2. The term "segmentary" has been used in reference to several types of social systems, but the essential features are the "nesting" attribute of segmentary series and the characteristic of being in a state of continual segmentation and complementary opposition. The series may be one of lineages, smaller ones nesting inside and composing larger ones, which in turn compose still larger ones, and so on; or it may be of territorial groups (hamlets, villages, sections, tribes, nations) or of others. . . . Segmentation should be distinguished from fission. By fission a group ceases to exist as an entity, becoming two or more new groups that are no longer in a state of complementary

bracing a larger number of generations descended from a common male ancestor. The range in size of such units is indicated by Fortes' usage of the terms minimal lineage, nuclear lineage, inner lineage, medial lineage, and maximal lineage. In a kinship-structured or segmentary society, each lineage group has a certain post designated in kinship terms, such as the senior male progenitor of the kinship group, which becomes the focal point for such purposes as the exercise of authority, the performance of ritual, and representation in relations with other groups, including the village. The values of the group are realized by the cooperation of kinsmen, whose manner of cooperation are indicated by their kin positions. Functions of a political, economic, religious, or conflict-solving character, which in modern society might be performed by corporate bodies specifically organized for the purpose, are in a segmentary society performed by social structures defined by kinship ties. The selection of the appropriate lineage group for the purpose of action is a matter of characterizing the particular situation in lineage terms, that is to say, whether it involves accepting the authority of the head of the family unit, the propitiation through ritual of an ancestor, or the settlement of a dispute between two opposing lineage groups which are distantly related.

The nuclear family of a man and his sons, or the extended family of a man and his sons and their families or, after his death, of the families of several sons of the same father, was the basic economic and jural unit. The extended family lived in a single compound and tilled the comparatively well-fertilized home farm and often brush farm land as well. The home farm was only a few acres in size, yet it provided a greater degree of security and comfort than the brush farm, which was the means for livelihood of families leaving their lineage homestead.

The extended family and its farmland formed a single working whole. The resources of human energy which such a family provided enabled its members to achieve survival over the generations, to perform their rituals, and occasionally to experience times of relative plenty. The head of this group was responsible for the welfare of the group and exercised authority to that end. He organized labor on the farm and controlled the distribution of its produce. He held

---

opposition; by segmentation a group merely divides in certain contexts but retains its corporate identity in others.

J. Middleton and D. Tait (eds.), "Introduction," *Tribes Without Rulers: Studies in African Segmentary Systems* (London, 1958), 7-8. For a fuller discussion of segmenting societies, see *infra* pp. 369 to 371.

the land as the lineage head. In this capacity, he was vested with rights over the farmland, livestock, and other valuables, together with rights to services and allegiance. He was the ritual head of the family and, as such, had the right to the custody of the ancestor shrines and other religious objects. He was the center of authority in the household and exercised authority over his wife and children. The wife was expected to perform the household tasks and to help with the harvesting of crops. The son was expected to obey his father, to respect him, and to be loyal to him to the point that he must take his side against the rest of the world. Yet there was no legal process or sanction, as we regard the machinery of law, to compel the father, wife, or son to adhere to their respective obligations and carry out their respective responsibilities. Reciprocity was an important sanction for the performance of duty. A father's failure to provide a bride-price for his son might lead the son to neglect his work on the father's farm or even to leave home. The basic pattern of family life was sustained by a system of mutual help, etiquette, and mutual tolerance.

A man had a duty to insure that the ancestor spirits and other mystical influences were kept in a beneficial attitude towards his family. In the event of illness, it was his duty to consult a diviner and perform the indicated sacrifices to help towards a cure. He was jurally responsible for his sons and unmarried daughters. While a nexus of rights and duties existed between a father and his children, he was, nevertheless, considered to own his children and even to have the right to pawn them for a debt. In earlier times he could even sell them into slavery. He could order his daughter to marry as he pleased and to use the bride-price he received for her in whatever manner he wished. He had full control over his son's labor, an over-right in any personal property his son might acquire, and the right to determine whether his son was to live with him or to set up his own separate household.

The very fact of birth into a family created an absolute moral bond between parents and child composed of devotion and duty on the parental side and filial piety on the child's side. The child must be fed, educated, and reared. The father looked after all the affairs of the child. He took care of the home, both in material matters and in the exercise of ritual. Upon his death, the child assumed responsibility for himself and lost the status of dependency in social, economic, and spiritual matters.

The authority of the father was not only reinforced by the son's dependency but also by the fact that through the father contact with the ancestors was reached. The existence or expression of resentment by a parent to a child was equivalent to a parental curse, which in any form was regarded to be the source of illness or other harm. A parental curse was to be used only in cases of gross affront or outright defiance. A more usual sanction was the father's legitimate power to inflict corporal punishment on his children.

Fortes says in this connection:

> . . . Respect, affection, a feeling of mutual identification, and a sense of dependence, supported by the whole strength of the lineage system and the ancestor cult, are mingled with great freedom in everyday intercourse, as we shall see shortly, and with the strain of latent antagonism. It is an indication of the strength and internal consistency of the social system as a whole that ruptures between father and son are not very common.

Filial piety is a significant element in all Tale genealogical relationships. A person's loyalty to and solidarity with his lineage springs from his relationship with his father, his ties with his matrilateral kin from his relationship with his mother. The founding ancestor of a lineage is visualized as its "father" and the progenitrix of a lineage segment as its "mother." A person identifies himself with his patrilateral kin through first identifying himself with his father, and with his matrilateral kin by extending his identification with his mother. Economic motives, jural rules, and ritual sanctions work on the individual through his sentiments of filial piety.

This can be seen clearly in the interlocking of land tenure, local cohesion, and clan solidarity. The land a man owns in his clan settlement is usually land that has come to him by inheritance from his father. It is hallowed land because it has come to him thus. This land is the basis of his local and economic ties with his lineage and clan. In psychological terms it stands for the most significant aspects of his own development and of his relationship with his father. It was here that he learnt to farm, working side by side with his father and thus coming to know every inch of it. His father's social personality is for him closely associated with this land, with the homestead which stands on it somewhere, and with the family graves including, in time, those of his parents, that lie there. When he inherits this land it is the principal sign that he has at length stepped into his father's shoes.[3]

Property fell into two categories, patrimonial rights and property, known as *faar,* and individual rights and property. *Faar* belonged to the lineage, whether minimal or maximal, and not to the individual. Its holder was free to use it but not to dispose of it. Individually acquired property, on the other hand, belonged to the individual, subject to the rights of his father. It became patrimonial property when

---

3. M. Fortes, *The Web of Kinship Among the Tallensi* (London, New York, Toronto, 1949), 181-182.

it was inherited. The holder of land in the *faar* might be said to stand at a point in time where he looked back to all the holders of the land who preceded him and all those who would follow him as constituting, with him, a single corporate group. He owed the duty to all such other holders not to alienate the *faar*.

The son grew up under his father's tutelage and direction. He learned from his father the details of the Tallensi culture and how to make the most of life. One who has been so reared was said to have "reached" his father. The period of adolescence to adulthood was perhaps the period of greatest harmony between father and son. It was the time when the son must closely identify himself with his father and yet it was also the time when the process of self-differentiation took place on the part of the son. The son could have fowls and livestock of his own or even his own private plot of land given him by his father or the head of the household. He was considered to be entitled to the fruits of such property. A father who interfered with his son doing as he wished with his "things" was considered to deprive him of a right. For example, a father could not rightfully forbid his son to use the proceeds of the sale of fowls raised by his son to buy desired clothing, though he had the naked power to do so. A father could not rightfully forbid his son to use products of his own labor as the son wished in the course of his courtship.

Other approved norms of conduct were more abstractly defined. For example, in distributing the fruits of the farm, the father was expected to respect the principle that "all those who work together to supply the needs of the household are entitled to a just share in the products of their labour."[4]

The child's desire for independence and the father's claims on his labor and property were not always contained in separate categories and came into conflict with one another. Rivalry between father and son was most marked in the case of his oldest son, who succeeded to the father's position and authority upon the latter's death. The son's desire for independence, particularly economic independence, reached its strongest point with his marriage and establishment of a family. As the son's children neared adolescence, he formally separated himself from his parental family, either by cutting his own gateway into his living quarters in the compound or by leaving the homestead altogether to create his own. Conflict with the father, including differences as to what was appropriate support for the son's family, led to separation from the family unit as the only solution.

There was an ideal pattern of interdependent relations whose

---

4. *Ibid.,* p. 204.

very interdependency or reciprocal nature was viewed to create obligations. It began with the proposition that a man "owned" his son simply because he begat him. There was then added the proposition that the dependency of the son made necessary the exercise of authority by the father. The fact that the son worked for the father was considered to create the latter's responsibilities for the son, including economic support and ritual and jural responsibilities. In other words, duties implied equivalent rights and powers.

The principle of reciprocity, or the duty to make equivalent returns for benefit received, was present in all kinship and family relations, as well as in interpersonal relations generally. When goods or services were received on the understanding that they would be repaid, a relationship in the nature of a debt was created and the duty of repayment extended to a man's heirs. But the borrowing of property from a member of an inner lineage or close relation created an obligation eventually to make some sort of an equivalent return. A grandson borrowing money from a grandfather did not create a debt but his act nevertheless created an obligation which was expected to be discharged by some such act as the later borrowing by the grandfather of a goat from his grandson. In the long run, mutual services or giving of benefits should balance.

In summary, the family provided the basic organization of Tale life. The father was the manager of the family unit, its authoritative decision maker, and its ritual head. He controlled, managed, and allocated its economic resources.

The economic basis of the kinship structures of Tale society was brilliantly delineated by P. M. Worsley.[5] He pointed out that the Tallensi were densely settled on their land. This had the result of placing a high value on a well-worked, well-mannered farm homestead, the *faar*. The compound farm worked by the extended family of a father and his sons and their families provided a surplus of grains that enabled them to surmount adversity in much better shape than the holders of small farms and to prosper. Hence the stability of the basic lineage unit of the Tallensi.

Religion

It has been seen that the holder of the *faar* was, by virtue of that fact, linked with all the ancestors who had previously held some part of it. This fact placed obligations with respect to its use upon the

5. P. M. Worsley, "The Kinship System of the Tallensi: A Revaluation," *Journal of the Royal Anthropological Institute,* LXXXVI (1956), 37.

particular holder in favor of the ancestors from whom it was received. A more universal link of an individual with his ancestors was found in the concept of the *Yin,* which was derived from the word *Naayin* or Heaven. The term *Naayin* related to all persons, but *Yin* only to one individual.

In order to arrive at an understanding of this concept, it should first of all be realized that death was not viewed as bringing an end to a person's membership and participation in the kinship group. The presence and influence of the ancestors as spirits was an accepted part of the environment to which one must adjust in an appropriate manner. They possessed power and control over an individual. A person was under the spiritual jurisdiction of the common ancestors of the kinship group to which he belonged. Everyone had his *Yin* of the mouth, that is, the destiny preordained from him before birth. This came to him when he " 'spoke when he was with Heaven above.' "[6] This was part of the spiritual forces which determined whether good or ill fortune would attend him in his life in this world. The most important aspect of his *Yin* was determined by his *Yin* ancestors. While all his ancestors had relevance to his life, some of them manifested themselves as being concerned particularly and solely with him. They were usually a select group of his immediate forebears. They were revealed to him typically in early manhood as a result of some accident, misfortune, or coincidence. The diviners whom he consulted upon such an occasion told him who they were and identified the objects by which they revealed themselves. He would then build a shrine dedicated to such ancestors. This became his means of communication with them and an instrument for securing their good will. The performance of ritual before the shrine was essential for all important events in his life in order that their outcome might be in his favor. Sacrifice to the ancestors on this shrine was required to minimize misfortune.

It was said above that the ancestors and other spiritual forces represented power and control over an individual. Here "power" connotes an ability to affect one's position, fate, or situation either beneficially or injuriously, while "control" implies the imposition of retribution or other sanction for misconduct. There was, for example, no legal process or sanction for murder. Compensation was not exacted by relatives of the injured. Murder might lead to warfare between clans, when killer and victim were drawn from different clans, but it did not lead to violence among the members of a clan.

---

6. Fortes, *op. cit.,* p. 228.

Spiritual forces, notably the Earth, visited the sanction of misfortune upon the murderer. Death would visit a particular family because the father had killed.

The preservation of the values of filial piety, parental affection and solicitude, friendly cooperation, solidarity, and good will in the kinship group was considered to fall peculiarly within the province of the ancestors and spiritual forces. The existence of blood ties between individuals or groups enabled them to collaborate in the performance of ritual to conserve these values. On the one hand, a person's conceptualization and worship of his ancestors represented a duplication on "the mystical plane of the tangle of attachments, reciprocities, tensions, and submerged antagonisms that bind parents and children to one another in life." On the other hand, ancestors were more prone to intervene in the lives of their living descendants "by the misfortune they inflict than by the benefits they bring. They emerge as sanctions of conduct more often by reason of the punishments they bring down on wrong doers than because of the benefits they confer for right doing." Upon the death of the father, he "becomes the paramount sanction of moral conduct" for the son and "this applies, *mutatis mutandis,* in only a lesser degree to the mother."[7] Performance of the son's duties to his father had a practical as well as a ritual sanction. The father might withhold economic benefits from the son to compel desired conduct. To a certain extent, the son could exert reciprocal pressure upon his father to compel adherence to desired norms. But the performance of socially recognized duties or norms by either was not subject to legal sanctions as we know them.

Individual misfortunes were viewed as a product of one's *Yin.* Public calamities were correspondingly viewed as a product of the mystical power of the Earth. As the ancestors determined the fate of the individual, so the Earth determined the welfare of the community. When men were good and were faithful in prayers and sacrifices to the Earth, it was benevolent to them and allowed them to succeed in their enterprises, the land to bring forth crops, and the women to bear children. When the relationship was broken, the

---

7. *Ibid.,* p. 235, italics supplied. The "punitive aspect of the ancestor figures has a disciplinary not a destructive function. It is the instrument of their justice and a measure of their sovereignty paralleling, on the religious plane, the usages and forms of family government we have previously described." The "lineage ancestors . . . are just; and their justice is directed to enforcing the moral and religious norms and values on which the social order rests. They do this through the power over life and death in which they are supreme." M. Fortes, *Oedipus and Job in West African Religion* (Cambridge, England, 1959), 77, 56.

Earth brought public calamities. The function of ritual, in relation to the Earth, was to help to prevent public calamity and to reintegrate the community after it had occurred. The earth was known as *teng*, and took different pronouns depending upon whether it was being referred to in its mystical sense. Chiefs and *tendaanas* had almost no temporal power, as we know it, but had instead the function "to prosper the community" through ritual. Within a particular clan and between clans, they formed "the axis about which the body of moral, jural, and ritual values that binds the community into a unity revolves." As they performed their complementary roles in ritual, they displayed "the fusion of the two principles that shape the total social field which ultimately determines the prosperity of the individual. One is the principle that the fate of the individual and of the community is determined by the practical and utilitarian concerns and needs that bind man to the earth and put him at the mercy of natural phenomena. The other is the principle that the attainment of prosperity and security, both for the individual and the community, depends upon the integration of the community."

The notion of chiefship

symbolizes the plexus of social relationships, based on lineage and kinship, which unites a defined group of people into a community; and tendaanaship symbolizes the bonds of men, as members of a community, with land, locality, and the material earth. . . . Both chiefship and tendaanaship are vested in maximal lineages and therefore have the ritual sanction of the ancestor cult; both are associated with the organization of the Tallensi into local communities and the utilization of natural resources, and therefore have the sanction of the Earth cult. But in the complementary conjunction the emphasis in the chiefship is on its linkage with the ancestors, while the emphasis in the tendaanaship is on its specific ritual bonds with the mystical Earth.[8]

The office of *tendaana* involved ritual bonds importing the highest values to the Tallensi, the bonds of a maximal lineage with its locality.

Interests, rights, and obligations in the land were sanctioned by mystical forces of the Earth and the ancestors, as well as by practical means.

Inherited farm-land is a sacred trust of the ancestors. Their labour won it for human use, hallowed it, and preserved it for their descendants. It belongs to them. To pledge it is a slur on them; to sell it is a sacrilege. "It will kill deaths *(de kura kum)*"—the offended ancestors will cause deaths in the family of the seller—the natives say. . . . Where land is

8. M. Fortes, *The Dynamics of Clanship Among the Tallensi* (London, New York, Toronto, 1945), 182-184.

concerned Tallensi always connect the fear of mystical punishment by the ancestors with obligations towards one's dependents and heirs.[9]

The system of ritual reflected the social system. A man did not attain the status of independence from his father and the capacity to perform ritual sacrifices to an ancestor until his father died. The performance of the mortuary and funeral ceremonies by the sons for the father marked the transformation of the father into an ancestor spirit and the assumption of jural and ritual authority by his sons.

The cult of the ancestors was important among the Tallensi because it defined "a person's place in society and his rights, duties, capacities and privileges" through precise genealogical knowledge. The ancestor cult reflected their social order and gave it a spiritual dimension and value. It provided the members of the society with the categories of thought and belief for organizing and interpreting their actions.

Filial piety existed to the point that fathers had an absolute power over their sons. The hostility that this engendered was handled by taboos binding on the eldest son, who represented all his brothers. Similarly the lineage ancestors were supreme in their power over their descendants. They were not always either benevolent or malevolent. Their ultimate power over life and death must be accepted as a fact and as just, since men were compelled to submit to their omnipotence. The punitive action of the ancestors was an instrument of justice and a means of bringing punishment for wrongdoing.[10]

The linkage of the ritual, social, and economic aspects of Tallensi life was symbolically exemplified in the cycle of the Great Festivals. This began with the celebration of the end of the rainy season. It included the harvest rites and looked forward to the sowing season. The ceremonies were "the joint responsibility of all the political-lineage and clan heads of the country. They are so concatenated that every ceremony is either the necessary preliminary to another, or the essential conclusion of another; and each such leg of a sequence is the responsibility of a different office holder, acting in his capacity as the jural and ritual representative of his clan and lineage." The rituals were intended to prosper the growth of crops upon the earth. The favor of the Earth and the ancestors was sought to accomplish this end. Thus all the holders of ritual office representing linkages with the Earth and the ancestors collaborated in the ceremonies. The ceremonies emphasized an order of peace and harmony. They could

9. *Ibid.*, pp. 178-179.
10. Fortes, *Oedipus and Job*, 27-31, 56-59, 78, quotation at 29.

be interrupted whenever a person holding some unresolved grievance involving the participating groups made his complaint known
and demanded its settlement.[11]

Witchcraft played a relatively small part in the Tale society. When
an event occurred for which the existence of a witch provided a
plausible explanation, the group would sometimes point to the oc-
cult powers of some one individual as its cause. "Most accusations
of this sort are in the first instance made by women against co-wives,
and are symptomatic of the tensions inherent in the joint family."[12]

Adherence to valued norms of conduct was not sanctioned by legal
machinery, as we know it, but instead by mystical forces. The pattern
of social control which emerged was one of ritual affirmation of the
values of kinship and the existence of an ideal society based on
amity, solidarity, loyalty among kin, harmony with the ancestors, and
the universal power of the Earth. When this ideal pattern was disrupted by deviant performance of a social role, such as departure
from one of the complex of norms inhering in the role relationship of father and son, the injured party used such practical means
to secure conformity as he possessed and otherwise left it to the mystical powers to sanction the wrongdoing in due course.

War

The Tallensi abhorred killing. The sin of visiting death upon another was not excused even by self-defense or justifiable anger. Yet
war between clans, notably those of the Namoos and those of the
first inhabitants of Taleland, occasionally took place.

War was a product of tension between clans and rarely spread to
involve the whole Tallensi people. Pillage, the acquisition of slaves
or territory, or calculated aggression were not motives for war. War
usually arose as a result of retaliation by one or more members of a
clan against attacks, frequently of a spontaneous character, made by
members of another clan. They would then spread along the basic
line of cleavage between the Namoos and non-Namoos. If hostile
clans were separated by the territory of a non-participating clan, it
was necessary for the latter to take sides in the war in order to allow
the warriors of one clan to cross its territory in order to attack the
other. General wars involving all the Tallensi were infrequent.

---

11. M. Fortes, "Ritual and Office in Tribal Society," *Essays on the Ritual of
Social Relations*, ed. M. Gluckman (Manchester, 1962), 73-78, quotation at 74.
12. Fortes, *Dynamics of Clanship*, 33.

Fortes reports that only three appear to have occurred in the last three or four generations.

The tendency of conflict between clans to be released through war was reinforced by the practice of raiding for cattle between clans as a measure of self-help for the enforcement of legal rights. There was no general judicial system among the Tallensi. An injury, such as adultery, abduction of a wife, or non-payment of a bride-price, sustained by one clan member at the hands of a member of another clan, created the right to resort to self-help in the form of a cattle raid if satisfaction were not forthcoming. This was legitimate action and gave rise to no right of reprisal by those who suffered the raid. Such action tended to foster a toleration of violence which was otherwise condemned in the moral system of the Tallensi.

During the time of the *Golib* festival, immediately before the rains, all fighting was prohibited. This festival emphasized the themes of food, harmony, fecundity, and the common interests of the people as a whole.

Thus war appeared to have two functions in Tale society. It emphasized the structural cleavages that existed in the society between certain clans and released tensions that existed between them and promoted solidarity and integration of the entire society as well. It was part of a sequence of events beginning with the presence of conflict and tension, which erupted into violence and war, and ended with affirmation of unity and reintegration.[13]

Conflict and Its Control

The preceding pages have already made it clear that social control in the Tallensi was exerted through such forces as parental authority, reciprocity, and the influence of the spiritual world. The functions of religion, self-help, and war as means for social control, were also indicated in some detail. The following discussion of conflict and its control within the Tallensi relates to disputes arising within a clan. The clan consisted of a number of relatively autonomous maximal lineages, identified by descent from a common ancestor, which were linked with one another. It was

> a set of locally united lineages, each of which is linked with all or most of the others by ties of clanship, which act together in the service of certain common interests indicated by the bond of exogamy, by reciprocal rights and duties in events such as the funeral of a member of any

---

13. *Ibid.*, pp. 234-239, 242-244.

one of them, and by the ban on intestine war or feud; and which act as a corporate unit in respect of these common interests in relation to such other units. . . . Clanship ties and cleavages mark out, for each lineage, one or more other lineages in relation to whose members its own members are automatically subject to the rule of exogamy, and have, in theory, the unconditional right to inherit widows.

A clan was identified with a specific locality. The "basic rule of inter-clan linkage is that spatial proximity is translated into terms of putative genealogical connexion." The clan represented a field of integration between its several constituent maximal lineages and a means for the due performance of the mutual obligations which they had to one another.

Disputes within a clan, as distinguished from disputes between clans, most frequently involved

rival claims to priority in the exercise of rights of a political-ritual nature, which are generally vested in lineages and are associated with the dominant values of the society. . . . Intra-clan discord is often due to the universal human propensity to resist infringement of one's recognized social rights or one's self-regard; or to the complementary tendency for individuals to assert themselves by aggressive action. But it is probably more often a phase in the structural development of a lineage or clan, a symptom of a hitherto unrecognized internal change in its structure.

Over the course of a number of generations, what was once a small inner lineage might have expanded its constituent branches to the point that it possessed *de facto* the status of a medial lineage. The importance of formally recognizing its claim to such a status might, upon occasion, be stressed by the fact that the succession to the headship of a more inclusive lineage was in issue, and the claim of the emergent lineage was opposed by other branches of the more inclusive lineage. If constitutive conflict was to be avoided, this claim must be recognized *de jure,* and the consequent redistribution of reciprocal rights and duties within the clan must take place. Without such recognition, stress and tension would persist.

For example, one maximal lineage might in fact have become autonomous of another in all matters save that formal dependency existed by its *tendaana* with respect to the *tendaana* of the other. The latter would demand the perquisites of the superior status which was formally his due and had been so recognized. Such perquisites would be given only most grudgingly because the superior status arose at an earlier time when a different situation existed, which was now superseded by a factual equality of the lineages. When such a situation occurred, some persons belonging to the emergent group would respect the original, formal pattern of institutional order and take part in ritual and ceremonial cooperation, such as funerals, just as if the formal supremacy of the older group still remained in fact. Others would refrain from so participating. The differing opinions on the propriety of such modes of conduct would create considerable tension within the respective groups. Behavior of this nature touched upon deeply felt sentiments associated with the values of how the respective groups should constitute or structure themselves.

The segmentary organization of Tallensi society became significant in disputes. Whenever a dispute arose, the lineage segments, which were linked with the disputing parties, supported each side in opposition to the other. Yet the opposing segments were also linked in a common lineage group of a larger size, tied by common descent from a more remote ancestor. The overriding value of integration and harmony within this larger group demanded a restoration of the order of peace. This order extended even to bridge the dominant cleavage between the Namoos and non-Namoos.

In one case, a man insulted a chief. The latter reacted by laying a curse upon the man, who then moved with his younger sons to the outer edge of the territory of the clan. The older son stayed behind, disassociating himself from his father's misconduct. The father not only continued to flout the authority of the chief, but his second son, upon the death of the father, withheld from the oldest son property to which the latter was the legitimate successor. The second son's action was in the face of a previous pronouncement by a diviner that the ancestors, whose norms had been violated by the father in his quarrel with his chief, had caused the father's death. The second son further refused to carry out the ritual expiation ordered by the diviner. Fortes made the very significant remark at this point that "There are no jural sanctions compelling a man to abide by custom in cases of this kind; and as the Tallensi often say, men do not fear to defy even the ancestor spirits, when their property or power is at stake."

Shortly thereafter the second son suddenly became ill and died. There was a second procedure of divination, which confirmed the public opinion that his death was due to his double sin of failing to carry out the ritual expiation and withholding property from its legitimate successor. The oldest son then performed the necessary ritual expiation, as well as such other acts as were necessary to effect a ritual reconciliation and restore the status required by the norms which had been breached. This erased the wrong and reunited the lineage on its proper basis.

A case having much wider ramifications and a much higher degree of tension was one which involved the custodianship of the shrine of the ancient Hill Talis. Such shrines in Tale society served as a focus of the maximal lineage as a whole and of the locality to which it was traditionally attached. The control of this particular shrine became enormously profitable as a result of expanding pilgrim traffic to the Tong Hills. The shrine was thought to bring wealth, power, children, and success in farming, business, career, or litigation. Payments of the pilgrims to the shrine brought to its holder the ownership of a huge homestead, eighty wives, sumptuous clothes, and an ability to distribute widespread largesse. Other clans of the region demanded a redistribution of the revenues of the system, urging a formal basis of clan relationships different from the current status to legitimize their claims. There was a struggle for power within the maximal lineages, as one group exerted pressure on another, which only subsided during the Great Festivals, when clan and ritual solidarity were reaffirmed.

The claimant groups may have had traditional norms opposed to them, with consequent risk of ancestral punishment. Yet this did not necessarily restrain them in the light of the pecuniary gains at stake. "Tallensi are not—so the old men say—restrained from doing something to their personal advantage by the fear of mystical penalties. 'Who fears death before death comes upon you.' It is only after a death occurs that the survivors see in it signs and omens referring to their social relations with one another."

Change in the significance of the various lineages within a clan was always occurring. Fission might reduce the importance of one, and growth might enhance the importance of another. As formerly close ties of cooperation disintegrated as a result of social change, the formal system of ritual and ceremonial cooperation in the ancestor cult and important public ceremonies, such as funerals, tended not to be adhered to in fact. When a member of a clan failed to perform an obligation of the group which embodied one of its important values, such as joining in the performance of ritual, much unease and disturbance resulted. Lineage solidarity was damaged, and an offense against the ancestors committed. In such a situation, Fortes said, the matter would be submitted to a diviner for a judgment. The invocation of the diviner, as decision maker, was occasioned by some misfortune, such as the death of one of the parties involved. The diviner was consulted to find the mystical cause. "The technique and social setting of the divining session make it a reflection of public sentiment. The diviner *brings the simmering conflict in the lineage into the open* and relates the death to it. *His verdict,* coming ostensibly from the ancestors, *concludes with commands from them to put the situation to right* by means of sacrifices and a ritual reconciliation. This is the commonest way in which the ancestor cult emerges as a sanction of reintegration in the lineage or clan."[14] (Italics supplied.)

This is a most significant statement. The Tallensi might not have a judicial system, as we know it. They nevertheless possessed, in the person of the diviner, a system of third-party decision-making dealing with problems of conflict arising as a result of the breach of basic kinship and ritual norms. Invocation of the decision-making process became possible when an event of serious misfortune occurred. The decision attributed the misfortune to some person's antecedent breach of a social norm, with the maintenance of which the ancestors or other spiritual forces were concerned, as well as the living. The misfortune thus became a sanction imposed by mystical forces which was punishment for wrongdoing. If a diviner was not consulted, the community could itself arrive at a similar common judgment as explanation for the misfortune. There were thus explicit or implicit processes for the support of adherence to norms of this character, consisting of breach of norm, imposition of sanction, and performance of measures of reintegration.

Release of tension arising in ambivalent social relations took place in forms of jesting and taunts. One of these was joking partners. Two persons who were members of different clans might find that their close relationships called for amity in one conflict situation and enmity in another. The tensions implicit in such opposing pulls of loyalties were released in teasing, mock abuse, and the snatching of meat or other food from the other person at a funeral ceremony which both attended.

When representatives of two clans met at some important occasion or ceremony, they would often taunt one another in a jesting manner. Such behavior occurred between clans—whose ties were ambivalent, sometimes calling for cooperation and at other times for enmity. The jesting operated to release the tension implicit in the situation.

---

14. *Ibid.,* pp. 247, 62-63, 87, 248-249, 251-258.

Law

Except for a possible study of marriage law by Fortes,[15] the literature on the Tallensi has no separate investigation of the topic of law. It is discussed incidentally in other contexts. It should be noted at this point that marriage law, in the sense of the customs relating to the creation and termination of the marriage status, is not within the purview of this book, although legal norms protecting the marriage interest, such as adultery and abduction of a wife, are comprehended. A brief summary of the relevant information concerning law among the Tallensi will now be made, which will, in part, consist of a recapitulation of points made above.

The extended family was the basic jural unit. The father allocated its resources to his sons and their respective families so long as they lived in the homestead. He had the right to their labor and an over-right to their personal property. The ownership of property inhered both in the lineage, subject of the right of its holder to use it, and in the individual.

Each kinship segment stood in opposition to its like segments and when a dispute occurred between segments of the same order, the linkages of each with lineage groups of a larger order were sought until a single comprehensive lineage was reached, which provided an ideal structure for the restoration of an order of peace. The outcome was support for the violated norm or a new alignment of structural relationships which cancelled the breach. The unity of the social order was highly valued. It was symbolically expressed in the cult of the Earth. Common interests in preserving the social order prevailed over those tending toward disintegration.

Violations of norms were believed to receive punishment through misfortune visited by spiritual forces. One who killed another would find that the Earth brought death to another member of his family as retribution. The ancestors were the principal sanctioning agents for wrongdoing. Diviners acted as third-party decision makers to discover the violators of norms and thereby enable a state of misfortune to be lifted. They linked the misfortune with the prior commission of misconduct or breach of norm.

Offenses committed upon members of one clan by members of another justified resort to self-help. The injured party could organize a

---

15. A reference to a publication in Accra by M. Fortes, *Marriage Law among the Tallensi,* failed to yield the volume for examination.

cattle raid against the clan of the wrongdoer. The victim of the raid could then demand restitution from the guilty person on the basis that common membership in the clan created a duty to compensate for the loss of the raided cattle.

Conclusion

The Tallensi, as a segmentary society, may be analogized to a stage performance. One looks at the proscenium, with the curtain raised, and sees a series of entrances from the wings projecting from the right and left which end with a painted backdrop. The entrances may be pictured as being marked by successive clumps of bushes or low trees. The backdrop changes from time to time to indicate, as necessary, the passing of the seasons, the village, the external shrine, the individual shrine, the family compound, warring groups, the festival, the family meal, the father's, mother's, or the son's portions of the compound, and a village belonging to another clan. With each such change of scene, a different set of actors emerges from its respective portion of the wings and carries out the appropriate performance. These actors may belong to the extended families in say the nearest opposing set of entrances, to inner lineages in the next, to medial and maximal lines in the next two sets, and finally to clans in the last. The backdrops change in a fairly repetitive pattern and each backdrop, as it reappears, is unchanged. The actors have learned their cues. When the appropriate backdrop appears to cue their entrance, they enter from their opposite wings, enact in opposition to each other the performances of eating, meeting, tilling, worshipping, marriage, funeral, festival, or war which is called for by the backdrop. Each performance associated with its respective backdrop is repeated time after time, substantially unchanged. As entrances are made from the wings toward the back of the stage, the stage becomes crowded with actors, until one reaches the entrances for the clans, when the entire stage is full. Yet each successive group knows when to respond to the cue given to it by its headman, chief, or *tendaana,* and they all act in unison in response to the cue. Action ebbs and flows across the stage. Sometimes it is crowded, sometimes it has only a few families in the front of the stage, each composed of a man and his children.

Yet upon reflection the analogy breaks down. For the actors are not in the wings. They are not segregated into different groups for all time. They compose a single people, a single society, occupying the entire stage. As the backdrop changes, the lights and the action reveal that this single society is segmented into groups and that each larger group is a cluster of smaller ones and that each is a reproduction, on a larger or smaller scale, of each other. Each segment, in other words, nests inside a larger segment until the largest segment or the whole is reached.

There is no stage director to call the actors forth from time to time. They need no central authority to enable them to respond appropriately to the cues which life gives them. Their traditional and appropriate kinship head and custom suffice. As problems arise in the political or economic sphere or in interpersonal conflict, the appropriate kinship heads step forward to handle the problems. The people have learned how to sort their problems, to class those which are appropriate for the clan head from those which are appropriate for the diviner or for the family head. They know those which are to be handled in this world and those which are to be handled in the world of the spirit. They know their roles, and frequently their roles are many. The family head is successively the manager and director of its affairs and personnel, the father, the husband, the judge, the priest, and the worker.

The Tallensi were a people without a temporal chief or council of elders to solve their common problems and inter-group conflicts. They were a people without judicial organs to handle their interpersonal conflict. They must, for such purposes, rely on intermediaries between this world and the mystical world. Otherwise, the handling of such matters was limited to those who were their kinship superiors. They were a people who saw themselves as living in two worlds, the world of the ancestors and the spirits and the world of tangible substance. Though they perceived the difference between each, the world of the spirit was considered to operate with real effect in the material world. The spiritual world must be propitiated, interpreted, and approached with due ceremony, if the world of practical affairs were to prosper.

There was a basic cleavage in the Tallensi between the Namoos and non-Namoos, or between the immigrant and older clans of the region. It is at this point that the cognition of common identity and belonging together in a single people became the weakest. Inter-clan tension and conflict would not be restrained from resort to war through the Great Festivals and other rituals emphasizing harmony and integration of the whole society. Kinship ties were at this point too weak to contain conflict. War between clans emphasized a basic structural cleavage in Tale society, released tensions arising out of conflict between clans which were socially distant from one another, and were a prelude to ritual affirmation of inter-clan solidarity. War was not an instrument for conquering or enslaving other peoples. It was instead part of the social process of the entire society, serving in last analysis to promote the ends of self maintenance and unity.

The Tale, as a stable, unchanging society, required little in the way of creative leadership to solve their political problems. Their society endured in substantially the same form it always had. They were fixed in their locality and fixed in their ways.

Conflict and tension arising through the violation of norms was handled by the mechanisms of self-help and war. Violation of norms within the clan led to measures of self-help by the injured party. Members of the lineage group which embraced the lesser groups of which the disputants were members also exerted pressures to resolve the dispute. Conflict and tension was otherwise handled through ritual and war, the latter always being followed by a ritual affirmation of unity.

Chapter 5

The Ashanti

Geography and Economy

THE Ashanti originally settled in their land as hunters. The land was a dense rain forest of great trees, lianas, riotous vegetation, matted undergrowth, and giant fallen trunks. They ranged for game and fish over a broad but, nevertheless, fairly well-defined territory. Roots, berries, and wild herbs provided other sustenance. Tradition has it that the Ashanti originally resided in a large town, from which they spread into the adjacent forest. The outlying farms which the migrating families created became the basis of new villages, as other farms clustered about them. Many came to the land of the Ashanti as immigrants, fleeing from their homes to avoid war and capture.

To clear the rain forest and make it into a tillable farm was such a herculean task, Rattray notes, as to require

> the collective efforts of the husbandman, his brother, sister, mother, and nephews and nieces. Crops and the fruits of the kola, plaintains, and palm oil, grown on the clearing, became the joint property of the kindred group which had assisted in the work, and were as far removed as ever from being the exclusive personal property, "in its strict sense," of any one individual.[1]

Communication and travel between villages was difficult. Each village was in large measure its own social, political, and jural do-

---

1. R. S. Rattray, *Ashanti Law and Constitution* (London, 1929, 1956), 349; see generally K. A. Busia, *The Position of the Chief in the Modern Political System of the Ashanti* (London, New York, Toronto, 1951), 3-5.

main. Its articulation with larger units was limited in nature and rather precisely defined.

The Elements of Individual Personality

It was seen above that the Tallensi considered themselves to live in a world of spiritual forces as well as a world of physical reality. The Earth and the ancestors, as spiritual forces, powerfully influenced the destiny and welfare of the individual. Certain of his ancestors determined his *Yin,* or the fate preordained for him at his birth. A vital part of life was communicating with the ancestors and endeavoring to influence favorably their temporal exercise of power.

The Ashanti shared a perception of the world as having both a temporal and spiritual nature, with the latter exerting a powerful influence on the lives of individuals. The Ashanti developed the linkages of the individual with the groups in which he acted into a comprehensive system possessing the neatness and intricacy of design of a Byzantine mosaic. The first aspect of the Ashanti's view of the interrelationships of man, society, state, and the spiritual world is that of the elements of individual personality. It will be seen that these elements define the individual as a personality and endow him with a clear basis of relationship with his father, his mother, and his clan. Moreover, they give him a place and a being in the world of spirit from which he came and to which he will return.

The Ashanti conception of the individual, as a physical and spiritual entity, was a product of the union of the male spirit (*ntoro*) with the blood (*mogya*). Both *ntoro* and *mogya* were spiritual elements. The *ntoro* was transmitted from the father to his children and was shared by them as a *ntoro* group, which performed certain rituals and observed certain taboos and totemic practices. The *mogya* was synonymous with *abusua,* or clan, and provided the child with its clan identity. Its presence made the child a human being, endowed with and amenable to reason. The *ntoro* was passed from father to son down the male line of descent as long as there were males to receive it. The female received the *ntoro* from her father but was unable to transmit it. Her children received the *mogya* from her and the *ntoro* from their father.

The *okra* was derived from the day of the week on which the child was born and was the spirit or soul of the child, as determined by the god or gods associated with that day. The *okra* came to the infant when it was already conceived, through union of the *ntoro* and the *mogya,* and was his guiding spirit or the determinant of his destiny in life. It left the person on death to become a part of the world of the spirit but subject to reincarnation in another life.

The *ntoro, mogya,* and *okra* were ineluctable, fixed elements of the being and were beyond the control of the individual. They were spiritual elements made manifest in individual life. They identified the child and placed it firmly in the respective spheres of his lineage, clan, and the spiritual world.

The *sunsum* was the closest counterpart of the ego of Freud in that it embodied a man's distinctive personality and character. It could make the character strong or weak, good or bad, and bring or protect against misfortune. Whereas the *okra* was divine, in that it came from and returned to the spiritual world, the *sunsum* died with the man. It could also leave the body during sleep, while the *okra* could not. The *sunsum* was the child of the *ntoro.*

Upon death, the *mogya* survived as a man's *saman* or ghost. This was not living substance but was the objective form of the dead as spirit. The *saman* could exert *sasa,* or invisible spiritual power, either for good or bad, upon the living. The ancestors, as spirits, exerted influence upon the living members of the lineage and must accordingly be communicated with and brought to favorable disposition through the performance of rites by the living. The *saman* may be reincarnated in another life through some woman of its own blood.

Since the *ntoro, mogya,* and *okra* were those elements of personality with which the individual was endowed at birth, they bear an analogy to the id of Freud. The id was everything psychological that was inherited and present at birth and was the source of psychological energy. The *ntoro, mogya,* and *okra* were the given elements of the Ashanti personality; they were not amenable to individual control. They were his link with the world of the spirit. They made possible his creation, in this world, from the world of the spirit and his return at death to that world. Upon his death he became for his descendants an ancestor which, in spirit form, influenced their fortune and with whom they could communicate.

The *sunsum* bore a certain analogy both to the ego, as noted above, and also to the superego. The superego, it will be remembered, controlled action of the individual in the light of cultural standards and ideals. It was the conscience. The *sunsum* was educable and had a moral operation as a system of reward and punishment.

The full significance of the Ashanti concept of personality and the social, political, and legal structure of Ashanti society cannot be perceived until comprehension is had of the Ashanti system of religion, which will accordingly be the next topic of inquiry. The set of relationships which comprised the Ashanti concept of personality was beautifully delineated by Busia in words which bear repetition:

Thus the members of the same *Ntoro* were linked by the observance of common taboos, and the use of common surnames and common forms of etiquette. All these served to strengthen the spiritual bond between father and son. The spiritual nature of the bond between them was again emphasized by the fact that a father was held responsible for his son's moral behaviour, and although a son belonged to his mother's lineage, it was the father who was liable for any damages that were claimed if his son committed adultery with another man's wife.

Social values and filial and parental bonds are thus given meaning within the Ashanti system of belief. Man as a biological being inherits his blood from his mother; this gives him his status and membership within the lineage, the clan, and the tribe, and his right and obligations as a citizen; moreover, as is discussed below, the concept of a life hereafter and of a spirit world, and the consequent worship of the ancestors, provides a religious link and an unbroken continuity with all one's matrikin.

As a spiritual being, a man receives a twofold gift of the spirit; that which determines his character and his individuality he receives through his father; but his soul, the undying part of him, he receives direct from the Supreme Being.

One part comes via his father from the father's *Ntoro* which, in turn, receives its spiritual power from one of the river sons of the Supreme Being. The blood that is transmitted through the mother, the personality that comes indirectly from the Supreme Being through intermediaries, and that "small bit of the Creator which is in every person's body" and which he receives directly from the Supreme Being, combine to make a man what he is.

These gifts, too, define his place in the universe, linking him with the world of nature and of man. All this is what the Ashanti mean when they declare: "All men are children of the Supreme Being, no-one is a child of the earth. . . .[2]

---

2. K. A. Busia, "The Ashanti," *African Worlds,* ed. D. Forde (London, New York, Toronto, 1954), 199-200; P. Abraham, *The Mind of Africa* (Chicago, Toronto, London, 1952), 59-63; R. S. Rattray, *Religion and Art in Ashanti* (London, 1927, 1954), 51-52, 152-155, 318-319; R. S. Rattray, *Ashanti* (London, 1923, 1955), 36-38, 45-46, 77.

Religion

The Ashanti world was one peopled by spirits and gods, as well
as by man. The lives of individuals were influenced by the spirits
and gods. They could be communicated with and favorably influenced by the performance of ritual. The close presence of the ancestors was revealed in the fact that the old Ashanti offered at meals
the first morsel of food to the ancestors. The ancestors were also
offered the first drops of the drink. Children were encouraged to
leave a small portion of food in the dish for the ancestors. An
Ashanti might remove himself upon occasion from a ritual ceremony because he felt uncomfortable in the presence of too many
spirits. Stories were told about how the presence of the ancestors as
spirits brought fortune or misfortune.

There was a supreme being or god identified as *Onyame*. While
some writers refer to him as a sky-god, the significant fact was not
that he was to be found above the earth and beyond the physical
reach of man, which was true, but that his was the supreme power
in providing bountiful protection to the people. The supreme being
created all things and exerted his power through many lesser gods.

The Earth possessed its own power or spirit, which was conceived
to be a female principle but not necessarily a deity or goddess.
Thursday was the natal day of the Earth. Work on the land was prohibited on that day, otherwise misfortune would result. The Earth
had the power of fertility and made all things grow. It was necessary
to propitiate the Earth to have a good harvest. In the *Adae* ceremony,
the drummer addressed the Earth:

> Earth, when I am about to die
> I lean upon you.
> Earth, while I am alive
> I depend upon you.
> Earth that receives dead bodies . . . .

The land belonged to the ancestors. The living received from
them the right to use it. The ancestors, as spirits, watched the use of
the land and insured, through their power over the living, that the
land was used in a proper manner. They also exerted power to bring
good or bad fortune in the diverse affairs of life.

The rivers, the trees, the rocks, and the animals were spirits, as
were also fairies, little folk, and forest monsters. The source of their
power was ultimately the supreme being and they were subservient

to it. They intervened either for good or for bad in the affairs of the living and must be propitiated in an appropriate manner and ceremony.

The interrelationship of the spirits and spiritual forces, misfortune, and ritual communication were reported by Rattray in a statement of an old Ashanti priest. Rattray had asked why reliance could not be placed on the one great god and the lesser powers ignored. The priest answered:

> We in Ashanti dare not worship the Sky God alone, or the Earth Goddess alone, or any one spirit. We have to protect ourselves against, and use when we can, the spirits of all things in the Sky and upon Earth. You go to the forest, see some wild animal, fire at it, kill it, and find you have killed a man. You dismiss your servant, but later find you miss him. You take your cutlass to hack at what you think is a branch, and find you have cut your own arm. There are people who can transform themselves into leopards; "the grass-land people" are especially good at turning into hyenas. There are witches who can make you wither and die. There are trees which fall upon and kill you. There are rivers which drown you. If I see four or five Europeans, I do not make much of one alone, and ignore the rest, lest they too may have power and hate me.[3]

This, then, was the world of the spirit, which the Ashanti found to be an essential part of their life. The spiritual made itself physically present and physically felt. It influenced fate and fortune. The Ashanti might well say: "From the world of the spirits thou comest and to the world of the spirits thou shalt return. Ever shall the spirits be with thee."

Contact with the supreme being was maintained directly in the household. Although the lesser gods had priests and shrines, there was no such shrine for God. The household maintained an altar to God, consisting of a pot or gourd placed between the forks of a three-forked stick cut from a certain tree known as the tree of God. Offerings of food and wine were placed in the receptacle. The common sharing of the ritual of *ntoro*-washing and certain totemic observances and avoidances by members of the *ntoro* group made it possible for the individual to have his unique tie with the world of spirit. Contact by the lineage with its ancestors was made through the lineage stool. When a new head or elder of a lineage was elected, the members of the lineage each swore to "serve you whom we have chosen to occupy the stool of our ancestors, so that you in turn may serve the chief." In other words, each lineage had its own stool,

3. *Ibid.*, quotation at 150, see 90-91, 214-217; Busia, *Position of the Chief*, 23-26, 40-43; Abraham, *op. cit.*, pp. 51-49; Rattray, *Religion and Art*, 25-38.

which was the focal point in ritual communication with the ancestors and served to identify the spiritual and temporal position of
authority and power of the elder. Similarly, the stool of the chief
identified his position as a link with the spiritual world and his post
of authority and power with respect to the tribe or division. The
Golden Stool of the Asantahene, or the chief who was also the head
of the nation, was the instrument identifying the spiritual power
and influence upon which his temporal authority over the nation
was based.

Wherever the spiritual world manifested itself and an intermediary was needed to bring its favor and avert its misfortune, one
was provided in the persons of the elder of the lineage, the chief of
the tribe or division, the chief of the nation, the medicine man, and
the witch doctor. The ritual which the elders and chiefs performed,
each for his particular group, were directed to express the linking of
the group with the spiritual forces and to bring about a favorable
outcome in the intervention of the spiritual into the temporal world.

The Apo ceremony was held once a year. This was an occasion in
which license and promiscuity were indulged and expressions were
made of hatred and resentments toward others, including their
causes. It was permissible even to tell the king of hatred held toward
him and his responsibility for such feelings. It was said of this
ceremony that its purpose was to cool the *sunsum* and to keep it
from becoming sick because of a person's keeping hatreds toward
others.[4]

Social Organization

The concepts of *ntoro* and *mogya* were the key elements for
arriving at an understanding of the Ashanti social organization. The
ntoro provided the bond with the spiritual and psychic worlds, the
mogya the bond with the world of the flesh. The *mogya* made the
child the member of its lineage, which was a group tracing descent
through a female line from a common original female ancestor.
The lineage group was a part of a larger group, the clan, which was
also composed of matrilineal descendants from a common single
female ancestor.

---

4. Busia, *op. cit.*, pp. 7-8, 26-27; Rattray, *Ashanti Law*, 1-7, 62-63; Rattray,
Ashanti, 153; Busia, "The Ashanti," 200-204; *cf.* E. L. R. Meyerowitz, *The Sacred
State of the Akan* (London, 1951), Chaps. 3-7, providing extensive but diffuse
data.

Membership in the lineage group, determined by matriliny, gave a person his political and legal status. It determined his property interests and his office and ritual status. Yet his patrilineal affiliation influenced his life in a subordinate way. He sometimes acquired a quasi-membership in his father's lineage group, including the use of its land. This membership was, however, always subordinate to his obligations to his matrilineal group. He looked to his father for education. A special relationship of loyalty, trust, and confidence existed between a father and his sons, which was lacking in his relationship with his sister's sons.

The head of the lineage group was its intermediary with its ancestors, administrator of its property, custodian of its traditions, and arbitrator of disputes among its members. His decisions in such disputes were not arbitrary commands of patriarchal authority but were reached after consultation with his household and were supported by religious sanctions. The authority of his post was supported by the spiritual order. He had an undisputed power over his slaves, which had no religious support. It should be realized, nevertheless, that the master-slave relationship was generally one of basic kindness and trust. The authority of the family head over his slaves and the children of his slaves was considerably greater than that over his wife or wives and his own children or grandchildren, since the latter group belonged to another clan by virtue of sharing its blood. It was merely the incident of marriage which brought them into his household. Thus, the appearance within a kinship structure based on matrilineal descent of authority vested in a senior male and of persons in the form of slaves disrupted the ideal purity of the kinship structure as a form of social action.

The lineage head or elder was elected by the senior members of the lineage. His role for the members of the lineage group living in the village corresponded to the role of the father in the family, together with the additional role of counsellor to the chief. He was the link with the ancestors of the lineage and administered the lineage property, including its stool. He decided disputes among members of the lineage. The men of the lineage living in the village ate their evening meal in the house of the elder. If they were married, their wives brought their meal to the house. Members of the lineage assisted one another in such matters as building houses, making farms, and clearing paths. They met together to perform funeral rites for dead members of the lineage and to share in the funeral expenses.

The clan was an exogamous division of a tribe, membership in which was determined by common descent from a female ancestor. A totemic aspect of clanship was provided by the notion that the ultimate female ancestor was descended from some animal. A village was composed of persons identified by memberships in various lineages or clans. Lineages and clans were not necessarily limited to any one community, though the clan, with its wider membership, was the more widely dispersed of the two. The clan had no political significance, although chiefs belonging to the same clan had a special feeling of kinship or brotherhood. Clanship worked a feeling of fraternity. A stranger who was a fellow member of a clan was given special hospitality.

Political Organization and War

The experience of the Ashanti reveals that a society may try to preserve its constituted order through the fixed responses of ritual performance, as well as by the process of making and performing decisions. The spiritual world is invoked to support order in the temporal world.

The Ashanti chief performed two roles. He was the performer of ritual designed to propitiate the spirits and the gods. In this role, only the performance of institutionalized patterns of behavior was seen. He was also the leader of his tribe in war, in which he manifested a most powerful authoritative role.

The Ashanti were a people of separate tribes, sharing a common culture and acting under the headship of chiefs and elders prior to the war against the Denkyira of 1669. Their final political order was assumed after the battle of Feyiase, when the several divisions under chiefs accepted the military and appropriate ritual paramountcy of the chief of the Kumasi division, known as *Asantehene*. The term *Asantehene* has been suggested to have the meaning of a chief appointed "because of war," that is, *osanti*.

The political organization of the Ashanti as a nation emerged after the battle of Feyiase. It embraced, at its largest compass, the Ashanti nation composed of tribes or divisions, at its intermediate compass, the tribe or division, and at its smallest compass, the lineage. It might be said that there was a typical model or structure of political action of the group, the headship of which was determined by a post identified in terms of kinship relations. This model was writ small in the lineage and successively larger in the tribe and the nation. The nature of the model was derived from the family unit. Each variant of the model, that is, lineage, tribe, or nation, was concerned with handling conflict resolution among its constituent groups and members, the violence of war, and the relation of the spiritual to the physical world. The relationship of nation, tribe, and lineage was in one sense hierarchical, in that there were different levels or extent of membership in each group. Yet the *Asantahene* had to procure the consent of the chiefs, and the chiefs the consent of the elders, in order to bring about group action. When such consent had been given, a chief could further strengthen his power through invoking spiritual aid to sanction his commands, such as orders to assist in putting out a fire, clear a path, or form a group to search for a murderer.

The relationship thus delineated was not one, strictly speaking, of a hierarchy of authority or a federal structure. One might refer, by way of analogy, to the process of democratic centralism in the sphere of the Soviet, in which decisions of policy democratically arrived at within the Communist Party are the subject of supreme authority in their execution within the party and the state. The concept of federalism was not an appropriate one to describe the Ashanti political order, in that it was not characterized by paramountcy in the exercise of a delegated sphere of authority. An image closer to reality is that of concentric groups of successively larger size yet with autonomous spheres of action or competence. The authority of the *Asantehene* to make war was dependent upon consultation with his chiefs. The procedure was closer to a confederacy than to a federal union. Similarly, a chief could not cause his tribe independently to make war upon another tribe without the consent of his elders and of the *Asantehene*. Nevertheless, a centralized authority structure was manifest in the conduct of war. The several tribes knew their posts and functions in the national army and the members of the army faithfully obeyed the commands of their superiors, subject, as will be seen below, to the imposition of sanctions for the offenses of treason and cowardice.

The *Asantehene* shared the performance of ritual with his chiefs to the end of preserving the nation as a whole. In his sphere, his person was sacred and so was his role. The chiefs in turn shared the performance of ritual with their elders for the benefit of the tribe. The elders similarly performed ritual for the benefit of the lineage. Each such sphere was independent from the others.

Each tribe managed its own affairs, had its own treasury, and performed its own ritual ceremonies. The village had its own head, or *Odekuro,* selected from one of the lineages there present. The village was an economically self-sufficient unit.

The chiefs of the tribes vowed military service to the *Asantehene,* who, as stated above, could wage war with the consent of his council of chiefs. The council met to perform certain rituals, which kept alive the sentiments of solidarity and of the nation. The council acted as a national tribunal and determined the enstoolment or destoolment of an *Asantehene.*

A stool symbolized a post of authority, its linkage with the super-natural world, and its ability to invoke supernatural power. In its presence, the ancestors were implored to bring blessings of health, long life, fertility, and abundance. The lineage was protected by its ancestors, the tribe by the ancestors of the lineage from which the chief was chosen, and the nation by the ancestors of the royal lineage. Busia summarized the situation as follows:

> An Ashanti chief is thus important not only as a civil ruler who is the axis of the political relations of his people and the one in whom the various lineages that compose the tribe find their unity; he is also the symbol of their identity and continuity as a tribe and the embodiment of their spiritual values. An Ashanti chief fills a sacred role as the "one who sits upon the stool of the ancestors."

> That stool, the symbol of his power, is what the famous Ashanti priest, Anoyke, described as "the soul of the nation." It is the sacred emblem of the tribe's permanence and continuity. The chief as the occupant of the stool represents all those who have occupied it before him. He is the link, the intermediary, between the living and the dead; for, according to the conception which the Ashanti share with other Akan tribes, the dead, the living, and those still to be born of the tribe are all members of one family, and it is the stool that binds that family together.

When a chief was installed, he was raised and lowered three times over the blackened stool of his ancestors. He thereupon became sacred and his office was a sacred one. Persistent failure to meet his responsibilities and obligations resulted in his destoolment. In other words, the stool was a symbol of office and role, analogous to the crown in Western cultures.

Just as the senior members of the lineage selected the elder who occupied the stool of the lineage, so the elders of the several lineages selected from one of the lineages the head of that lineage who would be the chief of all of them. He became the custodian of the tribal or division stool, and his land became the nucleus of all stool land of the tribe.

The chief had the capacity to make certain levies, with the concurrence of his council of elders and the approval of the people. These included such matters as paying for the expenses of a war, a chief's funeral, or a sacrifice of livestock on behalf of the tribe. The subjects of a chief also worked on his farm several days each year. The services and levies which the chief received were not his personal perquisite but were returned to the people in generous entertainment, the maintenance of the royal household, and the performance of the obligations of his office.

The functions of chiefs and elders were to maintain law and order in the community, to guard its security through the use of military force, and to preserve harmonious relations in the community and with the ancestors and gods. Public services, such as keeping the village clean and the roads in repair, were provided by communal labor.[5]

Law: Land Tenure

The existence and welfare of the Ashanti was dependent on the land. The Ashanti law of land tenure was one designed to insure the maximum use of the land for the common benefit. The law of the Ashanti was also designed to control the commission of acts which were to be seen as wrongful not only in the sense of being injurious to the preservation of valued and necessary social relations but also as striking at the foundations of the Ashanti world in its tie with the spirits and gods. Rattray put the matter as follows:

> The Ashanti law-makers' task entailed the ultimate acceptance of the responsibility for the even and normal working of forces which we regard as wholly beyond our power to control. They had to see to it that the "Constitution" of their Tribe was such that it would ensure, or at least not flagrantly militate against, the normal functioning of what we regard as nature's immutable laws. The assurance of bountiful crops; the continued fertility of the tribe; the even cycle of the seasons; the course of the heavenly bodies and the protection from some cataclysm which would destroy them and mankind; the control of other forces of nature —rain, lightning, floods; the onslaughts of wild beasts; sickness, and finally death itself—all these were concerns for which human beings were

5. Busia, *op. cit.*, pp. 200-205, quotation at p. 202; Busia, *Position of the Chief*, Chaps. 1, 2; Rattray, *Ashanti Law*, Chaps. 1-10, 15; J. B. Danquah, *Akan Laws and Customs* (London, 1928), Chaps. 1, 5; M. Fortes, "The 'Submerged Descent Line' in Ashanti," *Studies in Kinship and Marriage*, ed. I. Schapera, Royal Anthropological Institute Occasional Paper No. 16 (London, 1963), 58. For data on the structuring of household units of two generations, see M. Fortes, "Time and Social Structure: An Ashanti Case Study," *Social Structure: Studies Presented to A. R. Radcliffe-Brown*, ed. M. Fortes (New York, 1963), 54.

considered directly or indirectly responsible, for which in consequence of such beliefs, the Elders of the Tribe had to legislate.

Land which had been won from the forest by common effort and secured for the tribe by war could not be perceived to be owned in any individual capacity. Land was stool land, that is, land of the chief as custodian of the stool, which he held for the use of the members of the tribe. It was also land of the elder, as custodian of the lineage stool, which he held for the use of the members of the lineage. The individual's right to farm a piece of land was derived from his lineage, and a specific portion of the lands of the lineage was allotted to him by the elder.

When hunting was the primary source of sustenance, the land of the tribe was owned by the stool and the hunter was free to roam the land in the pursuit of game. When farming took the place of hunting, a family could create a farm sufficient for its needs by clearing the rain forest. It could assure its right to use the farm by a grant from the chief, but retention of this grant was dependent upon proof that the land was being used or had not been wholly abandoned and that the obligations owed the chief, such as military service and the payment of levies, were performed.

The land itself could never be alienated but the right to use it could be mortgaged or transferred. The mortgagee would receive a right to use the land for an indefinite term, and the land was always subject to redemption by the mortgagor. It was necessary to inform the chief, whose stool owned the land, of any transfer of land. If the transfer were made to a subject of the chief, the use of the land remained with heirs of the transferee. If the transferee were not a subject, the use of the land would revert on his death to the stool to which the land belonged.

It was possible for a person holding the right to use a piece of land in perpetuity to leave a small portion of the whole to one of his sons to take effect at his death. Consent of members of the lineage to the transfer was necessary and the presence of witnesses to the making of the disposition was needed. In such a transfer, the heirs of the donee would prevail over the heirs of the donor.

Succession to a man's property at his death was determined by blood or *abusua*. Thus a man's own children could not inherit from him because they were of their mother's *mogya*. Instead, his heirs were to be found among such persons as his maternal uncle, elder brother, successive brothers in age, his mother's sister's son, and his own sister's son, each in turn. Succession to the property of a deceased female went, among others, first to her mother then to her sisters by seniority, her own daughters by seniority, and her sister's daughters.[6]

An attempt was made to expound the principles of land law applicable to the entire state of Ghana. The author spoke of "our customary land law" and included therein the law of non-Akan, as well as Akan, communities, such as the Ashanti. He drew his description of the law from the reported decisions of established courts of Ghana, as well as other sources, such as the writing of Dr. Danquah.[7] The cautionary words seem appropriate that customary law is a product of the culture of a particular people and requires examination of that culture apart from that of other peoples. It would appear that there is no universal culture pattern of tribal behavior in Ghana or any other African state having more than one people within its borders.[8] The decisions of governmental courts describing native law are only valid to indicate the particular content of the law of the particular people whose law was determinative of the controversy. The search for a governing customary rule of law in a case involving the members of two or more peoples frequently requires application of a unique type of conflicts law. The law of the Ashanti is not the law of the Tallensi or other peoples of the north. Neither is it the law of the Gã or other peoples of the south. When a case is cited for a proposition of customary law, care must be taken to determine from what native culture the court derived the "customary law" which it made the basis of its decision. Unless this is done, it would not seem to be a precedent in any later case involving a similar issue of customary law. To cite a native chief, however illustrious, as authority for a proposition for a principle of customary law is only pertinent to the law of his people. To assert general principles of Ghana customary law requires that any generalizations thus made be supported by thorough comparative anthropological research throughout Ghana. It should be stated, however, that a study of Ghana land law, as it is applied in the Ghanese courts today, including their resort to sources of customary law, is entirely a proper objective.[9]

---

6. Busia, *Position of the Chief*, Chap. 3; Rattray, *Ashanti*, 39-44; Rattray, *Ashanti Law*, Chaps. 22, 23; Danquah, *Akan Law*, Chaps. 9, 10.

7. N. A. Ollennu, *Principles of Customary Land Law in Ghana* (London, 1962), citing Danquah, *Akan Law*, at pp. 5-6, 12, 13, 25-26, 42, 54, 63, 80, 83, 88, 94, 108, 116, 122, 131, 135-136, and 161.

8. S. K. B. Asante, "Interests in Land in the Customary Law of Ghana—A New Appraisal," *Yale Law Journal*, LXXIV (1965), 848.

9. See also K. Bentsi-Enchill, *Ghana Land Law: An Exposition, Analysis, and Critique* (London, 1964).

Law: Offenses

The management of conflict and tension in the Ashanti took place in a larger framework than in the Tallensi. This larger framework comprised a set of norms defining deviant behavior and institutionalized means for its control. Deviant behavior in such a context possessed not only the aspect of interpersonal conflict, including injury to persons affected by it, but it also possessed a quality of injury or threat to the preservation of harmonious relations by the group with the spiritual world. To arrive at an understanding of the Ashanti concept of bad behavior and the need and means for its control, it is necessary first to investigate deviant behavior in the lineage group, inasmuch as the structure and behavior of this group was the basic model for the tribe and the nation.

Within the lineage group, the taking of property by one member from another without the latter's knowledge or consent was not considered to be theft. A person committing such an act was merely called a bad or worthless individual. Such cases were not reported to the chief. A taking by one member of a lineage from a member of another lineage did, however, involve the lineage as a whole. Such an act gave the lineage a bad name. Usually the heads of the two lineages settled the matter between themselves. The offender might be handed over to the injured group to become its slave or pawn. Alternatively, he might be exposed to public ridicule, which was a most anguishing experience for the Ashanti individual.

A theft involving two lineage groups could also be reported to the chief for his adjudication. If, however, the property taken were under the protection of a god or spirit, then misfortune affecting the whole lineage might result. Such offenses were required to be reported to the elder, who might consider it necessary to inform the chief. The whole lineage might then be required to make reparation to pacify the injured god or spirit, such as by sacrificing a sheep or paying money.

There was also the offense of adultery, which was regarded as a theft or taking when it took place in such circumstances as to detract from the so-called "bride-price" paid for the sexual prerogative with respect to a wife.

The Ashanti individual had an extremely strong interest in the preservation of his good name and public esteem. He was most sensitive to personal abuse, invective, and public ridicule. Public ridicule would frequently drive him to suicide. Thus slander, abuse, and bearing tales about another were held to be offenses. Physical assault upon another was also an offense, which became most serious if the victim of the assault happened to occupy any position bringing him in close contact with the spiritual world.

Most offenses falling within the competence of the lineage group were not the subject of fines or physical sanctions. The elder or other senior member of the lineage group, who settled such disputes, acted more the role of conciliator than judge. Such punishments as he might impose were largely dependent upon group sentiment for their enforcement.

The concepts which made the above described conduct offenses subject to control by the lineage group made similar conduct tribal offenses when such conduct occurred in the context of tribal relations.

Theft or taking of property became a matter of tribal concern, if the property was that of a chief or of the *Asantehene*. Such a taking, however, was not regarded as stealing but rather the performance of an evil deed punishable by death.

Sexual relations by a man with a woman not his wife were not considered to be an offense, except where they involved a "theft," as above indicated in connection with the offense of adultery, or where the woman was the wife of a chief, or where they were committed under certain conditions which would be offensive to the spirit of the Earth or to the spirits of ancestors. Incest, or a violation of the blood relationship, was termed "the eating up of one's own blood," and was a tribal offense. Sexual intercourse with an "unclean" woman, or one in her menstrual period, was a crime against the ancestors. Adultery with the wife of a chief or *Asantehene* violated the sacred person of the husband and was an outrage upon his ancestral spirits. All such offenses were punishable by death.

To murder another was a tribal offense because it was a blow to the position of the chief and his elders, both in the temporal and spiritual spheres. The murderer was considered to have struck at the chief and the council of elders and to have treated them as if they were "brute beasts," in denying them their right to hear and judge the dispute and the justification for the act of killing. Moreover, if the chief should allow the act of murder to go unavenged, the spirit of the victim might take vengeance upon the chief. On the other hand, death by accident or negligence led only to responsibility to pay damages to the clan of the deceased.

Suicide or attempted suicide was a capital offense. If suicide were committed without proper justification, the *saman* or spirit of the deceased was considered condemned to wander about until the appointed time for death arrived. The person who committed suicide was found or presumed to have committed some offense and to have taken his life in order to avoid capital punishment for that offense. For denying the chief and the elders the opportunity to judge the commission of this offense and to execute him for it, the law reached him in death itself and the dead man was tried, judged guilty of an offense, and beheaded. If, however, the suicide was committed to avoid capture in war, to accompany a beloved master or mistress into the spiritual world, or to wipe out dishonor, it was not considered to be punishable.

It was also considered to be "murder" to have sexual relations with a girl before she reached puberty or with a woman while she was pregnant.

Abuse and slander of a chief or an *Asantehene,* assault of his person, theft of his property, placing a curse upon him, and treason and cowardice in his service were tribal offenses by virtue of his sacred position. The violation of any tribal taboo was a tribal offense, since it created the possibility of tribal misfortune.

The violation of any law or command which had been promulgated by the chief with the consent of his council of elders could be made a tribal offense if the chief invoked the sanction of spiritual forces for its violation. The chief, in such case, would swear an oath making the commission of the particular offense a disturbance of the spiritual world, with consequent imposition of sanction by it.

Any person could make a dispute or offense, which was otherwise subject to control within the lineage, a matter of tribal jurisdiction and concern by swearing an oath in which the other party joined. Such an oath referred in oblique terms to a tribal disaster connected with the ancestors. The very utterance of the oath was considered to recall the disaster to the ancestors and to create a risk that it might be revisited upon the community. It accordingly became necessary in such a case for the tribal authorities independently to inquire into the dispute in which the oath was declared and to determine which of the persons involved had justification in fact for his conduct in the situation evoking the dispute.

It may be noted that in more recent Ashanti history it became possible for the kin of a person guilty of a capital offense "to buy the head" of such person and thereby commute the penalty of death.[10]

10. Rattray, *Ashanti Law*, Chaps. 26-32; Busia, *Position of the Chief,* 65-75; Danquah, *Akan Law*, Chap. 8.

Law: Procedure

Slight disputes between members of the same lineage group were settled by any person whose wisdom and judgment were respected. More serious disputes could be brought before the elder for decision by declaring an oath having a purport for the lineage similar to the oath for the tribe discussed above. In such case, the elder endeavored to bring about a reconciliation of the parties. The formal acceptance of the mode of reconciliation indicated by the elder meant that the dispute was at an end and friendly relations resumed. The sanction for the elder's exercise of authority was primarily spiritual.

A dispute brought to a chief for decision, either by virtue of its tribal nature or the swearing of an oath bringing it within the chief's competence, was heard in a trial held by the chief and his counsellors. The plaintiff and defendant each gave his version of the facts, which was repeated aloud by the chief's spokesman. Questions to the parties could then be put by any one through the chief's spokesman. One and only one witness was heard to provide a third-party statement of the facts, if desired by either or both parties. He was sworn to tell the truth by declaring a sacred oath invoking, as a sanction, the intervention of two gods. The parties were not required to give their evidence upon oath. They were not even expected to speak the truth, if it were against their interest to do so. It was deemed impractical to place them under oath to a god to punish their lies, for any lie they might then make could not be punished by the chief until the god had first taken his vengeance. Hence, the solution was to place the entire burden of testifying the truth on the single witness, who, under the constraints placed upon him, could not conceivably be thought to lie. Unless a person were a witness in a trial, it was an offense, namely, that of tale-bearing, to report a bad deed of another person, even if it were true.

When a case was heard by a chief, as a result of invoking his action through an oath, the determination of guilt had the result of subjecting the guilty party to the sanction for the offense. However, the other party had also joined in the oath and exposed the tribe to danger. To expiate this act, he was required to pay an *asida,* or an offering of gratitude for having been spared his life. In addition to the sanctions which the spirits could visit upon persons committing tribal or lineage offenses, tribal offenses were subject to the sanctions of capital punishment, multilation, or subjection to slavery. It was also possible in some circumstances for a person under penalty of death to commute his punishment to a fine "by buying his head."[11]

Conclusion

A number of concepts or analogies come to mind, as a summary of the aspects of the Ashanti world is now made. Certainly the image of a stage and its actors, which was selected for portraying the Tallensi, is appropriate for the Ashanti as well. The Ashanti individual was simultaneously a member of his lineage, his tribe, and his nation. He knew the cues for his action and the role performance expected of him, whenever the backdrop of the stage indicated a situation of a lineage, tribal, or national character. Another useful concept employed above was that of the sphere of competence of the lineage, the tribe, and the nation. Each group represented a sphere in which action by an Ashanti was forthcoming in typical situations. An Ashanti chief or tribal member served the *Asantehene,* the Ashanti elder or lineage member served the chief, and the Ashanti lineage member served the elder, simply because his action in each case was what was necessary and expected in the circumstances. It was necessary because the spiritual world required and sanctioned it. It was expected because due form or custom had been followed in performing the cue calling for an established response.

The use of Western terms to describe non-Western cultures has long been a concern of anthropologists. The Western meaning for a term is not always congruent with the phenomena of native society which it is intended to describe. This might happen if the Ashanti people were identified as comprising a hierarchical state. The appropriate spheres of action of the *Asantehene,* the chief, and the elder were clearly perceived by the Ashanti. The authority of each in war and spiritual matters was clearly established without conflicts in jurisdiction among them. It does not appear, however, that the *Asantehene* was supreme over the chief and the chief over the elder by virtue of a delegation of authority from the superior to the inferior. If anything, authority was delegated from the smaller social units to the larger units and the larger could not act without the concurrence of the smaller. A more nearly correct way of putting the matter may be to say that the gods and tradition dictated the authority or sphere of competence of the leader of the particular group and when action under his leadership was called for and appropriate.

11. Rattray, *Ashanti Law,* Chap. 36; Rattray, *Religion and Art,* Chap. 22; Busia, *Position of the Chief,* 67-77.

The unifying themes in describing Ashanti behavior were, first, the supremacy of the spiritual world, second, the assumption of a particular form of political and social order because it was the appropriate mode of linkage with the spiritual world, and third, the universality of the model of action provided by the family or lineage as the means for organizing action in the tribe and the nation. Indeed, the authority of the *Asantehene* and the chief, each in his own sphere, rested precisely on the logic of the spiritual support of his authority once the area for its exercise had been defined, that is, war or propitiation of the gods.

The Ashanti may be said to have resorted to the solution of acting "as if," as the tribe encountered unforseen eventualities in the pursuit of its affairs, such as the misfortunes flowing from the vagaries of the weather and the violence of war. Some means of handling such unpredictable elements was essential. Their solution was to act, in the sphere of the tribe and the nation, as if they were acting in the family. The chief and the *Asantehene* acted, respectively, as if he were occupying the role of the elder in the lineage. This was, in essence, the nature of the political invention of the Ashanti chief of Kumasi who had the vision of the Golden Stool, purported to receive the stool from the spiritual world, and assumed its occupancy under conditions which made the several Ashanti tribes one nation under his leadership and in his sphere of competence. The relationship of the members of the several lineages in the tribe to the chief of the tribe and the members of the several tribes to the *Asantehene* were thereby automatically defined. All that was required, in the conduct of war by the Ashanti nation, was that each tribe should know its place and role in the national army and should accept its duty of following the leadership and commands of the *Asantehene*. This it did. Otherwise, kinship norms defined appropriate conduct in situations in the tribe and nation which were counterparts of familiar family situations.

The Western idea of a hierarchy of authority in the Ashanti state may not have been that of the Ashanti people, as they viewed their organization of political action. Rather, their perception may have been one of appropriateness of response in a given situation, once it was identified to belong properly to the sphere of competence of the *Asantehene,* the chief, or the elder. If the matter was one of his responsibility and spiritual control, the obligation of the individual was clear.

The Ashanti exhibited a marvelous sense of order and depth of perception in their concept of the elements of individual personality and the relationship of such elements to the world of human organization and the world of the spirit. Such elements provided a means for placing each individual in the world of his ancestors, as spiritual actors, and in the world of his family and clan. They also provided means for arriving at an understanding of his personality, as he acted in a world of spiritual and temporal forces.

The spiritual world was peopled by many actors, with each set of whom there was an appropriate intermediary in the form of *Asantehene,* chief, elder, priest, and the like. There were the supreme being, from whom all gods derived their strength, and the Earth. There were the gods and the ancestors, not to mention fairies, forest monsters, and witches.

The law and procedure which came into being in the Ashanti world was one designed to render secure the individual personality and its means of expression in a world which was partially temporal and partially spiritual. The individual, as such, had relatively little freedom of opportunity to act in an innovative manner. Life for the *Asantehene,* chief, and elder, on the one hand, and the individual, on the other hand, was very considerably a matter of performance of political and social obligations.

Land was held subject to the obligation to use it. Property was held subject to the obligation to use it generously for the benefit of those sharing one's blood. Tilling the soil, rendering services to those upon whose link with the spiritual world good fortune was dependent, rendering service to the chief or *Asantehene* in war, providing assistance in performance of ritual, making payment of levies duly imposed, and rearing of one's offspring, these were some of the principal obligations of the Ashanti male.

Norms for conduct designed to protect social order and avoid injury to the gods were laid down. Violation of them was the subject of regularized inquiry in the family and the tribe, as well as the nation. Tribal offenses were subject to severe sanctions because the risk of injury to the tribe through spiritual forces, which they entailed, was great. Thus a system of prohibited norms of fairly clear content and third-party decision making had developed for the control of deviant conduct. This system, and the society which it controlled, seems to have functioned with effectiveness.[12]

---

12. For a concise summary of Ashanti culture, see M. Manoukian, "Akan and Ga-Adangme Peoples of the Gold Coast," Ethnographic Survey of Africa, Western Africa, Pt. I, ed. D. Forde (London, 1950), 9-64.

Part Three

NIGERIA

Chapter 6

The Hausa-Fulani

Introduction

NIGERIA possesses, to a considerable extent, the same geographical belts characteristic of Ghana, that is, the savanna grasslands of the north, which merge into the orchard bush, then the dense rain forest belt, and finally the coastal region. The Hausa states of the north reveal the impact of Islam and outside cultural forces upon the peoples of the savanna. The open character of the savanna allows an extraordinary freedom of movement to both conquerors and traders. This region was the southern terminus of the Sahara caravans and the scene of mass migrations. The political organization of the Hausa states shares a number of basic features in common with peoples of the savanna grasslands, "namely the centralization of authority in a ruler with his councilors and sub-chiefs drawn from an aristocracy of birth; an elaborate etiquette of obeisance, expressive of ranking and subordination of classes in the social order; the collecting of tax and tribute to maintain the several organs of government and its agents."[1] The Hausa-Fulani, as found in the Hausa state of Zazzau or in the Zaria province in north-central Nigeria, will be selected for investigation because of the extensive literature of M. G. Smith and others. The study of the Hausa will be supplemented by a study of certain aspects of the life of the Nupe people, who were conquered by the Fulani. The Nupe are found to the south of the Hausa in an environ-

1. T. Hodgkin, *Nigerian Perspectives: An Historical Anthology* (London, Ibadan, Accra, 1960), 3.

ment which mostly lies outside the forest belt and is considerably comparable to the open lands of the Hausa. They provide a means for a greater understanding of the type of political organization and law found in the Hausa states and the impact of Islam upon these aspects of West African life. The writings of S. F. Nadel upon the Nupe are too valuable to be neglected.

The Tiv will be studied as representative of the peoples of the central territory. This region has been termed a cultural cul-de-sac, because of the survival of numerous archaic traits. Bohannan's work upon the Tiv makes their selection imperative.

The Yoruba of the southwest and the Ibo in the southeast will be the two remaining peoples studied. The political structure of the kingdoms of the Yoruba will throw light upon the centralized kingdoms of Western Nigeria. The impact of urbanization upon political and social structure and land law will be revealing. The Ibo will typify the tribes with villages and dispersed family homesteads characteristic of eastern Nigeria. They represent a type of culture particularly suitable for the modernizing process.

The Yoruba people extend to the coast at Lagos and the culture of the Yoruba and the Ibo extend to the coastal region. The Ibo in particular embody a type of culture found among the coastal peoples. There is only a slight literature on the peoples of the coastal region.

The peoples selected for study represent a fair sampling of Hodgkin's cultural divisions of Nigeria based on historical development.[2] They also reflect the Voltaic and Kwa subfamilies of the Nigritic stock of languages, with the Tiv belonging to the Bantoid subfamily.

Geography and Economy

The original seven Hausa states of northern Nigeria were located in the region to the east of the Niger and the west of Lake Chad. Their peoples speak a common language, Hausa, belonging to the Chado-Hamitic family, and represent a number of ethnic groups. One may distinguish the Habe or Hausa as the indigenous inhabitants, on the one hand, and the Fulbe or Fulani as the immigrant group, on the other hand. The Habe were a sedentary people, living in walled towns and villages as a means of protection against armed attack from the open savanna surrounding them. The Fulbe or Fulani were a nomadic, cattle-herding group, speaking the Fulfulde

2. *Ibid.*

language. They emigrated eastward from Senegal forming settlements from time to time as they did so. The Hausa are divided into pagan and Muslim communities. The Fulani are, in large measure, a Muslim people divided into bush nomads, semi-settled, and settled groups. Many of the pastoral Fulani remain pagan.

The Hausa are a highly developed people and possess skill and industry in agriculture, certain crafts, such as leather work, and trade. War and slave-raiding were characteristic forms of action by the state, and the use of slaves characterized political, economic, and social action. Islam had largely absorbed the town Hausa but did not effectively reach the farming Hausa until after the Fulani conquest of the early nineteenth century.

The land of the Hausa is that of the savanna and orchard bush country. Rainfall is not heavy, 35 to 40 inches for most of the region, and is confined to the months of May through September. The harvest takes place in October to December and is followed by a cold, dry season which merges into one of intense heat and drought prior to the rains. For the pastoral Fulani, this means that they must move to the north during the heavy rains but return close to water supply during the dry season. A symbiotic relationship developed of dependence by the Hausa upon the pastoral Fulani for meat and dairy supplies and by the Fulani upon the Hausa for food crops, grain, and other needs.

This chapter will investigate the former Hausa state of Zazzau, located in the center of northern Nigeria, of which Zaria was the capital, in the northern part of the province of Zaria. The chapter will also include a study of the Hausa state of Abuja, lying to the south, together with information concerning certain aspects of Nupe and Ruanda behavior.

Zazzau was conquered in 1804 by the Fulani under the leadership of Mallam Musa in a *jihad* or holy war. The Hausa king, Makau, fled with many of his followers and finally repelled the Fulani at the town of Zuba. In 1825, Makau's successor, named Abu Ja, built the town which bears his name and which became the capital of the state known as Abuja. It should be understood that the Hausa were by no means exclusively a pagan people prior to their conquest by the Fulani. The Hausa came in contact with Islam in the fourteenth and fifteenth centuries and rapidly absorbed Islamic culture. By the beginning of the nineteenth century this was manifest in many aspects of their life.

The unique developments shown by this study lie in the interrelationships of agricultural, pastoral, and urban cultures, and the impact of Islam upon African life, as revealed in the social, economic, and political organization of the Hausa-Fulani peoples. The Hausa-Fulani culture of Zazzau will be studied for this purpose as it existed prior to the establishment of the British protectorate in 1900. At certain points of this study, notably in the matter of political organization, attention will be given to the Hausa culture of Abuja. Investigation will also be made, for comparative purposes, of aspects of Nupe and Ruanda life. The terms Hausa or Hausa-Fulani will refer to the Muslim, Hausa-speaking population as a whole, the term Habe will refer to the non-Fulani portion of the Hausa, and the term pastoral Fulani will refer to the cattle nomads of the Fulani.[3]

Historical Background: Impact of Islam

A somewhat more detailed historical account of the relationship of the Habe and Fulani peoples with the Arab world is desirable. It will provide a perspective of the influences entering into their past and their cultural identities.

The Arabs divided North Africa into the Maghreb, or West, and Egypt. North Africa and the Sahara together comprised *Bilād al-Bīdān*, "Land of the Whites." The region lying south of the Sahara up to the rain forest, extending across Africa from the Atlantic coast to Abyssinia, was *Bilād as-Sūdān*, "Land of the Blacks." The Sudan, in turn, is divided into western Sudan, whose waters drain into the coastal rivers and the Niger, central Sudan, from the bend of the Niger towards the Chad, and eastern Sudan, consisting of the Nile basin.

Two trade routes led from North Africa to the Sudan, a western one from southern Morocco to the central Niger region and an eastern one from Tripoli to the Hausa country. A route from Egypt to the eastern Sudan also existed.

The Habe were largely a town-dwelling people, though they included agricultural groups, speaking the Hausa language, while the Fulani were originally nomadic herdsmen speaking a common language. The Fulani who settled in this land changed in course of time

---

3. M. G. Smith, *The Economy of Hausa Communities of Zaria* (London, 1955), 1-3; M. G. Smith, "Exchange and Marketing among the Hausa," *Markets in Africa*, ed. P. Bohannan and G. Dalton (Chicago, 1962), 299-302; J. S. Trimingham, *A History of Islam in West Africa* (London, Glasgow, New York, 1962), 126-136; Malam Hassan and Malam Shuaibu, *A Chronicle of Abuja*, trans. F. Heath (Ibadan, 1952), 4-10.

from a nomadic to more developed types of culture, including a ruling élite. While both Habe and Fulani were exposed to Islamic culture, it was the Fulani who considered themselves to be more faithful to the teachings of Islam and who achieved political control of the Hausa states through conquest. The Fulani appear to have had a longer contact with Islam by virtue of the fact that the western trade route across the Sahara was important in early times. Moreover, it was in western and central Sudan that stable Negro empires, such as the Songhay and Bornu, first developed, which promoted trade and intercourse with the Maghreb. The pilgrim traffic, trade, and political influence of Songhay and Bornu were the principal forces of islamization. The type of Arabic script used by the Hausa and the Malikite school of Islamic law adopted by the Hausa came from the Maghreb. Significant contact with Islam began in the fourteenth century and thereafter steadily increased. Armed conflict between the Sultan of Morocco and the Songhay at the end of the sixteenth century caused a shift from the western to the eastern trade route across the Sahara in the seventeenth century. Arab trade brought great prosperity and development to the Hausa states at this time. A movement of Islamic revivalism appeared toward the end of the eighteenth century, marked by the conquest of the Hausa states by the Fulani in a holy war, or *jihad*, at the beginning of the nineteenth century.[4]

Resistance to the acceptance of Islam and the integration of Islamic ways and teachings in a society appear to be a product of the degree to which the system of religion and authority and the social and economic structure constitute an organic, closely-linked whole. In the individualistic, trading, urban societies and the diffusely organized, nomadic societies, Islam has a greater appeal than in the agricultural societies, composed of closely-knit clans and families. When religion, in the form of spirits, ancestors, the earth, and the like, become a vital part of all aspects of life, as in many kin-structured, agricultural societies, the barrier to Islam is at its strongest. The agents of islamization are many: officials, policemen, soldiers, traders, and clergy. A society moves toward Islam at first in the acquisition of a veneer of Islamic forms and finally in attaining a synthesis of pagan and Islamic elements. The clan disappears, the family

---

4. J. Greenberg, *The Influence of Islam on a Sudanese Religion*, Monographs of the American Ethnological Society, No. 10 (New York, 1946), 1-9; S. J. Hogben, *The Muhammadan Emirates of Nigeria* (London, 1930), 25-27, 41-55, 87-88; Trimingham, *op. cit.*, pp. 1-33, 106, 126-136; J. S. Trimingham, *Islam in West Africa* (Oxford, 1959), 1-9, 11-12, 16.

assumes an Islamic pattern of authority and work, and religion assumes a dual character of pagan substructure and Islamic superstructure. The adoption of Islamic law, which is a theistic system of law, has a profound effect in vital aspects of life, such as changing matrilineal to patrilineal families, the status of women, and the nature of property.[5]

The Bush Habe

Before entering upon a study of the Hausa, that is, the Hausa-speaking, Muslim people of the state of Zazzau, it is desirable to indicate the character of the bush Habe and bush Fulani, who were and are important but declining elements of the population of Zazzau.

Two studies of the bush Habe are helpful for this purpose. Greenberg investigated certain Hausa-speaking pagans of Kano from the standpoint of the impact of Islam on their religion.[6] He also reported on the influence of Islam upon the clan organization of this people.[7]

Households were composed of brothers under the headship of the eldest, together with their sons. When the father of any such son died, the son could leave the compound if he wished, but not before. This was the basic landowning group.

The clan was a patrilocal organization exemplified in a collection of households claiming common patrilineal descent and living in a group averaging about ten in number.

The village had its "headman of farming," who was chosen by the household heads with the approval of the local Fulani headman. The post had no practical significance, for, although its occupant could nominally decide disputes over inheritance, the Fulani headman had the final power of decision.

At the time of the investigation, 1938–1939, the people had merged with the Muslim population to the extent that their language and material culture were practically identical. The group investigated lived in a small village of scattered compounds, some of which were occupied by Fulani. The latter were representatives of a headman living in a nearby walled city, who controlled both the city and the village.

---

5. *Ibid.,* pp. 24-42.
6. Greenberg, *op. cit.*
7. J. Greenberg, "Islam and Clan Organization among the Hausa," *Southwestern Journal of Anthropology,* III (1947), 193.

A compound was usually occupied by a group of males related in the paternal line. Farming was the principal means of livelihood. All land was inherited through the male line and could be owned only by males. Women were, however, given temporary holdings of land which they were expected to cultivate. A limited amount of marketing and industrial activity took place.

There was a more or less formal acknowledgement that Allah was the supreme power in the universe but, in general, Allah was regarded to be remote from and unconcerned with the affairs of men. The spirits, however, were many and had an important influence in determining health and welfare. They were found everywhere in the physical environment—the sky, the forest, the rivers, and the like. When they were identified by a name and definite locale and possessed a cult, sacrifice was made to them by the slaying of sheep, goats, or fowl. Sometimes they revealed themselves through taking possession of their worshippers. They were classified as white, or good, spirits and black, or evil, spirits.

Anyone could approach the spirits. Formal rites were held in the family, at which the head of the compound offered sacrifices for all members of the compound related to him on the paternal side.

Greenberg concluded that as a result of the impact of Islam upon the indigenous religion a new system was created, consisting of a synthesis of the elements of each. This came about as a result of the fact that the spirits of the bush Habe were identified by the Muhammadan *malams,* or learned men, as pagan jinn, recognized in Muslim religious doctrine. The actual existence and power of such spirits was thereby accepted, and the survival of spirit cults permitted.

The people were at the first stage of transition to Islam. Trimingham found three stages in the assimilation of Islam to exist. First, a stage in which aspects of Islamic life were incorporated in the indigenous culture, without displacing traditional religious rites. Second, a stage in which there was a formal adherence to the outward forms of Islam and discarding of fetishes. Third, a stage marked by a genuine belief in the power of the sanctions of the Islamic religion and change in conduct and social customs. Trimingham concluded that:

> The new culture which emerges as a result of this process may be compared to an embroidered textile. The basic fabric is the animist culture. Upon this is embroidered the Islamic pattern. In time this pattern is woven into the very texture of the background. The actual structure of the ground is no longer discernible, but it remains firmly rooted and provides the variation between different ethnic cultures. This reintegration is still in process, yet there is a recognizable West African

Islamic culture, different from that of North Africa, formed through the interaction of Islamic law and indigenous cultures.

The fact that this process of integration is rarely complete implies spiritual dualism. Religious life rests on a double foundation, the animistic underlayer and the Islamic superstructure. . . .

Old religious attitudes and customs rule in the sphere of village civilization and interwoven with this is the new civilization. But we can never generalize about the extent to which Islam is the supporting foundation of life for it depends upon the stage of integration reached. If we take a particular community, a Hausa or Songhay village, we may find that the main weight of everyday life rests more upon the old religion than the new. On the other hand, if we go to a Tokolor village we may find that Islamic law has had a profounder effect than upon Berbers of North Africa.

Retention of seemingly conflicting loyalties, attitudes, and institutions does not necessarily signify conscious dualism in people's lives. The African Muslim is not torn between two warring forces. In everyday life the two strands of religious inheritance are reconciled, for they are woven together like the warp and weft of different textures into a cloth of complicated pattern. . . .[8]

The effect of conversion to Islam upon clan organization should be noted. It caused the political and religious functions of clans to lose their significance. The economic organization of the society changed, in that women were no longer expected to work. The extended family disappeared as a functional unit. Clans increasingly assumed a shadow significance and finally disappeared, as the father ceased to tell his son of the name of his clan in order to cast aside his pagan past.

The Pastoral Fulani

The Wodaabe of the province of Bornu, west of the province of Zaria and north of the Benue River, will be chosen to illustrate the pastoral Fulani because of the extensive work of Stenning and the absence of any comparable work on the Fulani of Zazzau. Stenning described the family of this culture as a "herd-owning, milk selling enterprise."[9] This basic fact had an enormous influence upon family structure, patterns of actions, and the character of the ties of the people with the outside world.

---

8. Trimingham, *Islam in West Africa*, 43.
9. D. J. Stenning, "Transhumance, Migratory Drift, Migration; Patterns of Patoral Fulani Nomadism," *Journal of the Royal Anthropological Institute*, LXXXVII (1957), 58.

In early Wodaabe society, before the holy war in the first part of the nineteenth century, the basic economic unit was the nuclear and the extended family. This was a herd-tending group, which lived from the herd and sought to preserve and increase the size of the herd. To meet the vicissitudes of its existence, such a family usually acted in association with other families brought together by the principle of descent from a common male ancestor. Such an association of families was manifested in economic cooperation, marriage arrangements, inheritance, and leadership. Such an association or lineage group traced descent from a common ancestor usually not more than three generations removed.

Families of the lineage group located their homesteads together so as to form a camp. They travelled together with their herds, united to defend themselves, and cooperated to meet individual or common hardships. If a herd was deficient in certain types of stock, its owner could borrow the needed cattle. If a herd was depleted in numbers as a result of some catastrophe, other herd-owners of the lineage group were expected to make gifts to help restore the herd. The distinctive racial and lineage characteristics tended to be preserved by the principle of preference for marriages within the group or others related agnatically.

A father sought to build up his herd so that he might pass on to his sons more cattle than his own father had. At the marriage of each son, the father shared part of his herd with each son to the end that, at the last marriage of his sons, all his herd would be distributed among them. The family of husband and one or more wives and their children cared for its own herd, lived on its milk, sold milk for its needs, and slaughtered cattle only under necessity, since cattle were its capital. Milk production had to be adequate at all seasons to support the family. The family could be said to support or maintain the herd in its task by following patterns of transhumance, or search for adequate water and pastures, and taking care of the cattle.

The lineage group had an appointed leader, or *ardo,* who was selected on the basis that he embodied unusual attainment of the valued goals and qualities of the people. It was necessary, in his selection, that he should be a family head and unusually successful in the possession of wives, children, and cattle. He must be experienced and at least of middle age. He must be the closest in genealogical position, among his followers, of the *ardo* he succeeded. His attainment in an unusual degree, of a composite of the valued qualities, led to his selection by the "consensus of ten men." He was the spokesman of the group in dealings with other similar groups. He represented the group in its contacts with villages and arranged for pasturage rights. He generally supervised the making and termination of marriages. He was in charge of defense. His exercise of authority was mostly dependent on consultation with members of the group, weighing their views and experience, and reaching conclusions which were announced in terms of advice rather than command. If his leadership should prove unfortunate in its outcome over a period of time, he did not lose his office, but he might lose his following.

Constitutive conflict manifested itself frequently in the dry season. If the lineage group was of a substantial size, it was then necessary for the households to disperse rather early so as to obtain pasturage. At this time, the claim of a rival leader was more easily heard and followed. Fission of the group tended to take place on the basis of nearness of kinship ties, those who were the most distantly related were the most likely to separate. On the other hand, if a lineage group had an excess of cattle in relation to the number of persons able to care for the herd, it would accept as new members young men who were agnatically related but whose fathers were not able adequately to provide them with a herd upon marriage. Or it might accept a related household head who had lost his herd through misfortune.

In the wet season, it was possible and usual for a number of lineage groups to form a camp. The basis of their association was the putative agnatic relationship of several of their common ancestors with each other. The purpose of such a gathering was primarily to enable preferred marriages to take place within the families thus related. This cluster of lineage groups may be described as a clan.

The concatenation and meshing of the various rules or patterns of behavior that brought about successful goal attainment, namely, preferred marriages, numerous children to provide herdsmen and milkmaids, good husbandry, expanding herds, was collectively called the Fulani Way. It had three principal components which comprised the ideal personality type or the preferred social virtues. They were, first, modesty and reserve, second, patience and fortitude, and, third, forethought and prudent planning. The first category included correct conduct in personal situations, such as deference to elders and cooperation with equals.

Within the family, at first the mother and later the father instructed the children in the Fulani Way and its values. The *ardo* was the ideal figure to be emulated in the lineage group. The clan had a specific office known as the guardian of the Fulani Way, whose occupant was determined by descent in the purest line in the clan. He was the ceremonial leader and could also penalize for violation of specific rules of the Fulani Way. This usually consisted of temporary banishment from the group to the bush, ignominious treatment while in the bush, and later readmittance after repentance and ceremonies of abasement.

The Fulani Way was related to the human organism in that shame was felt in the belly, the place of secrets, the heart was the place of patience and fortitude, and the head the place of care and forethought. It was from the exercise of care and forethought that a man succeeded in the possession of wives, children, cattle, and the esteem and cooperation of kinsmen.

As contacts of the pastoral Fulani with the state and towns increased, the prized qualities of an *ardo* were not limited to his capacity as a camp leader but came to include his success as an intermediary with the state and a leader of irregular troops. As the people were drawn into the Islamic way of life through such contacts, the office of the guardian of the Fulani Way declined in significance. The effect of the movement to the state of Bornu was described by the Wodaabe as follows:

> Before we came to Bornu we were each under our *ardo*. That was the age of *pulaaku* [Fulani Way]; it gripped you by your little finger but you felt its force through your whole body. Then came the period of war, when our horses stood the whole day bitted and bridled, ready for action. This was the age of strength; it gripped you by the forearm, but you felt it only in your forearm.

New leaders emerged; these were the men who established and maintained relations with the Bornu state. In the latter part of the nineteenth century, the state appointed a head or leader known as the Laamiido, derived from the verb *laama,* "to rule." There were other officials or title-holders created as well, appointed from lineage groups. The Laamiido assisted in the ceremonials of the clan in the wet season, made gifts of meat for this purpose, and caused performances by his drummers and praise-singers. He was the chief slave-owner of the clan. He made gifts of horses to favored officials and followers and received gifts of horses and slaves from the Shehu of Bornu. Thus the pastoralists were drawn into the orbit of state authority and bounty. At the same time, they experienced, with increasing regularity, the deprivations of the tax gatherer of the state, as levies were made on their herds.[10]

---

10. D. J. Stenning, *Savannah Nomads* (London, Ibadan, Accra, 1959), 74; see also C. E. Hopen, *The Pastoral Fulbe Family in Gwandu* (London, Ibadan, Accra, 1958).

Social and Economic Organization of the Hausa

The Hausa were organized domestically into compounds or walled units, which were typically occupied by two or three groups based on marriage. The compound head was the head of an individual family. The members of the compound might or might not accept his authority in internal matters. In the latter event, the compound was simply a residential association of individual families possessing a head for the purpose of external relations. It was rather infrequent for kinship relations in a compound to extend more than two generations back.

The members of a compound were organized into work units on the basis that they produced food in common from a common farm and had a common granary, a common pot, and a single head. Such work units were termed *gandu.*

There was a close-knit intermeshing of *gandu* into communities and of communities with one another. From the standpoint of social relations, a community was distinguished by the higher frequency of the contacts of members with one another, as compared with their contacts with other persons more or less nearby, and the fact that social events affected them in common to a greater degree than other persons. From the institutional standpoint, a community was identified by the fact that its members recognized a common chief, regularly attended a common market, and accepted a common *limam* as their highest official religious authority. Local communities were bound by ties of interest to the state and to one another. They shared common political problems and interests and participated in a common group of rotating bi-weekly markets. Intermarriage, however, also took place between members of adjacent communities. Consultation of malams or Islamic scholars, magicians, and adepts at spirit-possession, also took place in different communities.

High achievement of admired values in social relations was termed *arziki.* Success in the attainment of wealth and influence, as a component of *arziki,* could be reached only through political office and trade. In earlier days, large scale slave-owning was another means. *Arziki* represented "general good fortune, a man's ability to have and enjoy all that he wants without prejudice to its continuation tomorrow; many wives and children, wealth, political security, a high standard of living, good crop-yields, success in his undertakings, high social recognition." It was a complex concept involving such elements as birth, prestige, political protection, large family, good farming, money, and wealth or greater than average consumption. There was a different degree or standard of *arziki* for each of the various occupations.

The division of labor between men and women was as follows:

> Men rule, farm, dye, build, work metals, skin, tan and work leather, slay and handle cattle and small livestock, sew all sewn clothes, make musical instruments and music, trade, keep bees, weave mats, may be *mallams,* wash clothes, weave narrow cloth on the men's loom, go on long-distance expeditions *(fatauci),* make pots, do carpentry, native and European, are the doctors and magicians, the barbers, employed farm-labourers *(kodago),* brokers and taxpayers. They also fish, hunt and do all the family marketing, keep goats, sheep, chickens, ducks, turkeys and pigeons, and took part in war.

> Women cook for their families, process and sell cooked foods (snacks) on their own behalf, sweep and clean the compounds, are solely respon-sible for delivery and safe care of children, draw wood and water, are the custodians of the cult of *Bori* (spirit possession), tease and spin cot-ton, weave cloth on the women's broad looms, thresh, grind and pound corn and other grains, process such sylvan produce as sheanut butter and locust-bean cakes, make pots, keep chickens, goats and sheep, trade in corn and food, and are, before marriage and when they are old, traders in the markets and from house to house. Women do one another's hair *(kitso),* may (but usually do not) farm, and help with the groundnut, cowpea, cotton and pepper harvests. Very occasionally women become *mallams* or professional musicians or magicians. In new towns where *karuwai* (prostitutes) are numerous, such as Kaduna and Bukuru, women sometimes work at the dyepits. Women may not inherit land nor houses where there are related male heirs, and under Maliki law daughters re-ceive half the inheritance of sons, but usually inherit the personal pos-sessions of their mothers. Women are expected to provide themselves with such luxuries and snacks as they require, and on the marriage of daughters, women of the paternal and maternal kin provide most of the dowry.[11]

Those who pursued nomadic or agricultural ways of life tended to resist Islam more than the town-dwellers and traders. Slavery could survive under Islam, though in a somewhat modified form as to the legal status of slavery. Hence, when slavery was abolished in modern times, it meant that many slave-supported Muslims, who spent their leisure hours at the mosque, were compelled to work for their living. Wives who worked as pagan Hausa retreated from the farm fields to the women's quarters of the home. Farmers who once pursued pagan cultivation rites to promote fertility turned instead to the Muslim

---

11. Smith, *Economy of the Hausa Communities,* 4-5, quotations at 15, 60; see also K. Buchanan, "The Northern Region of Nigeria: The Geographical Back-ground of its Political Duality," *The Geographical Review,* XLIII (1953), 451.

clergy for protection, though this stage was preceded by one of dualistic religious attachment.

The impact of the Islamic way of life upon the family was to promote the disintegration of the lineage group and to bring the nuclear family, consisting of man, wife or wives, and their children, into greater importance in the social structure. Pagan clans ceased to exist. The belief in the power of the ancestors in temporal matters diminished and, as a consequence, a considerable amount of the unity of the family. The authority of the head of the extended family decreased and that of the head of the nuclear family increased. The division of personal property among the children pursuant to Islamic law hastened this process of disintegration. The integrating force of the performance of common ritual by the members of the family disappeared as religious ritual became a personal matter. As above noted, clan relationships lost their significance and marriage prohibitions inculcated by pagan standards disappeared.

The impact of Islam upon towns was most significant. Trimingham stated:

> Islam as an urban religion cannot exist in its distinctive form without towns and only townspeople can conscientiously follow its principles. The farmer instinctively resists it as a disintegrative factor. On the other hand, in the town, where life and personal relationships are more secularized, Islam is an integrative factor. Town life and trading involve abandoning local religion, Islamic law can operate over a wider field of social relations, *qādī's* courts can function, and teachers attract pupils from a wide area. In the townsman class there are three occupational groups; clergy living on offerings and fees; men of business such as merchants and traders, craftsmen, shopkeepers, and street vendors, for if profit is meagre so is the expense of setting up; and, finally, artisans and manual labourers. The heterogeneity characteristic of towns, however, derives from differences of ethnic origins rather than from divisions of labour. Islam, with its power to call to the one *jami'* for Friday prayer, is the only integrative factor.[12]

Political Organization of the Hausa

THE HABE OF ABUJA

A brief sketch will first be made of the Habe of Abuja, who were driven by the Fulani from the state of Zazzau in 1804, made a successful defense at the town of Zuba in the south, and created the Emirate of Abuja. They were mostly town-dwellers, traders, and

---

12. Trimingham, *Islam in West Africa*, Chaps. 6, 8, quotation at 191-192.

brokers. They were successful raiders of towns and robbers on trade routes. Their prosperity was originally dependent upon the sale and other use of their slave captives but, with the outlawing of slavery, they turned to farming, weaving, tailoring, and trading.[13]

The state which they created in the nineteenth century was directed to the prosecution of war in order to capture slaves and enjoy the benefits of their sale and use. The maintenance of the political system required, however, that civil matters, such as police, prisons, markets, supplies to the capital and the army, be duly administered, and that justice be rendered through the courts. The holding and performance of office yielded economic rewards not otherwise attainable and provided high rank and status.

To understand the Habe political organization, and the Fulani as well, it is necessary to realize that they were political economies directed to the recruitment of slaves through war, the exploitation of slaves in working fiefs of land, which were also the reward of war and successful political action, the sale of slaves in markets, and the use of slaves as a means for the preservation of political power. Appointment to political office was dictated in part by tradition but was also influenced by considerations of maintenance of power by the king and his royal lineage. The structure of civil administration represented the setting in which a process of political competition and reward, manipulated by the king, took place.

The king did not represent the peak of political power and influence, it instead rested in his order of household officials. He was not the leader in war. It was instead one of his officials, the Madawaki, who was commander of the army and the head of the cavalry. Decision of major political issues rested primarily in his senior household officials and the senior order of public officials. The king was bound by their decisions; only where these two groups disagreed did he have an independent power of decision. The political supremacy of the order of household officials was marked by their veto power over proposals made by the public order of officials. There was also a concurrence of assent required among these groups, the details of which will not be described, for the appointment and promotion of officials. While the king enjoyed great administrative authority, he could not act politically against the joint decision of the public and household orders of officials.

The king was outranked in political power by, in successive order, the household officials, and the senior and junior public officials. On the other hand, he outranked, in turn, the *malams,* the slave-officials,

---

13. Hassan and Shuaibu, *op. cit.,* Part II.

and the chamber eunuchs. A reversal of this ranking of officials would indicate the degree to which the several groups of officials displayed administrative specialization in the performance of their tasks. Those at the bottom of the list reflected the greatest degree of administrative specialization in their task. The meaning of these categories of officials will be summarized below. M. G. Smith described the king's position in this context as follows:

> Kingship at Abuja was in fact an office with prominent administrative elements and functions, and as such its scope for free action was clearly limited and defined. Furthermore, as the pivotal point of the governmental system, being simultaneously the supreme administrative office and the central office of the political system, the kingship was basic both to the equilibrium and co-ordination of the total system. Hence, though itself involved in segmentary relations with other units of the political system, kingship exercised the least power over policy formation of any of the three units which participated in that process, except, significantly, when the equilibrium of the system was at stake through irreconcilable differences about policy between the public and household orders.

The order of public officials was divided into senior and junior orders. In the senior order, the Madawaki had a military role and the Galadima was responsible for a number of matters of civil administration, including the police. Each controlled a section of the junior officials. The junior officials were, among other things, responsible for administrative matters in relations with the chiefs. They were responsible for territorial administration, tax collection, and the execution of justice.

The household officials had no administrative functions within the state. They instead took care of various matters in the king's household and office. Yet they possessed greater political power than any other order of officials. The *malams* were the Koranic scholars and provided a majority of the electoral group which selected a new king. They officiated at rituals and advised on the content and application of Muhammadan law. Slave-officials possessed military, civil, and police duties. Chamber officials, composed of eunuchs, were the king's closest associates and dependents. Although they lacked the capacity of councillors and their advice was informed only, they were the first group consulted by the king. They were a distinct and specialized administrative staff.

Integration of the system of political and administrative action was brought about by the principles followed in the appointment to office and promotion. Slaves might secure manumission and thereby achieve elegibility for offices open to free men. Free men were mobile upwards, as government officials, from the household order to the junior public order to the senior public order and, finally, to the post of Madawaki. *Malams* could be promoted to higher office, if they gave up their religious status. Where fidelity and high standards of performance of administrative tasks were important, appointment tended to be made from the eunuch and slave groups. It was significant that three of the four senior officials of the public order were eunuchs.

Rewards of office were fixed in various ways. The king's chamber officials were provided rewards in the form of a share of the tribute and tax which they collected from vassal chiefs and others. Fief-holders were a relatively independent group, deriving their reward from their fiefs. Household officials relied on the king for support. The *malams* lived on the fees and donations which they received for the performance of their duties.[14]

The king received taxes from his people and tribute or gifts from the chiefs and officials, as well as a share of the spoils of war. From these revenues, he provided gifts to his officials on their appointment, built bridges, provided for the poor and strangers, and otherwise performed his duties to his people.[15]

M. G. Smith summarized the elements of office as follows:

> On these data from Abuja, the Habe concept of *sarauta* (ranked and titled office) involved the following elements: title, specified tasks, authority, and means of execution; supra-individual continuity; membership in a system of similar units, which was itself hierarchically ranked and organized in closed promotional series; political and administrative differentiation; differentiation according to the status conditions of eligible candidates; and appointment by selection, rather than on a hereditary basis. The material attributes of these Habe *sarautu* varied according to the particular office. It is likely that offices of all kinds had appropriate modes of installation, regalia, praise-songs, and perhaps farm lands. The more important offices also had compounds attached to them, wards, fiefs, benefices, rights and powers, set positions of precedence in the council and court, and on campaigns.[16]

THE FULANI OF ZAZZAU

The structure and process of government in the Fulani state of Zazzau of the nineteenth century evidence much the same premises as in the Habe of Abuja. There was the same motivation by those wielding the power of the state to use it in waging war for the pur-

14. M. G. Smith, *Government in Zazzau 1800-1950* (London, New York, Toronto, 1960), Chap. 2, quotation at 66.
15. Hassan and Shuaibu, *op. cit.*, pp. 83-84.
16. Smith, *Government in Zazzau*, 58.

pose of the capture and exploitation of slaves. There was the same striving for power and esteem. There were the same tasks of civil administration and law. The Fulani state, however, possessed an extra element of dynamism and its leaders possessed a unique attitude toward their domain not found in the Habe. Whereas competition for kingship took place in Abuja *within* a single royal lineage, in Zazzau it took place in a context of competition *among* dynasties. There were four Fulani lineages in Zazzau from which the king could legitimately be selected, although it was from the three most powerful lineages that kings were in fact selected. The outlook of the Fulani leaders, who held the bulk of political office and power, toward the Habe and the state was one of a people which possessed pride of race and religion and which had conquered a lesser people in a holy war. There was a basic racial, political, and social cleavage between the Fulani and the Habe.

Competition among the four dynasties for political ascendancy in the kingship and its rewards led to a distinctive pattern of political action. The person who succeeded to kingship established members of his lineage in office throughout his administration and otherwise selected incumbents for office on the criterion of their effectiveness in preserving him in power.

Clientage was a highly important and widespread political relationship. M. G. Smith stated that relationships of clientage were characteristic of all levels of office. In his view, clientage designated "a variety of relationships, which all have inequality of status of the associated persons as a common characteristic." In the political field, an official was loyal to the superior who appointed him and demonstrated that loyalty by the practice of *gaisuwa,* or making gifts. A stranger could assume the role of a client of a lineage group, in which he would occupy a junior status, as that of son to father or younger to older brother. The senior or superior would reward the junior or inferior as best he could. In political clientage, such reward might take the form of grant of office and title. In domestic clientage, such reward might be the provision of a kinswoman in marriage. A merchant might create a relationship of clientage with his agent, whom he would endow with capital to trade independently at a distance. The latter would act the role of client of the merchant. Such a relationship required much trust on the part of the merchant and loyalty and faithfulness on the part of the agent. In turn, a merchant might become a client of an important official who supervised an area of interest to the merchant. Clientage, in terms of chieftainship, was described as follows:

Chieftainship is a nexus of relations of clientage. This was true for Zaria at any political level, since the king himself, before 1900, was a client *(bara)* of the Sultan of Sokoto. Similarly before 1900 chiefs of vassal states under the suzerainty of the ruler of Zaria were clients as well as vassals of the king. The chief of a local community remains to-day the client of the administrative superior who appointed him and has power to dismiss him. He attains office, and maintains tenure of office by demonstrating his loyalty to his immediate political superior through the practice of *gaisuwa* as a means of showing allegiance or *cafka*. His interest in maintaining tenure of office leads the chief to avoid acting in a manner which conflicts with the interests of his superior, the *hakimi* (formerly the fief-holder, but nowadays the District Head). Thus the chief of a local community, as the client of an official who is the link between the community he controls and the state which sanctions his authority.

Within the community, officials and title-holders are clients of the community chief in the same way that the chief himself is a client of his political superior, and the chieftainship itself is an object of intense political competition between persons eligible by birth for appointment, who in turn attract clients in proportion to the local estimate of their prospects. Thus the institution of chieftainship, as the nexus of relations of clientage, contributes to the integration of the group under its authority to a greater degree than any other institution. At the community level the chieftainship in its range determines the boundaries of the community; in the competition, interest and activities it develops it activates and organises community sentiment; through its relations of clientage with superior authority, it subordinates and integrates the community of its concern into the life and structure of the state, and by its presence in the form and with the attributes of rank outlines above, it gives the community a hierarchic order and structure. The same is true, *in ratione ordinis,* of the state. A simple way in which these propositions may be tested is to try to imagine a chieftainless Hausa community, and to enquire, in the light of that experience, why such a thing is impossible.[17]

Whereas Abuja was an independent state, Zazzau was a vassal state under the suzerainty of the Sultan of Sokoto, who chose the king of Zazzau from one of its three principal dynasties. Zazzau also had states which were its vassal states but the king of Zazzau had less power of appointment to their chieftainships than did the Sultan of Sokoto over the kingship of Zazzau. Within his own kingdom, however, the king of Zazzau had vastly greater power over appointment and dismissal to office, promotion, and the creation of new office than did the king of Abuja.

The role of the Habe in the political system of Zazzau was confined principally to that of minor officials who were tax collectors.

---

17. Smith, *Economy of the Hausa Communities,* 12.

Both racial attitude and ideology, particularly the latter, justified placing the Habe in such a subordinate position. The Fulani achieved and maintained their power in a context of the mission of expanding and conserving the Muhammadan religion.

The senior officers of the state were *hakimai,* that is, territorial administrators or overlords of fiefs alloted to them by virtue of the office which they held. They participated in the division of the booty of war, notably slaves, by virtue of their military roles. They could profitably settle the slaves thus acquired in villages, which they also owned, where their labor was a continuing source of profit. An additional possible source of profit for the *hakimai* was in the role of tax collector, for they were privileged to take a certain portion of the taxes which they gathered before passing them on to the king. From their share, however, they were expected to pay the expenses of their office. The obligations of office included the maintenance of good order, the provision of military forces, the maintenance of public buildings, town walls, mosque, market, caravan routes, the observance of Muhammadan law and religion, and controlling within due limits the exercise of authority by local chiefs.

The rewards of slaves and slave-holding, the pecuniary advantages incident to tax collection, and the high value which was attached to the power and status of office, meant that the opportunity to hold office was much prized. Indeed, it was said that within a few years after the establishment of the empire of the Sultan of Sokoto, it had degenerated into "an assemblage of slave-raiding and tax-extorting fiefs."[18] Control of the political system, including access to office, rested in the king. His opportunities for gain from the political system were the largest of all, he was the wealthiest and most powerful of all men. Thus the dynasties competed for the kingship, and the king, upon his accession, rewarded the members of his lineage with office because they would then become his loyal supporters. There was a wholesale turnover in office with each new regime. Care in appointment to and supervision of office was, however, always necessary. The king must never permit the power of any person or group, including the military, to become so great as to become the starting point of a civil war. "Effective kingship included among its rewards the appointment of one's kin and supporters to office, the exclusion of rivals from such positions, and the accumulation of wealth and influence by military action, slave-raiding, taxation, and the like."

The total system of political action and administration was summarized as follows:

---

18. Trimingham, *Islam in West Africa,* 142.

Under the Fulani, office was an administrative organ, the king controlled the administrative structure, and the system of political relations was sharply distinguished from the administrative; at the same time, political considerations controlled administrative appointments, which were usually made and terminated on political grounds, and the administrative and political functions of government were closely identified. Within the limitations set by his dynastic context and his vassalage to Sokoto, the Fulani king ruled dictatorially; and although he had the power to decide policy, he consulted his officials on various issues as he saw fit. In the Fulani state officials were expected to execute the king's commands and to remain politically loyal. Although the Fulani kingship was the source of authority, authority was decentralized and delegated to fief-holders whose political relations with the king also gave them power. Effectively, the king and his officials formed a ruling bureaucracy, whose power, although neither total, absolute, nor indefinite in duration, was overwhelming while it lasted, and being legitimated by conditions of appointment, was in part expressed as authority.[19]

The doctrine of *imamci* enjoined obedience to the *imam,* or leader of the religious community. Those who questioned his authority and rulings were enemies of God. Ordinarily, however, it was a difficult task to refashion the Islamic ideal of a community of the faithful under the leadership of the *imam* so that it would become the ideological basis of a hierarchical state under a chief whose pagan spiritual authority supported his temporal exercise of authority. Dualism of religious attachment by the members of a state possessing a pagan foundation and an Islamic superstructure was the usual initial outcome.[20]

COMPARISON WITH THE NUPE POLITICAL ORGANIZATION

It is safe to say that consensus and authority are primary means for integrating human groups and coordinating their action. Consensus of values and goals and closeness of interpersonal relationships characterize the community to a much greater degree than does the exercise of authority. The use of force to support authority is much more a requisite for state action than it is for community action. The groups which a state must hold together have too diverse systems of values and hold their values with too great intensity for their control to be accomplished without the sanction of force.

The Tallensi and the Ashanti represented groups whose political organization reflected consensus, shared traditions, and common values to a greater degree than was present in the dominance of the Fulani and the Nupe. The conquering Fulani imposed on the conquered people of the Nupe a superstructure of political authority

---

19. Smith, *Government in Zazzau,* Chap. 4, quotations at 120-121, 124.
20. Trimingham, *op. cit.,* pp. 138-147.

supported by an alien religion and system of law. As in the Hausa-Fulani state, the Nupe state represented a system of political action the control of which was captured by a sub-system, namely, the dynastic families. These dynasties shared succession to the control of the apparatus of government in accordance with established principles.

Growth of the Nupe Empire in the days before the Fulani conquest took place toward the north. The Fulani expansion possessed a southward direction which continued after the absorption of the Nupe. Both manifested similar motivations. The desire for the booty of slaves, the need to pacify adjacent areas and to prevent raids by neighboring states and tribes led to successive steps of expansion beyond state boundaries. As conquered territories increased in relative size to the expanding core territory and people, force was increasingly used to preserve the authority of the conquering group. Thus war was the instrument both to constitute new political authority over conquered peoples and territory and to consolidate and support that authority.

The classification of the territories of the Nupe state reflected the above described mode of adaptation by the state to its surrounding territory. There was the kingdom proper, which consisted of, first, an inner core of countries which were the nucleous of the expanding kingdom, second, the town of Bida, the seat of the central government, and third, the remaining territories of the kingdom proper. In addition, there was a fourth zone of the conquered lands outside the territory of the kingdom. These were termed the Outside Peoples. They were considered to be dependent territories under the protection of Bida, but this protection meant only that they were given some assurance that other states could not raid or levy taxes upon them, but Bida remained free to raid her own territories. They were required to pay an annual tribute in slaves.

The relationship of clientage provided security and a means for social mobility upwards. A person who found himself in an exposed position as against one feudal lord could seek the protection of another by making a gift and a declaration of allegiance and by attaching himself to the household of his patron. The client received support, possibly rank, and an opportunity to better his fortunes. As a result of this process, the patron gained servants, soldiers, and followers, all of which added to his prestige and power.

Succession to the office of the king was regularized by a system in which the king was drawn from one of three royal houses on a rotation basis. When the head of one royal house was elevated to the office of *Etsu,* or king, the head of the royal house next in succession took the title of *Shaba,* which meant that he was the presumptive heir to the kingship, while the head of the third royal house was known as the *Kpotū.*[21]

COMPARISON WITH THE RUANDA POLITICAL ORGANIZATION

A study by Jacques J. Maquet[22] of the relationships between the Tutsi, the Hutu, and the Twa and in particular between the Tutsi and the Hutu in Ruanda illuminates the theme of Fulani domination of the Habe and the practice of clientage in Zazzau. The salient forces giving rise to the clientage system exist in Ruanda in such bold relief that it is possible to grasp the significance of the clientage system in a unique way. Its appearance in other societies is accompanied by ameliorating factors which tend to hide the stark realities which create it.

The Tutsi are a people who emigrated into Ruanda as part of a great southbound pastoral migration. They are a small minority. In 1956 they represented 16.59 per cent of the population, while the Hutu were 82.74 per cent and the Twa were 0.67 per cent. They were probably never more than 10 to 15 per cent of the population. The Twa were probably the first inhabitants. They are hunters and of pygmoid structure. The Hutu are agriculturalists, of middle stature, and have wooly hair, a flat broad nose, and thick lips. The Tutsi are slender, tall, and have a light brown color and often a straight nose. They are pastoralists.

The Tutsi conquest of Ruanda seems to have occurred as a consequence of gradual settlement and assumption of power. The resulting culture emphasized their superiority in race, type of personality, and characteristic roles. They held themselves aloof from the other races. They monopolized political power, administrative office—only a few minor offices were open to the Hutu—and the army. The most valued of all goods were cattle, ownership of which the Tutsi controlled through the clientage system and the overriding right of the king to dispossess anyone of his cattle, including a Tutsi.

Ruanda has an economy which has always been pressed to supply the demands of the Tutsi élite and the Hutu commoners. Indeed, much of the art of governing has been in knowing how closely to press demands for taxes or tribute to the point where they will cease

---

21. S. F. Nadel, *A Black Byzantium* (London, New York, Toronto, 1942), 24-25, 67-68, 84-85, 88-89, 114-115, 122-124.

22. J. J. Maquet, *The Premise of Inequality: A Study of Political Relations in a Central African Kingdom* (London, Ibadan, Accra, 1961), Chaps. 1, 5-8.

to be tolerated and will result in Hutu fleeing the territory. The political, administrative, and military systems have to be understood as consistently directed to levying toll upon the commoners for the benefit of the king, the great Tutsi families, and those participating in the administrative and military systems.

The army carried out a policy expressed in imperialism and ethnocentricism. The army existed to conquer adjacent lands, to preserve Ruanda dominance over them, and to make captives and take loot. The army also acted as an agency to redistribute wealth, principally in the form of cattle, the most prized possession. The Ruanda people were held to be different from those of other lands. The king had a divine origin. The land was the residence of the high god. The Tutsi were superior to all others.

The administrative system existed primarily to collect and distribute tributes and dues for the benefit of the king and the occupants of the administrative structure. It exploited taxpayers by gathering consumption goods for the benefit of the rulers. The land-chiefs exacted the dues from agriculture and the cattle-chiefs those from stock. They were assisted by the hill-chiefs as subordinates. Some Hutu were appointed land-chiefs and hill-chiefs but never cattle-chiefs. About two-thirds of the agricultural produce collected by the various chiefs were retained by them. Otherwise, the king and his spouses received the benefits of the taxing system. He used them for his personal advantage and to maintain the political structure and his paramount position in it.

In a world where the ability to exert dominance or social power was centered in the Tutsi people generally and was distributed among the Tutsi as individuals in varying degrees, the clientage system provided those who were weak in social power with a way of placing themselves under the protection of those who possessed power. The Hutu who had acquired an increment of cattle, the Tutsi who was at the lower end of social power in his group, each found it advantageous to identify himself with a person possessing higher social power. In a society whose norms protecting person and property from violent appropriation were not supported by authoritative courts dispensing equal justice to all comers, it was necessary for those who were vulnerable to power pressures to increase the amount of power at their disposal. Only by assuming the role of client of a strong protector could the weak escape the rapacity of the strong.

Clientage represented a type of feudality in that a socially inferior and weaker client offered his services to a more powerful superior in return for his patronage. The ceremony in which the respective roles and their accompanying obligations were assumed was marked by the symbolic offer of a gift by the client, a petition for milk, riches, and protection, and a statement that the patron shall be the father and the client his child (thereby indicating familiar roles to be the guides of action). The patron showed his acceptance of his role by the gift of one or several cows. The client enjoyed the usufruct of the cows, support in lawsuits, and aid in time of need. He thus participated in the control of cattle, as the highest economic good, and received a measure of protection against catastrophe. The lord enjoyed the attendance of his clients in his travels, their services in his fields, in tending his cattle, and in war, as well as other perquisities, such as a share in their agricultural produce.

The system made it possible for the dominant Tutsi class to enhance their power and to enjoy a leisure marked by comforts not available to the lower groups. It also secured their possession of such benefits by creating a check on those who might use their power to exploit the lower groups to a point of intolerability and resort to escape from the land.

The premise of inequality between the superior Tutsi and the inferior Hutu and Twa was culturally demonstrated in a number of ways, all of which served to perpetuate the system. Personality types were considered to reflect the social differences. The Tutsi were thought to be intelligent, astute, authoritarian, refined, courageous, and cruel. The Hutu were considered to be less intelligent, industrious, strong, obedient, and crude in manners. The Twa were held to be gluttonous, lazy, loyal to their masters, and courageous in the hunt.

Tutsi training of the young inculcated the virtues of self-mastery or control of the emotions in all circumstances, trustworthiness in keeping promises, generosity to friends, liberality to the poor, and courage in carrying out responsibilities. Instruction in war and raiding was given.

An ideology of superiority of the Tutsi existed in the divine right of the king and the innate superior endowment of admired cultural traits. The notions of superiority and inferiority infused many social relations. Paternalistic and dependent attitudes were typical of many role relations not limited to those of clientage. The superior was held to have the right to intervene in the whole of the subordinate's activities. The necessary foundations for a free contractual relationship based on the equality of the contracting parties were lacking. An inferior's verbal behavior toward a superior was supposed to express dependence rather than that of a truth distasteful to the superior. The superior manifested a tendency towards arrogance and command, on the one hand, and protection and compassion, on the other hand. Behavior of the inferior must conform to the superior's expectations.

It is interesting to note some parallels in the world today of unequal social power, the practice of clientage, and the struggles of rival groups for power, as revealed in Ruanda and Zazzau political action. The premise of inequality explored by Maquet is to a considerable extent found in the position of superiority and dominance in political and economic action enjoyed by members of the Communist Party in the Soviet and other Communist states. They represent an élite class enjoying a high standard of living, as compared with the proletariat, in an economy which has little reserves to meet its many demands. Their position is fortified by an ideology of mission, separateness from the rest of society, and creed of social responsibility, personal rectitude, and dedication. Struggle for power is marked by power cliques with which individuals must identify themselves. Escape from the system on the part of those dissenting from it is prevented by force, as well as a careful noting by the élite class of evidences of restlessness when pressures of exploitation become too severe.

The practice of clientage and the development of power groups with which the weaker might align themselves have their counterparts in the relations of states. In his study of the Kede, Nadel noted that feuds and factional splits within the hereditary ruling class became the means to limit the absolute power of the king and to achieve a "more equitable balance of power." He added the significant remark: "Attachment to one of the rival factions is also the only means by which the subject classes, the commoners with no rank and office, could exercise an indirect influence upon the political management of their country."[23]

The use of foreign aid by the United States, Russia, France, and China may be said to create a group of client states which will, at least to some extent and when no fundamental cleavage of interest exists, support the policies of the patron state. Alliances, balance of power groupings, and voting blocs exhibit something of an identity with the motivating circumstances of rivalry and feuding among groups in African political systems. The abuse of power by power-

---

23. S. F. Nadel, "The Kede: A Riverain State in Northern Nigeria," *African Political Systems,* eds. M. Fortes and E. E. Evans-Pritchard (London, New York, Toronto, 1940), 177-178, quotation at 178.

ful states in their external relations, and the absence of an effective supranational political and legal system, have their inevitable outcome in alignments of states designed to restrain at least some of the abuses of the uncontrolled exercise of power.

Religion: Impact of Islam

A description of the religious practice of the bush Habe prior to the Fulani conquest and the impact of Islam upon their religion and ritual was provided above in the section on the bush Habe. A description of the impact of Islamic upon the social and economic life of the Hausa was included in the section above entitled "Social and Economic Organization of the Hausa." This section will supplement such descriptions by directing attention to certain other major aspects of the Islamic way of life as it affected the peoples of West Africa with which it came in contact.

Islam provided in the *Shari'a,* or its doctrine of the whole duty of man, a new and comprehensive pattern for the conduct of the life of individual in all of its manifestations, in the relations of the family, of commerce, and in the spiritual realm. At all times, its teaching had the quality of revealed and immutable rules which could not be questioned and were open to learning and practice by any individual. The accessibility of Islam appealed to the town-dweller, the trader, the nomad, and the member of a society comprised of diverse peoples under uniform authority. It was a religion for the layman and made no severe demands for change in his outlook and way of life. Yet the agriculturalist, living in or near a village community, acting in kinship structures, having a system of religious beliefs which tied all the elements of his life and welfare into an organic whole, found little to attract him to Islam.

Islam was carried by the traders and the clergy into West Africa, and its first appeal was to the traders and the town-dwellers. It was also the religion of a conquering people. In the Hausa states, it was the Fulani engaged in a holy war who created the theocratic state typical of the West Sudan in the nineteenth century.

Once established in the political and legal system, Islam tended to erode old beliefs and rules of conduct. The process of islamization was slow and uneven in its impact, but it was steady. It was manifested in the acceptance of Islamic law at first in certain aspects of native life and then as a parallel system of law accompanying the customary law. There would ensue an acceptance of the basic "pillars" of the Islamic way, the confession of faith, the ritual of prayer, the periods of fast, the giving of alms, and the pilgrimage to Mecca. Other modes of Islamic conduct would be followed, such as in the rites of passage in naming, circumcision, marriage, and death, as well as the observance of other common rites and prohibitions. The spiritual power of Islam, as manifested in the actions of the clergy, would be accepted as a fact. Nevertheless, there generally remained a pagan substructure of religious beliefs not wholly destroyed by Islam.[24]

Law, Including the Impact of Islam

The system of judicial administration in the Hausa-Fulani state of Zazzau consisted of the chief of the village, the *hakimi* or fief-holder, the *Salenke,* and the *Alkali.* The chief decided land issues and minor offenses not carrying severe penalties, such as mutilation or execution. The more serious charges were referred to the capital at Zaria for decision.

The *hakimai* were responsible to the king for the observance of Muhammadan law within their fiefs. They were also obliged to make sure that the local chiefs did not exceed their authority. They had no officially constituted courts but frequently decided cases of magic, tyranny, and matters relating to land.

The Habe possessed the court of the *Salenke,* established in Zaria. The *Salenke* accompanied the army in war and decided all issues which arose there. In time of peace, he also sat in court in the capital and may have had jurisdiction over serious offenses.

The Fulani conquerors established a new court in Zaria under the *Alkali,* which heard offenses involving severe punishment, such as mutilation or execution, as well as appeals from the *Salenke.* The king decided boundary issues and such disputes involving customary and Islamic law as were referred to him. He acted as executive of the *Alkali* court, caused offenders to be brought to trial, and executed sentences through his police. The king was also responsible for the correction of abuse in the exercise of political or administrative power. However, the courts which were established to carry out this function failed in their mission, since dismissal from office was governed primarily by political or power considerations instead of malfeasance of office.[25]

---

24. Trimingham, *op. cit.,* Chap. 2.
25. *Ibid.,* pp. 90-106.

Examination should be made of the scope, meaning, and structure of Islamic law at this point. It is an important body of law in both West and East Africa. Where it has established itself in competition with native customary law, the breadth of its jurisdiction seems steadily to expand. S. F. Nadel described the process in the following terms:

> Two competing authorities of different range of power existing side by side and concerned with the same or closely similar domains of social life must be in danger of frustrating each other, as individuals dissatisfied with the decisions of one may be tmpted to obtain help from the other. The elimination or (as in Nupe) surrender of the weaker authority is the result. Family heads could maintain their paternal authority only by appealing for support to that authority which had superseded their own in other social domains. We may formulate it almost as a social law that an expanding system of jurisdiction, once it begins to supersede another weaker system of jurisdiction, is bound to expand further; culture change in this sphere appears to be carried on by its own momentum.[26]

The word "Islam" means to surrender completely to the will of Allah or God. This requires that a Muslim should pursue the beauty in life and character, as expressed in the revealed way of God. Every human action is deemed to possess an ethical quality; it is either beautiful and suitable or ugly and unsuitable. This quality is not to be determined by human reason. It is instead laid down authoritatively for all time through divine revelation. The law of God, as revealed to man, is obligatory, even though it is incapable of enforcement through the state or cannot otherwise be enforced.

Islamic law is a law of duties and these are a part of the *Shari'a,* which means the path to be followed or to the totality of God's commands to man. It represents an infallible guide to ethical conduct. The *Shari'a* covers all forms of action and indicates that which is (1) commanded, (2) recommended, (3) permitted, (4) reprehended, or (5) prohibited by God. Of these categories of conduct, the central norm is that of permission. All acts are permitted until some authority, the nature of which will be indicated below, can be found to place them in some one of the first two positive classes or the last two negative classes. The *Shari'a* alone expresses what is right and wrong. Since the law thus indicated is the word of God as revealed to man and concerns the relation between God and man, Islamic law is strongly individualistic in character.

Fiqh means literally intelligence or understanding and refers to the science of the law. The law was derived from four main sources,

---

26. Nadel, *op. cit.,* p. 168.

(1) the word of God as found in the Qoran, (2) the traditions, consisting of the practice of the Prophet and his companions, which appears to have been much more a product of fabrication than of historical fact,[27] (3) the consensus of the founders of the law or of the community as expressed by its most learned members, and (4) opinion, as reached by strict analogical reasoning.

The scope of law, as stated above, covered the entire field of human conduct. The end of law was to preserve the species and promote the welfare of the individual and society. The doctrine of the permissibility of human acts, as stated above, provided freedom for man under the protection of God from oppression by an irresponsible ruler. Yet the law never developed a constitutional check on the exercise of despotism.

Four principal schools of law developed, the *Hanafi, Maliki, Shafi'i,* and *Hanbali*. The *Maliki* school is the one almost entirely followed in Northwest Africa, from Nigeria to the Gulf of Tunis, as well as in certain other regions. It recognized custom to a greater degree than any other school. Its jurists have said that "customary law has the force of law" and that "ancient custom should if possible be brought under one of the known rubrics of law, but is valid even when it cannot be so brought." The *Maliki* school was introduced into West Africa at a very early time and developed fairly free from oriental influence.

West Africans were attracted to Islam because of its teaching that it was a great brotherhood. Uprooted individuals, torn from their community, are in particular attracted to Islam. The acceptance of Islam did not, however, imply full acceptance of the *Shari'a.* Islam has a breadth which enables it to absorb the detribalized in all ways of their lives but the will to undergo such a complete absorption seemed to be lacking. There was on the whole, little integration of the conduct of West African Muslims with standard Islamic practice. The resulting system was dualistic. Those who were pagans often did not accept the swearing of an oath and the rendering of a decree by an Islamic court as binding.

The rigidity of Islamic rules of conduct, a consequence of their divine prescription, made difficult adjustment by the Muslim community to changing conditions. There was accordingly a need for a basic reform of the Islamic legal system.[28]

---

27. J. Schacht, *Origins of Muhammadan Jurisprudence* (Oxford, 1950).

28. J. N. D. Anderson, *Islamic Law in the Modern World* (New York, 1959), 3-19; A. A. A. Fyzee, *Outlines of Muhammadan Law* (2d ed.; London, 1955), 15-18; M. Khadduri and H. J. Liebesny, *Law in the Middle East* (Washington,

Law: Comparison with the Nupe System

Most offenses in Nupe were subject to control by the coercive machinery of the state. At the local level, this was the chief and the elders and, in the fief, the delegate of the fief-holder, in consultation with the chief and elders. At the level of the central authority of the state, control was exercised by the *Alkali* and the king's court in Bida. Nevertheless, there was a body of offenses subject to control by other mechanisms outside the state, such as public ostracism or the intervention of the deity. These were religious offenses or kinship offenses, the latter comprising offenses limited to a single kinship group. Religious offenses included desecration of sacred objects or places, whether pagan or Muhammadan. Kinship offenses concerned friction within a kinship group, such as issues of inheritance, marriages in forbidden degree, and incest, and did not include offenses involving relations between kinship groups.

Within the state system, the local authority had jurisdiction over minor delicts where the penalty was not more severe than the imposition of reparation for damage done. Such offenses were small debts and thefts, seduction of a girl by an unmarried man who was willing to marry her, and adultery. The punishments were fines, flogging, and a formalized procedure of public ridicule. The central authority had the power to impose penalties, which included capital punishment. It had jurisdiction over cases involving large debts and thefts, certain types of adultery and seduction, murder, manslaughter, highway robbery, arson, high treason, and *lèse-majesté* or abuse of the king. Prosecution of an offense took place only when a plaintiff brought a charge, the state itself initiated action only in cases of *lèse-majesté*.

The clash between customary and Muhammadan law and the fact that the rules of each were appropriate to its particular type of order was revealed in litigation over inheritance. Customary law ruled that property and land should be inherited by the youngest brother of the

D.C., 1955), 85, 99, 106; A. Rahim, *The Principles of Muhammadan Jurisprudence* (London, Madras, 1911), 56; Smith, *Government in Zazzau*, 90-106; Trimingham, *op. cit.*, pp. 193-194, 205; S. Vesey-Fitzgerald, *Muhammadan Law* (London, 1931), 1-14; W. M. Watt, *Islam and the Integration of Society* (London, 1961), 136-138, 280-281; J. A. Williams (ed.), *Islam* (New York, 1961), 92-93. See also F. A. Ajayi, "The Future of Customary Law in Nigeria," and J. N. D. Anderson, "Customary Law and Islamic Law in British African Territories," in *Afrika-Instituut, The Future of Customary Law in Africa* (Leiden, 1956), 42, 70 respectively.

deceased family head. His sons and his brothers' sons were expected to stay and work the land under the new owner, who assumed in effect the role of a substitute father. Such a rule preserved the farming unit intact. The Muhammadan rule of inheritance, arising in an economy where property was mostly movables, that is, money, trade goods, or cattle, was that an inheritance of a father should be divided equally among his sons. The imposition of such a rule would destroy the farming unit when the father who owned it died. Yet, in modern Nupe, it is possible to cause the Muhammadan rule to prevail over the customary rule.[29]

Conclusion

The Hausa-Fulani states and the Nupe state revealed a new type of political system of extraordinary complexity. The operation of this system evidenced a number of most significant aspects. These states were the outcome of a situation in which one people, originally possessing a unique type of physical structure, language, way of life, religion, and law, conquered and ruled other peoples differing greatly in these respects. Rule by the conquering people was directed largely to exploitation of the subject peoples, instead of integration and shared opportunities for value realization. The states thus created embodied an alien élite whose philosophy was that of preserving their social distance or separateness from the underlying mass and their monopoly of political and economic advantage. The ruling Fulani class, as a group, were also characterized by a greater degree of islamization than the conquered peoples. Even when intermarriage with the latter had changed the physical characteristics of the Fulani stock and they had otherwise considerably merged with the conquered peoples, the Fulani still clung to an image of racial separateness and superiority.

The open savanna or orchard bush land made their dwellers vulnerable to armed attack and slave raiding. This insecurity led to the centering of life in villages and towns behind walls and the cultivation of outlying farms. Families lived in compounds of related households, which were clustered in such a manner as to provide security from attack.

---

29. Nadel, *op. cit.*, pp. 165-173. For the variety of influences affecting decisions concerning inheritance and succession in Hausa courts, see M. G. Smith, "Hausa Inheritance and Succession," *Studies in the Laws of Succession in Nigeria*, ed. J. D. M. Jerrett (London, 1965), 230.

The bush Habe were farmers, while the bush Fulani were pastoralists who were either nomadic or semi-settled peoples, following patterns of transhumance in the care of their cattle. Many Fulani, however, became settled in towns. The pastoral Fulani established patterns of trade of milk, and, to a certain extent, meat, with the agricultural bush Habe.

The system of political action was a balance-of-power system, the equilibrium of which was maintained by the following forces:

(1) The manipulation by the king of rewards and deprivations to his followers and opponents, through grants of office, fiefs, slaves, and gifts, on the one hand, and dismissal from office and removal of control of fiefs, on the other hand. The king was the most politically powerful and wealthy person in the kingdom and thereby possessed the necessary resources to make his influence effective in this manner so as to maintain the system and his paramountcy in it. While the king in the Hausa state of Zazzau had less effective political power than the king of the Nupe, both represented the most powerful single person in the state. The state was a monocracy in the sense that the king possessed authority to make appointments to offices of the state, though he exercised that authority in the light of power considerations.

(2) A system of control of succession to the kingship. The Habe state of Abuja had a monodynastic system in the form of a single royal lineage. The Hausa state of Zazzau controlled succession from four eligible dynasties through a set of constitutional rules, the most important of which were that a king should not be chosen from the dynasty of his predecessor and should himself be of royal blood. Succession in the Nupe state was handled by a system of rotation among three royal houses.

(3) The existence of a degree of social mobility to positions of greater power, prestige, and wealth on the part of those who were less well advantaged.

The political organization of the Hausa and Nupe states could well be described as representing a political economy. The state was an instrument which the ruling class used to achieve economic benefit in the accumulation, sale and use of slaves. The outlying territories of the state were linked with the territory of the state in a system in which war was waged to capture slaves to be sold in the markets and used in office, army, household, and farms. Steady expansion of the territory of the empire or state took place in the operation of this system. However, in the Nupe kingdom this process was regularized in a most unusual manner. Beyond the kingdom proper lay the territory of the Outside Peoples. This represented a preserve of potential slaves to be captured by raiding by the nominally protecting state. The protection which was extended was in fact merely against poaching on the preserve by would-be raiders from other regions.

The Hausa and Nupe states appear most closely to resemble the modern state in their political organization. Yet this resemblance was more a matter of form than of substance. The modern, welfare state typical of the Atlantic basin is characterized by widespread value realization, a considerable degree of social mobility and absence of social distance among classes, and a consensus upon national goals and a high degree of goal-attainment. Such a state does not require the measure of force to sustain authority which was utilized in the Hausa and Nupe states. The latter rather resemble the "veneer" states characteristic of the developing nations today. The author has elsewhere described them as possessing a thin veneer of élite of government personnel, businessmen, landowners, and the professions, constituting a superstructure over a submerged mass of industrial proletariat in the cities and peasants on the landed estates.[30]

The vicissitudes of a life in which a man would find himself in a secure position of political favor today and its loss tomorrow gave impetus to the growth of the institution of clientage. Those seeking political and social advantage otherwise denied them sought the protection of a patron, served him in his home or joined his military followers, and thereby often found a route to a modicum of well-being.

Slaves permeated life. Slaves held political office, formed armies, worked fiefs in slave villages, and carried out household tasks under their owner. Slaves were wealth, a liquid asset which could be readily realized through sale, and a highly profitable status-creating asset otherwise.

The ruling Fulani achieved power through a conquest professedly motivated by a holy war to bring Islam in a purer form to peoples who were pagan or only partially islamized. The resulting religious pattern was a dualistic one, in which Islam still had not permeated the kingdom and there was a situation of dualistic religious attachment. Islam tended to break down the clan and extended family structures and to promote the simple, nuclear family and the in-

---

30. K. S. Carlston, *Law and Organization in World Society* (Urbana, 1962), Chap. 4.

dividual in the society. It was difficult for Islam to destroy the unity of a religion in which family, kin, and tribal welfare were tied in with a world of spirits dispensing fortune, or at least averting misfortune, to those faithful in ritual performance.

Just as there was a dualistic religious system, so there was a dualistic legal system. In many situations, customary law was applied to pagan litigants, instead of Muhammadan law. Yet the scope of jurisdiction of Muhammadan law seemed, on the whole, to be expanding. Its law of inheritance was less suitable to an agricultural community than it was to an urban, trading community. Its central norm of permissiveness of action tended to provide a certain security of liberty in human affairs. There was a fairly clear delineation of offenses subject to judicial control. A defined system of judicial administration existed, ranging from the courts of the local chiefs and fief-holders to the courts of the *Alkali,* king, and *Salenke* at the capital. The courts of the capital had the more comprehensive jurisdiction.

It is surmised that the cleavage between the ruling town Fulani and the Habe of the provinces may have been the source of much tension. A situation in which a major group of society is denied in most substantial measure access to the full range of political and economic action is clearly an unstable one. When this is accentuated by a persistent attitude of separateness and superiority by the dominant race and ruling class, together with adherence by the latter to a different religion and law, the ensuing situation would appear to be one in which there was a lack of integration and cohesion. Attitudes of frustration and hostility existed on the part of the submerged people. It seems probable that the long period of British rule, the gradual abolition of the institution of slavery, and the growth of political and legal institutions less open to manipulation for private advantage by the ruling élite, considerably lessened this source of tension with the passage of time.

The need for a unifying principle to bring into a single group and common identification the many peoples of Africa is supplied by one of the basic principles of Islam, that of brotherhood. The Prophet taught: "The Arab is not superior to the non-Arab; the non-Arab is not superior to the Arab. You are all sons of Adam, and Adam was made of Earth. Verily all Muslims are brothers."[31] Unfortunately, the formal patterns of Islamic ritual were accepted by

---

31. Fyzee, *op. cit.,* p. 13.

its followers to a much greater extent than its inner meaning and substance. If the teaching of brotherhood could be grasped and held, a new path to African political unity would be opened. Without some such concept of common identity and interest, an Africa of many small, non-viable states and diverse tribal backgrounds may well become the Balkans of the future world.

Chapter 7

The Yoruba

Geography and Economy

THE YORUBA are a people who live in southwestern Nigeria and western Dahomey and constituted about two dozen tribes. They are an agricultural people, who are also shrewd traders and skilled in a number of crafts, such as weaving, dyeing, pottery making, and metal and leather work. They speak Yoruba, which is a dialect cluster of the Kwa languages of West Africa. The dialects are not wholly mutually intelligible.

The land which they occupy comprises a narrow coastal zone lying only slightly above sea level, a coastal plain, and an interior plateau, which becomes a forest, thins out, and ends in tall grass.

Wars with Dahomey took place in the eighteenth century, while the nineteenth century was marked by incursions from the Benin and the Fulani, civil wars among the kingdoms, and constant slave raiding. At times, whole towns had to be abandoned as a result of war, and new towns created.

The Yoruba are a people who have learned to live in towns, to engage in trade and pursue crafts, and to create a symbiotic relationship of town and farm. The literature on them does not create as detailed a picture as is provided for some of the other peoples of West Africa herein studied. It is significant, however, for the light it throws on the conditions of urbanization and the development of land law.[1]

---

1. D. Forde, "The Yoruba-Speaking Peoples of South-Western Nigeria," *Ethnographic Survey of Africa*, ed. D. Forde (London, 1951), Western Africa, Part IV, 1-10; P. C. Lloyd, "The Yoruba Lineage," *Africa*, XXV (1955), 234.

Religion and Concept of the Individual Personality

Morton-Williams' recent studies of the Yoruba belief system revealed a remarkable structure. The cosmos was composed of three
levels, the sky, the world, and the earth. The sky and the earth
embraced the world, which was the place of the living. It was the
ordered world where life was properly lived. The sky was the domain
of Olorun Oldumare, the supreme god. He was the source of the
power of his subjects, the *orisa* or gods, who influenced relations
between the sky and the world and thereby affected what goes on in
the world. The sky was also the dwelling place of the sky-people, who
were spirit doubles of the living and souls awaiting rebirth. The
earth was the domain of the goddess, Onile. The earth was the dwelling place of the ancesters and other dead. The ancestors bestowed
children, health, and prosperity and punished lineage members who
failed to maintain proper relationships with the community or to
observe proper behavior. The *Ogboni* was the earth cult and performed political and judicial functions, including ultimate power of
life and death over the *oba* for the proper performance of his governing role and offenses involving the spilling of blood. The principal
organ of the *Ogboni* was the *Oyo Misi* or council of state.

God determined the fate or distinctive character of a person before
he was born. Thereafter he was in the care of the *orisa*. The earth
goddess, Onile, interacted directly with men. Eshu, once regarded
by investigators as the supreme power of evil, seems to have been
the trickster, the messenger of the gods, and the bringer of misfortune. Ifa, the god of divination, revealed the intentions of the
gods. Oro could cleanse a town of witchcraft.

The three orders of the sky, the earth, and the world comprised
the cosmos. It was essential to maintain a proper relation among
them. There were two mediating agents influencing a person's relationship with the cosmos. Ifa, the god of divination, could enable
one to act so as to diminish the intervention of the gods. Eshu's reporting and misrepresentation of man's misdeeds to the gods, resulting in their punishing man, could be avoided by conformity to the
norms and standards of the community.[2]

Other gods were Obatala, the vice-regent of Olurun, and the gods
of lightning and thunder, of iron and war, and of the farm and

2. P. Morton-Williams, "An Outline of the Cosmology and Cult Organization
of the Oyo Yoruba," *Africa*, XXXIV (1964), 243 and "The Yoruba Ogboni Cult
in Oyo," *Africa*, XXX (1960), 362.

harvest. The worship of Oro among the Egba was centered in a cult known as the Oshuobo. Altogether, some 400 lesser gods and spirits were recognized. The spirits of the ancestors were also worshipped by their respective lineages.[3]

The Yoruba conception of the elements of the individual personality was highly refined and bore considerable resemblance to the Ashanti conception of the individual. Man was related to the gods through his spirit, which was the seat of life, and, in a rudimentary sense, might be regarded as similar to the superego or conscience. It was the divine element in man and controlled both the "heart" or "heart-soul" of man and his body. Its use of the body determined its fate when it left the body after death, that of reward, if good, and that of punishment, if evil. The "heart" or "heart-soul" was found in the material heart. It existed before birth and could be reincarnated after death. It left the body during dreams. It was the inner self and mind of man. Man was also found in his body, which was composed of his "physical body" and his "mental body" or mind. These and certain other elements were a unity which expressed itself through the body and the heart as "spirit" or "over-soul," that is, "the larger self which belongs to and is akin to the Supreme Divine Spirit."[4]

The performance of ethical and social obligations was strengthened by a ritualistic assumption of mutual convenants for their performance. The clientage relationship was also undertaken by the recitation of mutual covenants.

The Yoruba esteemed truth and rectitude and condemned the breaking of covenants and the utterance of falsehoods.[5]

Social Organization

The Yoruba were typically a town people, who farmed the outlying area and engaged in trade and the crafts. The town was designed for protection against attack and was surrounded by a wall or bank, an outer ditch, and often a belt of uncleared forest. A pattern of use of outlying farm land by the town dwellers developed, subject to the principle that each farm user had his farm located at not

---

3. J. O. Lucas, *The Religion of the Yorubas* (Lagos, 1948); E. B. Idowu, *Olódùmaré: God in Yoruba Belief* (London, 1962); D. Forde, *op. cit.*, p. 29.
4. Lucas, *op. cit.*, pp. 246-251.
5. Idowu, *op. cit.*, pp. 150-51, 169-62.

much more than one hour's walk, or about three miles, from his compound in town.

The Greek and Italian city-states are suggestive historical counterparts of the Yoruba kingdoms. In Yoruba there were metropolitan towns, which were the residence of the *oba* or king, a surrounding belt of farm land extending for about three miles or an hour's walk, continuing farm land associated with small hamlets, where those who worked the farms slept overnight, and finally subordinate towns which repeated the same organization of resources but on a smaller scale.

There were three types of settlement patterns. The first was the large central town surrounded by farm lands and hamlets, with the subordinate towns at the periphery of the kingdom. The central town was large and tolerated no rivals for its power. Only at an extended distance from the central town did conditions become suitable for subordinate towns.

The second type of settlement had plentiful land, and a man had considerable freedom in locating himself and his family. As land in one village became scarce, he could move to another where he had relatives with whom he could associate. The central town had a belt of farm lands extending for a short distance, but beyond this there were numerous independent villages with clearly defined boundaries.

The third type of settlement was a product of historical accident in that it consisted of central towns peopled largely by refugees and surrounded by farm lands extending over a wide area. There were no subordinate towns, only widely dispersed hamlets. The land held by descent groups was clearly marked. Hamlets served several descent groups but had no territorial boundaries themselves.

Although the Yoruba had achieved a form of urban life, their towns were simply clusters of compounds, each of which was the residence of a lineage group. Their social organization seems to have been little affected by the experience of urbanization, except as pressures on land through concentration of settlement had an impact on land law. The political organization, as will be seen below, assumed a structure which enabled the affairs of town and the state to be handled in bodies of a traditional African character.

Yoruba terms for identifying descent groups were used loosely but the principal types of descent groups seem clear enough. The smallest group was the domestic family of a man, his wife or wives, his unmarried children, and other persons, such as his mother or younger brother. Such a family identified itself with a larger group consisting of descendents of a common male ancestor. This group was a segment of the largest lineage group of all, identified by descent from a founding male ancestor, termed the *idile* or the *ebi*, which was considered to be a permanent entity. Intermediate ancestors might be forgotten as generations succeeded one another, but the identity of the common remote male ancestor of the *idile* remained fixed.

The *idile* was composed of intermediate patrilineal segments at various levels known as *isoko*. These typically consisted of three generations, a man, his sons, and their sons, although occasionally four generations were included.

The identity of the lineage was preserved by its name, myths of origin, songs, and facial markings. Each member of the lineage had his own song which linked him with the lineage. Membership in the lineage gave rise to the right to reside in the lineage compound and to use lineage land, determined one's occupation, importantly affected marriage, provided the link with the ancestor spirits and the gods, and determined political rank and power. The members of the *isoko* tilled the portions of the lineage land which were alloted to them, carried out a lineage craft, and participated jointly in worship of the ancestors and the gods. The above pattern of social structure was not uniform. For example, age sets played an important role in a number of Yoruba kingdoms.[6]

Political Organization

The head of a lineage, the *bale* or *olori ebi*, led the performance of ritual in which the link with the ancestor spirits and the lineage god was affirmed and their favor sought. He maintained harmony among the members of the lineage, arbitrated their disputes, and judged their offenses. He was their representative to the community at large and interceded on behalf of members of the lineage involved in external disputes. He was the final authority in the organization of work and the use of resources. In particular, he allotted the lineage land among its constituent groups and otherwise had final

6. P. C. Lloyd, *Yoruba Land Law* (London, New York, Abadan, 1962), 31-37; D. Forde, *op. cit.*, pp. 10-13; P. C. Lloyd, "The Yoruba Lineage"; W. B. Schwab, "Kinship and Lineage Among the Yoruba," *Africa*, XXV (1955), 352; P. C. Lloyd, "Agnatic and Cognatic Descent among the Yoruba," *Journal of the Royal Anthropological Institute*, I (New Series; 1966), 484.

disposition over the use of the land. The head of an *isoko* or lineage segment occupied a similar role to that of the head of a lineage. He was the repository of authority within the group and its link with the lineage. He determined the disposition of land within the *isoko*. The lineage head, by virtue of his authority as the head of the wider social group, could reject important decisions of the head of the *isoko* and also settle disputes between segments of the lineage. While the above pattern of segmentation was fairly typical, patterns of segmentation varied among the Yoruba people. Thus, in some kingdoms, age-sets were utilized to rank the male members of a society into groups to perform farm labor, road mending and other public work, war, and the holding of office. Titles to offices were distributed among age-sets, in which the senior titles fell to the more senior age-sets, and title associations.

The king was selected from a royal lineage. He was not necessarily the oldest male of that lineage.

A king or other person possessing power could be deposed from his office as a result of arbitrary or tyrannical action by a procedure known as *kirikiri*. A mob would parade through the town or countryside loudly abusing him and ending at his residence, which was pelted with dirt and stones. If he did not leave the country or commit suicide within three months, then a select band of men seized and killed him.

The government of the central city was also that of the state. The paramount ruler was quite generally called the *oba*. His decisions were a product of the deliberations of the council of senior chiefs. The subordinate towns had a similar structure of government and mode of selection of chief.

The *oba* had a sacred character and possessed ritual as well as temporal authority. He brought no property of his own to his office and left his property with his lineage as he assumed his title. He enjoyed a wealth which flowed to him through his office in an amount which evidenced the rank and prosperity of his town and kingdom. Compulsory labor, tithes, tributes, tolls, a large share of the booty of war, and the occupancy of the palace gave him a wealth approaching that of all of the chiefs of the kingdom as a group. When he grossly exceeded or abused his powers, his chiefs could ask him to die and, if he refused, cause his death.

The *oba* and his chiefs were concerned with the public affairs of the town and its relations with other kingdoms, including the power to wage war and to regulate the admission of refugees. They controlled much of the trading activity of the town. They also had certain superior powers in respect of the use of land, which will be described in the next topic.[7]

The political structure of the Yoruba town was linked with the lineage groups living in the town. The immigrant to a town severed almost all his ties with his original lineage, founded his own lineage and received a chieftancy title from the ruler of the town, and received a grant of land from the ruler. Each lineage structure was simple. It had its own compound. It was a patrilineal descent-group tracing its common ancestry for five generations back.[8]

Law: Land Tenure

P. C. Lloyd's *Yoruba Land Law* is a model of anthropological legal research.[9] The native law relating to the control, use, transfer of and succession to land is stated in the context of a careful elaboration of the system of political, social, and economic organization of the people. General descriptions and conclusions are made in Part One of the book, Part Two sets forth specific studies of the four kingdoms of Ondo, Ijebu, Ado, Ekiti, and Egba.

Two principal maxims in respect to the objectives of land law stand out. There must always be an identifiable authority having control over the use of land, and land must be used effectively.

There were three categories of land, first, public land used for a community purpose, second, unallotted land available for granting for private use, and, third, allotted private land in the control of lineages and families.

Those who exercised authority with respect to land were the *oba* and the chiefs, the lineage head, and the head of the lineage segment.

The *oba,* with the advice of his senior chiefs, controlled the use and disposition of public land. The chief, on behalf of the *oba* and senior chiefs, could allot vacant land within the territorial unit which he headed. The chief, in his capacity as head of the quarter in the town, could allot vacant land in the quarter. Finally, where a

---

7. Lloyd, *Yoruba Land Law,* 38-47; D. Forde, *op. cit.,* pp. 19-23; P. C. Lloyd, "Sacred Kingship and Government among the Yoruba," *Africa,* XXX (1960), 221; P. C. Lloyd, "The Traditional Political System of the Yoruba," *Southwestern Journal of Anthropology,* X (1954), 365; A. K. Ajisafe, *The Laws and Customs of the Yoruba People* (Lagos, 1946), 34; S. O. Biobaku, "An Historical Sketch of Egba Traditional Authorities," *Africa,* XXII (1952), 35.

8. Lloyd, "The Yoruba Lineage," 235.

9. Lloyd, *Yoruba Land Law,* 31-37. See also G. B. A. Coker, *Family Property among the Yorubas* (2nd ed.; London, Lagos, 1966).

lineage had a hereditary chieftancy, the chief could handle dealings in land of the lineage with non-members of the group, provided he obtained the group's consent. Ordinarily, however, it was the senior male of the lineage group who acted on its behalf in such matters.

The *oba* and the senior chiefs controlled the ultimate right to use land, including the grant of land to strangers, the power to take land for public use, and the right to the reversion of land which became abandoned for the lack of heirs. The lineage and its segments controlled the actual use of land and the power to dispose of the usufruct, or right to use it, to others.

The identification of permanent interests in land was a product of the availability of vacant land and the difficulty of clearing land. While the Yoruba town was permanent and did not shift its location, private control over the use of land upon a permanent basis did not exist when land was plentiful, except with respect to land which was actually in use. In such a situation, open land was cleared of its bush by a man, was farmed while its fertility remained, and was then abandoned. The community controlled all vacant land and the elders allotted new land to families or individuals when they vacated the old. The abandoned land was allowed to lie fallow until restored and needed again. In situations where clearing land of thick forest entailed tremendous labor, it was felt that the man who expended such labor had a priority to reclaim it after its fallow period and to clear it of its relatively light bush growth. This prior right extended to his children as well.

When land was very short, the lineage acquired permanent rights to the use of the specific portions of land. There was a certain pattern in the growth of interests of lineage groups in land. They might have merely a priority in the right to use land as against others but no power to alienate the right to use it to others. If not used, the land reverted to the community. The next stage was the acquisition of the ability to alienate the right of use the land to others, subject to the consent of the head of the community, if the grantee were a stranger. Finally, the land controlled by the group became fixed by definite boundaries and the group acquired the power to alienate to others any land within those boundaries, whether or not it had been used by lineage members. The power to alienate land to strangers was still subject to the condition that the strangers could and would in time be assimilated in the lineage. If not, the appropriate method for transfer was for the community itself to allot some of its vacant land to the stranger.

Even when private control of the use of land had ripened to its fullest extent, its holder held it subject to the rights of the community to hunt, collect firewood or stone, and pass over it for access to water. Also the *oba* and his chiefs had the governmental power to regulate its use of alienation or to take it over for a public use. In the latter event, however, the descent group which held it must be granted substitute land. It was considered that each descent group joined the community with the understanding that it would always be allowed sufficient land for it needs but no more than it needed. To deprive it of land was to banish it from the community.

Just as the community land fell into the categories of vacant, private, and public land, so did lineage land in an analogous sense. Vacant land was land over which the group had a right to disposition but which no member of the group was using in any specific way. Private land was land allotted to an individual lineage member. He had the right to the exclusive use of the rooms in the compound assigned to his family and the assigned land, together with the privilege to make improvements on the land. Any interference with his sole usufructuary right could be made the subject of complaint to the family meeting or ultimately to the native courts, though the latter were loath to intervene in family disputes. The public land of the lineage consisted of land held for lineage use, notably the compound reserved for the head of the group, and the shrine of the group's god and ancestors.

A man had a right to as much land of his descent group as he needed for his family. During his lifetime, he had a specific right to the land which he in fact used. As his sons matured, he gave them plots to till from his land until, in his old age, he was cultivating no land. Otherwise, his land would be partitioned among the children of each of his wives, the children of each wife being considered as a separate group, and, as such, sharing equally in groups.

The lineage group was a corporate body characterized by the exercise of authority, as it handled land and other matters of importance to the group as a whole. Family meetings were usually held in the portion of the compound occupied by the lineage head. In such meetings and after consensus had been reached to the point that all opposition had ceased, the family head expressed the common view in his rulings. The allocation of rooms in the compound, the allotment of family land, the transfer of land, the bringing of court actions to protect family interests, the settlement of family disputes, all these were handled by the family head, subject to the consent of the group.

The sale or transfer of lineage land to a stranger imported that the rights of the family in and to the land were extinguished, except the right of the reversion, if the land later became ownerless or abandoned. Such a transfer created similar rights in the grantee, including the power to alienate the interest thus acquired. The purchaser did not, as a result of purchase, automatically become a member of the community in which the grantor lived. This was a matter of time and the inclination of the parties concerned. He was usually gradually absorbed into the lineage group and community in which he lived. Until he was so absorbed, it was expected that he would pay the lineage group for the use of its land. Payment of the customary tribute to the *oba* by members of the community was ordinarily not made by the stranger until he had decided to give up his right of residence in his previous home and make the new community his residence and place of allegiance.[10]

Law

The lineage head not only exercised authority in lineage affairs, including marriages and the disposition of land, but he also settled disputes among its members and adjudged certain offenses, such as incest. The paramount sanction supporting the rules and judgments which he laid down was that of the power of the ancestors to bring misfortune. For example, expulsion from the group, which was the physical sanction for incest, was dreaded not so much for its physical deprivations as for the fact that it meant loss of communion with the ancestors and hence eternal misfortune. Nevertheless, the courts of the town and the kingdom visited severe punishments for the commission of offenses, including execution, selling into slavery, castration, imprisonment, and beating.

Appeal from decisions of the lineage head could be made to the court of the chief of the town and appeal from the latter existed to the council of state of the *oba* and his chiefs.

The council of state handled civil disputes between chiefs and a variety of offenses, including murder, manslaughter, treason, burglary, arson, incest, witchcraft, and sorcery. There was a considerable number of crimes, in addition to these. The ordeal was used to discover guilt.

A person having a complaint against another could present it to the head of the district or the appropriate chief and have a trial thereon by paying a fee. If the case involved a private wrong, the

---

10. Lloyd, *op. cit.*, 62-94, 281-282, 285-296.

defendant paid a fee in an equal amount. Both fees were for the benefit of the judge and his associates. The plaintiff testified first, followed by the defendant. Cross-examination of the plaintiff was permitted. On the settlement of the case, there was a ceremonial eating of kola nuts by the disputing parties and all important persons present, a sharing of a glass of wine or liquid, and payment of fine, if ordered. The fine went to the chief or head, unless it represented compensation for private injury, in which event it went to the plaintiff, with a small share to the chief or head. The defendant was required to make an appropriate apology. A failure to share in the kola nuts or drink meant that the case was unsettled and subject to appeal.

It is most significant that a law of contracts had emerged, probably as a consequence of the appearance of trade in Yoruba culture. Contracts could be made enforceable, if made in the presence of witnesses or if both parties admitted that they were in fact made.[11]

Conclusion

In the Yoruba, we have a people exposed to the vicissitudes of war and slave raiding in a fixed environment of towns and surrounding farm land. The country consisted of the three typical West African zones of coastal land, forest, and grass land. The mode of settlement was typically a walled central town surrounded by farm land and hamlets, beyond which lay subordinate towns with their associated farm land and hamlets. Sometimes there was only the central town and its surrounding farms and hamlets. The Yoruba spoke a common language but the dialects were not always mutually intelligible. There was no sense of unity among the people as a whole.

The pattern of government of the largest descent group repeated itself in much the same form as in the central city and kingdom. The head of the lineage was the eldest male, but the ruler of the kingdom was selected from a single royal lineage group. If the lineage head became unacceptable in his role of authority, he was not deposed. Another became the *de facto* head. If the king became unacceptable, he was asked to die. In each case, rule and decision by the head was a product of deliberation and consent by the representatives of the constituent groups of the corporate body.

A remarkable structure of beliefs concerning the supernatural

11. D. Forde, *op. cit.,* p. 24; C. Partridge, "Native Law and Custom in Egbaland," *Journal of the African Society,* X (1911), 422; Ajisafe, *op. cit.,* pp. 27-31, 35-41.

world existed. Man was placed in a relationship with the realms of the sky, the earth, and the world. A supreme god, whose domain was the sky, endowed the lesser gods with their power and determined the fate of man, while the lesser gods influenced his affairs. The earth was the domain of an earth goddess and the dwelling place of the ancestors, who brought fortune to their descendants and punished them for their misdeeds. Man could lessen the harmful impact of the supernatural world through Ifa, the god of divination, and by respect for social norms. Proper behavior averted punishment that might otherwise result from the reports of Eshu, the trickster and the messenger of the gods.

There was a judicial system of third-party decision making in the lineage, the town, and the kingdom at large. Offenses were defined and punishments appropriate to each were fixed, as a matter of custom. Capital punishment and severe physical sanctions were employed by the courts.

The land law was carefully developed to insure that land was always allocated to those who needed it and was kept in cultivation. Interests in land became increasingly well defined as the mode of settlement became more permanent, and land became scarce in relation to those who made claims for its use. The principle might be stated that, from the jural standpoint, lineage and individual interests in land multiplied and became more precise as a result of the permanency of settlement of land and increase in the numbers of users of land. The head of the lineage, the chief, and the *oba* and his senior chiefs, each had their sphere of competence as they made decisions concerning the allocation and use of land among the members of the family, the community, and the kingdoms, respectively. The exercise of authority in such matters was not arbitrary but was a product of joint discussion and consensus in the relevant group or its representatives.

The Yoruba had achieved the cultural innovation of the walled town as a means of protection against attack. The resulting concentration of settlement led to the development of hamlets and subordinate towns, as land near the central town became inadequate to support its population. The necessity of maximizing land use meant the development of a comprehensive system of land law, which emphasized the control of private land as land resources grew more and more scarce. Yet urbanization seems to have been achieved with but little change in social organization, which remained kin-structured. The political organization of king and council of chiefs, chiefs in their own right as heads of quarters or of subordinate towns, and lineage heads, dealt with problems of the town, land use, war, and resolution of conflict. Thus urbanization and the growth of crafts and trade did not produce and did not require any unusual innovation in social or political organization and had its central impact in law in influencing the character of the development of a system of land law.

Chapter 8

The Ibo

Geography and Economy

THE IBO are located in southeastern Nigeria and are among the most numerous of African peoples. They occupy a territory beginning close to the Guinea Coast in the south and extending up to the savanna and orchard bush in the north, bounded mainly by the Cross River in the east, and the Niger in the west. The land has a low elevation and is mostly in the rain forest belt. There is no single tribe but instead many local tribes or groups. The people speak a common language, Ibo, and possess a fairly similar culture. They are a farming people and engage in trade in central markets. It should be appreciated, however, that the cultures of their constituent groups vary considerably and the description made below reveals something of their central modes of behavior, rather than a universal culture pattern. They live mostly in villages. They lack centralized political authority, such as kingship and chiefship, yet kingship existed in one or two small communities, such as Onitsha. Their largest social unit is typically a village group, or a collection of villages in a single territory having a sense of unity.

Concept of the
Individual Personality

A man was perceived to be the union of three elements. His birth not only brought to the world his body but also his soul or personality centered in his heart, and known as *mmuo*. The *mmuo* meant the reincarnation of another being, usually an ancestor, and was subject to reincarnation after it left the body at death. Upon birth, Chuku or Cineke, the supreme being, sent down a portion of himself, known as the *ci* or *chi,* to join the body and the *mmuo*. This spiritual self determined a man's capabilities, faults, and fortune, as reported by Meek. On the other hand, Horton found that the *ci* determined a person's destiny or fate and the *mmuo* his potentialities.[1]

Social Values and Attitudes

Ottenberg reported that: "The Ibo are a highly individualistic people. While a man is dependent on his family, lineage, and residential grouping for support and backing, strong emphasis is placed on his ability to make his own way in the world." The society was so organized that it was possible for a man "to make his own way in the world." A man could become rich through the skillful use of the farming resources of his friends and relatives, trade, and use of loans. The attainment of wealth meant the attainment of prestige and influence, through respect, clientage, assumption of titles, and achievement of political influence. The competitive pattern in life was further manifested in rivalry among villages and other lineage groups for size, wealth, and influence.

A variety of paths led to success and prestige. One could become a wealthy farmer, trader, or fisherman. A person of a less aggressive personality type could achieve position through becoming a priest. A person who spoke well could achieve a position in the village moots or meetings.

Individuals were compelled to make choices as to the spirits they would call upon in situations of stress and conflict or the judicial procedures to be followed in disputes. Ottenberg stated that: "Ibo culture thus provides alternatives which the individual must decide upon in terms of his own skill and knowledge. Their significance for the individual is that he rapidly develops experience in making decisions in which he must estimate his own position and opportunities for success."[2]

---

1. C. K. Meek, *Law and Authority in a Nigerian Tribe* (London, New York, Toronto, 1937), 53-58; W. R. G. Horton, "God, Man, and the Land in a Northern Ibo Village Group," *Africa,* XXVI (1956), 17.

2. S. Ottenberg, "Ibo Receptivity to Change," *Continuity and Change in African Culture,* eds. W. R. Bascom and M. J. Herskovits (Chicago, 1959), 136, 138.

Strong emphasis was placed on achievement, and ways to achievement and leadership were open. Achievement was encouraged by many social groups, who aided their members as they sought to move upwards in status and influence. Achievement and initiative were permitted within many of the social groups and were facilitated by the number of contacts with social groups which were possible. The individual developed familiarity with working in and through groups. Groups not of a kinship character were manifest in the age grades, secret societies, men's societies, cooperative work groups, and title societies. An individual could turn to many different groups for land, political support, and other purposes. His initiative and shrewdness in doing so, together with his industry and judgment, determined his success. A man rose to leadership through his abilities to organize farming activities, to acquire the control of land, and to extend aid to his followers. He could use "a variety of techniques for increasing his social contacts and for ensuring the support of persons other than those of the groups into which he is born." Mastery of the technique of manipulation of social instruments and forces was highly esteemed. Men who were "skillful at making use of the network of social groupings and ties of birth and marriage in setting up relationships of mutual obligation between themselves and others, and in bargaining with others for support and assistance, are much admired and praised."

Leadership in Ibo society was not merely a matter of seniority but was dependent on an elder's knowledge of village and compound history and affairs, wealth, demonstrated capacity as a leader, ability to speak clearly, persuasively, and without offending others, and interest in local matters.

Emphasis was placed on the equality of members of a social group and of different social groups of a similar type. While differences in social rank and authority of course existed, there was a basic egalitarian attitude. Other prized values were property, money, honesty, and loyalty between kinsmen.[3]

The perspective of the Ibo of the external world was summarized by Horton as follows:

> So far as we can tell, the history of pre-Administration Iboland is one of spasmodic petty strife between one group and the next, often between

---

3. S. Ottenberg, *The System of Authority of the Afikpo Ibo in Southeastern Nigeria*, (Ph.D. Thesis, Northwestern, 1957), 349, 258-259, 197, 351, 85-86, 351, quotations at 347, 354-355; M. M. Green, *Ibo Village Affairs* (London, 1947), 88-89. See R. A. Levine, *Dreams and Deeds: Achievement and Motivation in Nigeria* (Chicago, London, 1966), which is concerned with the Hausa, Ibo, and Yoruba.

one village and the next. There were constant migrations, frequently from slave-raiding neighbours. Alliances were made, broken, and changed, confederacies formed and dissolved. So far as the immediate external relations of his village were concerned, then, the Nike man lived in narrow world a [sic] of flux and inconstancy. At the same time, however, his view of the world was far from parochial. A great trader, he would travel considerable distances to markets of those nearby groups which happened at the time to be friendly with his own; and early records show Nike to have been the crossroads of trade routes from such distant points as Idda, Awka, Bende, and the Cross River. Such trade was kept open firstly by exogamic ties whereby members of a group were custom-bound to select their wives from a neighbouring community, and secondly by safe-conduct passes from the ubiquitous agents of the *Aro Chuku* oracle. The latter alone, of course, attracted thousands of people annually from all over Iboland; indeed, the Ibo system of trading seems to have led to the extensive use of cults outside one's own group for purposes of propitiation or the taking of an oracle, for word of the efficacy of a given cult or spirit spreads very quickly in the markets.[4]

Religion

The Ibo recognized a supreme god, a number of lesser gods and spirits, together with the spirits of the ancestors.

Chuku or Cineke was the supreme being. He lived in the sky, and was the creator of the sky and the earth. He made the crops grow and was the source from which men derived their *ci*, or spiritual self. His two messengers, sun and moon, brought him news of happenings on earth. Some of the gods were his sons. He was not worshipped directly through sacrifices.

Anyanu, the sun god, was the source of good fortune and wealth. Amadi-Oha was the god of lightning. Chuku created all the spirits or *alosi*. Each spirit had a unique power to control some aspect of nature or the activities of men. There were numerous minor spirits, such as the guardian spirit of yams and the river spirits.

Probably the most important of the spirits was Ale, Ala, or Ani, the god of the earth. She was the mainspring of social life, the guardian of morals and law, the bringer of fertility, and the supervisor of farming activities as they succeeded one another through the seasons. The commission of murder, kidnapping, poisoning, theft, and adultery were offenses against Ale and had to be purged by the performance of ritual to her. Ale had the power to deprive men of their lives as a punishment for evil. In some communities, the priest of Ale was

---

4. Horton, *op. cit.,* p. 26.

a participant in the conduct of trials and had the power to call the elders to hold trials.

Each village had a shrine and a priest of Ale. She presided over the farming cycle, and performance of ritual to her was necessary for the fertility of the land in producing crops. Lesser spirits and the spirits of the ancestors were under the control of Ale.

The worship of the ancestors was one of the forces for maintaining group unity. They were the guardians of morality and owners of the soil. Any departure from custom was likely to lead to their displeasure and punishment through misfortune. Sacrifice to the ancestors was performed by the senior male member of the lineage group.

The sacred *ofo*, or staff, was the symbol of the ancestors and the symbol of authority of its holder, usually the elder. It was the source of sanctions for the exercise of authority. As handed down from generation to generation, it became the embodiment of all the spirits of the ancestors. It was made from a branch of a certain tree which was also held to grow in Chuku's garden. The taking of an oath upon *ofo* was the most binding of oaths. If death by *ofo* was invoked in the oath, upon failure to comply with the sworn conduct, retribution was held to be certain.

Oracles and diviners were consulted, and witchcraft was feared. Witches were considered to be controlled through diviners and medicine men. Certain renowned oracles also functioned in courts of the highest authority throughout the land. Disputes between individuals or villages were referred to such courts for decision.

There was a secret society, known as the Mmo, the members of which acted in the community as maskers and were regarded as ancestral spirits. They carried out sanctions in cases of adultery and witchcraft, expelling an adulteress from her husband's kin, requiring the trial of persons charged with witchcraft, or punishing those held guilty of witchcraft. An oath invoking the power of the Mmo compelled members to speak the truth. Another form of oath could compel non-members to obey members. Offenses against the Mmo were not a private matter but called for a meeting of the village and entailed a heavy fine.

Various other secret societies existed, were a powerful factor in maintaining law and order, and served to integrate the male members of the community and preserve male dominance over the females.[5]

---

5. Meek, *op. cit.*, pp. 20-48, 53-58, 61-66, 75-87; D. Forde and G. I. Jones, "The Ibo and the Ibibio-Speaking Peoples of South-Eastern Nigeria," *Ethnographic Survey of Africa*, ed. D. Forde (London, New York, Toronto, 1950), Part III, 25-26.

Age Sets and Age Grades

The institution of age sets and age grades appeared in Ibo society in varying forms and degree. The term age set refers to a group of persons who occupy an age relationship to one another of but a few years. An age grade refers to a group of persons having an age relationship of a wider span of years and usually encompassing a number of age sets. The groups perform social, political, and even legal functions in the societies of which they are a part. As the members of the groups move through life, their responsibilities increase with their age. Meek described their nature and function in Ibo society in general terms. Boys formed a group in an informal manner as they played together. When the members of such an informal group reached the age of fifteen to eighteen, they bound themselves together under some senior man as a captain or head. Aside from their functions of providing companionship, entertainment, mutual protection, communication between groups of different ages and social power, the groups had important political and legal functions. They acted as police in apprehending offenders and insuring their presence at a trial. They sanctioned decisions by the elders, such as collecting fines imposed. They declared rules for behavior, such as fixing the times for harvest and controlling fees for the exercise of office. They acted to prevent abuse of authority when the elders made unjust decisions. They performed public duties, such as clearing paths, cutting forest land, acting as market guards, and defending the village in time of war.[6]

Ottenberg described the constitution and functions of age sets and age grades among the Afikpo village group in eastern Iboland in considerable detail. It was seen that these groupings cut across the lineage groupings and joined with them in discharging social, political, and legal functions in their communities.

An age set was formed by young men in their twenties meeting together for work and entertainment. The members of such an informal group covered an age span of about three years. It coalesced into an age set through initiation ceremonies. In some sets, a single man emerged as a leader. In others, the tasks of leadership were divided among a small group of leaders.

In certain villages, the three age sets of middle-aged men assumed an executive function in the village government. They controlled the use of the village palm groves, organized communal labor, such

6. Meek, *op. cit.,* pp. 197-200.

as clearing village paths, carried out important ritual duties, such as those connected with farming, and conserved the firewood from waste. They did not usually initiate action or make decisions. Their function was to see that the decisions of the elders were carried out.

The senior sets of the elders' grade had the greatest authority. There were no chiefs; rule was by the elders as a group. Nevertheless, some villages had dominant individual elders in such a group. The senior members of such sets represented the village in inter-village affairs.

The younger age grade in the village acted as the executive for the elders, saw to it that their orders were carried out, reported violations of rules for behavior, and suggested needed public tasks. It also performed social functions and provided support for rituals. It exercised control over the behavior of women. It announced elders' decisions, and, to a certain extent, sanctioned compliance with them. If a person refused to pay a fine, it could seize his property. Repeated norm-violation might cause it to compel the offender to leave the community. It supervised the younger men and women in doing public work for the village.

The village group had its own age sets drawn from the members of the corresponding age sets of the villagers. The senior age grade acted as an advisory group for the two junior grades. The responsibility for making village group decisions fell on the middle age grade. It also acted in a judicial capacity. The junior grade was the executive grade. Meetings of the village group age grades as a unit were open to any man, and any person of the proper age could speak. Nevertheless, the three eldest sets dominated the meetings. Such joint meetings handled disputes between groups within the village group and acted for its general welfare. They represented the village group to the outside world. The middle age group was the primary regulatory, advisory, and judicial body of the village group. The whole middle age grade was used to settle disputes, although other alternative modes of settlement existed.

The junior age grade of the village group performed executive functions, collected fines for violations of rulings, and brought offenders to the senior grades for trial. They acted as police in the markets and as investigatory agents in cases involving women, such as adultery.[7]

Jones confirmed the division of age groups into a senior group of elders, a middle group of men, and a junior group of boys, with a

---

7. S. Ottenberg, *op. cit.*, Chap. 9, also pp. 78-85, 338-339.

corresponding basic grouping of women into senior female elders, women, and girls. He noted the further subdivision of such groups ideally into age sets of three-years span but in fact subject to variation in length of span of years. The governing body of the council of elders was drawn from elders who either possessed appropriate rank or natural leadership attributes. The groups otherwise engaged in recreational activities and performed public work with particular tasks being assigned to certain age sets.[8]

Social Organization

The largest social and political unit was the tribe or village group, consisting of a number of villages in a single territory whose members identified themselves as having descended from a common male ancestor. The members of a village shared this general identification and also had their own male ancestor, who was a descendent of the tribal ancestor. The basic social unit was a patrilineal group who lived together and were known as *ummuna*. A subdivision of the *ummuna* was the *ummune,* or children of one mother who had a common male ancestor.

The prevalent mode of social organization was for lineage groups to divide themselves into successive units of two, or halves of a larger whole. This process was used for political and social purposes and to some extent for the practice of exogamy. Thus a village might be divided territorially into two halves, each occupied by a separate kinship group. Each such half would trace its descent from a common founding male ancestor by way of two of his wives. Each such half would in turn be divided into smaller lineage groups consisting of the sons of a common father and their wives and daughters, all under the headship of a senior male, who held the family *ofo*. The heads of the larger group each had their own *ofo*.

The system of dual division of lineage groups became, in some communities, a means of cooperation to bring about the performance of village activities which might otherwise have required a chief or some other central authority. The joint clearing of village

8. G. I. Jones, "Ibo Age Organization, with Special Reference to the Cross-River and North-Eastern Ibo," *Journal of the Royal Anthropological Institute,* XCII (1962), 191. For a broad, cross-cultural study of age groups and youth movements drawn from an extraordinarily wide range of data, the reason for the selection of which is not entirely clear, except perhaps to sustain the categorizations made, see S. N. Eisenstadt, *From Generation to Generation* (Glencoe, Ill., London, 1956).

paths, attendance at the market, and the execution of justice were carried out or sanctioned by the organization of the village in two complementary and competing lineage groups.

The Afikpo village group had its own cultural and social unity in the form of owning land and shrines, having a central market, and possessing social groups, notably age grades. Linkages between villages existed on the basis of kinship, friendship, and special ties. All villages shared the use of certain land and other properties. Certain shrines and diviners played a part in all village life. One shrine was used for the purpose of putting oaths of innocence to persons whose guilt of an offense was in doubt.[9]

Political and Legal Organization

Those who made the rules for a community, whatever its size and character, were also those who handled cases of their infractions. In all communities, the principal governing authority for the making of rules and the decision of cases was the council of elders. It included the heads of lineage groups, rich influential men, certain title-holders, and priests of important cults. In some communities, there was a group of younger elders who exercised executive authority on behalf of the elders. They investigated cases, brought them to the attention of the council, when important, collected debts, and compelled thieves to pay compensation to the injured party. The very important role of age grades and age sets in legal matters was detailed above.

The council of elders had a type of legislative or rule-making power. They would determine the places where wood was not to be cut, measures for preventing the spread of an epidemic, the price for brides and burial-rites, and the degree of punishment for breaking the peace of the market. Forde and Jones stated that the concurrence of the community at a public meeting was necessary in the making of new laws. Sometimes the elders stipulated the penalty for breach of a rule, such as the payment of a goat. At other times, they would call upon the priest of Ale or of some other god to bring the power of his spirit to punish those who broke a rule.[10]

Ottenberg found three major types of authority to exist,

---

9. Meek, *op. cit.*, pp. 88-94; Green, *op. cit.*, pp. 15-17, 139-145; Ottenberg, *op. cit.*, p. 288. R. N. Henderson, "Onitsha Ibo Kinship Terminology: a Formal Analysis and its Functional Applications," *Southwestern Journal of Anthropology*, XXIII (1967), 15, indicates how kinship structures designate roles.

10. Meek, *op. cit.*, pp. 114, 206-208, 247-250; Forde and Jones, *op. cit.*, p. 21.

those who direct the affairs of the domestic and smaller lineage units and rely on informal social sanctions, those who lead the unilineal and residential units and have the force of law as well as informal sanction behind them, and those who wield religious authority. No one of these types of leaders dominates the Afikpo system of authority, but each plays an important role in it. . . . Leaders in all categories are mutually interdependent and require the support of each other.

The elders in the compound settled disputes among members, consulted a diviner when the group was experiencing misfortune, insured the upkeep of the shrines, handled the property of the lineage, and represented and defended it in disputes with other groupings.

The elders of the major patrilineal groups within the compound carried out for such groups, in large measure, the same functions performed by the elders of the larger groups and, in the exercise of their leadership, displayed the same personal qualities.

The elders of the village controlled the use of village land and property, regulated village groupings, such as age sets and grades, controlled individual members of the village, acted as judges, exercised responsibility for the general welfare of the village, and represented the village to the outside world. In their role as judges, they did not handle disputes within a lineage group. They heard appeals from decisions of the executive age grade, handled cases of fighting, and heard cases that the lineage groups were unable to settle within the group. When the village experienced decline or misfortune, they sought spiritual aid through consulting a diviner.[11]

The control of village affairs was also discussed above under the heading, "Age Sets and Age Grades."

The head of the household, known as the *okpara,* performed political, social, moral, legal, and religious functions. Meek stated that:

> The head of a household has numerous ritual, moral, and legal rights and obligations. He offers sacrifice for the welfare of the family, organizes the exploitation of family land, assigns kitchen-garden plots to wives, rations supplies in times of stress, helps members of the family who have got into difficulties, and bears a large part of marriage, funeral, and hospitality expenses. If the wife of any member of the household bears a child, the head of the household is expected to present her with a cloth and food, and to provide a goat for the naming feast. He himself confers the name. In short, the head of the household is the material and spiritual guardian of the group, and in external matters assumes responsibility for all, as far as he reasonably can.

---

11. Ottenberg, *op. cit.,* pp. 89, 105-106, 261-268, quotation at p. 354.

The *okpara* was the oldest male member of the household. He held the family *ofo* and was the intermediary with the ancestors and ritual head of the group. With his *ofo* at hand, he settled disputes within the household and joined with *okpara* of equal rank in settling disputes in the larger lineage group of which his group was a constituent part. He had the power to inflict physical punishment on persons found to have violated norms.

A lineage group was collectively responsible to others for norm violations of its members, such as killing a member of another lineage group.

A village composed of a single lineage group was "bound together by (a) the common possession of territory and consequently a common cult of Ale, and a common necessity for defence and particularly of defending its farmlands against encroachment; and (b) a sense of relationship based on the belief in descent from a common ancestor and cemented by the possession of a common emblem, tutelary genius, or taboo."

When the nominal head of a lineage group was unable to perform his several functions, a younger man having unusual ability might assume the *de facto* headship.

The custom of title taking prevailed among the Ibo. Societies existed to confer titles which had a political or social significance in return for gifts of items of considerable value or the provision of feasts. Persons of wealth typically acquired such titles and the exercise of the power of their office cut across traditional lineage lines of authority. Indeed, the views of title holders tended to prevail in the formulation of policy at the village meetings, as against the claim of formal authority by lineage heads.

Persons who possessed wealth could also acquire leadership by rendering financial aid and support to the members of a group. They were most influential in war-making activities, which could not be carried on without their financial support.[12]

Religious agents also acted in a judicial capacity. Diviners were consulted when trouble arose and prescribed ritual procedures as remedies. Powerful oracles were consulted to obtain advice and terminate disputes; their judgments were held to be final and binding because of their supernatural sanction. Such oracles were believed to have the power to kill or harm those who offended them. Meek stated that disputes between village groups were handled by an oracle. In Afikpo, disputes over land, trees, and water areas of the

---

12. Meek, *op. cit.,* pp. 98, 104-109, 119-121, 126-128, 138, 165-184, 111-114, quotation at p. 128; Forde and Jones, *op. cit.,* p. 19.

village group were referred to an oracle when they could not otherwise be settled. It was possible for a person who was dissatisfied with the decision of certain types of tribunals to take the case to courts of appeals. There was no single "highest" court, and, of course, there was no appeal from a decision by a supernatural agency. As noted above in "Age Sets and Age Grades," certain of the age sets in Afikpo possessed the power to decide cases, including cases of murder, theft, poisoning, sorcery, and certain abuses of community property. Such cases in earlier times had been handled through a certain major patrilineage known as the *amade* or freeborn.

Ottenberg had some general observations to make concerning patterns of legal behavior, which are of much interest. He stated:

A number of broad patterns in the exercise of legal authority should be noted. If a dispute involves two members of a particular social group, such as a compound or lineage, it will often be settled within that group, but if it involves individuals from two different groupings their leaders may settle it by calling in outside judges, by referring the matter to the middle village-group age grade, or by a variety of religious techniques, such as consultation with an oracle. Most of these judicial agencies can be used as a court of appeal. Cases generally start by being tried by the elders of the social groups concerned and they then may be appealed to other agencies. In general, the more serious a case or the more difficult it is to settle, the more likely that it will be judged by those representing a larger social grouping, such as the middle Afikpo age grade, or settled by resort to judicial procedures.

Judicial bodies invariably consist of groups, and judgements are not usually made by single individuals. This is perhaps nothing more than another aspect of a basic Afikpo pattern that major decisions, changes in rules and regulations, and the over-all responsibility for performing tasks involve groups of persons and not single individuals. The judging of cases by groups, particularly of elders, which is so characteristic of the residential units and the larger unilineal groupings, takes the responsibility from individuals and places it on the shoulders of groups who are perhaps more likely to follow and represent public opinion. Again this method diffuses the force of dissatisfaction. In terms of social harmony the system seems to prevent strong interpersonal conflict between the judges and the judged. The leaders—the groups of men who rule and judge—need no quality of sacredness to augment and support them, as single leaders sometimes possess in African societies.

Ottenberg noted that the practice of ignoring the decision of one judicial body and referring it again to another helped to prevent criticism of the judges but it had the detrimental effect of often perpetuating conflict for a long period of time. Such delays in decision frequently occurred when the disputants belonged to different social groups. Disputes, however, tended to be referred eventually to supernatural agents, and their decisions were usually final.

With respect to the qualities required for leadership in the judicial sphere, Ottenberg stated:

> The criteria for leadership in legal matters fall into two categories. In the first are those which are deemed to be essential. An influential leader in the compound, ward, unilineal descent groups, village, or village-group should be an elder, that is, a member of one of the village-group age grades. The more senior he is the more influential he will be until he becomes senile. Yet he must have a certain quality of aggressiveness to become an outstanding leader. . . . He must be diplomatic, a good speaker, and he should have a good knowledge of recent and past events in order to make use of them in carrying out his leader's role.

The second category, relating to success in leadership in legal matters, was concerned with a person's prestige and nearness to the location of the central villages of the village and social groups to which he belonged, wealth, position in his family group, and whether he was a son of a leader.[13]

Forde described the court system of the Ibo as consisting of a number of bodies having different criteria for their creation. If a dispute was viewed in lineage terms, then the senior elder presided over a council of household heads or component lineage heads or other representatives of constituent lineage groups. A group of elders could be constituted as a court on a territorial basis, that is, a decision of a village or even the whole village group. A person might acquire a high degree of prestige, power, and influence, not only in his own lineage groups, but also in adjacent lineage groups as well. He would then possess the ability to influence decisions. Such persons frequently decided private wrongs, as distinguished from public offenses.[14]

A number of institutions existed among the Abaja to prevent the outbreak of violence among a people who were excitable and had strong tempers. The false imputation of a commission of an offense was itself an offense. The office of diviner provided a means whereby a search for the guilty could be made without the risk of a charge of false accusation. Also persons who were engaged in a verbal dispute were subject to having their knives taken away from them.[15]

13. Meek, *op. cit.,* p. 47; Ottenberg, *op. cit.,* pp. 297-299, 353, 318, 116-117, 340-344, quotations at pp. 340-343; Green *op. cit.,* p. 54.

14. D. Forde, "Justice and Judgment among the Southern Ibo under Colonial Rule," *African Law: Adaptation and Development,* eds. H. Kuper and L. Kuper (Berkeley, Los Angeles, 1965), 80-86.

15. Green, *op. cit.,* pp. 92-96.

War

There were no military institutions or offices of leadership in the conduct of war. The age sets or age grades were not as such employed in war; instead, all able-bodied men were relied upon to repel attack or respond by force to other external threats or injuries.[16] Warfare reflected a regularized means of resolving conflict between villages arising out of norm violations and deeply felt tensions. Failure to pay a bride-price or homicide would bring into conflict two villages or two village-groups when the parties involved were drawn from different localities. When fighting occurred between villages of the same village-group, the weapons were limited to machetes and sticks, with the object of reducing fatalities. Guns were permissible in fights between different village-groups. Warfare took place by the warriors of one side leaving their village or villages in a disorganized mass and killing all they encountered. Each warrior endeavored to get an enemy's head. After a ritual performance, the skull was hung in the roof of his house.

Certain procedures existed whereby the losing side could sue for peace, the terms of peace made, and peace proclaimed.

The damages of the winning side, including the value of lost lives, were carefully calculated and paid by the losing side.[17]

Law: Land Tenure

The rules of land tenure, including inheritance of land, were a product of social structure, adaptation to ecological conditions, and density of settlement. As a system, the rules reflected "three cardinal principles: that the land ultimately belonged to the community and could not be alienated from it without its consent; that within the community the individual should have security of tenure for the land he required for his compounds, his gardens, and his farms; and that no member of the community should be without land." The term "community," as used in the foregoing, could mean the entire village-group, when, for example, there was a need to expropriate land for some public purpose. It could also mean a maximal, medial, or minimal lineage, depending on the context.

---

16. Ottenberg, *op. cit.*, pp. 236-237.
17. Green, *op. cit.*, pp. 63-65; Meek, *op. cit.*, pp. 242-247.

The village-group, typically numbering four to five thousand people, claimed the land in its vicinity, the boundaries of which became more definite as density of settlement increased. The pattern in which villages of the village-group were located reflected the need of contiguity for purposes of realization of a common identity and unity, on the one hand, and defense against attack, on the other hand. Each village was settled around one or more central meeting places and was given the right to occupy land extending in a specific direction away from the center or centers so fixed. Thus expansion was organized with a minimum of friction.

Two types of cultivation were evidenced. There was an inner zone of house land, which was permanently tilled in the form of oil-palm and other trees and shade crops. This was kept fertilized by the deposit of refuse from the compounds. Beyond the house land, and connected with it by a path through the forest, lay the farm land of the particular unit. Over the course of time and as settlement increased, the forest was first to disappear and eventually became entirely replaced by farm land. The final stage of intensification of use was reached when all land became house land and the village had to find some solution to the problem of feeding its members. There was a practical limit in the amount of time that could be allotted to transit to the outlying farm land. Further expansion of land by a lineage group, once it had occupied all the farm land within a few miles of the house land, could be achieved only in two ways. One was the absorption of the territory, and, usually, the personnel of an adjoining lineage group that had failed to expand in numbers. The other was emigration of the group to new land.

The ownership and use of the house land always appertained to an individual householder and passed by descent to his direct male descendants. Such land was permanently farmed by the family unit in question. The farm land was tilled on a principle of rotation, with periods when it was fallow, and the individual householder had the priority of use of specific plots of farm land when the time to use it came around. If, however, he failed to use it, the relevant lineage group of which he was a part could reassign it to others in the lineage.

Meek described the process of individuation of land ownership as one in which at first the village had the power to determine whether a person clearing adjacent forest land for farming purposes was interfering with use of the land for public purposes, such as a source of wood. The village, as a lineage group, held its own farm land, which was allotted anew each time it was to be farmed. As settlement grew, such land diminished in quantity until it entirely disappeared. Smaller lineage groups also held their ancestral land, which was apportioned annually among the members of the group. This land, too, diminished in the course of settlement until situations were reached in which all land was individually owned.[18]

Jones described the sequence of steps involved in the settlement of land as beginning with a colonizing stage, in which the community held vacant land which could be assigned to any members of groups which were short of land. When such vacant land substantially disappeared, save only for substantially unusable plots, ownership by the village, except for the power of eminent domain by the village, was supplanted by smaller lineage groups, which acquired the power to control the use of specific plots of land. The final stage was the conversion of all farm land into individually owned and used house land.[19]

The final stage in land use was described in some detail by Green. In the community which she investigated, no village land remained. Land was owned individually by small lineage groups consisting of from one to a half dozen or more close male relatives. Priority of right of cultivation of specific plots on the part of individual members of such groups was recognized, even though the practice was professed to be that any family member could cultivate the land of the group. There was a division of labor between the sexes in the cultivation of the crops, and members of the lineage group could call upon one another for needed aid in cultivation. Husbands and wives cultivated specific crops; for example, the husbands cultivated the yams. Each owned the crops which they cultivated. Inheritance of land was by father to sons, with seniority determining the size of the share of land inherited. Land could be pledged for a debt. The practice of transferring land by pledging it for an amount representing the value of its permanent use was developing. Land could be leased for a season for farming as a way of increasing its use for the benefit of all.[20]

Individually held land was acquired by clearing virgin forest, by inheritance from father to son, and by receipt as pledge for a loan. When land was pledged for a sum considerably in excess of its normal loan value, the creditor would, with the passage of time, acquire perpetual rights in the land. This was the usual method for transfer-

---

18. *Ibid.,* pp. 100-103.
19. G. I. Jones, "Ibo Land Tenure," *Africa,* XIX (1949), 314.
20. M. M. Green, *Land Tenure in an Ibo Village,* Monographs on Social Anthropology, No. 6 (London, 1941).

ring land, although outright sale was practiced in some localities. Land could be pledged for a loan and could also be leased for a season or longer.

Public lands included sacred groves devoted to the gods, as well as taboo lands or "evil bush."

The right of an individual to be provided with land for his needs was recognized through the rules governing the devolution of the lands held by a householder to his sons. When his sons reached maturity and again when they were married, portions of his lands were allotted to them. On his death, his remaining lands were divided among his sons, with the eldest usually taking the largest share. If, however, he left surviving wives and their children, the lands were divided among such wives, with the sons of each wife taking individual shares of each allotment. Land was thus ordinarily held by men, and husbands were expected to provide their wives with land for themselves and their children. The wife was expected to provide food for her husband. Women were free to acquire land in their own right.

In the early period of land settlement, it was possible for entire lineage groups and even villages to settle on vacant land of other groups, and eventually to be assimilated into such groups as members. As farm land became scarce, at first permanent transfers to strangers were prohibited, and later such transfers were forbidden between members of the same land-owning community. Finally, when practically all farm land had disappeared and only house land remained, permanent transfers of such land were forbidden.

Transfers of land of a temporary character tended to promote land use and were always permissible. Such transfers could be for a single farming season or could be for an indefinite period, in the latter case with the intention that the grantor or his heirs could recover the land. Seasonal transfers could be given, on the basis of a token rent or an economic rent. Indefinite transfers usually took the form of pledge or mortgage. In the latter case, the land could be redeemed upon payment of the debt by the pledgor or his heirs. Farm land could be pledged with the consent of the land-owning group which held it.

Permanent transfers of land, which were made in the early stages of colonization, were usually accomplished by gift with or without conditions attached. Such transfers could be made only to persons which the community was willing to absorb. Transfer by sale or by pledge for a larger than usual loan value was also possible in some regions.

The land on which a compound was built and its adjoining plots were considered to be owned by the lineage group which occupied it. This ownership, or priority of claim, persisted even after the group moved to another site.

Land disputes, in some communities, were settled by a body of men who had obtained the heads of enemies in war. They were best able to handle the physical violence which often occurred in such cases.[21]

Law: Offenses

There were norms adherence to which was considered necessary to preserve the unity of the community with the spirit of the earth and the good fortune which attended such a state of affairs. Their violation was considered to offend Ale, the earth goddess, or to have "polluted the land." Murder, suicide, incest, adultery within the lineage group, and the sale of a fellow kin member to effect payment of a debt were examples of such offenses. The mode of trial and the punishments visited upon such offenses were different from other and lesser offenses.

Green stated that there were two different approaches to handling the commission of offenses, dependent upon whether the culprit was known or suspected or whether he was unknown. Where the culprit was known or suspected, a range of procedures were open. The dispute could be submitted to the settlement of a few individuals as arbitrators. The more formal mode of judicial settlement was by the elders of the village, who would sit in judgment at a trial at which any interested person could be present and even gain a hearing in the proceedings. In exceptional cases, the sacred spear of the yam cult might be invoked and its custodial village might be required to hear the litigation and decide the dispute. When an offender was caught in the commission of an offense, such as stealing at a market, he could be dealt with on the spot by those present. With respect to the second category of offenses, namely, situations where the offender was unknown, a diviner could be consulted.

Murder was an offense against Ale, and the murderer was expected

---

21. Jones, *op. cit.;* Meek, *op. cit.,* pp. 101-103, 229; see also L. T. Chubb, *Ibo Land Tenure* (Ibadan, 1961). For a carefully outlined and thorough statement of Ibo law relating to land and other property, see S. N. C. Obi, *The Ibo Law of Property* (London, 1963). On succession to land and other property, see S. Ottenberg, "Inheritance and Succession in Afikpo," *Studies in the Laws of Succession in Nigeria,* ed. J. D. M. Derrett (London, 1965), 33.

to hang himself immediately. If he did not, sanctions were applied by the community to his kin, including the destruction and appropriation of their tangible property.

Suicide was also an offense against Ale and was followed by the performance of ritual to appease the anger of Ale.

Assault might lead to retaliation upon the party committing the injury or his kin, or the elders might order the payment of compensation and the services of a diviner to aid the recovery of the injured.

Theft was subject to severe punishment. If the identity of the thief were known, the exaction of compensation and the infliction of punishment could be made by the kin of the injured party. Otherwise, a public trial by the elders took place.

Adultery within the lineage group was an "abomination" and offense against Ale. The guilty parties were subject to banishment and ritual purification by the priest of Ale was necessary. Adultery outside the lineage group was merely a private offense. Incest was an offense against Ale, and the offenders were subject to punishment by killing or sale.

A number of other offenses may briefly be noted. The birth of twins and cripples was regarded as abominable and they were destroyed. The use of witchcraft was an offense subject to public trial by ordeal. Persons committing trespass were required to make good the damage done. Disputes over inheritance were settled by the elders. Defamation of another could lead to the payment of heavy damages. To curse another was a serious matter, and attempts were made to cause the withdrawal of the curse.

Non-payment of debt was subject to public trial by the elders. Measures of self-help could be taken by the kin of the creditor to recover property of the debtor to pay the debt.[22]

Conclusion

The Ibo possessed a pluralistic, achieving, competitive society. Individuals were free and were motivated to employ their talents to maneuver and manipulate in order to attain position, power, wealth, and prestige. They were a people admirably suited for the

22. Meek, *op. cit.*, Chap. 10; Green, *Ibo Village Affairs*, 99-101; *Cf.* S. Ottenberg, *System of Authority*, 318. See also N. W. Thomas, *Anthropological Report on the Ibo-Speaking Peoples of Nigeria* (London, 1913 and 1914), Part I, 108-122, Part IV, Chap. 5.

modernizing process. Admired personality traits in their culture were industriousness, achievement, ability to handle and maneuver persons and social groups, social aggressiveness, persuasiveness, accumulation of wealth, and acquisition of social and political power. Reciprocity, bargaining, persuasion, and working in and through groups were characteristic forms of social action. Group decisions were the typical mode of procedure in the lineage and village institutions. The society was relatively open and offered opportunity for mobility of movement upwards in social status and wealth. A wide variety of social groupings existed. These were of an associational character as well as kinship groupings. There was an egalitarian attitude. Leadership was based on an individual's personal qualities and not merely his seniority and kinship status.

There was a hierarchy of gods, including a supreme being, and recognition of the existence and influence of the spirits of the ancestors. Diviners and oracles were employed. The gods, spirits, including the ancestor spirits, oracles, diviners and priests possessed a variety of roles in the constitution of the courts and the conduct of trials.

The society was mostly organized into groups of villages in close territorial relationship to one another. These broad structures of social action were in turn organized on religious and secular lines, on the one hand, and kinship and associational lines, on the other hand. Kinship structure manifested a dual division which was significant, not only for purposes of exogamy but more importantly for political or public purposes as well. Cutting across the kinship structures were the age grades and sets, which performed social, political, and judicial functions.

The council of elders was the typical governing body for the lineage groups. Inasmuch as the members of a village were also conceived to be composed of descendants from a common male ancestor, they too were governed by a council of elders. This body made the rules for the respective groups which they controlled and also performed a judicial function with respect to norm violators and cases of trouble in their own group and between lesser constituent groups. Other judicial bodies were principally oracles and age grades.

The outbreak and amount of violence was controlled by certain procedures designed to control resorting to dangerous weapons. The Ibo were not institutionally organized for war and pursued it mostly by way of defense or response to injury rather than aggressively and for profit. All able-bodied males were expected to become warriors.

Offenses were generally classified into two categories, those which disrupted the harmony of the relationship of a community to the earth goddess and those which did not. When guilt was established, immediate physical sanctions, as well as possible future spiritual sanctions, were visited upon the offender.

The mode of settlement was in villages and village groups. The village possessed the character of a major patrilineage, and the village group could be viewed as a tribe or clan. Each village grew in a specific direction from a central meeting place, thereby minimizing inter-village friction resulting from expansion. There were outlying zones of house land, which was in intensive and continual cultivation, and farm land, which was tilled on a rotating basis. As settlement became dense, house land tended to replace farm land and individually-owned land tended to supplant land held by larger lineage groups. The rules governing the use of land were designed to achieve three objectives: first, ultimate ownership or control of land within the community; second, security of tensure for the individual user in the land which he required for himself and his family; and, third, provision of needed land for all members of the community.

The Ibo were, in short, a viable, resilient, industrious, tenacious, achieving people, and experienced in the ways of group life, including groups other than those of a kinship nature.

Chapter 9

The Tiv

Geography and Economy

THE TIV are the largest tribe of the savanna country of Northern Nigeria, located on both sides of the Benue River, some 140 miles north of its confluence with the Niger. They speak a semi-Bantu language. They are mostly subsistence farmers, engaged in growing yams, guinea corn, and bulrush millet. Their land is an undulating plain descending from high land in the south down to the broad basin of the Benue and the flat sandbanks of the river. Another plain rises toward the north until it reaches the escarpment of the Bauchi Plateau.

Social Values and Attitudes

The Tiv were a people who lived in fear of power and were compelled to place themselves under the possessors of power for protection against its abuse by others. As they steadily migrated to new lands, they lost their ties with the land of their birth and found themselves in more or less continual conflict with other Tiv and adjoining tribes. They could be considered to be a highly egalitarian people but their preference for equality seemed to be less a product of the ideal of equality in its own right than envy and fear of those who rose in importance. Misfortune, illness, and deaths were held to be ultimately caused by some human enemy using witchcraft for his malevolent ends. It was thought that individuals who rose above the general level of the group could not have achieved power without an ability to call upon magical forces to promote their advance.

The emergence of an individual above the general level of the group was viewed with fear, malice, and hostility. As a person developed political skills of an ability to discuss group problems, oratorical capacity, tact, persuasiveness, he acquired moral and secular influence or power. As he accumulated wealth through industry and sagacity, and used his gains generously for the benefit of the group, he acquired prestige, power, and followers. Yet such achievement was feared and hated in the very moment that its protection and advantages were sought by the less successful. The Tiv interpretation of such a rise to power was that it was achieved by success in witchcraft.

Kinship groups were postulated to be potential enemies. The greater the genealogical distance between two lineages, the more likely were they to view each other as enemies. Also the more remote the relationship, the wider the options to use deadly weapons. If the relationship were close, fighting with club and stones might be permissible. If of a greater depth, bows and arrows could be used. If remote, the use of poisoned arrows and Dane guns was permissible.

When the Tiv looked at one another as members of a common lineage group, it was not with the comforting thought that one found among his close relatives his truest supporters. The disquieting thought also lurked that these were the persons who, above all others, had the power to inflict harm through witchcraft.

The Tiv were highly mobile and considered themselves always to have been a migrating people. Children at the age of seven or eight were often sent to visit kinfolk. Among many Tiv, a pattern of wandering endured into middle age. Whole lineages, as well as lineage segments, would move to new lands occupied by their kin, who were regarded as "enemies," or by foreigners. It is highly significant that a migrating people consistently gave as the reason for their move the fact of political influence of a man or group of men who were considered to be tyrannical or the desire to escape from the activity of witches. Long and bitter wars took place with other peoples whose lands lay in the pathway of Tiv migration.[1]

---

1. L. and P. Bohannan, "The Tiv of Central Nigeria," *Ethnographic Survey of Africa*, ed. D. Forde (London, 1953), Western Africa, Part VIII, 7, 11, 13, 25, 32-37, 79; P. Bohannan, "The Migration and Expansion of the Tiv," *Africa*, XXIV (1954), 11, 13; R. C. Abraham, *The Tiv People* (2d ed.; London, 1940), 49.

Religion and the Concept
of the Individual Personality

The heart was considered to be the focal point of the individual in that it was the means whereby he perceived, understood, and knew the world about him. There was a substance which grew on the heart and was known as *tsav*. Its color and configuration were indices of its good or bad influence. If its edges were notched and its color mixed, its influence was evil. It was the seat of the ability to exert witchcraft and the source of personal power, talent, and ability. A person's success in life, in the possession of wives, children, large farms, followers, and good fortune in general, was a product of his *tsav*. His misfortune was a product of the *tsav* of others.

Every man had his own shade, shadow, or reflected being, which accompanied him everywhere, mirrored his every motion, and departed from him at death. In waking hours, information was transmitted to a person's heart by his eyes and ears. When he slept, his shade received information, as a result of the *tsav* of others or the activity of shades of those recently deceased, and conveyed such information to the heart.

The hypothesis has been advanced, with some but not considerable evidence to sustain it, that the Tiv once had an ancestor cult but that it became forgotten, and other beliefs and practices were substituted in its place. The Tiv did not recognize ancestral spirits as the source of favor or misfortune. Instead they believed that ordinarily one should enjoy continued life, good health, and fortune and that a failure to do so was the product of evil supernatural forces.

There were invisible animate forces associated with illness, birth, hunting, fertility of crops, the obtaining of wives, and other important aspects of life. These could be given material form by the making of an *akombo*, or fetish. The *akombo* did not imply the attribution of life or force to an inanimate object but represented instead the belief in the existence of a vital force which could be made manifest in physical form in the fetish itself and could be subject, to some extent, to the will of its maker and holder. Their use in ritual was designed to avert misfortune in the particular category of events or actions over which the *akombo* had a special and unique power.

Each community had among its membership those who possessed *tsav* to an exceptional degree and used it to exert power over others and bring them misfortune, on the one hand, or to bring good fortune to the community, on the other hand. Such persons were known as the *mbatsav*. Akiga, a Tiv, said of them:

> It is the *mbatsav* who kill people. No man ever dies a natural death, it is always the *mbatsav* who have killed him; and if any man falls sick it is often the *mbatsav* who have bewitched him. "Bewitching" means the process by which the *mbatsav* bring about a man's death, or give him a disease. The Tiv do not bewitch people indiscriminately. You only bewitch a near relative, on your mother's or your father's side, who has done you some wrong. The bewitching is not always intended to kill; sometimes it is used by a grown man against a child who has been very impudent to him.

In other words, not even within the family was the Tiv free from the fear of witchcraft. It was instead the very place in which it was to be most feared, because it was the sanction for violation of family norms.

The *mbatsav* were considered to have a considerable degree of organization as a group, to have officials with specific tasks, and to meet and exert their power at night. Rank in the *mbatsav* reflected the degree of power in the form of *tsav* which a member possessed and varied from time to time as the amount of such power varied. Whereas other African peoples tended to regard misfortune as a type of retribution for misconduct, the Tiv believed that misfortune was visited by the possessors of *tsav,* who did so mostly for their own benefit. Only rarely were they thought to use *tsav* for the benefit of the group as a whole. Since those who were influential in the community were those who possessed *tsav* in an unusual degree, political rebellion and uprisings took "the form of witchcraft or anti-witchcraft uprisings, depending on the men in power."

The impersonal, sacred powers of *swem* and sasswood acted as control agents over the *mbatsav*. *Swem* was the power found in the sky and the earth and was manifested in a material symbol of a pot containing ashes, canewood, two types of leaves, and sometimes a stone celt. *Swem* represented absolute, impersonal justice, which restrained the power of *mbatsav* as they used their *tsav* through *akombo* and other means. Sasswood was a poison which was administered as an ordeal in the administration of justice and operated with greater swiftness as an agent of justice. If its taker vomited and survived, he was innocent of guilt. If he died, he was guilty.

There were also sprites of great power to be found in the woods of stream beds and hills who could cause dumbness, a certain kind of madness, and monstrous births. There were lesser sprites in other forms, such as ape-like creatures, who could cause malicious or mischievous harm.[2]

Social and Political Organization: Lineage

The Tiv were remarkable for their lack of development of political institutions. The study of their social and political organization cannot be made by a neat classification of data into their respective categories. The solution of political problems was reached among the Tiv by a variety of means which must be studied in their interdependent functioning.

Anthropologists have observed a unity in the relation of a kinship-structured group to the land which it occupied and tilled. There was an optimum to be achieved in the meshing of rights, obligations, and exercise of authority within a lineage group, as it lived in its compound and worked its farm land. The Tiv had a symbol for this idea or ideal situation. They named it *tar.* When there was a breakdown in the working relationship of the lineage group and land, it was necessary to "repair the *tar.*" *Tar* "refers to people, their farms and compounds. . . . *Tar* is a social matter. To repair the *tar* is to govern and to ensure that all the activities—political, social, economic, and mystical—of the people of the *tar* are in good running order."[3]

Tar, then, is a term referring both to a lineage group and the land which it occupied. Genealogically, it meant the agnatic descendants of a common ancestor. Territorially, it meant the land occupied by such a descent group. Socially, it meant a good, working relationship between these two.

The Tiv people, as the descendants of Tiv, were a single family or whole. Viewed in relation to the land which they occupied, they were divided into lineage groups, or *tar,* of varying depth or numbers of generations. As one moved downward in the scale of generations linked and identified by descent from a common ancestor, from a greater to a lesser number, one reached the minimal *tar.* Below this point, genealogical identification was made in terms of a segment-within-the-hut. At and above this point, identification was made in terms of *tar* of varying genealogical depth. The identification of a particular *tar* was the product of the nature of the particular situa-

---

2. L. and P. Bohannan, *op. cit.,* pp. 80-93, quotation at p. 92; L. Bohannan, "Political Aspects of Tiv Social Organization," *Tribes Without Ruler: Studies in African Segmentary Systems,* eds. J. Middleton and D. Tait, 54-56; R. M. East, *Akiga's Story* (London, 1939), 179-180, 240-241, quotation at 246; Abraham, *op. cit.,* pp. 84-85; R. M. Downes, *The Tiv Tribe* (Kaduna, Nigeria, 1933), Chaps. 4, 5.

3. L. and P. Bohannan, *op. cit.,* p. 22.

tion. The use of the concept of *tar* was limited to those situations in which a lineage group's relationship to the land which it occupied, that is, the territorial aspect of lineage, was significant or important. Such situations characteristically raised political issues but *there was no legitimate political authority for the Tiv people as a whole or for any division or segment of them to solve such issues on the basis of the authority of office.*

The last sentence is the key to the understanding of much of Tiv behavior, including its concepts of leadership and kinship relations, and its institutionalized patterns of migration. Whereas in the Yoruba kingdoms there was a system of hierarchically related systems, including principles of land law, whereby a man could be assured of the right to occupy some piece of land in case of need, among the Tiv a man's right to live on and farm land was limited to "the *tar* associated with the smallest segment to which he was filiated by birth—usually this is the lineage of his father."[4] Only in his agnatic minimal territory or *tar* did he have a right to sufficient land for himself and his dependants. This right, so-called, was something less than a complete and perfect right. Bohannan said in this connection: "There is no one in authority within the minimal segment to assign land—the minimal segment has no office of leadership; no head with constituted authority. Neither, in the traditional system, has any lineage at any other level."[5] Only the compound head assigned land to the members of his compound. If there was no open land, it was taken in the migration process described below.

When issues arose of the placement of the individual for purposes of identifying whom he might marry from the standpoint of avoiding incest or other objectionable lineage relationship, who could bewitch him, to whom he might turn for his allotment of land, with whom he might perform ritual, who among his kin might be his potential enemy, and from whom he might expect aid in the event of attack upon or from an enemy, the problem was first to be solved in terms of lineage relationship itself, namely *ityo* or the relevant agnatic lineage segment. When the relevant *ityo* was determined, membership in the corresponding *tar* was clear. Resolution of conflict as to what decision should be made in situations involving issues of this nature was made in terms of genealogies. Given a certain state of genealogical facts, the answer to any such question was clear. All Tiv became increasingly versed in their genealogical ties as they

---

4. P. Bohannan, *Tiv Farm and Settlement*, Colonial Research Studies No. 15 (London, 1954), 14.

5. P. Bohannan, "Migration and Expansion," 4.

grew older and encountered an increasingly greater number of situations demanding genealogical knowledge in order to deal with them. When the parties lacked sufficient knowledge themselves, they turned to elders who were learned in such matters to provide the required genealogical background. While *in form* the search was for the required genealogical information independently of the particular situation and such information purported to be formulated on the basis of its historical truth, the search and decision were in fact dictated by the necessity to find a genealogical relationship which would validate the outcome which the cultural necessities of the situation demanded. The consequence was that often fictional relationships were introduced into genealogical history in order to serve the interests of the parties in a particular case. Since genealogies were used to sanction or validate desired social relationships, it was essential that genealogical lore should be preserved and applied by oral means, which made truth a relative matter, and not by some written historical chart, which made truth absolute and eternal. If a written historical record had existed and had been rigidly applied to all cases without regard to its impact upon the preservation of desired values, than a rigid decision-making system and a correspondingly rigid social system would have ensued.

The separation of the concept of lineage segmentation from that of *tar,* and the situations in which lineage identification became significant, were explained by Bohannan as follows:

> In all local areas of Tivland, different and varying depth and span of lineage are associated with units within which court cases must not be called, units within which fighting of any sort must not take place, and within which fighting with clubs must not take place, and within which fighting with deadly weapons must not take place. But these criteria for singling out lineages do not systematically coincide with any other set of criteria for singling out lineages. There are units within which it is a sin to murder, but within which no vengeance takes place; there are units within which one must, under no conditions, steal. All of these activities are associated with the lineage system, and the groups which form by means of it. In *no* case, except by mere coincidence or by design of a foreign administration, do two of these functional criteria of groups adhere to the same depth or level of lineage in all areas. Tiv "use" their lineage system to adjust these matters, but in no case do these matters affect the structure of the lineage system. The lineage system is constantly expressed in terms of marriage, political action, crime and (in the old days—and still, occasionally) warfare. But it is conceptually independent of any of these activities.

> The other important characteristic which Tiv lineages do *not* have is this: there is, in the indigenous system, no office or status of any sort,

which is connected or associated with a lineage of any specific depth or span. Fortes has shown that, for the Tallensi, the hierarchy of lineages, so to speak, is paralleled by a hierarchy of office holders relevant to earth and ancestral cults, and that a ritually significant office is correlated with each lineage in the system. This is precisely *not* the case among Tiv.[6]

Tar identified a specific piece of land or territory by the name of the lineage group which occupied it. The question of whether the lineage group was perceived to have the right to occupy it was a relative one, the answer to which was dependent on whether the speaker was a member of the occupying lineage and was speaking of his *tar,* or whether he was speaking of the right of a member of another lineage to occupy land. In the latter event, the perceived right to continue to occupy the *tar* was one of degree. The more distant the relationship between the *tar* of Ego and the *tar* of Alter, the more likely it was that Ego might press his land use into the land occupied by Alter, if the two *tar* adjoined each other. In such case, Alter belonged to a lineage which possessed a greater degree of potential enmity by virtue of its remoteness.

The minimal lineage segment associated with the minimal *tar* was one whose founding ancestor was some three to six generations removed from the living elders of the kinship group. Its numbers might vary from two hundred persons to over a thousand. The territory it occupied ranged from less than two square miles to well over twenty. Land was settled in accordance with lineage patterns, each minimal segment adjoined the territory of its sibling minimal segment. It should be appreciated that a minimal segment, for purposes of association with land and for political purposes, was not equivalent to the smallest lineage group. On the other hand, the Tiv identified *tar* larger than the minimal segment. The agnatic descendants of persons 1, 2, 3, and 4 could be identified respectively as belonging to the respective *tar* of such persons. The fact that 1, 2, 3, and 4 were also related as descendants of A and B became the means for identifying the relevant kinship groups, as related to land. In still other situations, the fact that A and B were the descendants of the common ancestor of all, namely, I, led to the identification of the *tar* of I as that which should be the controlling factor in handling the situation.[7]

------

6. P. Bohannan, *Tiv Farm and Settlement,* 13; see L. Bohannan, "A Genealogical Charter," *Africa,* XXII (1952), 301.

7. See generally L. and P. Bohannan, *op. cit.,* pp. 19-25; P. Bohannan, *Tiv Farm and Settlement,* 3-4, 8-14; P. Bohannan, "Migration and Expansion."

Social and Political Organization: Authority and Leadership

The only person who possessed legitimate authority, which he held by virtue of his traditional role, was the compound head. This was the oldest man in the compound. He might not in fact be the person who actually exerted authority or handled the affairs of the compound. If, upon the death of a compound head, a younger brother of the oldest man was preeminently the better suited, such younger brother would possess actual authority while his older brother would possess only nominal authority.

The compound head coordinated farming activity, assigned land to the men who lived in the compound with their wives, controlled the magical forces, *akombo*, to bring prosperity to the farms, and settled disputes among members of the compound. It was the compound head of whom the Tiv thought when they were asked to identify someone who was "responsible."

The fact remained, however, that political and legal action was performed within and on behalf of a lineage group by its elders and men of affluence, prestige, and power. The dwellers of a compound were primarily within the same line of descent but strangers to the lineage were permitted to live in the compound. The lineage group itself had the need for posts to perform ritual, control *akombo*, and exercise *tsav* for the benefit of the group, to lead the discussion of group problems, to settle disputes, and to decide issues of theft, homicide, and widow inheritance, and to make peace and treaties. Such posts were occupied by elders and men of wealth, social esteem, and power. A man who, in addition to his seniority in age within his lineage group, possessed knowledge of the genealogical history of the lineage and its individual members, oratorical skill, ability to discuss and persuade, wisdom in settling matters of conflict, and unusual *tsav*, became a leader of his group. If, in addition to his personal qualities, he had affluence and prestige, could perform the ritual of the great *akombo,* and had *swem*, then he indeed possessed influence among the people. Elders of such stature "acted as arbitrators in quarrels within their lineage and between strangers, sat on moots, acted as spokesmen, representatives, and leaders in external affairs, and, as unusually influential elders, in all internal affairs."

The acquisition of wealth alone would enable a man to rise to a position of importance and prestige, to acquire the position and regalia, including drums, of a drum chief, and also to acquire *akombo* and titles. Such a person would develop a type of clientage relation with those who sought his protection. He would be expected to be generous with his wealth to others, to make gifts, and to serve large quantities of food and beer at secular gatherings.

Leadership became most important to the Tiv when relationships with other groups were involved. The leader was there acting as a leader *against* some foreign group rather than as a leader *within* the group. In other words, unity of the group under leadership reached its highest point when "foreign" affairs were concerned.[8]

Downes found lineage councils of elders to exist, of whom one was regarded as more important than the others.[9] Others have noted the existence of groups of elders and others for arbitrating disputes.[10]

In summary, a position of leadership was achieved primarily by ability and personality and was not held merely as a result of age or traditional office. Leadership was held only so long as a man's personal ability justified it. A leader was feared for the *tsav* which enabled his rise to a position of power and influence. He was perceived to use his power for his own benefit as much as possible. Even as his protection was sought, it was feared that his self-interest might lead him to act against the interest of those who were his followers.

The Migration Process

When a man had a need for land but no legitimate way to satisfy that need, then he must take the desired land by force—either by his own force or by means of some social process whereby he can bring to bear the force of others in addition to his own. The Tiv developed such a social process with extraordinary ingenuity.

The Tiv had no perception of the permanency of the line separating different *tar*. The idea of a "boundary" was not accepted. One's land would either "come to an end" or it would "march with" or be "next to" another's. To "divide" land, in the sense of a division or splitting of the *tar* into two groups was bad or most unfortunate.

As social demand for land increased, which was particularly the situation in the south, pressure for additional land would be exerted by a minimal segment upon the land of the adjoining *tar* which was

---

8. L. and P. Bohannan, *op. cit.,* pp. 31-37, quotation at p. 36.
9. Downes, *op. cit.,* pp. 27-28.
10. L. and P. Bohannan, *op. cit.,* p. 29.

occupied by the lineage segment most distantly related to the expanding lineage group. A group did not expand at the expense of those who were closely related but rather at the expense of those lineage segments occupying adjoining or other lands which were most distantly related. If adjoining land was occupied by a people other than Tiv, then it was preferable to advance at their expense. As different lineage segments occupied new land, they always tried to establish the same pattern of territorial relationships to one ananother in the new land which was established in their older residence. The governing principle for expansion was described by Bohannan as follows:

> This principle of maintaining one's own rights and at the same time maintaining as large a group of supporters as possible is crucial at the level of the minimal *tar*, where it is associated intimately with migration and movement. When a Tiv whose fallow bounds the *tar* of another lineage extends his holdings in that direction, he is in fact exercising his rights to sufficient land and at the same time making sure that his own lineage is entirely in his support. Unless, however, he expands against a companion lineage to his own minimal segment, he is expanding against a lineage which is larger and at a higher level than his minimal segment: that is, when a man of MbaGor extends his holdings at the expense of MbaGbera (several times the size of MbaGor), all MbaGbera oppose him. This brings all MbaDuku (which subsumes MbaGor) in on his side. But MbaGbera and MbaDuku, as part of the expanding Kunav (their subsuming lineage and tar) and as part of an expanding Tiv nation, agree that all MbaDuku should be expanding toward the Udam, instead of toward other Tiv. When migration takes place, then, and possibly leads to war with the Udam (who are defending their territory), MbaGbera joins him and his lineage in exercising his right to sufficient land. He has, in fact, exercised his right against the world to sufficient land, and done it in such a way as to ensure the largest possible support and backing.[11]

In other words, the principle for selecting land for migration was to move to the adjoining land of the person who was most distantly related to the person who wished to enlarge his holdings. This would bring to the support of the aggressor the largest possible number of people who were related to him and would support him in any fight which might ensue with the person who was losing his land. Bohannan described the process in the following concrete terms:

> We can illustrate again, starting with MbaNyam, a segment of Mba-Duku (see fig. 3). If a man of MbaNyam wants to increase his land holdings he will do so, if possible, against the territories either of MbaYongo or MbaGbela, for they are his most distantly related actual neighbours.

11. P. Bohannan, *Tiv Farm and Settlement,* 59.

However—and this point is crucial—MbaGbela and MbaYongo do not see it as mere expansion of MbaNyam, let alone of that individual. To them it is "MbaKuku encroaching." There are, thus, two points of view: the original man, *qua* individual farmer, expands his holdings against his genealogically most distant neighbours (MbaGbela, say) but that MbaGbela people affected immediately see the situation in lineage terms, and it is "Mbakuku shoving *(kpolom)* MbaGbela."

Now, though MbaGbela are the most distantly related neighbours from the standpoint of MbaDuku as a segment: from that view point the Udam, being non-Tiv, are the most distant of all neighbours. Therefore, MbaGbela people say—and, when put into these terms, at this level of the lineage system, MbaKuku people agree that MbaDuku should expand into Udam territory, not into MbaGbela territory.[12]

All Tiv would potentially unite against a foreign people, which in the above example would be the Udam.

While inter-lineage land pressures were a characteristic aspect of Tiv life in all regions, the migration process, as described above, was particularly strong in the south where the population was most densely settled. In the north, where land was more plentiful, migration would still take place but here political tyranny was more of a motivating force.

It should be noted that it was also possible for a migrating group to move beyond, instead of on, the adjoining land of other lineage segments in order to place themselves on a new site. Such a type of migration usually took the form of a small group or, infrequently, an elementary family or single man leaving its home land for new land to become the nucleus for further expansion.

The Tiv looked upon themselves as a people given to migration as a part of their very nature. The need for new land and a desire to escape political tyranny and witchcraft were the principal reasons advanced by the Tiv as causes of migration.[13]

War

War between Tiv groups or between Tiv groups and foreign peoples was typically a product of the migration process, although other

---

12. P. Bohannan, "Migration and Expansion," 8-9.
13. See generally, P. Bohannan, *Tiv Farm and Settlement,* Chaps. 10, 13; L. and P. Bohannan, *op. cit. Cf.* M. D. Sahlins, "The Segmentary Lineage: An Organization of Predatory Expansion," *American Anthropologist,* LXIII (1961), 322, in which the thesis is developed, on the basis of the expanding tendencies of the Tiv and Nuer, that segmentary societies develop practices and systems of expanding into occupied neighboring territory as open and uncontested domain disappears.

acts, such as theft and abduction, could also lead to war. As noted above, once fighting broke out it brought in more and more lineage groups until equivalent segments of opposing lineage groups were opposed to each other to the degree that all the segments of the same order, as found in a particular territory, were involved. The situation was described as follows:

> The spread of war is determined by the segmentary order of the groups involved. The fighting spreads until equivalent segments are engaged and is limited to them. . . .

> The personnel involved in Tiv warfare is dictated by the segmentary order of *uipaven*. The territorial position of the segments dictates the battlefield, and the combination of territorial juxtaposition with social distance determines the focal point of enduring hostility. . . .

> The degree of hostility between segments is a function of the social distance between them, which determines (1) the manner of fighting—with clubs, arrows, poisoned arrows; (2) the bitterness of the fighting—"close" segments fight but do not attempt to kill in the fighting; (3) the frequency and seriousness of provocative actions, such as theft, abduction, etc.; (4) the degree of looting, burning and farm damage in time of war; (5) head taking and slaving in and out of wartime; and (6) the moral, social and religious consequences of homicide (Bohannan 1953: 25-30).[14]

Treaties

Conflict and war between remote lineages among the Tiv were regulated by treaties, which were entered into with ritual, including ceremonies involving the mingling of blood and resort to *swem*. The opposing groups agreed by such treaties no longer to wage war or commit bloodshed or adultery between them and to display an unusual degree of hospitality to one another. The principal purpose of the treaties was to render safe travel across areas in which the traveller might be killed because of the distance of his lineage to that of the dwellers of the land. Lineage groups would also unite in pacts designed to secure peace in a market to which they commonly resorted.[15]

---

14. L. Bohannan, "Political Aspects," 46-51, quotations at 46, 47, 50.
15. L. and P. Bohannan, *op. cit.,* pp. 30-31, Abraham, *op. cit.,* p. 122; Downes, *op. cit.,* p. 73; L. Bohannan, "Political Aspects," pp. 61-64.

Law: Land Tenure

Every man in a Tiv compound had a right to have sufficient land to enable his wives and their respective dependents to support themselves. Every woman in a Tiv compound had a right that her husband would provide her with such land and perform those tasks upon it, notably work of a heavy nature, which custom allotted to the male. The source of a man's right was his membership in the lineage associated with the minimal *tar* by which the dwellers of the compound were identified. It could also arise from the simple fact that he was permitted to dwell in the compound. The sanctions for his right consisted of certain lineage procedures which were brought to bear by moving out of the compound when he was denied needed land. The sanction for the woman's right, as against her husband, consisted in leaving him and the compound. This would mean not only the loss of the woman but also her children and the bridewealth paid for her.

When a compound head died, whether the membership of the compound persisted unchanged depended on the ability of the new head, the oldest male remaining in the compound, to exercise leadership. If he was unable to hold its members together, then after a period of time and with due attention to the proprieties and custom, the compound would split into new and smaller ones and the land controlled by the former compound head was divided among the full brothers who were his sons. This division took place on the basis of the principles that (1) a man had a right to that portion of his father's fields which was farmed by his mother, and (2) if full brothers divided their land, they did so on the basis of the land which had been farmed by their respective wives. The objective to be achieved was not to divide lands on the basis of an equal amount to each claimant but rather to allot land on the basis of assuring that needs were equally satisfied.

A man could go to live with his non-agnatic kinsmen and acquire a right to till land which the head of the compound of his new residence would give him on a temporary basis. Tenancy on the basis of rental was unknown; strangers could be given land on which to live but their right to do so was temporary. The concept of an ability to sell land was completely alien to Tiv culture. Bohannan explained this as follows:

> Any resident has a right to sufficient land; it goes with residence. However, it is impossible to acquire a permanent, inalienable right in any

way other than by filiation; and one cannot buy or change (by sale) one's filiation.

The important point is that everybody has a right to sufficient land in the minimal *tar* in which he is recognized as a resident: a right acquired by "gift" if it is not a man's agnatic minimal tar, or a right acquired by birth if it is. No one can buy land in a *tar* in which he is living; he has a right to sufficient land already. No one can *buy* land in a *tar* in which he is not living, because he is not living there.

If lnad runs short in one's own *tar,* one takes land from an adjoining tar. All Tiv sees the tar as expanding with the synchronous processes of passage of time and increase of population (proved to Tiv satisfaction by reference to lineage genealogies). This has led to the doctrine, *not* of transfer of land, but of movement of people and social groups.[16]

Law and Procedure

Tiv concepts concerning law in its social setting started with an ideal personality of a "man who knows things," a person whose relations with others showed that he was well versed in Tiv custom and belief and that he conducted himself in accordance with their teaching. The stupid, neglectful, or bad man was one prone to commit faults or offenses.

The Tiv language was rich in words expressing prohibition of conduct. There were many rules in its culture indicating acts one must not perform in particular types of situations. The notion of offenses, or what we would term criminal law, was based on the idea that there were acts which were bad or morally at fault, that is, *dang,* and that there were other acts which went beyond this in the seriousness of their implications and possible consequences and were mystically dangerous, that is, *bo.* The idea of crime or offense was identified by the word *ifer.* This implied the breach of a norm which was of a sufficiently serious character to justify corrective acts consisting of self-help, the performance of ritual, or resort to a *jir.* The term *jir* identified either a court or a case being heard by a court.

The function of the court, in deciding a dispute, was to indicate the right way for the litigating parties to act in the future in accordance with Tiv custom. For such a solution to be complete, it was necessary for the parties to concur in it. Not until then could it be said that the proceeding was brought to an end. There was then no problem of enforcing the decision. Concurrence of the litigants in fact meant the reaching of community consensus as well. If any por-

---

16. P. Bohannan, *Tiv Farm and Settlement,* Chaps. 5, 7, quotations at 39.

tion of the community still supported a litigant, he would not be ready to accept the court's action. It was community opinion which compelled acceptance. Finally, the outcome of the case was not necessarily permanent but instead represented a *modus vivendi* which would endure while conditions remained the same but could change if conditions changed.

The norm which the court took to be significant for purposes of the case was not seen as part of a comprehensive body of the law which it was the duty of the court to apply solely on the basis of logic. The norm was rather seen in the context of the situation, which in turn was viewed in the light of a shared culture of common standards and values. In affirming that a certain norm should have been followed, the court was simply stating a truism of conduct which was right and proper in the situation and which no one could deny.

The courts possessed power to impose certain fines and punishment. In a court consisting of elders of a lineage which was handling an internal problem of the lineage, the elders might threaten to withdraw their protection from a litigant who held out against all others in accepting their decision.

While Bohannan averred at one point in his study of Tiv law that the purpose of a court was "not to apply laws, but to decide what is right in a particular case . . . usually . . . without overt reference to rules or 'laws,' " this remark must be understood in the context of the foregoing analysis. Norms, standards, established expectations, customary notions of right and wrong conduct undoubtedly played the central part in indicating the right path to be followed in the particular case.

Where patterns of behavior were at their highest frequency and institutionalized norms had emerged, where, in addition, the expectation that norm performance would or should be forthcoming was reinforced by values of high priority or importance, then breach of a norm led to further action which Bohannan characterized as counteraction and correction. A jural institution was, in Bohannan's view, characterized by a breach of norm "followed by a counteraction which (if successful) leads to reparation of the original breach or other sort of correction." In other words, the basic elements of the sequence were breach of norm, counteraction, and correction. Such a sequence might take place through court action or, alternatively, a person could resort to self-help to determine responsibility for the wrong done him, such as theft of his property, and apply corrective measures of punishment or direct taking of equivalent property to effect reprisal or reparation for the injury suffered at the wrongdoer's hands. If his measures of self-help stepped outside this orbit and did not "even the score" but instead exceeded it, it was regarded as impermissible action or vengeance. Resort to self-help and the personal exaction of reparation or punishment did not, however, have the effect of "repairing the *tar*," or restoring the original equilibrium or harmony of the relationship of the lineage to the land which it occupied. This was effected only by recourse to the traditional procedure of the *jir*.[17]

To understand fully the functioning of the *jir*, it is necessary to explore its operation within a lineage group in disposing of lineage cases. Most problems requiring settlement by the *jir* arose within the minimal tar. Whatever the size of the group involved in the dispute, all the elders of the particular group composed the court. The issues which such a court considered were viewed in mystical terms. Disharmony among relatives might lead to one placing a curse upon another, which would bring mystical forces to bear and thereby cause illness or death. *Tsav* was a source of tension in the society in that the *mbatsav* were thought often to exert their *tsav* for personal instead of community ends. The operation of *akombo* or fetishes were also considered frequently to cause illness or misfortune. Failure to perform norms associated with debts, which were obligations of a broad range not necessarily of a pecuniary nature, and with marriage wards, could also result in a curse or some sort of witchcraft which could produce harm to the norm violator. The Tiv held a view of life as involving relations with the living and with mystical forces as well. Misfortune could be a product of witchcraft or fetishes, or it could be the result of a person's own evil *tsav*. Before a *jir* within a lineage was convened, it was necessary to consult a diviner, report to him the facts of the matter, and receive from him his interpretation of the type of mystical cause which brought about the misfortune. It was then left to the elders of the *jir* to ascertain the identity of the person, if any, who had brought about the misfortune by mystical means.

The *jir* of a lineage was always convened by an elder who was an

17. P. Bohannan, *Justice and Judgment among the Tiv* (London, New York, Toronto, 1957), 33-34, 55-59, 61-68, 100-101, 138, 150-151, quotations at 19, 151. For a further development of the concepts of breach of norm, counteraction, and correction, see P. Bohannan, *Social Anthropology* (New York, 1963), 284-285. Counteraction was there defined to be acts of societal agents "designed to counter the original breach of the norm," while correction meant "either a return to the *status quo ante* or else the establishment of a new *status quo* from which normal action can again proceed."

agnatic member of the lineage associated with the *tar*. No mere
member of a *tar* had the capacity to call it into operation except in
most unusual cases. However, when a treaty existed between lineage
groups, as described above, it was possible for a person to bring a *jir*
into being to hear his case by following a stipulated procedure involving the "*swem* of the treaty."

A case was initiated by the person acting the role of plaintiff, who
gave a recitation of the facts, to which the other party would respond.
The elders questioned the parties and witnesses to arrive at the
nature of the dispute. Witnesses were sworn by magical means, but
the principal parties were not put under spiritual control through
the taking of an oath because it was felt that the latter step would
oust the court from performing its function and substitute for it
complete spiritual control of the case. When the decision of the
elders was formulated and communicated, ritual was performed to
bring the spiritual world into an order of peace and harmony and to
dispel the possibility of its further harmful intervention in human
affairs, as they were involved in the case.

A *jir* could also sit independently of any particular *tar* to hear
such disputes as were brought to it. It would hear cases, upon the
payment of a fee, at the first meeting of the court when the parties
and witnesses could be called together. Hearing of a case could be
refused by a court, and it could be referred to some other more appropriate court. In general, a *jir* preferably took place in the *tar* of
the defendant. As noted above, witnesses were sworn not to tell
falsehoods under oath, but principals were exempted from this requirement. Traditionally, however, a principal could resort to the
ordeal of taking poison in the form of drinking sasswood. If this was
vomited and the taker survived, his version of the case was considered proved. After hearing the case and rendering a decision indicating the right way for the parties thereafter to proceed in the
light of custom, the *jir* was not considered to have ended its action
until its solution was accepted by the parties. As evidence of such
acceptance, one or both of the parties might be required to pay a
fine. To bring about an acceptance of a decision which a party was
reluctant to make, the elders might threaten to cease protecting him
from the forces of witchcraft.[18]

Typically, a *jir* dealt with misfortunes, such as illness and bad luck,
which were of such a character as to be caused by witchcraft. If a
dispute not involving witchcraft arose, an elder might be asked to

---

18. See generally *ibid.*, Chaps. 9, 4.

arbitrate between the disputing parties. If a theft occurred and the thief was found, the head of the compound of the latter might be asked to make recompense. If damage to property occurred as the result of acts of another, the wrongdoer might be asked to make the damage good. It is also to be observed that a special form of proceeding by the elders took place when a person wished to place a charge of witchcraft against a man of very great influence. In such cases, the plaintiff's age set and members of his mother's lineage group came to his support in raising the question before the elders why they were allowing him to be bewitched.[19]

Bohannan had some illuminating remarks to make concerning the somewhat vague development of the law relating to debt and obligation in comparison with the rather precise notions of duty involved in marriage relations:

> It is becoming evident that Tiv rules of property management and financial transaction are not nearly so rigid or so generally agreed as those of marriage. There may be differences of opinion about marriage norms; there are seldom differences of principle. In regard to property, however, the rules are very imprecise, and rights and duties are not nearly so clear-cut. This observation may be correlated with another: Marriage is highly important to Tiv, and involves very broad-scale and far-reaching relationships. These relationships are themselves very dense, each having many strands and many implications. Debt, on the other hand, is much less far-reaching in its social consequences. The relationships between debtor and creditor and between pledger and pledgee involve fewer people and can be broken with less disruption to the social order and to the lives of individuals and families.[20]

It should be noted that some development of what we would conceive to be the idea of contract had appeared in the practice of private understandings between two men to undertake mutual help in farming.[21]

Offenses which were subject to legal control included murder, theft, adultery, incest, assault, and arson.[22]

Law: Comparison with the Barotse System

The insights which Paul Bohannan developed in his study of law among the Tiv should be compared with Max Gluckman's study of

19. L. Bohannan, "Political Aspects," 54-57.
20. P. Bohannan, *Justice and Judgment,* 109.
21. Abraham, *op. cit.,* p. 125.
22. Downes, *op. cit,* p. 72-76.

law among the Barotse.[23] The latter study is comparable in depth
and thoroughness to Bohannan's and should be examined in order
to render precise Gluckman's use of the concept of "the reasonable
man" and to compare his view of the Barotse approach to the resolution of disputes by the use of a court with Bohannan's view of the
Tiv. In so doing, it will be found that Gluckman's use of the symbol,
"reasonable man," was perhaps unfortunate, at least in the later use
of this symbol made by others.

As a matter of fact, Gluckman and Bohannan perceived the tribal
behavior in question in much the same way. Gluckman's symbol of
"reasonable man" had considerable congruence with what a Tiv
court would consider to be proper conduct. It was conduct which
was correct, appropriate, and customary conduct in the circumstances. It was conduct which reflected established standards and
norms. The values held by the parties, expressed in conduct which
could rightfully be expected to be forthcoming in the circumstances,
were the basis of judgment by the court. The function of the judgment and the judicial process was to reaffirm those norms to the
parties and to the community at large and to effect a reconciliation
of the parties so that they would thereafter perform their relevant
roles in the community in a way satisfactory to all. The process and
goal of reconciliation and restoration of harmonious social relationships demanded that the violators of norms be identified and
shown where they fell short of community standards and expectations, to the end that they might be thereafter effective or "upright"
participants or role performers in community activities.

Gluckman developed his notion of the "reasonable man" as a
basic premise for judicial decision with the initial statement that
judges searched for evidence and explored its significance so as "to
catch persons in departures from usages and norms." This is precisely the starting point of Bohannan's categorization of the elements of the legal process—breach of norm. Gluckman explained
that: "Some of these usages are definite, in the sense that a person
either has or has not conformed with them. But many norms of behaviour are of the general pattern: 'respect and help your father';
'treat the headman of your village properly'; 'treat your wife
well.' . . ."

The norms to be applied, therefore, may range from those which
describe fairly concrete and narrow sequences of behavior, such as

---

23. M. Gluckman, *The Judicial Process among the Barotse of Northern Rhodesia* (Glencoe, 1955).

homicide or incest, to those which refer to broad and general types of behavior. Gluckman affirmed that in all cases involving norm fulfillment there was a certain standard of performance of norms which the culture expected of the parties and which was applied in the judicial process. When that standard was not met, he was regarded as a deviant performer and subject to control or sanction. Gluckman said that: "This standard is 'the reasonable and customary man and what he would have done.'" In the next sentence, Gluckman affirmed the universality of this standard: "The reasonable man is recognized as the central figure in all systems of law, but his presence in simpler legal systems has not been noticed." In the footnote supporting this statement, he acknowledged that there was a paucity of references to the "reasonable man," except for citation of a reference to the works of the British humanist and satirist, Sir Alan Herbert. He stated that the concept of the "reasonable man" appeared in most textbooks of jurisprudence not, indeed, as a central concept or even as an all-embracing figure in the law but only "under separate heads, such as proof of guilt, responsibility, intention, negligence, etc." This is indeed the case. In certain aspects of the law, such as in torts, contracts, and equity, the law has had to be content with such general standards of desired conduct as "reasonable care," "due diligence," "reasonableness," and "prudence." In these specific and rather localized contexts, one might say that the courts resort to somewhat *ad hoc* appraisals of conduct as to whether it should be held permissible on the basis of community standards, expectations, and that which was, in general, reasonable or rational conduct in the circumstances.[24] This is not at all to say, however, that: "The reasonable man is recognized as *the* central figure in all developed systems of law." (Italics supplied) The asserted fact, as a proposition of law in Anglo-American jurisprudence, is flatly denied. Moreover, Gluckman's term, the "reasonable *and customary* man" (italics supplied), is a term believed to be unknown in Anglo-American law. Gluckman seems later to have considerably relinquished his use of the concept "reasonable man" and to have substituted for it the "reasonable brother, sister, uncle, nephew, or general dependent of the new headman." The "standards of 'the reasonable man'" were those "specified in particulars for incumbents of varied positions in

---

24. See discussion of the "reasonable man" in W. L. Prosser, *Handbook of the Law of Torts* (3d ed.; St. Paul, 1964), 153-168. He is "a personification of a community ideal of reasonable behavior, determined by the jury's social judgment." (P. 154)

social life." In other words, the standards of performance of a particular role are now held to be the expectations of performance of the "reasonable man."[25]

Gluckman stated that the role of the judges was one of "adjusting the underlying and multiplex relationships which are still basic in tribal society." The judges were said to proceed with an "awareness, often subconscious, of customs, standards, and ways of life of the people to whom they have to administer justice."

The meaning which the Lozi of Barotseland gave to the concept of a "reasonable man" was that he was a "sensible" and "upright" man. This was embodied in the term *mutu yangana.* Yet "Lozi judges do not make continual explicit use of the general phrase of reasonable man." In other words, not only was their referent for Gluckman's "reasonable man" a different one from the Anglo-American referent for the term, but the Lozi concept did not appear to be central to the Lozi judicial interpretation of social action. Instead, Lozi judges appeared to be more frequently concerned with defining what was desirable and approved *role* behavior in the circumstances. They were "in most cases" concerned with "the behavior of people occupying specific social positions." They were "chiefly concerned with the relationships of status." They "more often work explicitly with the phrases, 'a good husband,' 'a sensible induna,' and so on." Judges use the "common practice" of the people to refer to such specific roles as "chief," "headman," "fisherman," "herdsman" and "in doing so they are setting up the differentiated standard of the reasonable and perhaps even upright incumbent of a particular social position."

The term accordingly had the referent of role performance as being carried out in either an approved or disapproved manner. "The concept of 'reasonable' measures the range of allowed departure from the highest standards of duty and absolute conformance to norm, and the minimum adherence which is insisted upon." "If 'the reasonable man' is more precisely the man who conforms reasonably to the customs and standards of his social position," clearly he corresponds closely with the concept of "the role of a particular *status,* which has become so important in current anthropology and soci-

---

25. M. Gluckman, *The Ideas in Barotse Jurisprudence* (New Haven, London, 1965), 16, 21. The congruence of Gluckman's concept of the "reasonable man" and the concept of the protection through law of norms of behavior established through role performance is further borne out in M. Gluckman, "Reasonableness and Responsibility in the Law of Segmentary Societies," *African Law: Adaptation and Development,* eds. H. Kuper and L. Kuper (Berkeley, Los Angeles, 1965), 120.

ology." It is believed that precision in the use of terms, conceptual analysis, and clarity of communication might have been better served if the symbol of "reasonable man" had not been adopted and a simple dichotomy used instead of reasonable or desirable role performance, on the one hand, and deviant or undesirable role performance, on the other hand. The term role is, as Gluckman admits, sufficiently well established in the social sciences, including "current anthropology and sociology," to justify such a step. Thus desirable and undesirable role performance was, in the Lozi view, not solely to be seen in terms of "a narrow, legally enforceable claim" but more generally in terms of "whether the parties observed the obligations due to each other" as they performed their roles in specific situations.[26]

Conclusion

The Tiv were a maladjusted society, crowded on their land, restless, ridden with fear, and migrating to other lands. They were lacking in adequate authority to organize action, torn by conflict within and between groups, characterized by the use of violence, and without adequate measures for resolving disputes and sanctioning offenses. Authority within the compound was vested in the oldest male member, but, upon occasion, a younger brother would exercise actual authority while his oldest brother retained only nominal authority. Authority was minimal and diffusely exercised by the elders and men of influence and power. Consensus, rather than binding authority, was the means for dispute settlement. The ambivalence and frustrations of life led to an almost unbearable perception of magic and witchcraft as instruments for achieving wealth and power or bringing evil. Of the peoples so far studied, none exhibited to the same extent as the Tiv the acceptance of witchcraft and mystical powers as a part of their life. Even the members of a family feared the exercise of witchcraft against one another.

Ancestors were not perceived to possess the power to bring fortune or misfortune. Ancestors were used to identify lineage groups. Lineage groups, in turn, were perceived in terms of potential enmity and alliance in the event of conflict. Coherence and integration of the society were at a low point. There were no significant offices of a political and jural nature above the minimal *tar,* or lineage group,

---

26. Gluckman, *The Judicial Process among the Barotse,* 49, 80-83, 95-96, 125-129, 138-140, quotations at 82-83, 95-96, 126-129, 139.

and the *jir,* or court. Leadership existed in the elders and men of affluence and prestige. Leadership was held to flow from the possession of *tsav,* or witchcraft power, as well as the personal qualities of judgment and knowledge of the world. Leadership was feared and hated, even though its necessity, in a world of menace, was acknowledged. The *jir* was the actual political-legal mechanism.

Spiritual forces were principally manifested in and through *akombo,* or fetishes, and *tsav.* The maker or holder of an *akombo* was able considerably to direct its unique mystical power. The *mbatsav,* who possessed *tsav* or witchcraft power to an unusual degree, were able to use it for good or evil. There was also *swem,* a superordinate and impersonal sacred power. Sprites existed who could cause dumbness, madness, monstrous births, and malicious or michievious harm.

Life, health, and good fortune were thought ordinarily to flow toward a person. However, this flow was frustrated and death, illness, and misfortune occurred as a result of the intervention of the supernatural forces of life. These forces were under the control of those who were one's superiors in the kinship group and those who held positions of authority and power in the community.

The Tiv had two basic concepts of lineage. *Ityo* expressed a person's status or position in terms of lineage for purposes of marriage, performance of ritual, and armed support. *Tar* expressed the relationship of a lineage group to the land which it occupied and the idea of harmony, perfection, and balance among the various ways in which that relationship was expressed. When that harmony was disturbed through the commission of offenses or the like, it was necessary "to repair the *tar.*" The *jir,* which was the court or moot, was the social means to that end. The cases which it heard were also known as *jir.*

There was no central political head for the people as a whole. The head of the compound coordinated farming activity, allotted land, controlled magical forces for the benefit of the compound group, and settled disputes among its members. However, sage elders and men of affluence and prestige handled problems between and within lineage groups. The *jir* was the mechanism for dispute settlement and control over the commission of offenses.

The absence in Tiv society of a territorial or kinship structure which controlled a larger amount of land than that held by a compound, *from which allotments of land might be made to lineage groups as needed,* was the primary cause of the phenomenon of the movement of Tiv lineage groups to other lands, even those of related kinship groups who were, however, distantly related. Faced with the fact that the head of a compound was the only source for the *allotment* of land and that he had none to allot, confronted with tyranny and witchcraft, the Tiv migrated with the inexorable force of a glacier. They were good farmers and prided themselves upon their ability to till the land and upon their industry. As their numbers expanded and land was needed, as political tyranny, unresolved conflict, and tensions symbolized in witchcraft made life intolerable, they moved upon the land of another lineage group, to which they were most distantly related, or upon the land of foreigners. The concept of *tar* was significant for the purpose of the migration process. The land which was appropriate for migration was identified in terms of *tar*, with its occupying lineage group being viewed as potential enemies, and the *tar* of more closely related lineage groups as potential allies.

The commission of offenses or the occurrence of disputes disturbed the *tar* and it was necessary that it be "repaired" by the operation of the *jir*. The elders of the *jir* would hear the case, listen to the parties and the witnesses, cross-examine them in an effort to arrive at the truth, and indicate the right way for the parties in conflict to conduct themselves or decide upon the offense and its penalty. Even though valued norms of conduct might be pointed out by the court to have been violated by one of the parties and his fault clearly revealed, the action of the *jir* must be seen in the context of effecting corrective action and restoring the harmony and balance of the *tar*. Ritual to that end was necessary in some circumstances, but above all it was necessary that the parties and the community at large should accept the judgment of the *jir*. Performance of its role was not completed until this took place.

As one considers the patterns of Tiv life, they fall into a large, overall pattern in which Tiv society is manifested on two planes, each mirroring the other and each inexorably linked with the other to form an organic whole. One is the face of reality. The other is reality mirrored in the supernatural world. The combination is an organization of society under the holders of authority, whose positions are supported by supernatural power.

The Tiv can be said to be a people who transformed a kinship structure of social action into an organizational structure by endowing those who held positions of authority with a power to inflict supernatural harm. Those who occupied positions of leadership and authority were required to be persons of ability. The senior elder of the compound who had only his seniority to justify his exercise of authority found himself shoved aside by a younger man of ability exercising *de facto* authority. Those who came to the fore in the community and were its important leaders and controllers of conflict were men of demonstrated ability as well as elders. In addition, all those who exercised temporal authority were able to bring to bear their possession of supernatural power, in the form of *tsav*, to reinforce their authority. *Tsav* was linked with the heart, which was the means for knowing the world. Such persons also possessed *akombo*, through which they could influence the affairs of life. Powerful possessors of *tsav* were known as the *mbatsav*. The *mbatsav* were perceived to be structured into an organization acting at night in which there were officials possessing rank and authority. *Swem*, symbolizing impersonal justice, operated to control the abuse of power by its possessors.

Tiv society, as it endured and grew with the passing generations, exhibited four principal aspects of maladjustment to its environment.

First, a Tiv had a most inadequate conception of a social order. The pathology of his ways of meeting life was revealed and reflected in his image of the supernatural world. The resulting order of supernatural power, linked with temporal authority in structures of social action, failed to satisfy his needs for the development of a healthy personality. In short, his cognitive map of the cosmos, his temporal world, and his place therein was a bare working minimum for an enduring social order. A Tiv was an isolated person, exposed to evil forces mostly beyond his control and living in fear of his fellows and the supernatural world.

His fate was determined by his *tsav*. His failures and misfortunes were not the product of his actions but were instead the product of the *tsav* of others. Those in his immediate lineage group whom he loved were also those whom he feared for their possession and use of *tsav*. Related kinship groups were viewed in terms of their potential enmity in war. Those who were his leaders were perceived to attain and keep their leadership by virtue of their unusual *tsav*. His conception of the supernatural world and his relation to it was most inadequate.

There was no supernatural power which he could invoke to bring him good fortune or avert misfortune, except by resort to fetishes or *akombo* for specific ends. The gods brought him harm, such as dumbness or monstrous births. Indeed, the supernatural world as a whole brought misfortune to man, whose natural condition it was to enjoy good fortune.

Second, authority was most minimally developed and supported. It appeared primarily in the head of the compound and secondarily in the *jir* or court.

Kinship-structured societies, other than the Tiv, were supported by a belief system in supernatural power manifested in independent, impartial entities, bringing both good and bad fortune to man. Good fortune was dispensed as a reward for ritual correctness and respect for temporal authority and norms. Bad fortune was a punishment for lack of observance of ritual prescriptions and lack of respect for temporal authority and norms. Rewards for good conduct and deprivations for bad conduct flowed independently and impartially, although it was possible for man, through observance of ritual, to lessen the impact of misfortune.

Not so with the Tiv. *Tsav,* or supernatural power, was personal to its holder and consisted of a power to inflict evil. It could be used for personal, arbitrary purposes. It could be used to achieve power in temporal affairs. Those who possessed temporal power by definition possessed *tsav* in an unusual degree. Since authority resided in persons possessing *tsav* in an unusual degree and since the *jir* or court was composed of persons also possessing *tsav* in an unusual degree, authority was supported by fear of *persons* possessing a supernatural power to inflict evil, instead of a supernatural entity independently and impartially exercising the power to inflict deprivations as a sanctioning process.

Third, when open land was not available for needed family use in many situations, there was no procedure, other than that of force to secure needed land. When no land was available within a minimal *tar* for the lineage segment associated with it, adjoining kinship groups were perceived either as potential enemies withholding needed land or as potential allies in a war for its possession. Kinship groups larger than the family were important for purposes of dispute settlement and war. The family, the dominant social structure, was inadequate for the purpose of satisfying the basic needs of Tiv society. It was replete with interpersonal tensions and surcharged with fear.

Fourth, there was an inadequate structuring of the legal system. Disputing parties were limited in their capacity to invoke action by the *jir,* and the *jir* was limited in its capacity to render binding decisions—the consent of the disputing parties was necessary to implement its action. Self-help, in the form of individual resort to supernatural or physical power, was the principal sanctioning process. There was little of an independently functioning sanctioning process.

Part Four

UGANDA

Chapter 10

The Ganda

Geography and Economy

UGANDA, Kenya, and Tanzania were selected for study from the East African states for the reason that this group of states was under British administration prior to independence and possessed a somewhat common structure of economic organization. It was thought at the time of their independence that they might move toward federalism, but this does not now seem likely to occur. An additional people, the Nuer in the Sudan, were selected because of the outstanding quality and comprehensiveness of the literature on them. The peoples investigated in these states provide a fairly wide sampling of East African cultures.

Uganda lies in tropical Africa but its altitude provides an equable climate. The Republic of Congo bounds it on the west, Ruanda Urundi and Tanzania on the south, Kenya on the east, and Sudan on the north. The north is a hot, dry savanna. The typical vegetation is long elephant grass or shorter grass, but tropical forests grow in the west, which looks upon the Ruwenzori mountains. The country is divided into the Western, Northern, and Eastern Provinces, with Buganda Province occupying the center, south and southeast, including Lake Victoria.

Farming and the raising of livestock characterize the economy. Plantains or bananas are the principal foods in the well-watered areas near Lake Victoria; millet, peas, and beans in the uplands of Ankole, Toro, and Bungoro in the west; milk, blood, and grain in the pastoral regions of the southwest, supplemented by sweet potatoes, cassava, and other vegetables. The principal export crops today are coffee and cotton.

Six peoples of Uganda will be investigated, the Ganda, the Soga (Appendix B2), the Nyoro (Appendix B3), the Amba (Appendix B4), the Lugbara, and the Alur (Appendix B5). The first three belong to the Bantu-speaking peoples, the fourth to the Nilo-Hamitic linguistic group, the fifth to the Sudanic linguistic group, and the sixth to the Lwo group of the Nilotic languages. The first three were kingdoms, the next two were organized on a segmentary lineage and age-set basis, and the last was organized into chiefdoms of a rather unique type. The Ganda, Soga, Lugbara, and Alur were agricultural societies, the Nandi were a pastoral society, the Nyoro were a people who once had been considerably a pastoral society. A further reason for the selection of these peoples is that the literature on them is fairly complete.

The Ganda are a Bantu-speaking people living on a plateau lying between Lake Victoria and Lake Kyoga, with the Victoria Nile River to the east. The average elevation is about 4,000 feet. The land consists mostly of flat-topped hills descending into swampy valleys and sluggish streams, usually filled with papyrus or reeds. The annual mean rainfall ranges from 45 to 55 inches and is well distributed throughout the year. The lowest mean annual temperature is 65°F.

The principal food was bananas, supplemented by beans and millet. Chickens were kept for meat, and other meat was obtained through hunting and gifts and feasts by the chiefs. Fish was obtained by those living near the shores. Cattle and goats were owned by the wealthy. Reliance upon bananas as the chief source of food meant that adequate food for all at all times could be obtained with but very little work and that agricultural work was chiefly done by the women.[1]

Individual Values and Attitudes

The literature on the Ganda affords insight into the individual mostly from its description of social and political life.

The Ganda constituted a warring, authoritarian, achieving, and competitive society. These traits, and the patterns of behavior which

---

1. D. E. Apter, *The Political Kingdom in Uganda* (Princeton, 1961), 30-36; M. C. Fallers, "The Eastern Lacustrine Bantu (Ganda, Soga)," *Ethnographic Survey of Africa,* ed. D. Forde (London, 1960), Part XI, 32-33.

they engendered, formed an interdependent, complex whole. They were a predatory society. War brought them additional territory, slaves, women, power, and individual rise in position. Through prowess in war, individuals could achieve a rapid advance in status. War became a standard norm of external relations. Not until the latter half of the nineteenth century did external trade develop. Sir Apolo Kagwa, a prime minister in the early twentieth century, said that: "This custom of robbing the surrounding nations brought wealth to the Buganda, but it also meant the loss of their ability to trade. These expeditions had to be made quite regularly about every six months, and sometimes resulted in considerable loss of life and no particular gain."[2]

Heavy reliance on the easily-raised banana as food freed the men to engage in war and to make and maintain a system of roads over which armies could assemble and move rapidly and thereby preserve the internal and external power of the king. The necessity of unquestioning obedience in war created patterns of authority in the king which emphasized his complete control over the lives and fortunes of his subjects. Support of any one chief was voluntary on the part of his followers. The necessity that chiefs have followers to support them in war and to enable them to meet the demands of higher authority for labor supply curbed their tendency to abuse their authority in their relations with followers. It also led to a system under which the king and his chiefs distributed largesse among their followers and exceptionally able followers were rapidly promoted.

Within the family, the father was a very authoritarian figure. Wives and children were expected to show marked humility and submission to him. Restraint upon his power over wives existed in their ability to return to their own relatives should he treat them badly. Children were expected to give unquestioning obedience and were severely punished for failure to meet desired standards of submission. Moreover, a father could discriminate arbitrarily in giving favors to his children. The pattern set in the home foreshadowed the mercurial shifts in favor by the king and his savage displays of power in killings, beatings, burnings, and mutilations of his followers.

Typically, a man placed himself in a relationship of clientage with a patron or lord. During the ages of three to seven, his children were sent away from home to the homes of relatives. There they received

---

2. A. Kagwa, *The Customs of the Baganda,* ed. M. M. Edel, trans. E. B. Kalibala (New York, 1934), 92-93.

a stern training and gained experience in living a life of adjusting to the will of their superiors. Adolescent children were sent to the residences of chiefs, the king's ministers, or the king himself. The boys became pages and the girls became household servants, concubines, or wives. The result was to promote the political and economic fortunes of the giver, on the one hand, and to open the possibility of an advance in status to the children, on the other.

The situation has considerable coincidence with aspects of achieving societies in the modern world. The emphasis upon the value of position and rise in status, the possession by the élite of cultural knowledge of how to promote achievement, the training of children in modes of conduct which would facilitate achievement, the personal dedication of individuals to achievement, all these were aspects of Ganda life which are familiar patterns in modern society.

The king displayed whimsical patterns of favor, persons were rapidly advanced and demoted in office, thereby promoting authority and power through fear, dependency, and submission. A slight departure of behavior from one of abject humility and submission would lead to loss of position or even death. In these circumstances, there was an extremely strong emphasis on politeness and courtesy in person relations. "The physical survival of a young courtier might depend on his docility, and his judgment of his superior's character and mood; his promotion certainly did. . . . Attention to appearances and the saving of face is a reflection of the Ganda social order. . . . Baganda were also praised for being adaptable, intelligent, shrewd, efficient and far-sighted."[3]

An achieving and competitive society, in which man strove to achieve higher status and its attendant rewards, was accordingly created. It is obvious that, in all societies, man displays the requisite degree of industry called for by its level of culture and physical resources. In Ganda society, it was possible for man to be slothful and survive, yet he was not.

Competition for advancement and the securing of achieved position from loss in favor of rivals not only led to patterns of politeness and deference but also deception and intrigue. Cunning and cleverness in outmaneuvering others were admired virtues. Truth was not a virtue in its own right.

The supremacy of the king's will in peace and war was maintained by a continual display of his absolute power over the lives, bodies,

3. A. I. Richards, "Traditional Values and Current Political Behavior," *The King's Men: Leadership and Status in Buganda on the Eve of Independence,* ed. L. A. Fallers (London, New York, Nairobi, 1964), 294, quotations at 297, 299.

and fortunes of his subjects. The palace was the scene of constant killings and mutilations of courtiers, wives, concubines, and servants of the king who had incurred his disfavor. Men and women were casually selected for sacrifice in ritual carried out to safeguard the king's health and to prosper the kingdom. Men were killed arbitrarily merely to show the king's power. Cowards in war were burned.

The society of the Ganda was one in which advancement in status was achieved on the basis of individual accomplishment in war and able performance of office and not merely as the result of hereditary position. An outstanding warrior could, at the end of a battle or campaign, be made a chief as a reward for his accomplishments or receive lesser rewards. The ability to recruit and hold followers, who could be used in war and in building roads and the king's dwellings, was essential to retain office. Clients were free to leave their patrons. A lord who demonstrated his skill in holding office and rising in the hierarchy of office attracted followers. A lord who fell into disfavor with the king or his superior found his followers leaving his service.

Relations between superiors and inferiors, that is, lord and subject, were marked by patterns of behavior of impassivity, dignity, and casual notice of inferiors on the part of the lord and mute acceptance of the lord's will on the part of followers. The lord was expected to be bountiful in his hospitality, but the degree of hospitality extended was determined by the status of the visitor. Important guests received food as well as drink, those low in the social scale were served only a cup of tea.[4]

Religion and Magic

Buganda was a kingdom established by conquest. The myth of divine origin of the king and the close articulation of political and spiritual forces so characteristic of African life, including the Bantu, did not appear. His selection to the office of kingship was not based on his sacred descent but instead on his temporal ability to lead his kingdom. The ceremony of his accession to office took place under priestly guidance and appeals to the appropriate gods to reinforce his authority, but he was no son of the gods. After the assumption of office, it was, however, the duty of the king to invoke the gods for the good of his people.

Religion was not identified by clan but by locality, in the sense

4. A. I. Richards, "Authority Patterns in Traditional Buganda," *ibid.*, p. 256.

that the spirits were consulted and invoked by turning to the local prophet of the particular spirit whose aid was sought. The only public ritual of tribal unity in Ganda did not affirm a mutual dependence upon the king, as linked with the tribal god, but instead simply expressed a common fealty to the king.

The spirits were not held to be a source of fortune but rather of misfortune. They were not thought of as the source of bounty for those who served them faithfully. Their favor was invoked when their malevolence was made manifest in illness or other evil. They were, in short, forces to be placated rather than loved.

The Buganda divinities included ancestors who had in their lifetime displayed special supernatural powers. After their death, they were consulted through prophets and mediums. Kibuka and Nende, the gods of war, Mukasa, the god of children and fertility, the gods of the elements—rain, lightning, earthquake, and drought—the gods of the plague and smallpox, and the god of hunting were the gods whose influence was largest in the affairs of men. On every important undertaking and as misfortune occurred, the prophets of various spirits were consulted on the basis of their reputation for "speaking well" or accomplishing a desired outcome. Certain gods, such as Kibuka, had definite categories of action as their special province, such as national success in war and individual success in hunting and fishing. Kibuka was propitiated by human sacrifice, as was also a certain river god.

A spirit expressed its power by visiting misfortune upon a person who had in some manner wronged it. Certain types of illness were attributed to such a spiritual cause, and it was necessary to propitiate the spirit by an offering. Such wrongs to a spirit consisted in wrongs done to it before death and in its lifetime, wrongs to its heir, or wrongs done by its heirs to its relatives.

The prophets who served particular gods were consulted at times of danger or upon important occasions either by way of precaution or to alleviate evil. Purificatory rites were performed when a village was threatened with calamity. Magical rites were performed during pregnancy or to avert damage by rain or hailstones. Cures were obtained from the prophets for barrenness and illness. Magic to produce courage and success in hunting was sought.

The prophet had a most important role in warfare. He was consulted by the general of a war party as to whether the day was unpropitious for fighting and gave other advice daily to the general. His advice was also sought on where and when a war should be undertaken.

The Ganda believed that magic was used to inflict upon persons. Sorcerers could exert their force upon their victims from a distance, as well as near at hand. Individuals resorted to sorcerers out of envy, spite, and anger against others. Sorcery and supernatural sanctions also operated in the legal sphere. A person with a legitimate grievance which was left unremedied would resort to sorcery to punish the one who had injured him wrongfully. Certain types of sacrilege and breaches of sexual regulations were held to bring retribution automatically to the person who committed them.[5]

Social Organization

The Ganda were divided into a number of patrilineal clans, each identified by common descent from a single male ancestor and common totems consisting of a principal totem and a lesser totem. The men of the same generation called each other brothers, the women called each other sisters. They called the male members of their senior generation fathers and the female members mothers. Parentage of two or more persons was identified by asking whether they had the same father or the same mother. A person did not marry into the clans of either his father or his mother. A clan had its own estates which contained the burial grounds of its members. Branches of a clan could also secure freehold ownership of land when three or four generations of its members were buried there.

Clans were a part of the political organization of the kingdom. They were tied in with its history and performed special duties for the king. For example, one supplied the chief herder, another a certain official for the coronation ceremony, another a certain gatekeeper, another the keeper of a certain national shrine, and still another the keeper of the bark cloths. All candidates to succession to the headship of clans had to be approved by the king.

The clan was significant for purposes of endogamy, funerals, and end-of-mourning ceremonies. The head of a clan held court over cases of incest, inheritance, succession, bridewealth, and other kin-

---

5. L. P. Mair, *An African People in the Twentieth Century* (London, 1934), Chap. 9; J. Roscoe, *The Baganda: An Account of their Native Customs and Beliefs* (London, 1911), Chap. 9; *cf.* T. Irstam, *The King of Ganda: Studies in the Institutions of Sacral Kingship in Africa,* Ethnographical Museum of Sweden, Stockholm, New Series, Pub. No. 8 (Lund, Sweden, 1944); see also D. A. Low, *Religion and Society in Buganda, 1875-1900,* East African Studies No. 8 (Kampala, Uganda, 1956).

ship matters. Appeal from his decisions could be made ultimately, through the prime minister, to the king.

The royal family belonged to no one clan. Children of the king took the clan of their mother. Any son of the king, except his firstborn, was eligible for the kingship. The king could marry the women of any clan.

Homesteads were rarely occupied by extended families. Young men established their own homesteads where, if they were able, they brought plural wives. Polygyny was favored over monogamy, although the latter was common.[6]

Clientage relationships were found throughout Ganda life. A person seeking land or opportunities for advancement in status attached himself to a superior by action termed *kusenga*. The two roles were named "my lord" and "my servant."[7]

Political Organization

The king, or *Kabaka*, was selected from the royal family, and the office went in direct descent from the father to one of his sons other than the eldest. Upon the death of a king, the succeeding king was named by the chief minister, or *Katikiro*, and the official in charge of the king's fetishes. Accession to kingship thus tended to emphasize capacity to rule, in place of such formal criteria as primogeniture. His office symbolized his power over the country and his representation of its military exploits, superiority over other tribes, and system of administration.

In the coronation ceremonies, his role as guardian of the welfare of his people was emphasized in the abjuration: "Look with kindness upon all your people, from the highest to the lowest; be mindful of your land, deal justice among your people." His role as supreme authority and the source of military power was indicated by giving him spears and a shield, accompanied by the explanation: "With these spears you will fight those who scorn you, who trouble you, your enemies. The king is not despised, he is not thwarted nor contradicted. You are to overcome rebels with these spears and this shield." His role as the dispenser of justice was symbolized by the *Katikiro* handing him a rod and saying: "With this rod you shall judge Buganda; it shall be given to your *Katikiro* to judge Buganda,

---

6. Roscoe, *op. cit.*, Chap. 6; M. C. Fallers, *op. cit.*, pp. 52-55.
7. L. A. Fallers *et al.*, "Social Stratification in Traditional Buganda," *The King's Men*, 73-74.

you shall both judge Buganda." The rod was thereafter returned to the *Katikiro*. The king was also given a two-edged knife to symbolize his duty to "cut cases" or decide disputes impartially. He was held to be above bribery.

As he was led to the throne, he was proclaimed to the people with the statement: "This is your king, hear him, honour him, obey him, fight for him." Mair draws the conclusion that:

> From this ceremonial emerges the idea of a monarch having not only rights but obligations. His subjects' duties were given in the expectation of a return from him; their obedience was the counterpart of his leadership, both being necessary to make the people victorious over his enemies. Absolute as was his power he was expected to respect established rights, to uphold justice, and to behave with "kindness" or generosity in rewarding the deserving. This reciprocal relationship was explicitly affirmed before the active obligations of chiefs and people, in abeyance since the death of the late king, were resumed.[8]

Save for a few hereditary chiefships, the king was the source of legitimate authority. He made an extraordinarily wide range of appointments to office and confirmed appointment to still other offices. The clan heads were at an earlier period of time held to be considerably independent from the king. They then looked at him as first among equals. By the nineteenth century, however, his concurrence was necessary to their appointment, and he had very considerably occupied their field of authority. Thousands of officials were dependent upon him for appointment and were part of his system of patronage. This system was manipulated to maintain his power, as officials strove to rise in office and royal favor. A balance of power among competing groups was maintained through allocating posts in favor of one lineage as against another on the basis of their respective power and loyalty, on the one hand, and the avoidance of jealousy, on the other hand. Southwold found the following principles to govern the use of the appointive power so as to maintain sovereign power:

(1) The subordinates of the administrator should be appointed by and made responsible to the Lord himself, not the administrator.

(2) The formation of local groups loyal to the administrator personally should be frustrated by the frequent transfer of administrators from place to place.

(3) The aggregation of descent of kinship groups loyal to the administrator personally should be checked by avoiding the succession of kinsmen to any post.

(4) The Lord should acquire and maintain both the right and the

---

8. Mair, *op. cit.*, pp. 180-182.

power to appoint whatever persons he chooses as administrators, and to dismiss them as he sees fit.

It was also pointed out how an administrative system under the authority of the king was used to supplant and restrict the power of a hereditary aristocracy:

(1)   Even if the new Staff is appointed to a new set of offices alongside the old ones held by the Aristocracy, the relative power of the latter is weakened.
(2)   If the new Staff is appointed to offices formerly held by the Aristocracy, the latter may be wholly or largely driven from positions of power.
(3)   At the least, the new Staff serves as a check upon disloyal activities of the Aristocracy, if only by reporting on them.
(4)   The new Staff can be used as the instrument for direct attacks on the power and privilege of the Aristocracy, or at least as a support when such measures are carried out by other means.
(5)   If the new Staff and the Aristocracy exist side by side, they can be played off against each other, thereby weakening the independent power of each; the Lord, as arbiter of their disputes (which he may foment), has a position of exceptional power. To this end, it is advantageous for him to leave the respective spheres of authority of each group indistinct and even confluent.[9]

When the king's power of appointment and removal from office was used wisely, the result was: "The Kabaka was admired for his domination over all the authorities in his kingdom, as this was thought to give security to the country as a whole and to make possible the rule of law. This seems to be what is meant by the phrase *ensi eteredde:* 'The country is put to right.' "[10]

The country was divided into ten territorial districts or *ssazas,* the chiefs of which were appointed by the king. Within these territories and representing a second level of authority were a number of great chiefs, or *bakungu,* who exercised authority over a third level of chiefs, known as the *batongole* and *bataka,* except such lesser chiefs as were appointed by the king directly. This is not to imply that there was a hierarchy of the three levels of authority in the sense that a chief of a senior level could simply, by virtue of that fact alone, issue commands to a chief of a lower level. The order of seniority indicated the path communication should follow. A messenger from the king was sent to the *ssaza* chief, who would then appoint his own messenger to introduce him to the chiefs under him.

---

9. M. Southwold, *Bureaucracy and Chiefship in Buganda,* East African Studies No. 14 (London, 1961), 3-4.

10. A. I. Richards, *op. cit.,* p. 284.

The administrative system was organized for the purpose of providing labor and warriors to the king, collecting taxes, building and maintaining a network of roads, rendering justice to the people, providing opportunity for advance in status by subjects, and extending gifts and food to subjects and followers of chiefs.

The administrative system provided labor for constructing the buildings of the royal enclosure at the capital. The great chiefs each had a quota of men to supply for this purpose. The important chiefs were expected to spend a great amount of time at the palace and to maintain homes there as evidence of their dependence on and loyalty to the king. The *ssaza* chiefs were required to keep in repair a road from their seat to the capital and the lesser chiefs were similarly responsible for the roads from their enclosures to that of the *ssaza*. Over these roads, chiefs and their entourages passed back and forth on their visits to the king, and armies were gathered and sent on their way to conquer and plunder.

Warfare was a way of life among the Ganda in that it was not so much a means of alleviating tension and conflict as it was a meaningful opportunity to rise in importance in the community, achieve chiefship, rise in importance in chiefship, and to become wealthy. War had dimensions of personal glory and personal gain, as well as national glory and prowess. A man who displayed special prowess in war could achieve promotion to chiefship on the spot.

Taxes and the booty of war were used not only to maintain the administrative system and reward warriors but also to provide gifts and food to those who labored in building dwellings and roads, as well as feasts for the subjects generally. Liberality was expected by the peasants from their chief in the form of "beer, meat, and politeness."

Control over the abuse of power by chiefs was effected by a number of mechanisms. The leading *ssaza* chief, the one holding the highest degree of precedence, had the title of *Sabadu* in his service of the king. The king's *Sabadu* held a particularly close relationship with him and could loosely be said to represent the king's conscience. They were regarded as brothers to the point that their children could not intermarry. The *Sabadu* of a chief, in turn, could not only advise, but he could criticize his chief for abuse of authority. Peasants who felt that they had been mistreated could complain to him so that he might reason with the chief concerning their complaint. The king, through his royal council headed by the *Katikiro,* heard cases involving charges that chiefs were failing to carry out their duties properly in governing their people and were abusing them.

The king would remove such a chief from office. In fact, the king had the power to discharge a chief from office, other than the chief of a clan, without a trial. Finally, peasants always had the refuge of leaving the service of an arbitrary chief and entering that of another. Southwold describes the effectiveness of this limitation upon the arbitrary power of lower chiefs as follows:

> The number of chiefs, and the intensity of competition between them, on the one hand; the abundance of land and of chiefs competing for followers, on the other; these factors would suggest that the chief had greater need of keeping his *musenze* than the latter had of staying with the chief. The *musenze* lacked constitutional checks, not because his position was too weak to obtain them, but because it was too strong to require them. We may be sure that the village chiefs who survived as chiefs were those who ingratiated themselves with their people by their efficiency, justice, wealth, generosity, and humanity.[11]

Law: Land Tenure

Land was distributed and used to enable the holders of office and heads of clans to carry out their traditional roles and to provide sustenance to peasants and their families in reasonable security. Those who received land from a chief in assuming the clientage relationship denominated as *kusenga* were obligated to serve him loyally in performing the chief's obligations to the king to provide men for waging war, building the dwellings in the royal enclosure, and maintaining roads. They were also expected to provide labor in building and maintaining the dwellings in the chief's enclosure.

The king, his relatives, the queen mother, princes and princesses, the chief minister, the keeper of the king's fetishes, the *ssaza* chiefs, and their sub-chiefs, all held estates located at various points throughout the kingdom. The holding of such estates was attached to the particular office, the benefits flowed to the holder of the office, and terminated, insofar as the individual holder was concerned, when he ceased to hold the office. The sub-chiefs in such estates were directly appointed by the holders of the estates and were removable by them. The estates of the king's relatives and the more important chiefs were not subject to regular taxation, but their holders were expected to give presents to the king.

---

11. M. Southwold, "Leadership, Authority and the Village Community," *The King's Men*, 210, quotation at 214. In addition to references cited *supra* notes 8-10, see Roscoe, *op. cit.*, pp. 184-196; Mair, *op. cit.*, Chap. 7; L. P. Mair, "Baganda Land Tenure," *Africa*, VI (1933), 187.

The heads of clans derived rights in land by virtue of long-held grants from the king or undisturbed occupation for a period of time during which the land became the burying place of the ancestors. Clan lands were not a large, continuous territory containing a number of contiguous villages. They were instead hill tops or single villages scattered throughout the country, with their greatest concentration near the residences of the kings as located at various times. Only rarely did villages reflect predominant settlement by the members of a single clan. As new families came into being, they tended to settle on other lands than those of their own clan, with the result that village membership was dispersed among a number of clans. Moreover, when chiefs were rewarded with a higher office and its attendant estates, their kinsmen and followers frequently accompanied them to their new residence and took up land.

In certain instances, individuals acquired hereditary rights in small parcels of land by virtue of the fact that they were a direct grant from the king as a reward for service. Their holders were free from the obligation to contribute labor otherwise due to the chief, but they were subject to military duties. It was also possible for chiefs to make small grants of land to provide for their sons.

A peasant who held land from a chief who was also a fellow clansman had a greater security in tenure and freedom from interference than one who held land from a chief who was of a different clan. In any event, either in his capacity as a member of a kinship group or as a subject of a chief, a man had the right to occupy open land under the control of a chief in the amount needed for his family. So long as he cultivated the land, he was secure in his holding, but unused and abandoned land reverted to the chief for redistribution. A man's rights in his land were subject to succession in his family, and, as the land became marked by the graves of ancestors, the permanence of his interest in the land became fixed.

All holdings were subject to the overriding consideration that their effective use or tilling should not too long be postponed. Moreover, the king had the power to dismiss a chief and appoint another in his place, thereby succeeding to his holdings. Similarly, a chief had a residual power to evict any peasant in his service from lands held by him for almost any reason. The taking of such land was held to be justifiable, however, only when the peasant was remiss in rendering service to his lord.[12]

---

12. A. B. Mukwaya, *Land Tenure in Buganda: Present Day Tendencies*, East African Studies No. 1 (Kampala, Uganda, 1953), 5-14; Mair, *op. cit.*, pp. 154-164; M. C. Fallers, *op. cit.*, pp. 34-36; L. P. Mair, *op. cit*, p. 187.

Law

The Ganda may be described as "litigation-minded." Quarrels were prone to be argued before nearby third parties. Disputes were brought so hastily to chiefs for decision that often the issue in dispute had not yet been recognized. Such a situation may be symptomatic of a great deal of latent tension in the society. The pressures of attaining or preserving social position, the menace of arbitrary exercise of power by the king and superiors, the exposure to sudden loss of status as a result of palace changes in the political system, the repercussions of the power system upon the lives and welfare of the peasants as well as the élite, all point to a society characterized by insecurity and tension.

Cases were heard by a chief in the presence of any peasants who happened to be there at the time. Anyone present at the court could express his views and ask questions. Cases heard in the courts of village headmen and sub-chiefs were appealed to the court of the *ssaza* before going to the courts of the *Katikiro* or *Kabaka*. Roscoe describes the court system as follows:

> The King's reception-hall was the highest court in the land. It was there that the King met his chiefs and discussed State-business with them, and it was there too that all appeal cases were heard. In the Council (Lukiko) anyone might speak; indeed several people would often be talking at the same time. These gatherings were held almost daily, they were summoned sometimes by the *Katikiro,* and sometimes by the King. . . .
>
> The majority of appeals ended in the *Katikiro*'s court, which ranked next after the King's court; it stood facing the King's entrance. This court-house appears to have been a survival of an old custom, according to which the King sat under one of the sacred trees at the entrance of his enclosure, and tried all cases brought to him. The *Katikiro* tried the more important cases in person, but deputed an assistant to try others; the assistant had to report the result of his examination, and the *Katikiro* then gave the decision. In each court a fee of twenty cowry-shells was paid by the plaintiff when stating his case, and a further fee of a goat and a barkcloth, before the accused was summoned to appear in court; the accused also paid a goat and barkcloth before the case was tried; these sums were called the *bitebi*. When sentence was given, the judge fined the offender two goats and one barkcloth, which were given to the plaintiff in addition to the whole amount which he claimed from the defendant. When an appeal was made from one court to another, ending in the *Katikiro*'s, the plaintiff paid the fee of twenty cowry-shells, a goat, and barkcloth to each of the lower courts, but to the *Katikiro*'s court he paid ten goats and five barkcloths. If it was a case of cattle-

lifting which was to be tried, the *Katikiro* fined the offender a number of animals, in addition to ordering him to restore the full number which he had stolen. The *Katikiro* was given one-fourth of the fine, besides his original fee, and the party against whom the sentence was given had to refund al the court fees. Corruption was rife in these courts. If a man thought that he was losing his case, he would endeavour to bribe the judge; if he proposed to give him a slave, he would place his hand flat upon the top of his head as if rubbing it, when no one but the judge was looking; this signified that he would give the latter a man to carry his loads. If he proposed to give him a woman or a girl, he would double up his fist and place it to his breast, to represent a woman's breast; if he proposed to give him a cow, he would place his fist to the side of his head, to represent a horn; if it was a load of barkcloths, he would tug at his own cloth. These signs were made secretly; if the judge accepted the bribe, he pronounced sentence in the man's favour.[13]

The chief acted to decide "cases where a crime was denied, where responsibility was disputed, or where there was a question of fixing compensation." Cases between members of a clan, particularly if they involved issues of kinship, inheritance, and marriage, were decided by the head of the clan. A chief never decided a case the day it was brought. He would wait to see if the parties changed their accounts of the episode or to give the parties an opportunity to bribe him. If only one party offered a bribe, decision was invariably given in that party's favor. If both gave a bribe, then the chief's council made the decision without his participation.

Punishment consisted of confinement by having one or more limbs placed in the stocks, mutilation, and death. The ordeal was used in cases of sorcery to find the guilty person. This consisted in requiring both the accused and the accuser to take a highly intoxicating drink and to decide in favor of the person least affected by it.

A person who was "robbed or cheated" began his suit by payment of a certain number of cowry-shells. The chief then sent for the defendant and both sides pleaded their cases. At this point, a larger payment was demanded from both sides before the court would proceed. The chief thereupon reviewed the case as presented by each side and obtained the verification of his presentation from both sides. The decision was then rendered. If appeal was desired, the losing party refused to pay the fine and costs and went before a higher court, charging the lower court with reaching its judgment wrongly.

The principal offenses included adultery, theft, treason, murder and accidental death, sorcery, and arson. Self-help, that is, war be-

---

13. Roscoe, *op. cit.*, pp. 258, 260-261.

tween clans, could be used in cases of murder until the number of deaths in each clan was equal. In cases of murder and adultery, when the guilty party was caught in its commission, and theft, when the thief was caught with the stolen goods in his possession, the guilty party could be killed on the spot by the injured party. It was considered preferable, however, to obtain the chief's consent before such a resort to violence took place.[14]

Conclusion

The Ganda established an organizational, achieving, war-making society. War determined the form of their political structure and led to the growth of a bureaucracy of administrative officials. The gains of war maintained their political and administrative structure. War largely supplanted trade in their economy. The conduct of war developed an achieving, competitive society, with emphasis on power in social relationships. The Ganda admired power and developed highly the techniques of acquiring and using power. The economy created surplus labor. That labor was used to provide the panoplies and perquisites of power in the élite groups and to maintain the administrative and war-making machines. An élite was established which had its own system of manners and perceived superiority over lesser folk, yet entrance to the élite was relatively open. Indeed, the society was characterized by both social and spatial mobility on the part of individuals.

Criteria of excellence in performance of administrative or military roles determined both recruitment to and retention of such roles. Excellence in performance led to favor and advance, failure led to ignominy and sometimes to death. The king displayed at times a certain degree of caprice in removing persons from positions of power.

The favor of the gods was sought on important occasions. The spirits were considered to punish failure to adhere to certain basic standards of conduct. More frequently, however, the intervention of the spirits was seen to be expressed in bringing misfortune than good fortune. Each day a man was exposed not only to the risk of ill favor of the spirits but also to the malevolent use of sorcery by those who would do him ill.

---

14. Mair, *An African People,* 184-191; Kagwa, *op. cit.,* pp. 128-133; M. C. Fallers, *op. cit.,* p. 63. For a comprehensive statement of customary law in its historical and modern setting, with references to judicial precedents, see E. S. Haydon, *Law and Justice in Buganda* (London, 1960).

Social mobility existed for individuals to achieve higher roles and status. Entry to the élite was not closed to the peasant, though it was becoming increasingly difficult for him to do so, as families of the élite grew in numbers and the favor of superiors tended to be more easily attained by children of the élite who were trained in the outlook and performance of élite roles.

War provided a constant stimulus not only to maintain the system but also to centralize power in the king, to deprive the clan aristocracy of power and position, and to develop a sense of national superiority.

Spatial mobility for individuals existed. The pressures of population upon land had not yet reached the point where rigidity had begun to appear. Peasants could change their dwelling place freely. Indeed, large bodies of people, consisting of a chief and his followers, could move freely to new lands.

The king was the symbol and repository of political, military, and judicial power. He could appoint and remove chiefs, and his concurrence was necessary to the appointment of heads of clans. He had the war-making power and appointed the generals of war-making forces. He could display his ultimate power over the lives of his subjects in an arbitrary fashion, as well as in ritual killings. His court and that of his chief minister were the courts of last resort for appeal from the judgments of the courts of chiefs.

The administrative system, coupled with the system of land tenure, enabled the king to make war, to maintain his royal residences, and to build and keep in repair the network of roads whereby war and travel to and from the capital could be accomplished. Tribute of food, bark cloth, beer, timber, and firewood was collected for the benefit of the king and the chiefs but food, meat, and beer were rapidly redistributed, at least in part, to peasants in form of feasts and gifts as a reward for labor or simply as evidence of a generous spirit on the part of the holder of office.

Checks on the arbitrary exercise of power by those holding office by the office of the *Sabadu,* by hearings of complaints of abuse of power before the king's council, and by simply leaving the service of an unpopular chief. The political organization was of a highly authoritarian or totalitarian character. The king was the legitimate source of power for most political, military, administrative, and judicial roles and exercised his power to maintain his authority system. It was possible for him to be either a wise or a vengeful, arbitrary wielder of authority.

The commission of offenses of murder, adultery, theft, and the like was sanctioned both by a system of self-help and by the courts. A definite procedure of arriving at a final decision after hearing the parties governed the action of the courts. Appeal from the decision of lower courts to higher courts was possible. Impartiality in decision making was fouled by the prevalence of a system of bribing judges. Certain offenses were viewed to be sanctioned by intervention of the spirits. The existence of tension in the society was indicated by the proneness of individuals to enter into disputes and litigation.

The Ganda possessed a secular view of authority, an organizational way of life, and a culture characterized by the values of achievement and social and spatial mobility. Much of their life would readily lend itself to the modernizing process.

Chapter 11

The Lugbara

Geography and Economy

THE Lugbara are a Sudanic-speaking people living along the line of the Nilo-Congo divide, with the Nile River as their eastern boundary. In 1963, they numbered about 242,000, of which about 183,000 lived in northwestern Uganda and the remainder in the Congo. The Sudan lies to the north and Lake Albert and the Congo to the south. The northern and eastern parts are relatively low, 2,000 to 3,000 feet in elevation, and are very unhealthy. The Lugbara mostly live on open, rolling plains, which take the form of small ridges between which streams and rivers flow. This land is at an elevation of between 4,000 and 5,000 feet. Rainfall is adequate. The people were agricultural and raised millet, legumes, and root crops. Cattle, goats, and fowl were kept. There was little trade outside the area.

Sleeping sickness was widespread along the Nile and up most of its tributaries, often almost up to the watershed. The tsetse fly of sleeping sickness soon disappears, however, when an altitude of 4,000 feet is reached. Malaria, elephantiasis, and leprosy were common diseases.[1]

---

1. J. Middleton, *Lugbara Religion: Ritual and Authority among an East African People* (London, 1960), 1-4; J. Middleton, "Witchcraft and Sorcery in Lugbara," *Witchcraft and Sorcery in East Africa*, eds. J. Middleton and E. H. Winter (New York, 1963), 257; P. T. W. Baxter and A. Butt, "The Azande, and Related Peoples of the Anglo-Egyptian Sudan and Belgian Congo," *Ethnographic Survey of Africa*, ed. D. Forde (London, 1953), 120-121; E. Ramponi, "Religion

Individual Personality and Religion

A man's body was a temporal thing, which, after death, "goes" no-where but simply rotted. A man's *oindi*, or soul, was located in his heart and survived his death. It went to God in the sky and then re-turned to the shrines and to live under the earth, beneath the com-pound. A man also had his *adro*, or guardian spirit, and *tali*, or personality.

The ancestors were thought of as individual personalities as well as a group. They consisted of all the forebears of a person through all lines of descent. The term ghosts will be used to identify ancestors as individual personalities. Shrines were erected to ancestors in both these capacities, that is, to particular ancestors, on the one hand, or to the ancestors of a man's direct line of descent within his minimal or, sometimes, inner lineage, on the other hand.

God was the ultimate source of all power and of the moral order. He had a transcendent aspect, where he was thought as being in the sky, and an immanent aspect, where he was thought of as living on earth, in rivers, large trees and thickets, high mountains, and rocky places. He was feared in his immanent aspect as the source of mis-fortune and death and as linked with witches, sorcerers, and divina-tion. He was also recognized to be concerned with the well-being of the entire tribe and the bringing of rain.

There were two mythical heroes, Jaki and Dribidu, from whose sons the several clans descended. Witches and sorcerers were also held to exist and to bring harm to individuals. Witches were in-verted beings who had perverted relations of kinship and authority. They destroyed ties of kinship and neighborhood. Their physical characteristics were abnormal. They preferred to be alone but would mask this by excessive cordiality and friendliness of manner. They could bewitch both kin and non-kin. Elders were feared as witches, a man could be bewitched only by a man older than himself. Witch-craft was practiced only between men, for it was mainly between men that orderly social relations existed. A witch was a person with *ole* (indignation), which was the psychological product of situations involving envy and frustration, that is, the inability to accomplish one's desires or to enjoy the good fortune of another.

A witch was defined by Middleton and Winter to be a person who

and Divination of the Logbara Tribe of North-Uganda," *Anthropos*, XXXII (1937), 571-572, 849; R. E. McConnell, "Notes on the Lugwari Tribe of Central Africa," *Journal of the Royal Anthropological Institute*, LV (1925), 439-441.

had an innate magical power to do evil. They defined a sorcerer to be a person who acquired knowledge in the use of medicines and the like and used it to bring harm to others.

Witches and sorcerers attacked the order of Lugbara society. Witches were persons who were members of a local community. They represented internal threats to a community and reflected internal tensions. Sorcerers, except for sorcery between co-wives, were persons living outside the community who threatened persons within it. Witches attacked kin who violated kinship obligations and neighbors who were guilty of unneighborly conduct. They operated as a sanction to support kinship and community standards of behavior. Sorcerers attacked kin and non-kin, neighbors and non-neighbors, and acted indiscriminately against people, whether they knew them or not.

Those who lived outside the local community and the neighboring lineages were held to display inverted or antisocial behavior according to the degree of their remoteness from the local group. "The more remote the being, the more its behavior is conceived of as being the utter negation of that to do with kinship." The mythical heroes were not thought of as ancestors in any way, their connection with the existing Lugbara society was too remote. Their behavior was characterized by "physical inversion, cannibalism, incest, miracle working, absence of bridewealth, no fighting, living outside the bounds of society." Those who lived beyond the territory of the neighboring lineages were believed to be sorcerers, magicians, and persons evilly disposed to the Lugbara. Beyond these were people of even more inverted characteristics, who walked on their heads, were cannibals, eaters of "bad" meat, such as night creatures, and practitioners of terrible methods of sorcery.

The dead of a lineage, as personalities and as a group, formed an entity with the living members of a lineage. The ancestral spirits were actors in the temporal world of a lineage. They were concerned with the behavior of the living, watched over them, guarded them, and punished them when their actions struck at the foundations of lineage authority and the system of role-relationships within the lineage. There was an ideal pattern of lineage conduct which was held to be exemplified by the ancestors in their day to the maintenance of which the ancestors remained dedicated. The living were the temporary custodians of the welfare of the lineage. By adhering to the ideal pattern of lineage conduct, the living would cause the lineage to prosper. By departing from the ideal pattern of conduct, harm would follow. If it was merely an individual who failed to maintain the traditional standards, some particular ancestor would punish him, usually in the form of illness. If the lineage as a group departed from traditional ideals in some manner as a general practice, the group would be punished, but this time the punishment was by God instead of an individual ancestor or ghost. Thus a long series of sins, or departures from basic ideal lineage patterns of conduct, was believed to offend God and to lead to a condition known as *nyoka*. The lineage would in such event find itself visited with a continuing series of misfortunes, usually manifested in the sterility of its women, livestock, and fields.

The performance of rituals at shrines symbolized the ideal order of the lineage or community, preserved that order by thoughtful, frequent repetition and repaired the breach of that order in the event of misconduct by the individual or the group.

There were two types of shrines. The first was the internal agnatic ghost shrines dedicated to particular ancestoral spirits of the lineage, and, second, the external lineage shrines symbolizing the lineage itself as an entity. Congregations at the internal ghost shrines were termed *awi'buru*. These were composed of the lineage members and representatives of immediately continuous lineages, whether or not agnatically related. The purpose of attendance was said to be to "rejoice with their kin." The gathering at the shrine emphasized the uniqueness, the exclusiveness, and the harmony of relationships within the lineage and its attendant groups. The second type of shrines was a set of external lineage shrines which represented the lineage of the elder who had their custodianship and the wider lineages of which his lineage was a part. Only elders of minimal lineages could have such external shrines. They symbolized the linking of the basic lineages of the people in a territory with their next higher level and the unity of the entire minimal lineage of which they were a part. Congregations at these shrines were called *awiamve* and consisted of the elder of the minimal lineage, acting in that capacity as well as the representative of his own segment, and the elders of the other segments which, together with the first segment, constituted the minimal lineage. At the sacrificial rites in the first category of shrines the meat was offered to the dead who had visited punishment upon one who had violated lineage standards. At the sacrificial rites involving the second category of shrines, the meat was not so offered because the dead were not involved in the situation. The purpose of sacrifice in the second category was to restore the harmony of a minimal lineage impaired by feud and conflict in marriage relations.

The distribution of the meat in both cooked and raw form revealed in symbolic form the kin structure of the group participating in ritual sacrifice at the internal ghost shrine. The cooked meat was distributed to and consumed by the true agnates who were members of the same minimal lineage as were the ancestors. They sat near the shrines and received and ate the meat cooked at the shrines and drank beer together. The uncooked meat was distributed to the entire congregation, including the same agnates and the accessory kin and clients. The representatives of the accessory lineages of the minimal lineage which acted as host took the uncooked meat to their respective homes. At each home a new distribution of the meat took place at a common meal at which some received and ate cooked meat and others received raw meat.[2]

Social and Political Organization

The Lugbara did not settle in villages surrounded by open country but instead in homesteads scattered across the country and typically located on ridges of land. They were organized into family clusters or local settlements, consisting of a group of elementary and polygynous compound families under the authority of an elder. The family cluster was based on a minimal lineage. The head of the lineage acted as the head of the cluster. The composition of a family cluster was fluid. Members moved to other communities, where they became tenants, and members of other communities moved in and became tenants. As time passed and members multiplied, segmentation took place.

Clans, descended from the sons of the two culture heroes, Jaki and Dribidu, were divided into sub-clans which were the agnatic cores of tribes. A tribe was a territorial group within which fighting, if it should break out, was to be settled by discussion. Permanent fighting was permissible only between units of different tribes. The tribe had no head with authority.

Sub-clans were divided into major, minor, and minimal lineages. Each of these lineages was the agnatic core for a territorial group or section. The structure of social action through which the people

---

2. Middleton, *Lugbara Religion*, 29-34, 52-54, 238-247, 252-258, 25-27, 22-23, 61, 119, 126, quotations at pp. 238, 236; J. Middleton, "The Concept of Bewitching in Lugbara," *Africa*, XXV (1955), 252; J. Middleton, "Witchcraft and Sorcery in Lugbara," 272-274. For definitions of witch and sorcerer, see J. Middleton and E. H. Winter (eds.), "Introduction," *Witchcraft and Sorcery*, p. 3.

organized their lives and worked the ground was the family cluster. Authority within it was formally determined by lineage criteria.

The smallest segment of a lineage was identified by descent from a wife of an ancestor three or four generations removed. Her sons and their male descendants constituted the segment.

The ideal pattern of authority within the family cluster posited that there was the family head, or elder, who was the eldest son of the senior wife of his predecessor. He was viewed to possess complete authority over his agnatic dependents. Other heads of families in the group were the "men behind." The more junior men were the "youths." The Lugbara name for elder meant literally "big man." In theory, a segment consisted of three generations and divided after three generations but such division did not always occur. A segment could in fact be as small as a single compound family.

Authority relationships were identified by the use of such terms as "big" and "small," "strong" and "weak," "a man stands before another" and "a man stands behind another." A man, his family, and his lineage were the focal points of a field of social relations which were authority relations validated by genealogy.

Ownership of a shrine marked a man's responsibility as head of a unit, which could be a minimal lineage, component family segment, or set of full brothers. Such ownership also indicated the validity or legitimacy of the position he thus occupied from the standpoint of his genealogical status. Other factors than his actual genealogical status would influence his assumption of the post indicated by his ownership of a shrine. When a *de facto* status of authority was in fact inconsistent with genealogical history, the latter was re-framed to validate the *de facto* status.

The ancestors entered into the lives of the living, communicated with the living, and responded to invocation by those of the living who had legitimate authority to do so. Shrines were "signs of ritual status *vis-à-vis* both the dead—the higher the status the closer the contact with them and the more numerous the shrines—and the living."

> In the totality of shrines is represented what might be called the total lineage personality as it is relevant to the members at the present time. In them the living members see their lineage past incapsulated, with differences in their importance (for the living) of the ancestors made clear. They see themselves as having reached a particular point in their lineage history of development. . . . The contemporary alignments of intra-lineage authority and ambition and rivalry between family segments and their heads are reflected in the distribution of shrines.

Conflict and Its Control

The meaning of Lugbara authority relations and conflict will be much clearer if their description is preceded by a statement of certain basic propositions concerning order and conflict in Lugbara society. These propositions reveal a society characterized by constitutive conflict.

1. The assumption of a legitimate post of authority was held to be an inevitable outcome of genealogical history and status. When a person possessed certain traditional relationships with the ancestors, he was automatically entitled to the occupancy of the post indicated by such relationships.

2. The retention of a legitimate post of authority so defined became increasingly subject to stress as the social and economic conditions of the relevant groups changed, demanding the recognition of an occupant of the post other than the person indicated by tradition. Such stress was manifested in conflicts presented and resolved in ritual terms and performance.

3. The constitutive conflict in the struggle of the traditional head to retain authority on the basis of the legitimacy of his occupancy of the post, as against a claimant supported by the social and economic necessities of group life, took place in a repetitive pattern ending finally in the ritual assumption of *de jure* authority by the emerging *de facto* repository of authority.

One must understand that among the Lugbara interaction by an individual with others was with persons who were viewed as either kinsmen or non-kinsmen. Sexual relations which took place outside marriage but within the lineage, homicide and assault which took place within the lineage, represented misconduct which struck at the foundations of the lineage group and, in that sense, could be called a sin. If the same behavior involved members of a related lineage, such as a segment of the same maximal lineage, then the misconduct was handled by feud or payment of compensation. If no kin relationship existed, then fighting, with no obligation to terminate it, was a permissible outcome.

The manner of control of disputes over land, livestock, and women, together with the handling of such offenses as incest, adultery, homicide, and assault, depended on whether or not such matters were viewed to impair the existing authority structure.

Most social interaction took place among kinsmen and within a structure of authority relationships defined in kinship terms. It was essential that this structure be maintained, if orderly social relations were to be preserved. Yet individuals within this structure changed their status, or set of statuses, as time passed, some within the group died or moved away, while still others were added to the group through birth or immigration.

The authority structure was supported by the concept of *ru*. This implied the observance of "respect" by a junior to a senior supported by "fear" of a senior. Politeness and decorum were inherent in giving respect. Outrageous breaches of respect, such as killing or striking a senior kinsman, quarreling with him, or committing adultery with his wife were considered to be conduct which "destroyed" the lineage or the community. The term *eza* and *ezata* were used to describe such conduct. *Eza* meant to "destroy" or "spoil" and *ezata* meant "destruction" or "destroying." It was believed that ghosts would punish such conduct by sending sickness to the offender or his family. Sanctions emanating from God, the ancestors, and witches were a means for maintaining traditional authority patterns.

Sickness was a frequent and substantially universal aspect of Lugbara life. Its appearance was often interpreted as a penalty for a sin, or offense striking at the authority structure of the lineage group, visited by an ancestor upon the offender. Such a perception of sickness took place in a sequence of events which included, first, the occurrence of an offense, not limited to offenses of the serious nature of sins, but also consisting of conduct simply implying lack of respect for authority; second, secret invocation by the elder of punishment for the offense by the dead ancestors; third, the consequent rendering of punishment, in the form of illness, by a particular ancestral spirit or ghost; and, fourth, the validation of the truth of the foregoing interpretation of events by a diviner or oracle who was consulted by the elder. Part of an elder's established performance of his role involved the invoking of ghostly sanctions against those who flouted his authority and the bringing of the fact of such invocation to the attention of the group by the elder openly consulting a diviner after the offender had experienced sickness. The diviner decided upon the propriety of validity of such invocation.

The Lugbara had a clear perception of the nature of the emotion aroused in situations when established norms of behavior were not respected or when a person experienced frustration or disappointment. It was expressed in the term *ole,* meaning, in general, indignation. For example, it pointed to the sentiment experienced by an elder when he encountered action impairing or questioning the foundations of his authority. The word *ole* was otherwise used to refer to such sentiments as the feeling aroused when one saw a man eating rich food who failed to invite the viewer to share the meal or the sentiment experienced in seeing a dancer succeeding with impressing girls with his agility while the viewer stood alone. *Ole*, in its present context, referred to "a feeling of indignation or outrage at sins or immoral behavior, using 'immoral' in a limited sense to refer to behaviour directed against recognition of orderly ties of kinship and usage."

While elders were typically persons who invoked ghostly sanctions, any person whose father was dead could invoke ghosts to reinforce his authority as a family head. Most cases of invocation occurred within the family cluster to maintain authority within the cluster. Ghostly sanctions could be applied to the offender or any member of his family who was his junior.

The act of invocation consisted of deliberate thought by an elder near the shrines about the bad conduct of a child or dependent. If such thoughts were expressed orally in an appeal to the ancestors, they would amount to a curse. Instead, such thoughts were secret and were not revealed until after the sickness had occurred. It was admitted that such sickness need not necessarily have been brought about as a consequence of the invocation by the elder. There were a variety of situations or alternatives which might have induced it, and it was necessary to put these before the diviner for interpretation and final decision. These alternatives and the choice among them made by the diviner reflected the existing tensions in the relevant lineage group or groups.

The elder, in consulting the diviner, was expected to make a full disclosure of the facts to the diviner and the latter, on his part, further explored the facts. The experience and technique of the diviner, in interpreting the particular situation and ascertaining its true facts, operated as a control measure to insure that authority was not abused and that new authority relations were legitimated in due course.

The convenience and usefulness of such a procedure is apparent. The occurrence of the act of invocation prior to the illness was not revealed until after the illness had taken place. Whether invocation had in fact occurred as reported could never be known, since it was secret and a rationalization for the secrecy of the act was supplied. The illness in such circumstances could be an opportune event of which to take advantage. The third-party decision by the diviner validated the propriety of the act of invocation, when it was apparent that existing relationships and tensions within the lineage required the support of lineage norms.

The purpose of the elder in invoking ghosts was "to purify the territory (of the lineage), so that the home may be all clean." Middleton stated:

> Lugbara say that the purpose of ghost invocation is "cleaning the territory" *(angu edezu)*, that is, to purify the lineage home and to mend the breach in lineage relations that has been caused by the original offence. There is also, conjointly, the purpose of "cleansing the body" *(rua edezu)*, which refers to the individual patient and the members of his immediate family.
>
> The concepts of "cleansing" and "repairing" are both included in the Lugbara verb *ede*. It also means "prepare" or "make ready." A person or territory (especially in the sense of a lineage home and so of the collectivity of lineage members) is cleansed of sin, and the network of social relations that compose a man's status or a group's position in its social system is repaired.

The process of invocation of ghosts and ghostly punishment took place typically in situations involving either (1) disobedience to legitimate authority, when a senior invoked against a junior, or (2) impiety and refusal to make sufficient sacrifices to the ancestors, when a senior invoked against a person of equal generation. The most frequent cause of invocation was rivalry between elders for authority. Middleton stated in this connection:

> In short, a family cluster that is about to segment may be characterized by a high frequency of claims to ghost invocation. . . . The process reaches its most critical stage when sacrifices are made at fertility and external shrines, which are responses to a realization that orderly relations within the lineage have reached a stage of general disintegration, and when accusations of witchcraft under the guise of invocation start to be made against an elder.
>
> Within the minimal lineage accusations of witchcraft are of two types: a son accuses his father who claims to have invoked against him of being a witch; and a senior man claims that the elder, from whose authority he wishes to free himself, is a witch. . . . These two types of accusation tend to occur at different stages within the development cycle of any given segment, whether a minimal lineage or a component family segment. Accusations by a son against a father—real or classificatory—occur mainly during the earlier stages; those between equals in generation occur mainly during the later stages. The former occurs when the person against whom the invocation is passing from one age-grade or family status to a higher one. . . .
>
> Accusations between men of equal generation, "brothers," tend to occur at later stages in the cycle of development of a lineage, when the heads of large segments wish to become independent. Such accusations are an extreme way of denying the authority of the elder.

The sequence of events consisting of misconduct striking at the foundations of Lugbara order, ghostly invocation by an elder, sickness of the sinner, and validation of the invocation by a diviner consulted by the elder, did not end at this point. It was necessary to restore order and harmony within the group and to reaffirm the bases of its solidarity. This was done at the ceremony of sacrifice described above. The rite of sacrifice marked the purification of the sinner, who had been cured of the sickness visited upon him, and the repair of the relations with his lineage and community which had been broken by his sin. The commensal meal and the ritual addresses there made were the means to this end. The total sequence of events constituted "a logically consistent system and explains most sickness and provides a social and psychological response to it; it also provides sanctions against anti-social behaviour." It was the latter aspect of the institution here described that was most significant from the social and political point of view. It was the sanction for maintaining authority and also operated from time to time to recognize and legitimize the transfer of authority in a system that formally could not admit of change in authority structure. The second address of the elder at the commensal meal performed the function of restoring harmony in the group. At this stage, an opportunity was afforded for all the repressed animosities and conflicts to be openly expressed and released. It reached its full significance in the fifth stage of the sequence of events outlined in the next paragraph, that of segmentation. By its recitation of genealogical and traditional experience of the group, it reminded the members of their past history and formulated that past history in terms that validated the realignment of relations occurring as a result of segmentation.

The typical cycle of constitutive conflict consisting in the establishment of a constituted order or authority structure, conflict and disintegration within the order, and restructuring of the order, took place in the following successive phases:

1. *De facto* authority patterns and their legitimacy or *de jure* genealogical validation closely corresponded.

2. Conflicts of interest within the family arose, principally in the claims of married sons for livestock and land. The exercise of authority by the family head to resolve such conflict was accepted.

3. Increase of population, decrease in fertility of land, death of older men and maturing of younger men, the growth of families of younger men, led junior men, on the one hand, to question the authority of elders as they carried out the allocative process of distributing land, and led elders, on the other hand, to respond to such

a challenge and reinforce their authority by invoking the sanctioning power of the ancestors. Conflict in this stage was largely between senior and junior age generations.

4. Conflicts of authority increased in seriousness and frequency and included rivalry for recognition of the status of elder by heads of component segments. Charges of witchcraft were raised by those under authority against those exercising it.

5. Segmentation occurred, usually precipitated by the death of an elder. The new distribution of authority was legitimated by a re-ordering of genealogies. Alternatively, the dissident segment might move elsewhere to escape the authority of the elder.

In Lugbara society, men matured and acquired descendants, dependents, and property, yet their social and ritual status remained unchanged. As the new social reality departed more and more from the traditional authority structure, elders whose *de jure* authority was threatened responded by asserting the legitimacy of the formal order in which they held an office. Sooner or later, and usually at the death of an elder, the emergent *de facto* authority was accepted as *de jure* authority. At the ritual address delivered at the ceremony of a sacrifice, a new genealogy was formulated to validate the new order and was accepted by the group. The ideal and the actual order then became coterminous. The Lugbara had no system of perceptions whereby they could accept gradual change and reorganization of authority relationships. New structures of authority emerged as social facts but were not formally admitted to exist until validated by a radical restructuring of the relevant groups, which usually took place at the death of an elder.[3]

A series of cases involving the sequence of events described above and revealing constitutive conflict was reported by Middleton. Some of them will be briefly recapitulated in order to bring into relief the actual episodes upon which the above description of Lugbara social and political behavior was based.

CASE 1   A family cluster named Arake, based upon a lineage of the same name, had grown to the point that land was becoming short. The elder was Ondua, who was head of the Lari'ba segment. His formal assistant was his senior brother, Olimane, head of the Nyaai segment that was considering becoming a distinct lineage. His actual assistant was his half-brother, Oguda.

---

3. Middleton, *Lugbara Religion,* 5-23, 78, 34-45, 78, 84-85, 214-226, 264-266, quotations at 75, 71-72, 39, 101-102, 226-227, 128; J. Middleton, "Some Social Aspects of Lugbara Myth," *Africa,* XXIV (1954), 189.

Oguda had charged that Ondua's sickness was a consequence of a failure to offer animals for sacrifice. The diviners confirmed that Ondua's sickness was a result of the ghostly vengeance of his dead father. Ondua accepted the verdict, sacrificed a sheep, and, in his second ritual address, brought the quarrels of the Nyaai segment for land into the open as a basic factor in the situation. The sacrifice was attended by all the men of Araka and the elders of its coordinated lineages.

CASE 2   Oguda's grandson, son of his son Jobi, became sick. Oguda sacrificed a goat to effect his cure. Oguda claimed that the sickness was the result of his invocation against his son, Jobi, for Jobi's bad conduct. The diviner gave the verdict that Ondua had invoked the ghosts against Jobi. Ondua admitted this.

In this situation, Ondua had by invocation asserted his authority as lineage head to sustain his position, while it would have been more appropriate for Jobi's father to have done so.

CASE 3   Obitre, a member of the Nyaai segment, sacrificed a goat on behalf of his son. Olimani claimed that he was the agent for ghostly vengeance against Obitre, because Obitre had refused to accept his authority as elder in a number of rites. The diviner confirmed that it was Olimani who had invoked the ghosts, thereby validating Olimani's authority as head of the lineage.

Olimani's invocation was part of a pattern of an increasing number of invocations against the Nyaai, which had led to three Nyaai households moving across their boundary stream and apparently defecting. Ondua needed all possible families to maintain a lineage large enough to maintain itself by force of arms against attack on its land. The only way he could maintain his authority to accomplish this end was by the diviner decreeing that it was his invocations which were heard by the ghosts, rather than those of Ondua.

Charges of witchcraft by Olimani were made by the young men of the Nyaai segment but were disregarded.

CASE 9   Olimani, head of the Nyaai segment, became seriously sick. Ondua, as head of the Araki, consulted a diviner and reported the history of the disputes between the two segments, referring to disputes over land, inheritance of widows, and livestock. Ondua expressed a fear of *nyoka*. Ondua questioned the manner in which Olimani had exercised his authority as head of the lineage. He reported to the diviner that he had discussed with another person Olimani's failure to offer adequate sacrifices to the dead. The diviner's verdict was that Olimani had so failed and should now make a large offering of a bull at his senior ancestral shrine.

Olimani was angry that Ondua had presumed to consult a diviner on his behalf but, after recovery, accepted the verdict and sacrificed a bull. All the men of Araka and the elders of coordinated lineages attended the sacrifice.

One of the men of Nyaai reported to the diviner that Olimani had been thought of as using witchcraft for his own ends and was unjust and quarrelsome.

CASE 14   Olimani made an offering of a goat at a fertility shrine, to which he called the senior men of Nyaai, Lari'ba, and the elders of the coordinate lineages of Araka within the same minor lineage. His ritual address at the sacrifice was that he was performing the ceremony because Ondua had been remiss in making offerings in performance of his duties as elder.

CASE 17   Ondua voluntarily consulted a distant, renowned diviner about the hostility occurring in Araki, principally between the men of the Lari'ba and Nyaai segments, and the lack of acceptance of authority of senior men by their sons. The verdict of the diviner was that the sickness of Olimani, head of his segment, and Ondua, elder of Araka and head of his segment, was caused by an ancestor who was the founder of the minor lineage, together with the ancestor who was the founder of Araka, and, finally, the apical ancestor of the Lari'ba segment. The verdict thus supported Ondua's claim to authority, notwithstanding the radical changes in lineage patterns of authority in fact.

A sacrifice of a goat was made at an external shrine shared by the Araka, Ambidro, and Ombavu lineages, attended by the elders of these lineages and their ritual assistants. Ondua's ritual address described the history of Araka genealogy in such a manner as to validate his claim to authority and pointed to a variety of serious catastrophies as warnings of the consequences of dissension. The distribution of the meat confirmed the validity of Ondua's claim and the error of Olimani's assumption of authority by conducting a sacrifice at a fertility shrine. The effect was to reestablish to a considerable extent Ondua's lessening authority, which ended with his death the next year, followed by segmentation.

CASES 33 AND 34   Ondua died but before death named his eldest son as the future elder of the Araka. Within a few months, however, Olimani became the elder of a new minimal lineage, the Nyaai. This was validated by the acceptance by other elders of his new ritual status in the performance of sacrifice.[4]

In interpreting the meaning of the above cases, Middleton had the following to say:

> And it must be emphasized that if a man does not invoke against his son when he should, he risks losing the support of the dead for his authority as their representative. It is said that a father must sometimes say "I cannot strike with my hand, the ghosts must strike for me." In the cases from Araka, there were two invocations of the ghosts by men against their own sons, by Draai (Case 5) and by Olimani (Case 7). In both of them the reasons given were that the sons behaved in a way likely to harm the segment and the lineage by refusing to share their labour earnings: to share wealth among the members of one's lineage is one of the primary obligations of lineage membership. But in both cases there were undertones, in that the invokers were using these offences as pretexts in order to show that they had ghostly support for their pretensions to higher status.
>
> *   *   *
>
> As each young man grows adult and becomes a full member of the society the small segment consisting of himself, his wives and children, and perhaps his brothers, becomes in his view a separate entity. But his elders do not usually consider this segment as such to be separate, and his aspirations are seen by them as merely disruptive and directed at weakening their authority. These aspirations and the opposition to them are played out largely in ritual terms. The younger men can acquire status, which is validated in terms of the system itself and cannot be taken away from him, by the possession of junior ghost or ancestral shrines, or both. To do this he must be given sickness by the dead. This sickness must come directly from them, as part of the process of ghostly vengeance. This shows first that he has not been invoked against by his seniors, so is to an extent free of their authority, and also that the dead regard him as the head of a small segment or at least as an adult person in his own right. Almost all the cases of sacrifice at the *andesia* and *a'biva* shrines made in Araka were by men in this position. There is often opposition from senior holders of authority against this interpretation of the sickness. The oracular interpretation of the situation is, of course, the vital part of the process, and, as in Araka, there is usually considerable competition as to who shall be chosen to consult the oracles. Here however, the authority holders have both the right and the duty to consult them.
>
> This conflict is repeated at higher levels of authority. When a man dies, his son takes over his generation status in the lineage, if he inherits the shrines. The elder brother inherits the father's senior shrines, and the junior can set up only junior shrines. There is usually little conflict between the brothers in their own generation, since the tie between them is very close and only comparatively rarely do they dispute for authority. But in the following generation their sons may dispute, since

---

4. Middleton, *Lugbara Religion,* 134-146, 146-154, 164-167, 176-181, 192-210.

by then they may all be the heads of segments of some size. Thus in Lari'ba, Abiria is said to have quarrelled with Dria, and in the second generation Draai has quarrelled with Ondua. Status is achieved mainly by showing that such a man is able to invoke the ghosts, against his own dependants, thus demonstrating that he is considered a responsible and mature man by the ghosts, who listen to his invocation. Once it is accepted that a man has authority over a large segment—the acceptance being also shown by his being treated as such in the distribution of sacrificial meat and by his being allowed to make ritual addresses—then he is regarded as equal in generation to the elder in most situations of lineage authority. This was the case in Araka with Olimani, and on some occasions with Draai and Otoro, whose position was not yet firmly accepted.

* * *

Only the elder is the direct representative of the dead, and only he may sacrifice at the external lineage shrine. But for him to invoke the ghosts against the segment heads directly would bring "shame" to them and he would be open to charges of witchcraft for abusing his position. A man can invoke the dead against a junior, in terms of kinship, but not against a "brother," except in only the most serious situations of stress.[5]

The above pages reveal an order of which constitutive conflict was an enduring part. There was an established procedure for handling its occurrence and outcome, whether that outcome should be a reaffirmation of unity of the kinship groups or a fission of the original kinship group into new and separate kinship groups.

It should be observed that release of tensions within a social group took place in the form of dances after the death of an important man. Normal behavior standards were then completely relaxed, except in the extension of hospitality, and license in sexual behavior was permitted.[6]

Conclusion

When one considers the totality of the traditions, beliefs, and practices of the Lugbara, the conclusion is compelled that, for a segmentary society, they had created a design for living of unusual breadth, intricacy of detail, and articulation of the parts into a working whole. The conditions of their environment, their way of life, and their interpretation of their way of life were integrated into a meaningful and coherent system.

---

5. *Ibid.*, pp. 219-221.
6. *Ibid.*, pp. 202-203; see also J. Middleton, "The Political System of the Lugbara of the Nile-Congo Divide," *Tribes Without Rulers*, eds. J. Middleton and D. Tait (London, 1958), 203.

The Lugbara were organized on a segmentary basis, the smaller kinship groups, that is, the family, including the extended family, performed reproductive, economic, educational, and dispute-settlement functions. Larger lineage groups extending finally to the clan and the tribe, performed exogamic, political, dispute-settlement, and warmaking functions. Ritual served to identify the respective groupings and to reinforce their authority and the attachment of their members to them.

In other words, the organization of a society into kinship and segmentary groupings, whatever particular form they take, is a cultural invention which enables a society to establish an order and means of cooperation to accomplish the necessary objectives for its continued existence. Thus the number of types of lineage groups—family, minimal, medial, maximal, and the like which the anthropologist as an observer is able to discern is simply a product of the various functions which such groups are called upon to perform. In last analysis, they are a means whereby individuals can identify themselves as members of diverse groups for the purpose of performing the diverse functions of such groups and thereby enable the society to endure.

The Lugbara believed that the personalities or souls embodied in the living persisted as actors in the society after death. With the maturing and death of new generations, they mostly subsided into the background of ancestral spirits in general and were forgotten. The ancestral spirits supported the exercise of authority of those legitimately entitled to possess authority. Ghosts punished with sickness those whose acts struck at the foundations of the existing authority structure. Yet the contact of the living with the ancestors was flexible enough to permit change to take place and new occupants of authoritative posts to assume their roles on a basis of legitimacy. Lugbara society presented the paradox of legitimacy supporting an unchanging formal structure of authority and system of statuses yet at the same time accommodating change. It accepted changed conditions and allowed them to assume a new formal structure of authority and system of statuses, which, although expressed in traditional terms, embraced new authoritative roles and new occupants of authoritative posts. In other words, the traditional system was the legitimate system, legitimacy supported authority, and change was accommodated within the legitimate structures.

Upon death, a man's body became nothing but his soul persisted and returned eventually to the living as an ancestral spirit. Beyond the spirits of the ancestors was God, the source of all power. Both

God and the ancestors were concerned with the well-being of the lineage or tribe as a group and were aroused when it was guilty of impiety or the like. At the edge of the group of the living, who had a defined system of kin relationships with one another, were the witches and sorcerers. Beyond these were strangers who bore no relationship to the living group, and, finally, beyond these were people of a fearsome, alien character. Each successive external group possessed increasingly inverted characteristics.

Social and political action were primarily structured through a lineage group which was the core of a family cluster of a number of homesteads found in a territory but not settled in a village. Harmony within a lineage group and with its related lineage groups was a valued social ideal. To preserve that harmony when it was impaired by deviant conduct striking at its structural rules, a unique system of social control developed. This consisted of (1) the recognition by an elder of conduct which was deemed to be an offense against the existing authority structure and questioning its legitimacy, (2) ghostly invocation by the elder against the offender or sinner, (3) visitation of sickness by an ancestor as penalty for the offense, (4) after the recovery of the sick person from his illness, consultation of and validation by a diviner that the sickness occurred as assumed in (3) above, and (5) a rite of sacrifice purifying the offender and restoring the relations within the community impaired by his offense. In course of time, the fifth step would mark and validate a realignment of lineage relationships and the emergence of new authority patterns as segmentation of the lineage group took place.

The handling of disputes over land, women, and livestock and the control of such offenses as incest, adultery, homicide, and assault were made a part of the process of preserving authority.

Lugbara society carried its heavy burden of sickness and its occurrence was used in a symbolic system supporting its system of authority, controlling constitutive conflict manifested in questioned claims of the exercise of authority, and acknowledging and legitimizing change in the possession of authority.

Part Five

KENYA

Chapter 12

The Kikuyu

Geography and Economy

KENYA is bounded on the west by Uganda, on the south by Tanzania, on the east by the Indian Ocean and Somalia, and on the north by Ethiopia. It includes parts of the great African lakes and the great volcanic mountain of Kenya, as well as other peaks. The land in which the peoples studied dwell are the highlands or plateau regions. The economy was mostly agricultural but the cattle culture was found among some peoples.

The Kikuyu, the first Kenya people to be studied, are among the largest of the northeast Bantu-speaking tribes. They possess common physical characteristics, culture, and language. Their land is a high plateau, dominated by Mount Kenya and the Aberdare range. Cultivation took place up to a height of almost 7,000 feet on Mount Kenya. They dwell on a series of undulating hills and ridges ranging from 200 to 600 feet in height, with valleys between them which are well-watered.

They were an agricultural people who raised sorghum, millet, and perhaps beans and sweet potatoes. Their livestock was sheep and goats, with some cattle. Markets were held for trade among the Kikuyu. Trade with the Kamba and Masai tribes also took place.[1]

---

1. J. Middleton, "The Central Tribes of the North-Eastern Bantu," *Ethnographic Survey of Africa*, ed. D. Forde (London, 1953), Part V, 11-24.

Individual Personality
and Social Attitudes

The Kikuyu perceived the individual to possess significance through his relationships with others. Kenyatta stated:

> According to the Gikuyu ways of thinking, nobody is an isolated individual. Or rather, his uniqueness is a secondary fact about him: first and foremost he is several people's relative and several people's contemporary. His life is founded on this fact spiritually and economically, just as much biologically. . . . His personal needs, physical and psychological, are satisfied incidentally while he plays his part as member of a family group, and cannot be fully satisfied in any other way. . . .
>
> This vital reality of the family group is an important thing for Europeans to bear in mind, since it underlies the whole social and economic organisation of the Gikuyu. . . . The Gikuyu does not think of his tribe as a group of individuals organised collectively, for he does not think of himself as a social unit, It is rather the widening-out of the family by a natural process of growth and division. He participates in tribal affairs through belonging to his family, and his status in the larger organisation reflects his status in the family circle.

The father was the authority figure in the family. Relationships between the father and his children were characterized by respect and obedience to his authority. Conversation between them was gentle and polite in tone on both sides. A much warmer and closer relationship existed with the mother.

The proper attitudes and manners to be adopted in role relationships were emphasized in the education of children. The age-set system reinforced adherence to common standards of dress and deportment. The significance of particular kinds of personal relationships was made clear, and the importance of adherence to social obligations was demonstrated. Loyalty and devotion were important values for persons in the same age group. The individualist and the selfish person were decried. The appropriate behavior in the concrete situation and the importance of personal relations were the dominant themes in training the young.

There was an openness and frankness in accepting the sex relation and seriousness in realizing the procreation function as important aspects of life. This is not in the least to imply licentiousness; the virginity of a bride was a critical matter.[2]

---

2. J. Kenyatta, *Facing Mount Kenya: The Tribal Life of the Gikuyu* (London, 1953, first printing 1938), pp. 8-10, 105-121, quotation at pp. 309-310.

Religion

There was a supreme god, named *Ngai,* with whom it was essential to maintain harmony and have communion. He was the creator of the world and was manifested in the sun, the moon, the stars, and rain. The lightning was his weapon, the thunder the cracking of his joints. His concern was for the people, not the individual, yet the individual should manifest, in ritual, communion with him at the four important events of life, that is, birth, initiation into the age set, marriage, and death. The sacrificial ceremonies for these occasions were conducted through the family group and elder, not by the individual. God brought fortune or misfortune to the people. Sacrificial services in which communion with God took place upon occasions of importance to the tribe. These were the planting and harvest ceremony and the ceremonies to bring rain or eliminate an outbreak of illness. Such ceremonies were conducted by the elders.

There were three significant social groups, each of whom had their counterpart in the spirit world. In life, one had his soul or *ngoro.* After death this became his spirit or *ngomo* and joined the underworld of spirits. These spirits were recognized as (1) the spirits of the father and mother, which were directly concerned in their living children, (2) the spirits of the clan, and (3) the spirits of the age-group, which were concerned with the fortunes of the tribe.

When misfortune struck a family, and in any event periodically about every three months, the head of the family communed with the spirits of its ancestors at the family shrine. Kenyatta spoke of the role of the elder as intermediary with the ancestors:

> The function of an elder, both in his own family group and in the community, is one of harmonising the activities of the various groups, living and departed. In his capacity of mediator his family group and community in general respect him for his seniority and wisdom, and he, in turn, respects the seniority of the ancestral spirits. This is because he realises that his present elevated position is due to the care and guidance rendered him by his departed ancestors, and whatever he gives them, he gives them not in a form of prayer, but in gratitude and to hold their memory green.

The ancestors were linked with the control of behavior in the group. "The Gikuyu believe that the spirits of the dead, like human beings, can be pleased or displeased by the behavior of an individual or a family group, or an age-group. In order to establish a good relation between the two worlds the ceremony of communing with the ancestral spirits is observed constantly." The family was considered to consist of "all members both living and dead. Anything that disturbs that fellowship is evil, and nothing disturbs the dead more than an offense against family unity and loyalty." Medicine men acted diviners to search out the fault which was committed, when misfortune or illness struck a person or a family. This would enable the family to re-establish good relations by appropriate ceremony.[3]

The ability to influence the realization of important values by magic, that is, the use of magical powers by medicine men and sorcerers through the employment of ceremony and fetishes, was a significant factor in Kikuyu life. The role of the medicine man was to perform ceremonies and provide charms whereby important personal values of his clients could be realized or protected. He acted to purify ritual uncleanness resulting from failure to observe rules of ritual avoidance, to divine the causes of misfortune, and to accomplish a variety of objectives of his clients. He was sought for protective magic, magic to inflict harm or inculcate love, and magic to bring good fortune. Sorcerers or witches were perceived to use black magic to bring about death.[4]

Social and Political Organization

The father was the head of the polygynous family, consisting of himself, his wife or wives, and children. Upon his death, the eldest son succeeded to the post of authority as head of the family group, unless it broke up. In the latter event, the head of each segment assumed the post of authority for its members. The disposition of the control of land followed several rules upon the death of the head of a family. The sons of each wife shared in the property associated with their mother. This included cultivated land, livestock, and movable property. Control over unallotted land and care of the deceased father's widows remained with the new head of the family group.

The *mbari* was the largest local kinship group, formed on the

3. *Ibid.,* Chap. 10, quotations at pp. 265, 266, 115; J. Middleton, *op. cit.,* pp. 65-69; J. Kenyatta, "Kikuyu Religion, Ancestor-Worship, and Sacrificial Practices," *Africa,* X (1937), 308; W. S. Routledge and K. Routledge, *With a Prehistoric People: The Akikiyu of East Africa* (London, 1910), 225-228, 239-244.

4. Kenyatta, *Facing Mount Kenya,* 299-308; C. W. Hobley, *Bantu Beliefs and Magic* (Rev. ed.; London, 1938), Parts I and II, J. Middleton, *op. cit.,* pp. 69-71; J. Kenyatta, "Kikuyu Religion," 308.

basis of common descent from a single male ancestor. The senior elder of this group was its ceremonial head and represented the group as it participated in larger social groupings, such as the district.

The *mbari* had significance primarily by virtue of its relationship to the land which it used and controlled. It was the governing structure for the village or *itora,* that is, a group of people living on a ridge of land and identified through their acceptance of a particular *mbari* for associational and political purposes.

The different *mbari* of a particular district would act together in certain political and ritual situations on the basis of territorial nearness to one another and convenience and not on the basis of common kinship. The most notable of these occasions was the *itwika* ceremony, or circumcision ceremony marking the passage of a child, either male or female, to the status of adulthood.

The largest kinship group, which had no territorial identification, and was characterized by common descent from a remote male ancestor, was the clan. There were nine clans. These were divided into sub-clans, which were the exogamous groups. Their principal significance was their common acceptance of mutual responsibility for a killing committed by a member and the payment of compensation for it. In a broader sense, they were identified by "whether they continue to take part in common initiation ceremonies, family and 'group' sacrifices, contribution to blood-money, eating of sacrificial animals in marriage transactions, and family ceremonial eating of meat."

Kenyatta described the Kikuyu organs of government as follows:

> The starting-point was the family unit. From the governmental point of view members of one family group were considered as forming a family council *(ndundu ya mocie),* with the father as the president. The father represented the family group in the government. The next group was the village council *(kiama gia itora),* composed of the heads of several families in the village. The senior elder acted as the president of the council and this group represented the villages in the government. Another wider group was formed, and named, district council *(kiama kia rogongo),* in which all the elders of the district participated; this council was presided over by a committee *(kiama kia ndundu),* composed of the senior elders of the villages. Amongst these elders the one most advanced in age and wisdom was elected as a judge and president *(mothamaki* or *mociiri)* of the *ndundu.* From the district council a national council was formed, composed of several *ndundu,* representing the whole population. Among the judges, a president was elected at the meetings of the national council. All these councils were composed of men from the age of about thirty onwards. But there was a very important council of

young men known as *njama ya ita* (council of war), its members were between the age of twenty and forty. This council, apart from its military activities, represented the interests of the young people in the government.

The status of being an elder was the terminal stage of a succession to a series of roles embodied in the age sets and generation sets of the people. The significance of such roles in the social and political constitution of the people will be made clear from the following statement of Kenyatta:

1. Freedom for the people to acquire and develop land under a system of family ownership.
2. Universal tribal membership, as the unification of the whole tribe, the qualification for it to be based on maturity, and not on property. For this reason it was then decided that every member of the community, after passing through the circumcision ceremony as a sign of adulthood, should take an active part in the government; and that males should go through this initiation between the ages of sixteen and eighteen, and females between the age of ten and fourteen.
3. Socially and politically all circumcised men and women should be equally full members of the tribe, and thereby the status of a king or nobleman should be abolished.
4. The government should be in the hands of councils of elders *(kiama)* chosen from all members of the community, who had reached the age of eldership, having retired from warriorhood. And the position of elders should be determined by a system of age-grading.
5. All young men between the ages of eighteen and forty should form a warrior class *(anake)*, and be ready to defend the country, and that the country should respect them and have pride in them.
6. In times of need, the Government should ask the people to contribute in rotation sheep, goats, or cattle, for national sacrifices or other ceremonies performed for the welfare of the whole people.
7. In order to keep up the spirit of the *itwika,* and to prevent any tendency to return to the system of despotic government, the change of, and the election for, the government offices should be based on a rotation system of generations. The community was divided into two categories: (a) *mwangi,* (b) *maina* or *irungu.* Membership was to be determined by birth, namely, if one generation is *mwangi,* their sons shall be called *maina,* and their grandsons be called *mwangi,* and so on. It was further decided that one generation should hold the office of government for a period of thirty to forty years, at the end of which the ceremony of *itwika* should take place to declare that the old generation had completed its term of governing, and that the young generation was ready to take over the administration of the country.
8. All men and women must get married, and that no man should be allowed to hold a responsible position other than warrior, or become a member of the council of elders *(kiama)* unless he was married and had established his own homestead. And that women should be given the same social status as their husbands.

9. Criminal and civil laws were established and procedure clearly defined. Rules and regulations governing the behaviour between individuals and groups within the Government were laid down.

The age sets and generation sets cut across all Kikuyu society, without regard to clan or district application. Each age set consisted of all youths, boys and girls, who went through the initiation ceremony of circumcision in the same year. Boys were initiated between the ages of 15 and 18 and following instruction achieved the status of a junior warrior. Girls were initiated between the ages of 10 and 15 but did not marry until 16 or 17 years of age. Men of the same age set had a very close relationship with one another, they were "like brothers."

About six years after his initiation, the male became a senior warrior and a member of the war council. Each age set became a regiment. The war council and a war magician made decisions in war. The raids upon the enemy were led by three leaders chosen by the war magician for their ability. The purpose of warfare was to capture the livestock of the enemy.

When a man married and established his own home, he took the first step in becoming an elder. On the birth of his first child and payment of one goat, he became known as an "elder of one goat." This gave him the capacity to listen to cases as the senior council of elders sat in judgment. His role was to act as a messenger for the council and assist in preparing its feast. After the initiation ceremony of his first child, he became a member of the lowest grade of the senior council of elders. At this point he ceased to be a warrior and assumed the role of peace-maker in the community. He then acquired the capacity to join in the decision of cases by the senior council of elders. When most of his children had undergone the initiation ceremony, his wife had ceased to bear children, and he had passed through all of the age grades, a man could, upon payment of the appropriate fee, become a member of the sacrificial or religious council and, as such, was invested with the power to conduct sacrificial ceremonies for the people. This last-mentioned council had the power to promulgate laws binding upon all within their sphere of jurisdiction, to participate in the judicial function, and, as stated, to conduct religious ceremonies.

The age sets were combined into a generation set, which ruled the country for a period of about 20-30 years, or perhaps longer upon occasion, when the powers of government were turned over to the alternate and succeeding generation at the *itwike* ceremony.

The age-set system meant that leadership was secular in nature and was recognized on the basis of ability, instead of descent. Within the age-set group, natural leaders emerged. Their qualities became manifest in a wider setting as they became actors in inter-group relations. The admired qualities of a leader, represented "a complex of intelligence, personality, good reputation, social and economic success, and a sound heredity." He might develop a talent for warmaking or he might reveal a capacity to judge wisely in disputes.[5]

Law: Land Tenure

Control over the use of land in the sense of ownership was acquired by the purchase of land or the clearing of unclaimed land. Any such land was uniquely the land of the person who acquired it to the point that it did not fall into the land of the family or clan of which he was a member. It was instead the land of a new family unit of which he was the original head. This will be made clear as the typical history of such an acquisition of land is traced.

The land so acquired was regarded by its holder as *his*. When he allotted portions of it to his wives, they regarded it as *ours,* that is, the land of the family. As sons were born, became mature, married, and received allotments from it, they regarded it as *ours*. The land did not need to be one contiguous piece. Usually it was a number of plots of land located at different points. It could be cultivated land, fallow land, bush, or forest.

The man who held the land as outlined above controlled its allotment and use by virtue of his authority as head of the family. When he died, however, a family-land unit came into being known as the *mbari*. The land which it controlled was known as the *githaka*. The eldest son of his senior wife assumed, on the man's death, the role of controlling the use of land by the surviving members of the family. This post was known as the *muramati* and the family-land unit was, as stated above, the *githaka*. As grandsons of the founding head of the *mbari* were born and the family enlarged, it still remained the same *mbari*. It held together as long as the group acknowledged common descent from a single male ancestor for land-use purposes.

---

5. Kenyatta, *Facing Mount Kenya,* 188-206, quotation at 188-189, 194-195; J. Middleton, *op. cit.,* pp. 27-38, 64, quotation at 32; H. E. Lambert, *Kikuyu, Social and Political Institutions* (London, New York, Toronto, 1956), 8-106, 131-144, quotation at 101; Routledge and Routledge, *op. cit.,* pp. 142-146, 195-202; A. H. J. Prins, *East African Age-Class Systems* (Groningen, Djakarta, 1953), 4-57, 98-118; C. Cagnolo, *The Akikiyu: Their Customs, Traditions and Folklore* (Nyeri, Kenya, 1933), 119-125.

With the death of the founding father, the authority to control the use of land of the *githaka* within the family vested in the *muramati*. The *muramati* had the privilege to cultivate the lands which were his, as his father's son, but not the lands belonging to the other sons. Such land of the *githaka* as was available could be allotted by him for use within the family or by outsiders as tenants. He could not sell such land. Other land could be sold, however, after the purchase price had been agreed upon. It was transferred by a formal ceremony known as marking the boundary, in which the bounds of the transferred land were permanently marked. It was also possible for a man to acquire and hold, upon a basis of friendship, land from another as tenant. As long as the tenant used the land, he was generally secure in its enjoyment.

Public lands, consisting of grazing lands, salt-licks, sacred groves, public meeting places, public dancing places, and public roads and paths were under the control of the elders. Any person had grazing rights on fallow land of any *mbari* and unclaimed land.

Land-use disputes were decided by the elders of the district.[6]

Law and Procedure

The elders in the age-set system were those who were qualified to decide disputes. The elders who were selected to decide a particular dispute were determined on the basis of family relationships between the disputing parties. Disputes in the family were decided by the father. Upon his death, the eldest son of the senior wife assumed the authority to decide minor disputes but, in disputes of a somewhat serious character, he was usually assisted by other elders in the family. As different families became involved in a dispute, the heads of the families of the disputing parties joined in the court, together with the heads of related families. The rule for selection of judges was put as follows:

If the two families immediately concerned cannot settle a dispute, it is the business of the family heads of all the kin to do so. Authority had been distributed in much the same proportion as the common blood. In general all heads of families with a share of the blood of the nearest common ancestors of the disputants equal to that of the disputants themselves share in the authority once vested in that ancestor and may

6. Kenyatta, *op. cit.*, pp. 20-40; J. Middleton, *op. cit.*, pp. 52-56; Routledge and Routledge, *op. cit.*, pp. 142-146; M. Beech, "Kikuyu System of Land Tenure," *Journal of the African Society*, XVII (1917-1918), 46, 136.

take part in the meetings to achieve a settlement of the dispute, provided that they are senior enough, that is, are members of the appropriate grade of the *kiama* (the second grade in the Embu district and Kikuyu).

The rendering of justice was not free. It was dependent upon the payment of stipulated fees such as livestock or sugar-cane beer, which had to be paid at successive stages of the judicial proceeding. These fees were then consumed in a commensal meal. "The essential idea at the back of such fees is the binding force of commensality. Those who eat or drink together thereby express their common interest and their intention to arrive at an agreement amicably; they, unlike the disputants themselves, do not divide into contending parties."

A dispute between two persons who were members of the same *mbari* would have normally come before the kinship court, the *kiama kia mbari*. The next court was the *kiama kia mwaki*. It had "jurisdiction over the area in which live the people who joined in the commensal meals following the payment of the various 'entrance fees' paid in the different stages in social status by the individual" (i.e., the age-set ceremonies). A dispute between two persons who were not related but lived in the same *mwaki* was handled by this court. If feelings between the disputing parties or the groups to which they belonged were high, outside judges might be called in to add their authority to the acceptance of the judgment. In exceptional cases, the dispute might be referred to another court.

When neither kinship nor domicile could be the basis for bringing a case before a court, the disputants could establish an *ad hoc* court by agreement. Proceedings before this court took place in two stages, in each of which the court was differently composed. The first stage was open to the public. The purpose of the first stage was to insure that the subject matter was properly presented from the standpoint of both sides and that the issues for decision were fully and clearly developed. The court at this stage consisted of two or three judges chosen by each side and such additional outside judges as the court might select. The second stage was held before a court of final judgment. About four judges for each side were chosen, together with independent judges. The parties told their stories and were questioned by the judges. The court then held a secret session, calling such witnesses as it might think helpful, deliberated the case, and reached its judgment. In the meantime, the animals which had been paid as fees were killed and roasted. The gallbladders of these animals were ritually broken to reinforce the secrecy of the deliberations. The roasted meat was then distributed among the court according to the rank of its members and was eaten. The decision was then ceremonially announced.

Since the object of the proceeding was to restore harmony between the disputants and their respective groups, a party who was dissatisfied with a judgment had one and only one opportunity to have a rehearing and a new decision by a wider court than that which originally heard his case. Thereafter the matter was finally closed.

A system of judicial ceremonial oaths and ordeals was used to insure the telling of truth in the trial. A ceremonial curse, invoking poverty, sickness, and calamity upon all who unreasonably failed to obey the court's decision was used to bring about compliance with the court's judgment. Two elders were appointed to insure that the judgment was performed by the parties. Property which a judgment ordered to be transferred to a disputing party was not paid over to him directly. It was instead transferred through the hands of the appointed elders, who brought to bear the authority of the entire court to compel compliance with the judgment. If a party refused to comply with a judgment, he and his wife would be ostracized by the community. If the case were an important one and had come before an independent court, there was a ceremonial form of ostracism for failure to comply. It should also be noted that the persistent wrong-doer, guilty of repeated theft or sorcery, was put to death. Consent of his nearest relative was necessary for such a killing. This step was taken "only when no other course could ensure the security of the community. The necessary consent of the relatives, and the secrecy observed regarding the occurrence, convince me that it was not regarded as a legal measure, but rather as a violation of law made necessary for self-protection against a dangerous character, who, by his misdeeds, had deprived himself of the protection of the law."

Persistent offenders might be handled within the group of which they were a member of being beaten with stinging nettles or birches or being subjected to the bites of tree ants.

The judicial system reflected a number of principles. Its cardinal objective was the restoration of peace and harmony within and between groups, once it had been disturbed by deviant behavior. Lambert stated in this connection:

> The essential meaning at the back of "fines" as distinct from compensation to the injured party is the reinstatement of the offender in society, from which he has virtually expelled himself by some anti-social act. The method of the reinstatement is the eating of the animals paid as "fines," another instance of the binding force of the ritual meal. Close relations

are expected to assist the offender to find the wherewithal to pay the
"fine" and compensation unless he can do so readily himself, and it is no
doubt this fact which to some extent induces a sub-clan to punish the
offender when his offense is frequently repeated. The habitual offender
whose actions are a constant threat to the wealth and well-being of his
clan or sub-clan may be summarily expelled or put to death.

The elders "will always say that their chief duty was to prevent strife
between creditors and debtors, and to prevent both from resorting to
supernatural powers and open hostilities; nor was it their duty to
condemn and punish this one or that."

It was observed among the Kikuyu that:

> The maintenance of peace depends upon the recognition of three
> principles: first, settlement by deliberation and discussion instead of
> seeking settlement by force; second, the correction of imbalance by
> compensation rather than by talion; and, third, an impersonal adjudica-
> tion and assessment by the aged (in social grade) who are deemed to be
> beyond the partialities and impetuosities of self-interested youth.
>
> Three stages in the mode of settlement, particularly in cases of homi-
> cide, appear to be traditionally remembered. These are settlement by
> force, settlement by talion, and settlement by compensation. The first
> of these involved the taking up of arms and generally ended in a blood
> feud, the second was an attempt to put an end to feuds by limiting the
> retributory action to the magnitude of the offence (the murder of a man
> was settled by the killing of the murderer or of his equal in the kinship
> group or, alternatively, by handling him or his brother or son over for
> adoption into the damaged group), and the third meant payment of the
> murdered man's equivalent in stock.

The three principles of dispute settlement noted above were illustrated in the three stages in the private settlement of cases of homicide. Warriors of the clan of the murdered man invaded the clan of
the man of the suspected murderer and cut down plants in its
gardens but otherwise committed no violence. The warriors of the
invaded group then appeared, armed for battle. Elders of the two
groups intervened at this point and tried to settle the matter by discussion. If responsibility for the killing was admitted, a promise to
pay the requisite compensation was made. If the killing was denied,
there was an agreement to have the case heard by an *ad hoc* court.

Compensation for certain offenses, notably homicide, injury to the
person, and theft was fixed in a table of damages for each offense.

The Kikuyu system of justice was designed to secure wisdom and
impartiality in adjudication through the mode of selection of elders
to decide cases. Regularity in the application of norms was secured
through the resort by judges to their recollection of applicable past
precedents and their knowledge of custom. The application of strict

law was tempered with equity. "Every tribe has a code, but it is a code of general principles, not of detail. Every judgment must conform to it, though the principles are applied with a latitude unknown in European law. The rights in property vested in the kinship group, for instance, may not be invaded. But within the group equity and equilibrium may be powerful determinants in the allocation or redistribution of property." Knowledge of the facts of the case on the part of the court was insured by the fact that it was drawn from the neighborhood, if not solely from the village. "A court which of its own personal experience and environment has the facts at its finger tips has a better knowledge of them than one which has to depend on a string of individually garbled versions. And a judgment arrived at by agreement between the elders of two contending parties is more likely to be satisfying in the long run (that is, equilibrium maintaining) than one arrived at by an independent court which has no immediate concern with equilibrium."

An important defect in the Kikuyu system of justice was its overemphasis on the fee system of administering justice. This meant in practice that the poor were unable to invoke judicial proceedings to safeguard their interests. The existence of this defect was openly acknowledged among the people.

Turning now to the realm of offenses, homicide was an offense but not because the killer was an evil person to be restrained and punished. Indeed, a killing could be entirely by inadvertence and excusable in terms of Western morality and still be wrongful in Kikuyu terms. Provocation, self-defense, and absence of culpable intentions were of no consequence in assessing responsibility. Any killing meant that the perpetrator, or more precisely, his kin group, must pay the compensation stipulated as blood money. If this was not forthcoming, a retaliatory killing by the injured group through blood feud could be expected. The significance of injury to the group was brought out by the fact that a man had greater value to his group than a woman. The blood money for killing a man, therefore, was over three times that for killing a woman.

Injuries to the person were wrongful on the same basis. Compensation on a fixed schedule was payable according to the nature of the injury, without regard to whether it was intentional or avoidable. Adultery, rape, and theft represented private, rather than public, injuries. On the other hand, one who persistently stole or committed sorcery was subject to be executed, as indicated above. Unpaid debts arising from transactions involving land or bridewealth were also brought before the courts to compel payment.

Lambert notes that the senior rank of the council of elders had the power to legislate concerning matters of general concern not falling within the province of the clans. Orders so issued were considered to have a supernatural sanction. Examples of legislative action were found in the spheres of the prevention of witchcraft, theft, and famine, as well as the reservation of land for public purposes and the conservation of firewood.[7]

Conclusion

The Kikuyu are a Bantu-speaking people living on a high plateau next to the slopes of Mount Kenya. They were primarily agriculturists.

The individual in Kikuyu society had a clear perspective of himself in relation to others. Role and status were central concepts in the organization of action. Action was structured in part through the family and clan and in part through age sets. The latter emphasized the roles of the warrior and the elder outside the context of kin. The father was the focus of authority for the family, the council of elders for the village and district. Education emphasized the content and propriety of role performance. Loyalty, devotion, and adherence to social standards were important values.

The supernatural was a part of life, of course, but it did not manifest itself as a control of deviant or wrongful behavior to the extent that it did in other African societies. God brought fortune or misfortune to the people as a whole. The performance of ritual was important to preserve a good relation with the supreme god and the spiritual world. Established ceremonies were performed by the senior elders and participated in by the family or the group. These took place at the central points in the life of the individual, at planting or harvest times in the life of the group, or at times of misfortune for the individual or the group. There was a constant communion between the living members of a family and its ancestral

7. Lambert, *op. cit.*, pp. 100-144, quotations at pp. 107, 108, 113-114, 115, 118, 121; Kenyatta, *op. cit.*, pp. 214-230; Cagnolo, *op. cit.*, pp. 147-159; J. Middleton, *op. cit.*, pp. 43-50; Routledge and Routledge, *op. cit.*, pp. 204-221; C. Dundas, "The Organization and Laws of Some Bantu Tribes of East Africa," *Journal of the Royal Anthropological Institute*, XLV (1915), 234, quotations at 260, 261; C. Dundas, "Native Laws of Some Bantu Tribes of East Africa," *Journal of the Royal Anthropological Institute*, LI (1921), 217; H. R. Tate, "The Native Law of the Southern Gikuyu of East Africa," *Journal of the African Society*, IX (1909-1910), 233.

spirits. The ideal was to preserve harmony in the relations of the living and the departed. Witchcraft and magic were recognized as forces influencing the fortune of the individual, acting either for good or bad.

The age sets, family, sub-clan, village, and district operated to structure action in an overlapping manner. Kin relations to land were structured through the *mbari,* which had an associational, economic, and political significance. Leadership for purposes of political, judicial, and warmaking action, and, to a considerable extent, economic action, was recognized on a basis of ability. The council of elders carried out legislative and judicial functions and secured the community interest in public lands.

The rendering of justice was on a secular basis and was invoked by the payment of fees, typically in livestock, which were consumed in commensal meals symbolizing the preservation of harmony within the group as the basic objective of the judicial process.

The judicial decision-making process took place in two stages, the first of which was designed to develop the issues presented by the case and the second to reach a final decision. The facts and issues were thoroughly explored. The elders vested with the authority to decide the case had the power to question those who gave testimony and to call witnesses. The proceedings were, through the taking of oaths and the placing of curses, invested with supernatural sanctions. Ostracism was a group penalty for failure to comply with a judgment. Repeated offenses of sorcery or theft would subject the offender to the penalty of death, with the consent of his group. Persistent offenders of a lesser degree were subjected by their family group to beatings or to the bites of tree ants.

The basic objectives of the judicial process were the determination of improper conduct on the basis of custom and the restoration of group harmony disturbed by deviant conduct.

The council of senior elders also had the power to legislate, or issue orders to the group, in matters of general concern, such as the prevention of witchcraft, theft, and famine, and the use of public lands.

In general, the Kikuyu displayed considerable success in secularizing authority in the sense of selecting its decision makers in politics, war, and justice on the basis of ability, as well as minimizing the impact of the lineage upon such decision making. It was a society that had achieved a considerable degree of psychological health and social integration. Its ways of behavior adapted well both to its internal and external environments.

Chapter 13

The Nandi

Geography and Economy

THE NANDI live in the southwest corner of the Uashin Gishu Plateau, a table-land bounded by the escarpment of the Rift Valley on the east and the Nandi escarpment on the west. Mount Elgon, over 14,000 feet high, rises in the northwest and the Suk mountains in the northeast. The land of the Nandi begins in the south a few miles to the northeast of the Kavirondo Gulf of Lake Victoria. The elevation is about 5,500 to 7,000 feet high, the average being between 6,000 and 6,500 feet. Much of west and southwest Nandi is forested. The northern, central, and eastern parts are a sloping parkland, well-watered and drained, and with abundant rainfall. There is no need to move the herds of cattle during the dry season. The Nandi are part of the Nandi-speaking peoples and their language is more developed than any other of those peoples. They are members of the Nilotic division of the Negro race and possess a Hamitic origin.

The Cattle Culture

The Nandi were a pastoral people. Their central interest was cattle. They existed for their cattle, though they also kept goats and sheep. Agriculture was secondary. Milk, blood, and meat were their principal foods, supplemented by millet and eleusine grain for women and old people. Care of the cattle was the principal occupation and concern of the men. Tribes which did not possess cattle were held in contempt. A Nandi who did not possess cattle had little social or political status. He could not speak at the council meetings. Personal names were frequently connected with cattle. Cattle was the only form of property that mattered. A man could not sell the cattle which he inherited, only the cattle which he acquired by himself. The payment of cattle was essential for bridewealth and, hence, marriage. Cattle were used for gifts between relatives and for compensation for offenses. Milk, grass, and dung had a sacred quality because of their connection with cattle. The hides of cattle were used for clothing and covering in sleep. The dung was used for building and medicinal purposes. The Nandi were, in short, absorbed in cattle.

A large part of a man's cattle, unless he owned only a few head, were distributed among relatives and friends for care. The advantage was that the risk of loss of cattle through epidemic or raids by the Masai was lessened. The result was to provide ties which linked many people together throughout the tribe.

The Nandi considered themselves to be a most superior people. They had no word for tribe. They had their own name, the Nandi, but other peoples were referred to by group-names, covering in each case a group of tribes. One who was not a Nandi was of no consequence. They were a community, superior to all others, having a common name and territory.

Land, the central concern of an agricultural society, was for the Nandi not a property shared with the ancestors in the same way that cattle were. It was true that land had a ritual value because the ancestors had lived and died on it and thereby hallowed it. But land existed for cattle grazing. Accordingly, the rules governing its use had to be simple and to promote widespread grazing. There was no litigation over land as land, only over the crops grown on the land. Land was held by the whole people, rather than by individuals. Ritual involving land had value for the purpose of producing crops. Sale of land within the Nandi did not really occur.

The Nandi were a self-contained, self-supporting unit, needing little or no commerce with other peoples. "These three occupations, cattle, war, and agriculture were the mainstay of tribal life, war entering the economic sphere because it was the means of increasing the numbers of stock owned by the tribe. . . . "[1]

---

1. G. W. B. Huntingford, *Nandi Work and Culture* (H.M.S.O., London, 1950), 81.

Religion

Every person had a body and a soul. The body had a shadow-soul, which lived in the shadow and died with the body. The heart was the other aspect of the soul. It was the vital part of man, the personality. It survived death. As the dead body was consumed by the hyena, which was the method of disposal of the corpse, the heart used the hyena as the means for entering into the land of the spirits, where it became the *oiindet* (pl. *oiik*). The spirits lived underground, in a region similar to that of the earth, and occupied a status equivalent to their physical and material condition at the time of their death. They used snakes and sometimes rats as vehicles for travelling to visit the living.

The ancestral spirits were part of the cosmos. The Nandi had a term, *kiet,* which referred to that which, in the beginning, God set in order. The *kiet* was the world order, consisting of the sky, the heavenly bodies, the weather, and the whole of nature that could be seen and felt. Nature was perceived in terms of whether it had a practical benefit or disadvantage and how it affected the realization of values. Huntingford had the following significant remark to make in this connection:

> We can in fact say that things which are useful to man, and which are likewise necessary to him for his existence, acquire a practical value which may be called a social value; and because of this social value certain of them also acquire a ritual value, since apart from their effect on people's material well-being, certain acts of a spiritual nature must be done to ensure the continuity of this well-being, while other things must not be done for the same reason, lest the invisible link which connects the living with the Other World be broken.

There was a harmony and order in the interrelationship of God, the spirits, and man in his material world, which must not be broken. The preservation of this order was central to the maintenance of law. A deviant act which disturbed the foundations of this order led to a reaction in the spiritual realm which brought retribution to its performer.

The *kiet* embraced

> the concept of Asis, 'God,' an element which can be reached only through some form of mediation, the principal mediating agent being the body of the spirits of the dead, the *Oiik,* who though no longer present in the flesh, *are still members of the tribe.* Without some understanding of the great part the *Oiik* play in tribal life, and in the preser-

vation of public order, it is impossible to realize the true nature of the foundations of public law. (Italics supplied.)

There was a supreme god, named Asis, whose being was identified in the sun, *asista*. He regulated the balance between man and nature. His beneficent influence was accordingly invoked by ritual at the harvest ceremony, to bring rain in times of serious drought, and when a herd of cattle was attacked by disease. He was thanked when there was a successful war raid, and his forgiveness was asked when a raid was unsuccessful. Misconduct entered the sphere of Asis when it was so widespread or repeated as to arouse his displeasure and sending of punishment. Asis represented a force or element which, when disturbed, did not confine its reaction to punishing the offenders but instead to punishing the people at large.

The ancestral spirits were

the principal mediators between man and God. They are the guardians of public morality. They are the driving force behind customary law. Violation of the law by the commission of crimes against the tribe brings down upon the criminal the wrath of the *oiik*, partly because their law has been transgressed, and partly because the regulating element, Asis, has been offended and may itself send punishment. By this punishment not only would the offenders be destroyed, but the *oiik* themselves would be hurt as well for they are dependent upon the living for the continuation of their own existence [i.e., through the offering of food].

The ancestral spirits were held to be motivated by love toward the living. The visitation of punishment by them, which usually took the form of illness or of death, was the consequence of some omission in expressing regard for them, such as the failure to make a usual food offering, the denial of a ceremony which was their due, the killing of a snake at night, or the commission of certain crimes which struck at the tie between the temporal and the spiritual worlds. Diviners were used to ascertain responsibility for offenses to the spirits whose anger had brought death, illness, or misfortune to the living.

Thus the meaning of religion to the Nandi was to be found in the mystical relations between the living and the dead which entered into all aspects of life and which reinforced the authority of elders, who would be puny figures indeed without their closeness to the world of the dead and their support by that world. The *oiik* inspired

both through the elders and the knowledge of their power, a fear which keeps people from doing wrong. For the principal significance of the *oiik* in the public life of the Nandi is their part in exacting obedience to law and custom. These are founded on public opinion, and behind public opinion are the *oiik:* "our fathers did this, and if we do not do it, the *oiik* will be angry." Therefore men must obey the elders, according to custom, or the anger of the spirits will be turned upon them, whence the strength of a political system which appears superficially to be so full of weakness.[2]

Social and Political Organization

The Nandi countryside was not organized into villages, with open spaces between villages, but instead consisted of scattered homesteads. There were almost always ten or twelve homesteads in view. There was, however, a local grouping of homesteads called a *koret,* which was the basic political unit. The *koret* has been translated as "parish." It had from about twenty to a hundred homesteads. The members of the homestead were not identified by lineage interrelationship but by territorial location. Each *koret* had its governing and judicial council of elders called the *kokwet.* The next larger division represented a territorial grouping of warriors and was called the *pororiet.* This term originally defined a group of warriors, or a regiment, and as applied to land, meant a regimental area. The *pororiet* had its council. There were sixteen *pororiet.* The last and largest territorial division was the *emet,* of which there were six, now reduced to five. This had no political significance and simply referred to a defined region.

The Nandi, with their pastoral outlook, were a restless people and frequently changed their dwelling place, even though the home site might be moved only a couple of hundred yards.

The Nandi were organized into clans but the clans were not segmented into lineages. Clans were patrilineal and totemic. They had an exogamous significance and provided a link among their members, which were dispersed throughout the country. They also furnished a means of identifying the interrelationships of persons brought into the *tiliet* by marriage.

The *tiliet* was the means for organizing social life. It may be translated as the "relationship system." It referred to "all those who are bound to a man by descent and marriage, and who call each other by relationship terms." The *tiliet* did not refer to a lineage but rather to a group of people united by both blood and marriage and who identified each other in relationship terms. For this purpose, the

---

2. G. W. B. Huntingford, *The Nandi of Kenya: Tribal Control in a Pastoral Society* (London, 1953), Chap. 7, quotations at 128, 122-123, 145, 156.

relevant relationships were those on both the father's and mother's side. The term *tiliet* meant "peace" and embodied the values of good will, good feelings, congeniality, and "getting on with people," which were important to the Nandi. The *tiliet* was the framework on which was hung the family behavior code.

Finally, the Nandi were organized into age sets. These carried out the military and governing functions in the society on a non-kinship basis. The age sets also provided a disciplinary factor in relationships, such as emphasizing the superior status of a senior brother belonging to a senior age group over that of his younger brother belonging to a junior age group.

The Nandi had no centralized political organization or chiefs. They were ruled by the elders. The key elements for purposes of political organization were the behavior code within the *tiliet,* the universal fear of the ancestral spirits, which compelled respect for the laws, and the clan system, which linked and identified in a significant way persons scattered throughout the country.

The *koret,* or local group or parish, was governed by the *kokwet,* or council of elders. The principal figure or leader of discussion within the *kokwet* was the *poiyot ap kokwet,* or "the elder of the council." He was described in Nandi terms as "the most important old man who takes counsel, and leads the business with the other people in the *kokwet.*" All the men of the *koret* could attend the *kokwet,* but younger men were not to speak unless asked by the elders to do so. The *kokwet* met under the shade of its council tree, with the elders in more or less of a circle and the *poiyot* under the tree. The *poiyot* opened the discussion. When he was finished, each elder spoke in turn until all who wished to speak had done so. The *poiyot* then expressed the opinion of the assembly, for which the traditional formula was: "We the old men agree that so-and-so should do such-and-such a thing."

The principal items of discussion were cattle disputes, offenses, calamities, such as a drought, and public matters, such as roads and the use of salt-licks.

The decisions of the *kokwet* were accepted by those to whom they were addressed because of the force of public disapproval, if compliance were not forthcoming, and public esteem, when compliance took place, fear of the power of the spirits, and the compelling strength of a personal acknowledgment by each individual of guilt, even though he might make a public denial of such guilt.

The principal concern of the council of the *pororiet* was war, but it also decided on matters which affected all the local groups within its area, notably the time of performance of the ceremony of circumcision, which defined the age sets, and planting. Any decision to fight had to receive the approval of the *orkoiyot,* the tribal ritual expert or head medicine man.

The office of the *orkoiyot* may have had a recent an origin as the middle of the nineteenth century and was borrowed from others, rather than being of Nandi origin. It is found in only one other tribe of the Nandi group. While the Nandi did not like the *orkoiyot,* he was firmly established as the principal human intermediary between Asis and the people. War, circumcision, and planting could not take place without his sanction. He was an expert in rainmaking. He was a diviner who could practice all forms of divining. He was also a witch, who could bring harm to individuals. Although he was not a chief, he provided "a mystical focus for public activities" and a means for rendering more certain the beneficial outcome of war, planting, and the circumcision ceremony.[3]

War

The Nandi waged war not to acquire land or slaves but rather cattle. Other motives were that war represented a sport and sometimes vengeance. It was also necessary to defend the people and their cattle from raids by the Masai. Widespread ruin and destruction were not its outcome, although sometimes a raiding-party might itself be almost completely destroyed. The *pcroriet* system intermeshed with the system of age sets, and coordinated by the *pororiet* council and the *orkoiyot,* constituted the warmaking structure. Discipline in waging war was built up and supported by "education in boyhood, the age-set system, the discipline of circumcision, tribal spirit and pride in being a warrior, the leader's personality, fear of disapproval, shame, and fear of magic and of the *orkoiyot.*" The disobedient or cowardly warrior could be beaten or even killed by the members of his section in the *pororiet,* since he endangered the enterprise of war.[4] In other words, when the individual assumed a role subject to authority in a group where interpersonal relations were not perceived in kinship terms, a sanctioning process of a physical rather than a supernatural nature appeared.

---

3. *Ibid.,* Chap. 2, quotations at pp. 22, 24-25, 58; E. E. Evans-Pritchard, "The Political Structure of the Nandi-Speaking Peoples of Kenya," *Africa,* XIII (1940), 250.

4. Huntingford, *op. cit.,* Chap. 4, quotation at p. 89.

Law: General Principles, Including Offenses

The legal system and rules of conduct were a part of the Nandi view of the universe, religion, and tribal organization. All of these were a composite, interdependent whole. The tribe was regarded "as a metaphysical entity comprising the persons and collective opinion of contemporary elders and deceased ancestors, which together with Asis constituted a wholly conclusive repository of authority and a compelling sanction for reverence, thought and conduct." Asis, or God, was "the source of all power" and "the final arbiter of justice and upholder of tribal sanctity." The incorrigible wrongdoer was committed to the final judgment and punishment of Asis. The repentent wrongdoer was committed to the forgiveness and rehabilitation of Asis.

> Asis was responsive to intercession and his displeasure could be appeased by sacrifice. In general his activity was beneficent, and active evil was due to the influence of malignant or discontent ancestral spirits. . . . The general social order—clans and families—of the tribe was believed to be perpetuated in the spirit underworld; the spirit of a naturally ill-disposed persons or a person ill-treated before death might cause evil to the mortal members of his clan on earth.

Conduct which impaired the constituted order, that is, the social, political, and spiritual order, formed the most serious category of offenses. Conduct which disturbed "the spiritual and material security" of the members of the social order, conduct which "violated the social and political structure, the moral discipline and the religious sentiments of the tribe was wrong. . . . The treatment in turn of wrong was directed at restoring the balance in the social equilibrium occasioned by disturbances of it."[5] Conduct that in western usage might be called a "crime" or "offense against the tribe" was conduct which disrupted the harmony of the temporal and spiritual world. Conduct that in western terms was a "tort" or "civil wrong" was conduct which injured primarily the living and was subject to control through compensation or physical punishment.

More precisely, sacrilege, that is, impiety directed against the *orkoiyot,* persistent failure to follow the decisions of the *kokwet,* incest, witchcraft, and ritual uncleanness created by the bearing of a child by a woman who had not been initiated, were offenses that disturbed the relationship of the tribe to the world of the spirits and,

---

5. G. S. Snell, *Nandi Customary Law* (London, 1954), 3-8, quotations at 3, 7-8.

thus, were likely to bring harm to the tribe as a whole. These offenses were subject to physical punishment by representatives of the group or even killing in the case of witchcraft. On the other hand, homicide, theft, and assault were offenses against the individual and did not create the risk of intervention and punishment by the spirits. Compensation to the injured Nandi group to which the individual belonged, rather than ritual ceremony or purification, was typically the outcome of the commission of such offenses. When offenses were committed against an individual, self-help was much more likely to occur than immediate recourse to the *kokwet* for its decision and control. When matters were submitted to the *kokwet,* the elders and the assembly were already familiar with most of the facts of the situation. When the *kokwet* decided, the sanctions for compliance with its orders were principally in the realm of group pressures, group opinion, and the wrath of the spirits.

Compensation for injury to the individual was expected when the individual was a fellow Nandi and a member of a different clan. When the injury was by another clan member to a person who was not a Nandi, it was outside the sphere of community control. In the first case, it was a matter for the clan itself. In the second case, it was outside the sphere of social control.

The relationships established in the *tiliet* were linked with a behavior code, which told the members of the *tiliet* how to behave toward their relatives, the duties which they owed them, and the specific behavior they could justifiably claim in return. The Nandi developed a system of approved standards of behavior, which they called *karuret,* or "custom." The term was derived from the verb *rur,* meaning "to become mature." It meant "something that has grown and become accepted by all as a standard of behaviour."[6]

Law: Property and Inheritance

The Nandi were a somewhat nomadic, pastoral people, living in a region where fertile, well-watered land was in sufficient supply for purposes of grazing and the little agriculture that was practiced. Since there was no shortage of land for its use in the Nandi economy, disputes concerning land use were very rare.

Grazing land fell into three categories, (1) the area immediately surrounding a dwelling which was used for early-morning and late-

---

6. *Ibid.,* pp. 55-66; Huntingford, *op. cit.,* pp. 99-119, quotation at p. 100.

evening grazing, (2) the main, all-weather grazing grounds of the community, and (3) the land beyond the tribal frontiers and un-settled land within the frontiers. This last category of land, *kaptich* or *kaptic* land, was used between rainy seasons. Warriors were sent to herd the cattle on those lands. A man's herd was divided for this purpose.

Cultivated land consisted of tilled land immediately adjacent to a dwelling. The right so to till land was an implied right of each house-holder, provided it was exercised within not much more than two hundred yards of the dwelling. Married men were also allotted each year additional land as needed by the elders of the *kokwet*. Each family was allotted as much land as could be cultivated by the wives and children and as was needed for subsistence and hospitality pur-poses. Holding of cultivated land was on the basis of a right to occupancy, which existed until the land was abandoned. Such occu-pancy rights could be inherited, again, if there was no lapse in the cultivation of the land. The land descended to a man's widow. If she should die, her eldest son took it, subject to the overriding principle that he needed it, otherwise it went to a younger son who had been supporting her.

Inherited cattle were held in trust, that is to say, a man could not sell them, although he could give them as bridewealth for his sons. Cattle were inherited by a man's sons on the basis of recognition of the interests of each of his "houses," that is, each of his wives and her sons, with precedence among sons on the basis of seniority. The rules for the inheritance of other property, including other livestock and chattels, were clearly defined.[7]

Law: Procedure and Sanctions

The hearing of cases before the *kokwet* council took place in an open assembly. The adult males of the *kokwet* sat in a large semi-circle facing a small group of elders acting as judges. The facts of the case were usually already known by the community. Nevertheless, one or more firsthand witnesses were generally called. The witnesses sat apart, where they could not hear what was said.

The party bringing the case first appeared and told his story, to which the other party replied. The witnesses of the plaintiff and

---

7. Snell, *op. cit.*, pp. 43-55; G. W. B. Huntingford, "The Southern Nilo-Hamites," *Ethnographic Survey of Africa*, ed. D. Forde (London, 1953), Part VIII, 23-24.

defendant followed, each group in turn. No interruption of witnesses was allowed but parties could ask questions or make statements after a witness had spoken. The parties then left the assembly. Any adult member of the meeting, senior to the age group of a warrior, could speak during the ensuing deliberations, but the decision was made by a group of three or four elders who were known for their judicial ability. As noted above, the *poiyot* announced the decision.

A dissatisfied party could complain of the decision to the elders in another *kokwet* in the *pororiet,* who, if they agreed, would discuss the matter with the elders of the *kokwet* who had made the decision. Important matters could be brought before the elders of several *kokotinwek* (plural of *kokwet*).

Oaths were used to elicit admissions from a party as to whether he was responsible as charged. If an oath was taken and guilt existed, it was believed that disaster would be visited on the guilty party and his relatives. If the oath was refused, guilt was assumed to exist. All parties involved in a case were expected to attend its trial, subject to the penalty of the elders' curse for their failure to do so. Serious disobedience of the elders' authority or of the *orkoiyot* was controlled by the tribal curse.

Persons who had suffered a wrong would resort to a recognized witch as a means of self-help or sanction. The witch was frequently asked to punish those who had failed to perform some obligation, such as the payment of bridewealth or the return of cattle held for another.

The use of sanctions and other remedies was summarized by Snell as follows:

> Social conformity was ensured by positive sanctions (the desire to stand well in public opinion, for instance) and by negative ones (such as the fear of public condemnation, the denial of the help of neighbours in time of need, and the hostility of ancestral spirits). Torts and "criminal" offences were in general regarded as disturbances of the social equilibrium and treatment was therefore concerned fundamentally with restoring the *status quo ante.*

The principles employed may thus be summarized in the following order:

(1) reconciliation;
(2) restitution;
(3) compensation to the individual or his family;
(4) compensation or fine to the community;
(5) if an offender were too poor to pay compensation, corporal punishment;
(6) social ostracism and public ridicule;

(7) protection of the community from the hostility of ancestral spirits (through the kokwet elder's repudiation in the curse);

(8) protection of the community from direct physical harm (through expulsion or execution);

(9) formal reconciliation of the offender to the community wherever possible.[8]

Conclusion

The Nandi were representative of the cattle culture of the Nandi-speaking peoples. Their land begins a few miles northeast of the Kavirondo Gulf of Lake Victoria. The average elevation is between 6,000 and 6,500 feet. Agriculture was practiced but it was secondary.

The people were organized into local units or *korotinwek* (singular, *koret*) for political and judicial purposes, and into *pororiet* for military purposes and for certain other purposes as well. Each of these had its governing council, that of the *koret* was known as the *kokwet* (plural, *kokwotinek*). Relationships of a social group were organized into a system known as the *tiliet,* on which a behavior code was hung. Age sets provided the means for dividing men into warrior and elder groups. The latter group was the cource of the governing bodies. Families were the smallest social group, and clans were means for identifying relationships among persons for exogamous and other purposes. The *orkoiyot,* or ritual expert, had only a limited appearance among the Nandi-speaking peoples.

The living, the dead as spirits, and Asis were linked together. Asis acted to reinforce the moral and legal standards. While physical punishment and execution for offenses took place, fear of anger of the spirits and Asis was a much stronger sanction in tribal behavior.

Land was plentiful and was principally valued for its use to graze cattle. There were different types of grazing interests in land, which a man held simply as a member of the community. Cultivated land was held on a basis of occupancy and use. It was hereditable as long as it was used. Inherited cattle could not be sold, but they could be transferred for bridewealth for a man's sons.

Offenses were divided into those which affected the tribal group, as a whole, in its relationship with the spiritual world, which were subject to physical sanctions, and wrongs which affected only the group or private interest. The latter were subject to control pri-

8. Snell, *op. cit.,* pp. 79-86, quotation at pp. 84-85; G. W. B. Huntingford, "Nandi Witchcraft," Witchcraft and Sorcery in East Africa, eds. J. Middleton and E. H. Winter (New York, 1963), 175.

marily by payment of compensation. A general standard of approved behavior had developed and was referred to as *karuret,* or "custom." Behavior in conformity with desired norms was sanctioned principally by group opinion and pressures and the anger of the spirits bringing harm when norms were violated. Oaths were used to ascertain the identity of offenders, and curses were employed to compel compliance with the orders of the council of elders.

In Nandi society, the basic elements of family, *koret* and *pororiet* were held in position, and conduct was controlled by the concepts of *tiliet,* or relationship system, *karuret,* or custom, and approved norms of behavior departures from which were considered to be subject to control by the supreme god, the ancestor spirits, and public and private procedures. Offenses were classified for purposes of control by social and spiritual means on the basis of whether they injuriously affected the temporal and spiritual order of the people or whether they merely affected the interest of a particular group identified by its kin status.

Part Six

_____

TANZANIA

Chapter 14

The Arusha

Geography and Economy

TANZANIA is located to the south of Uganda and Kenya, to the east of Ruanda Urundi and the Republic of Congo, to the north of Northern Rhodesia, Nyasaland, and Mozambique, and to the west of the Indian Ocean. The country is mostly a plateau having an elevation of 3500 to 4500 feet. The Great Rift valley runs north and south through the middle of the country. The mountain ranges are mostly in the northeast and southwest. The peaks of Kilimanjaro (19,565 feet) and Meru (14,980 feet) are in the north. There are three principal geographical zones, the coastal belt, the lake region, including Lakes Victoria and Tanganyika, and the massive interior plateau. There are few permanent rivers, and most of the central plateau has no running water for about half the year. The monsoons are an important aspect of the climate.

The country is primarily agricultural, with considerable emphasis on livestock, but the mining industry is growing steadily.

With respect to the tribes selected for investigation, the Nyakyusa and Sukuma (Appendix B7) are Bantu-speaking peoples, while the language of the Arusha belongs to the Nilo-Hamitic linguistic group. The Nyakyusa and Arusha reflect a combination of segmentary lineage and age groups, while the Sukuma have chiefs. The literature concerning these peoples is somewhat more complete than that of other possible peoples for study.

The Arusha settled on the lower, southwestern slopes of Mt. Meru, at an elevation between 4,400 and 5,300 feet, in the second quarter of the nineteenth century. They speak a dialect of the Masai language in the Nilo-Hamitic linguistic group and are often referred to as "agricultural Masai." Their settlement took place with Masai approval, since they provided trade, labor for herding cattle, and new water supplies. The land was practically a virgin forest, with good rainfall and many streams and springs. As the forest was removed, settlement rapidly increased. The Arusha were farmers and raised bananas, maize, beans, millet, and a number of lesser crops. Settlement tended to take place on the upper portions of the ridges of the mountain slopes. Streams flowed between these ridges.[1]

Values and Personality Traits

The Arusha were a people who placed a cultural premium on individualism. Hostility between the age groups was expected verbally and in fighting and brawling. On the other hand, age-mates held the ideal of brotherliness in their mutual relations, and brothers were close to one another. It was shameful for agnates to quarrel among themselves. The people showed a strong attachment to egalitarianism.

Violence in interpersonal relations occasionally took place. Arusha men were quick to take offense and to act to protect their honor and their own interests. Fighting among them was accompanied by the use of sticks, which sometimes resulted in death, as well as injury. It was held to be immoral to resort to self-help and physical coercion in disputes. Resort to violence was an admission of weakness in one's case. There was a very strongly held value that disputes should be settled peacefully by persuasion and by resort to the established procedures for settlement. It was particularly important that disputes between members of the same group should be settled within the group. Group solidarity was an important value.

The Arusha valued the preservation of peaceful relations among themselves more than the recognition and enforcement of norms for conduct. They had no word equivalent to the western symbol of justice. To insist upon one's rights when a reasonable settlement was at hand was to depart from an established community norm. Yet it was realistically perceived that the process of dispute settlement could not restore close relations where none previously existed. Re-

1. P. H. Gulliver, *Social Control in an African Society, A Study of the Arusha: Agricultural Masai of Northern Tanganyika* (London, 1963), 5-14.

conciliation was an important goal of the dispute-settlement procedures only when there were in fact friendly relations between the disputing parties to be restored.[2]

Religion

The people worshipped a supreme god name Engai and performed rituals to him to secure their general welfare and the fertility of the women. Other rituals were performed to avert catastrophes such as epidemics and drought. The rituals were conducted by the senior diviner in the parish. A ritual against witchcraft was performed every two or three years.

The family head had a shrine to his ancestors, notably his deceased father, where ritual was performed to secure their favor. Diviners were consulted to determine the ancestors responsible for a particular misfortune. Ancestors were considered to become angered and to send misfortune as a result of discord among their descendants but they were not thought of as punishing the commission of offenses. Their conduct had no jural significance.[3]

Social and Political Organization

THE PAIRING PROCESS

As characteristic of Maa-speaking peoples, the Arusha organized themselves into pairs of units in the types of social and political organization which they displayed. The pattern of division of corporate groups and other categories of persons into two parts appeared in the family unit. One of the two units into which the polygynous family was divided was referred to as *olwashe* (plural *ilwasheta*). This dichotomous structuring of the family was not perceived to exist when a man had only two wives. In such a polygynous unit, the senior and junior wives occupied a simple reciprocal relationship, even though their children were differentiated for a variety of purposes. When the family unit increased in size to one in which there were three or more wives, however, one of the wives took a certain responsibility for each new wife entering the group. The first two relationships of patroness and junior wives thus established

2. *Ibid.*, pp. 103, 45, 108, 220, 103, 236, 242, 277-78.
3. *Ibid.*, pp. 20-21, 83, 288.

determined the two *ilwasheta* divisions and later new wives were assimilated with one or the other of the two original *ilwasheta* divisions. The concept was useful in family relations, not only for the purpose of introducing a new wife into the polygynous family unit, but also for cooperation in domestic and farming work, the allocation of land to sons, division of bridewealth, inheritance, and future lineage structure.

The whole people was divided into two moieties or divisions, each of which was composed of two clans. Each clan was divided into a pair of clan-sections, which were in turn divided into a pair of sub-clans. The sub-clans were divided into two *ilwasheta*, composed of the various maximal lineages.

Each maximal lineage was composed of a number of inner lineages, each of which was divided into two *ilwasheta*. Each of such two divisions of the inner lineage was not divided into two parts but simply consisted of a number of families. Each family, however, was divided into two *ilwasheta*, as indicated at the beginning of this explanation.

The pairing process appeared in substantially all the important groupings of the Arusha. The Arusha saw themselves as a single people or *olwashe*, which was territorially divided into two sub-tribes. Each sub-tribe recognized a single leader in war chosen from the senior age group of warriors. The sub-tribes were divided into local territorial units, or parishes, which were a local grouping of family homesteads, the male heads of which were organized into age groups important in governing and in war.

The pairing process provided a frame of reference for perceiving the character of disputes as a matter of their relevance to the social structure, e.g., whether they were to be characterized as appropriate to settlement by the parish assembly or the lineage moot, and for handling such disputes in the settlement procedures. While opportunism influenced parties, as they sought the dispute settlement procedure which would yield the most advantageous outcome for their respective sides, the actual disputes tended to emphasize either conflict in an age-group setting or conflict in a lineage setting and thereby to limit the parties' freedom of choice in the selection of a forum for settlement.

PARISH AND AGE-GROUP STRUCTURES

The parish was a territorial structure of action. The families of the parish were neighbors rather than kin. The collection of homesteads in the parish was more scattered than the dwellings of a village, but it had many important functions in Arusha life. Each parish had two geographical divisions determined as a consequence of the settlement pattern on the mountain slopes. The lower slopes were settled first and a parish was accordingly divided into two units as settlement progressed up the mountain. The second division of the parish was located higher on the mountain slopes and was composed of the sons of the first settlers or other young men from older parishes lower down. Parishes were in turn grouped into pairs, and these pairs were grouped into still larger pairs. Raiding took place by pairs of parishes. Major war parties consisted of a sub-tribe.

A parish was also organized into age groups. These became the basis for the administration and integration of the parish, as well as the waging of war. The age groups of a parish were in turn loosely organized into age sets, each of which consisted of all concurrent age groups of the several parishes which were initiated during the same period. The age groups consisted of youths, junior warriors, senior warriors, junior elders, senior elders, and retired elders. It should be appreciated that individuals in their maturation proceeded at different rates through the formal stages of age groups. For example, some individuals would in fact be performing to a considerable extent the role of a particular age group, even though they were not as yet formal members of it, as a result of their earlier maturation than other members of the same age group.

The junior elders' group was linked with the junior warriors' group, and the senior elders' group was linked with the senior warriors' group, in that the older group guided and assisted the younger group in performing its new role. This linkage of alternate age groups was perceived to continue in time and to include the dead as well as the living. The result was to create again two major divisions or streams of Arusha men. Each age group had three circumcision-sections corresponding to the three stages in the performance of the circumcision ceremonies. Two of these sections usually became dominant in the age group, once again reflecting the principle of dichotomy in organization of the Arusha people.[4]

The parish was a territorial unit within which the age-group system principally operated. Males living and tilling land within its boundaries were automatically brought into the age-group system by initiation ceremonies. The age groups provided a set of roles whereby the functions of public labor, war, dispute settlement, and other matters of governance were performed. Each parish was the setting

---

4. *Ibid.*, Chap. 7; P. H. Gulliver, "Structural Dichotomy and Jural Processes Among the Arusha of Northern Tanganyika," *Africa*, XXXI (1961), 19.

for the performance of ritual and ceremony. There was always the ritual grove dedicated to Engai, the high god. Drives against witches periodically took place. Parish members were free to attend the personal ceremonies of any one parish member, such as his initiation ceremony or pre-marital feasts.

The males of a parish were organized into age groups and through these groups into age sets, as explained above. A more detailed explanation of the significance of the several age groups will reveal their importance in the life of the parish. Youths were initiated into an age group by circumcision ceremonies, which took place in three stages and created three circumcision-sections. Identification by members with the whole age group was a gradual process, the first stage of which was identification with the circumcision-section whose members shared a common experience of growth and initiation ceremonies. The circumcision-section was structurally important in the selection of spokesmen for the purpose of dispute settlement.

Members of the same age group had a sense of close fraternal relationship and recognized obligations of loyalty and support in the dispute-settlement process. Age-mates referred to one another as "brothers" to exemplify the fraternal quality of their relationship. There was a privilege of occasional sexual access to the wife of any age-mate. On the other hand, sexual relations with an age-mate's daughter were denied because she was "like your own daughter." A man usually found his closest friends among his age-mates. They publicly mourned his death.

The imposition of public responsibilities upon the several age groups was a gradual process. Youths mostly engaged in play, but they also herded cattle and acted as servants for older members of their families. Junior warriors were not considered to be fully adult or experienced warriors. They assisted in public work on parish roads and paths. The senior warriors were experienced in war and were privileged to attend parish assemblies, but not even their spokesmen were allowed to speak unless it was necessary to represent the interests of their age group. (It is to be observed that Gulliver identified the warrior groups as "murran," derived from the Arusha term *olmurrani,* perhaps in order to avoid an undue emphasis upon the warrior role. The latter had become anachronistic at the time of his investigation after sixty years of peace). The senior warriors were heads of families and carried out certain police functions in connection with the dispute-settlement process. They performed heavy laboring tasks.

The junior elders actively participated in the dispute-settlement process in the parish assembly. Their spokesmen could call and conduct parish assemblies and take an active role in bringing disputes to an end through discussion and agreement. They no longer performed heavy labor. The senior elders were beginning to withdraw from an active public life, but they were the wise men who had knowledge of the past and were experienced in the technique of dispute settlement. They were expert in ritual performance. The retired elder was wholly outside the stream of active life, responsible for nothing and "too old for anything." They were still entitled to respect and to food and beer, without the obligation to contribute to the group's interests in some manner.

The public affairs of a parish, such as questions involving roads and the settlement of disputes among its members, were handled by the parish assembly. Meetings of this body were held as required and were usually called by spokesmen of the junior elders' grade. The assembly was attended with a high degree of frequency by spokesmen and notables of the senior and junior elders and with a somewhat lesser degree of frequency by spokesmen of the senior warriors' group. Ordinary members of these three groups were privileged to attend whenever they might so desire. Although disputes arose between individuals, in the assembly they were typically cast in terms of conflict between age groups. Kinship ties may have had an influence in certain cases but, if such ties became dominant in a dispute, it was expected that it would be handled within the lineage or clan structure.[5]

LINEAGE AND CLAN STRUCTURE

Lineage relationships were determined on the basis of descent from a common patrilineal ancestor. This meant, for the "true Arusha," descent from one of the original settlers who came to the slopes of Mt. Meru in the second quarter of the nineteenth century. Lineage systems were accordingly very shallow. Two principal lineages were identified. The first was a maximal lineage based on descent from the earliest known male ancestor, almost always a first settler. The second was an inner lineage composed of the heads of families who were sons of the same father, now dead. The family, of course, was composed of a father with one or more wives and their children.

Each Arusha individual was born into membership of the whole tribe, a moiety of it, one of four clans, a clan-section, a sub-clan, and a lineage. The moiety was divided into two clans, each clan into two clan-sections, and each clan-section into two sub-clans. The sub-

5. Gulliver, *Social Control in an African Society*, Chaps. 2, 3.

clan comprehended a varying number of maximal lineages, up to a total of ten, and organized them into two sets. Clans had no exogamous significance. When agnatic links existed between a man and a woman, their marriage was prohibited. Membership in a particular clan group had some significance for the purpose of extending hospitality, but its primary significance was its influence in determining the locus of dispute settlement, as explained below.[6]

A PLURALISTIC SOCIETY

The foregoing description of the manner of organization of Arusha society reveals that it was a pluralistic society. Kinship relations were significant for marriage, economic, educational, religious, and dispute-settlement purposes. Age-group and parish relations were significant for public affairs, warfare, religion, control of witches, and dispute settlement purposes. The social, political, and legal functions of the society were distributed among a wide variety of groups.

War

Warfare and raiding was conducted on a localized basis until the eighteen-eighties. Until then, a war party was recruited from a linked pair of adjacent parishes or by two linked pairs. In the eighteen-eighties, the Arusha adopted a method of offensive warfare on a tribal basis. A "great-spokesman" was then selected in each sub-tribe to lead it in war. These military leaders led their groups in raiding and in resisting unsuccessfully conquest by the Germans.[7]

Law: Spokesmen and Counsellors

A number of conflict-solving bodies existed in Arusha society. Leadership in the settlement of disputes by these bodies was exercised by a limited number of spokesmen and counsellors. Their function was to handle the cause of a disputing party and to try to bring about an agreement for its final disposition which would be the most advantageous that could be procured. Any peaceful means of persuasion, including lies, was used to bring both sides to a final agreement disposing of the dispute.

---

6. *Ibid.*, pp. 69-116.
7. *Ibid.*, pp. 150-151.

Each age group within a parish was expected to select a total of six spokesmen to act for its members. This was on the basis that each of the two parish divisions was entitled to have one spokesman for the three circumcision-sections into which it was divided. Ideally each maximal lineage should have two counsellors, one an experienced person in the grade of senior elder and the other a learner in the grade of junior elder. In fact, each maximal lineage always had one counsellor but not always two. There were never more than two counsellors. Calmness and deliberateness of action were important qualities for a counsellor.

> He must be a physically active man of manifest intelligence and initiative; he should always have shown forensic skills in public discussion and assembly; he should have a good knowledge of the people and affairs of his lineage, and of Arusha custom and precedence; he should be diplomatic and persuasive in argument, able to assess individuals and situations, and prepared to depend on patient debate without precipitately taking inflexible positions likely to hamper his work.[8]

The lineage counsellor performed his role in the lineage moot or meeting, where he sought to prevail upon the opposing side, and also his own side, to accept the settlement that he thought was the best that could be achieved for the kinsman on behalf of whom he acted. He also had a role in important transactions and events within the lineage. It was expected that he would be informed of betrothals, marriages, bridewealth, loans, and the tenancy and pledge of land. He was supposed to witness the marking of boundaries, the sale of land, and the transfer of bridewealth cattle.

Law: Procedures for Dispute Settlement

The parish assembly was a forum in the sense that it was a meeting place where age groups, whose members were in conflict, could conduct a procedure for the settlement of their disputes. The parish assembly was not a corporate body empowered to decide disputes and enforce its decisions. Each party to a dispute appeared at the assembly, together with the spokesmen and notables who supported his cause and any members of his supporting groups who might wish to be present. The spokesmen took the lead in presenting and arguing the cause of their respective clients and endeavoring to bring about the most advantageous settlement possible.

---

8. *Ibid.,* pp. 38, 101-109, quotation at p. 103.

Conflict, which was characterized in kinship terms, was handled through a moot or meeting of the spokesmen, notables, and supporters of each disputing party. It was at this point that the social significance of the above-described pairing process became evident. It was necessary to characterize the parties to a dispute in such a manner that they fell into the two opposing sides of the same social unit. When this was done, the persons who were expected to aid each disputant as a matter of social obligation automatically became clear. For dispute settlement was accomplished through advocacy, negotiation, discussion, and agreement, instead of decision by superior authority. If the relationship between the protagonists in the struggle to reach agreement was marked by the fact, for example, that they were members of the same clan, it then followed that their respective supporters belonged to each division or clan-section of that clan. If it happened that the disputants were related only as members of the same sub-clan, then their respective supporters were members of each division of that sub-clan. The characterization of disputes in such terms sought to ascertain the kinship group to which both of the disputing parties belonged in order that their supporters might be automatically defined on the basis of their membership of the two divisions of that group.

An Arusha endeavored to characterize his dispute in such terms that it would point to the selection of the persons who would come to his support and who would be the most likely to yield a settlement in his favor. He would in general try to reach the *olwashe* or division which had the closest ties of kinship and geographical nearness. The members of such an *olwashe* would be his most loyal and active supporters. His search for supporters did not stop at that point. In selecting the members of, say, a sub-clan to support him, he would search for those who were persons of importance and were his nearest neighbors. He would turn to the members of his inner lineage and expect the highest loyalty and assistance from them. He would request the assistance of spokesmen who belonged to his supporting lineage units and had the best reputation for success in moots, as well as were nearest to his residence. A man's ability to enlist active supporters of his cause definitely influenced the outcome of the moot in his favor. A disputing party had a *structure* of related groups to which he belonged which were significant for the settlement process. The persons whom he called to his support were oriented to him and were drawn from that structure. They acted for him and not for the groups from which they were drawn.

A dispute between two members of an inner lineage was expected to be settled within the lineage. The division of the inner lineage into two parts was not utilized for the purpose of such settlement, in order not to impair the unity of the group. A maximal lineage was weakly integrated, however, and its *ilwasheta* became important in dispute settlement.

When disputes could not be settled at the lineage level, which was often the case, the intervention of "outsiders" consisting of counsellors and notables at the higher levels of the sub-clan or even the whole clan were called in to induce an agreement.

Certain other procedures for the settlement of disputes should be mentioned. Gulliver defined conclaves in the setting of the parish or of the lineage, respectively, as "either the members of a single age-group, or—where disputants belong to different age-groups—they comprise some of the age-mates of each man, together with relevant men of influence. . . . A conclave comprises either the members of a single inner lineage, or—where disputants belong to different inner lineages—it comprises a few close agnates of each man, together with their respective counsellors." Conclaves were used in parish assemblies or lineage moots as a part of the procedure of settlement, as well as the means for settlement of disputes within a single age group or inner lineage.

Homicide appears to have been a matter which was considered to affect the whole tribe, inasmuch as the procedure for handling it focused upon the two moieties of the tribe. The moiety of the killer was responsible for and contributed to the payment of the blood-wealth, which was distributed among all the sections of the moiety of the victim. Forty-nine cattle represented the bloodwealth. Nineteen of these were contributed by the maximal lineage of the killer, and the remainder was contributed from other parts of the moiety.

In a parish assembly, the personal interests of the disputants were intertwined with their respective age groups and also, though to a lesser extent, with those of the pertinent major streams with which the age groups were linked. As the spokesmen, notables, and other members of a party's age group came to a disputant's aid in the course of the proceedings, the dispute assumed a new hue, namely, that of inter-group conflict. A price was paid by the disputant for their support. The leaders of a party's supporting groups sought settlement itself, and his supporting groups exerted pressures upon him to accept a reasonable settlement acceptable to the opposing sides.

The parish assembly and the moot each began with an invocation to Engai, the high god, for his blessing on the gathering, thereby symbolically expressing the value of unity. In the parish assembly, the presiding junior elder called upon the plaintiff first to state his case. In a moot, the plaintiff himself, or sometimes his counsellor, opened the proceedings. The defendant was then heard. Witnesses thereafter arose to be heard but not in any particular order. Each main speaker stood as he spoke, usually in an open space in the middle of the gathering available for that purpose. Speakers could be questioned and interrupted, but they were allowed to complete their statements and to be fully heard, although pressures were applied to loquacious secondary speakers. It was important to give a hearing to any one who wished to speak. The phase of arriving at an agreed settlement, consisting of offers and counter-offers, did not tend to begin until the facts were as clear as they could be made, although the two phases of fact clarification and negotiation toward settlement often took place together. A definite proposal for settlement called for express rejection or a counter-proposal. Silence to a proposal implied consent. Indeed, agreement was marked by a stopping of discussion rather than express acceptance of a proposal. If rejection of a proposal or counter-proposal was not followed by some new suggestion, then it was evident that no agreement could be reached.

In both the parish assembly and the moot, a party's supporters tended to gather around him, although they might intermingle at the edges. They would from time to time give verbal approval or disapproval of varying degrees of loudness on his behalf to points made in the proceeding. The vigorousness of such support was an important factor in reaching a favorable settlement.

The procedure in a conclave was marked by considerable informality and ease. The persons present were seated and did not rise to speak. There was almost no oratory, discussion was of a more conversational quality. The atmosphere was one of privacy and a degree of cordiality was promoted by drinking beer or honey-wine together and by exchanging tobacco and smoking.

While a disputing party would call to his support age-mates at a moot and, conversely, kinsfolk at a parish assembly, each procedure had its unique character which should not be violated. An "assembly" was for disputes between residents of a parish, and a "moot" for disputes between members of different lineages.[9]

---

9. *Ibid.,* pp. 53-58, 121-140, 223-230, quotations at pp. 174, 175.

Law: The Meditation Process

The goal of the dispute settlement procedures of the Arusha was the final elimination of a dispute by reaching an agreement for its settlement by the disputing parties and the performance of such an agreement. The dispute-settlement procedures did not partake of a third-party decisional process, although third-parties participated in the procedures and most importantly influenced their outcome. The norms of conduct whose violation created the dispute were not all-important in determining the outcome of the cases. The agreement, which was the goal of the procedures, was not a binding decision but was instead often regarded as a burden to be escaped by the losing party, if at all possible. Persons who breached norms for conduct sought to evade the procedures established to support the observance of those norms. Parties and their supporters lied when it suited their purpose to escape the imposition of relief for their breach of norms. Parties delayed and failed to perform the agreements reached to resolve disputes arising from their breach of norms. Yet Arusha behavior in the settlement of disputes was logical in the light of the need for the control of violation of norms in a chiefless, individualistic, aggressive society, without belief in the sanctioning power of the gods or the ancestors for such violations. Compromise in the settlement of disputes and the reparation of injury sustained as a result of wrong was not necessarily valued for the harmony which it restored between the disputing parties. Compromise was frequently the outcome of disputes where no harmony between the disputing parties previously existed and where none was created as a result of the settlement. Compromise was valued simply because it was necessary to effectuate the peaceful settlement of disputes in some manner so as to reduce violence within the community.

While Gulliver referred to the dispute-settlement procedures as jural processes, he also stated that they were closer to the political processes of settlement imposed by power and dominance than the judicial process of third-party decision.[10] There is no process in western society closely comparable to the dispute-settlement procedures utilized by the Arusha. In Arusha society, the power or bargaining positions of the parties and their skills in dissembling, lying, and negotiating tended to have a much greater influence upon the outcome than the fact of the breach of the norm. This is not to say that

---

10. *Ibid.*, pp. 116, 297-299.

the breach of the norm, when the defendant was compelled by clear circumstances and convincing evidence to admit the breach, had little or no significance. The clearer the fact of the breach of norm, the more restricted the defendant's ability to maneuver. But the overwhelming differences were that the Arusha were not given to emphasize their rights and obligations in the dispute-settlement process to the degree that western society does and, moreover, they had no notion of the impartial, third-party decisional process. Sanctions were not imposed for wrongs but for failure to respect the settlement process.

One is struck with the comparability of the Arusha settlement procedure with international law and the diplomatic settlement of disputes in the international society of today. In dispute settlement in international society, norms for conduct are a factor in the outcome of diplomatic negotiations but not necessarily the most important factor. Power and dominance frequently play a greater part. The settlement process is carried on with little or no attention being given to the existence of the judicial process as means for settlement. The international society, however, does not have the compelling community pressure and institutionalized resort to third-party settlement procedures when the parties are unable to settle their own disputes, which the Arusha possess.

It is difficult to find the most appropriate western symbol to identify the Arusha dispute-settlement process. It partook of an informal concensus in that discussion took place until an agreement was reached. It partook of a bargaining process in that offers and counter-offers were made until agreed terms were reached. It partook of a negotiating process in that persuasion, artifice, and strategem were employed to reach an agreement. It partook of an adversary process in that each disputant was represented by spokesmen or counsellors. The term mediation seems to provide the closest analogy because of the importance of third parties in effectuating the final settlement, which was based on agreement between the disputing parties. Mediation represents the settlement of disputes by agreement through the counsel of a third party. Yet the spokesmen, counsellors, supporting groups, and community gave more than mere counsel. They exerted strong pressures on the disputing parties towards settlement. Moreover, Arusha society consistently and highly valued the peaceful settlement of disputes, which is not always true in mediation in the west.

The mediation process in Arusha society was a jural process in the fact that it recognized that disputes most frequently arose out of the breach of valued norms for conduct, that it was important to preserve these norms, and that injuries resulting from their breach must in large measure be repaired. Its coercive sanctions were principally those necessary to maintain the process itself as a viable process. The absence of centralized authority in Arusha society, its highly individualistic nature, its egalitarianism, the absence of coercive measures against norm violation, the absence of even the typical African belief that the ancestral spirits would punish wrongdoing, created a most unusual problem in tension management in the society. The resulting system for the control of conflict by the peaceful settlement of disputes was an extraordinary achievement. It was a complex system of interdependent parts of much ingenuity and sophistication.

With these explanatory and cautionary remarks, it is now possible to describe the Arusha process of dispute-settlement and to state some of the principles of social control which it reveals. The mediation process of the type employed by the Arusha for the settlement of their disputes may not represent the bare minimal conditions necessary for its use as a system of legal control in a society. It may possess features which could be eliminated without a breakdown in the society occurring. It seems reasonable to assume, however, that if the mediation process is to be used as the sole means of legal control in a society, as many as possible of the features of the Arusha mediation process listed below should be adopted.

In order that the mediation process may be successfully employed as the sole method of legal control in a society, the following conditions appear to be necessary or desirable:

1. *The mediation process should be so conducted that it (a) recognizes that conflict in a society typically arises out of the breach of valued norms for conduct and (b) satisfactorily repairs the injury resulting from such breach.* An examination of the various cases reported by Gulliver reveals that they all arose out of the breach of valued norms for conduct and that the discussion centered about the proof of the violation and the reparation which should be made in the circumstances of the case. A plaintiff might be bitterly disappointed over the compensation which was the agreed outcome of the case but when this occurred it was accompanied by circumstances that he felt there might be bias against him or that prior relationships between the plaintiff and defendant were rancorous. Even though the result of the proceedings was very frequently an agreement for compensation which was considerably less than would be required to repair the fault, the parties, including the plaintiff, would usually be satisfied with the outcome in the sense of a readi-

ness to accept it. One might find a plaintiff, who had done rather badly in the proceeding, drinking beer with his friends after the event and taking the outcome as a matter of course.

The norms relevant to the dispute were guides to its solution rather than absolute and exclusive criteria for decision. There was a strong insistence upon rights during the negotiations. The norms were viewed to be important and to have been established by the ancestors. But the end of the discussion was the agreement for settlement rather than the enforcement of the violated norm. To reach that end, concessions were made. Nevertheless, proposals and counter-proposals for settlement took place with a mutual appreciation of what was reasonable and tolerable in the circumstances.

Gulliver, in his examination of the dispute-settlement process in Arusha society, did not find it possible

> either empirically or analytically valid to adopt Gluckman's hypothesis of the "reasonable man, incept insofar as the concept 'corresponds closely with the *role* of a particular status' . . . Among the Arusha there is, too, a commonly accepted range of toleration allowable in the behavior of a person in a specific role—an integral attribute of the "reasonable man" which can be described as reasonable expectations.[11]

Gluckman later responded to these remarks with statements indicating that he was essentially in agreement on the meaning of the concept but differed in the choice of the symbol to refer to it. Gluckman stated that the ideas of "reasonable incumbents of various positions" and "reasonable standards of performance in different roles" influenced the "bargaining process" among the Arusha.[12]

The Arusha held the view that a satisfactory outcome was not so much the strict enforcement of the breached norm but a mutually acceptable solution of the dispute. They wanted "a reasonably satisfactory conclusion of an unpleasant situation." The disputing parties might live a considerable distance apart and have relatively little interpersonal relations which it was important to restore. It was always important to achieve the end of conflict. Thus the above stated principle reads "satisfactorily repairs the injury resulting from such breach."

Yet at the same time the Arusha clearly perceived and highly valued their inherited and established norms for conduct.

---

11. *Ibid.*, p. 300, citing M. Gluckman, *The Judicial Process Among the Barotse of Northern Rhodesia* (Manchester, 1955), 129; see *supra*, pp. 230-233.

12. M. Gluckman, "Reasonableness and Responsibility in the Law of Segmentary Societies," *African Law: Adaptation and Development*, eds. H. Kuper and L. Kuper (Berkeley, Los Angeles, 1965), 145, 146.

They are, then, guided by their principles of right behaviour, and they use them as the bases of claims to rights; but they accept an imperfect world in which an individual does not and should not expect to gain all the ideal rights prescribed by the approved norms. But equally, men hope to be able to avoid some of the obligations implicit in those norms. . . . Every dispute begins as the plaintiff contrasts, directly or by implication, the divergence between the defendant's behaviour and the relevant norm. The defendant's reply is usually to attempt to show that no real divergence exists; or, if it does, that some overriding and more general norm necessitates it. The process of negotiation continues from there.

In this process of negotiation, which might continue upon occasion for a long time, "it is what a plaintiff *can* obtain, . . . which is important, rather than what he *ought* to obtain." When the disputing parties were rather distantly related to each other, either as a matter of geographical distance or lineage ties, the breached norm was considerably more influential in determining the outcome as against bargaining power, though the latter was still important.

2. *The mediation process should be generally recognized in the society as a conflict-solving procedure preferable to face-to-face confrontation and violence in interpersonal conflict and unaided individual attempts to reconcile differences. Common value attachment to the mediation process should exist to the degree necessary to support the sanctions required to maintain the viability of the process* (propositions 14 and 15 below). The preceding discussion has revealed the value which the Arusha placed upon peaceful settlement of disputes in a society which was highly individualistic and inclined to aggressive behavior. It was a most important means for preserving integration and managing tension. The instant proposition is stated in full detail in order to make very clear the importance of the aspect of strong value attachment to the process of mediation, if it is to be an effective conflict-solving process in a society.

3. *Either party to a dispute should be able to invoke the mediation process.* The Arusha did not distinguish between a plaintiff and a defendant; each was considered a party to "a matter in discussion." The term plaintiff, as used herein, refers to a person who initiated the proceeding in order to remedy a wrong, while the term defendant refers to one who has committed the wrong and should respond to the proceeding. In the Arusha mediation process, either disputing party could choose and initiate the particular procedure, but it was usually the person who desired positive action in his favor who did so.

4. *There should be a plurality of mediation procedures, each with*

its own unique character derived from the types of conflict which it is its function to handle. While Arusha practice did not insist that each kind of mediation should preserve unimpaired the purity of its particular meaning and relationship to its social context, there was a certain minimal adherence to logic and rationality in resorting to any one procedure. It could loosely be said "that a parish assembly takes disputes between members of the same parish; that a moot takes disputes which, pertaining to kinship relations, are more critical, such as those concerning inheritance, land, marriage, bridewealth and the like." When, for example, an inappropriate person raised an issue which appeared to be outside the customary sphere of control of the assembly, those present would say, "Who is this man?" "He is not one of us. We do not know him here." "Let him go to his counsellor if he has a matter (to discuss)." Or the more emphatic statement might be made: "Go to Namuka! (the plaintiff's lineage counsellor). Do not bring the shame of brothers (i.e. agnates) quarreling here. We know nothing of all this." In other words, the Arusha had a fairly good concept of "jurisdiction," or the sphere of the capacity to act of a dispute-settling body. Jurisdiction comes from the Latin term *jurisdictio,* meaning a speaking of the law. This was not held by the Arusha in a precise sense, but the relevance of the dispute to the character of the dispute-settling body had real meaning.

Gulliver laid down the principles governing the jurisdiction of the dispute-settling bodies as follows:

[1.] A parish assembly, or conclave with spokesmen, deals only with disputes between members of the same parish.
[2.] Disputes between age-mates should be dealt with by a conclave of the age-group.
[3.] Disputes between kinsfolk should be dealt with by a moot or a conclave with counsellors.
[4.] Disputes between members of a single parish who are not kinsfolk should not be dealt with by moot or conclave with counsellors, but by intra-parish procedures.
[5.] A conclave is preferred to a moot, and sometimes to a parish assembly, when the dispute is of a minor kind, or where speedy settlement is important. Conclaves are also convened to deal with an impasse arising in a public assembly, or to execute the details of a settlement in an assembly, or to establish an injunction pending in assembly hearing.

5. *The foregoing principle 4 should operate so as to permit some degree of flexibility of choice in resorting to the several mediation procedures and varying degrees of advantage in pursuing them. A disputing party would always seek the forum for settlement of his*

disputes which seemed to him to be the most advantageous, "taking into consideration the nature of the relationship between himself and the other disputant, the nature of the matter in dispute, and the advice, support and constraint he receives from his close associates." While there were limits of rationality upon his choice of forums, in that respect had to be observed to a certain minimal relationship of the interests involved in a dispute to the forum for its settlement, the concept of jurisdiction was loosely applied.

The defendant, in responding to the plaintiff's choice of forum, did not always have to submit to his choice. While a defendant had to appear in response to plaintiff's invocation of the procedure, he was free to suggest another procedure. Sometimes he was successful in bringing about mutual consent to remove the case to another forum. Practically he could not do so in the face of the opposition of his own supporters and the opposite side.

The latitude of choice of forums and the factors influencing that choice were illustrated in a case involving the repayment of bride-wealth to a man whose wife had deserted him. This would normally be a matter for hearing by a moot, but lineage relationships and ties in the particular case were very brittle. The plaintiff hesitated to place it before the lineage, fearing that it might cause the lineage to break up into a number of new groups. Moreover, the plaintiff was doubtful of the degree of support he might receive from his kinsmen. It happened, however, that the disputing parties were so aligned as members of different age groups, between which considerable tension existed, as to make it possible for the plaintiff to cast the dispute in terms which made it acceptable for hearing by the parish assembly. The latter means for settlement was accordingly chosen.

The handling of disputes by different procedures also moved flexibly from one type of procedure to another as the parties continued in their efforts to bring it to an end. Thus, Gulliver reported a case in which, among other things, the proceedings ran through a counsellor's conclave, an internal moot, a parish assembly, a second and expanded moot, an abortive attempt at another conclave, and a different type of a conclave.

In general, a plaintiff would tend to choose the parish assembly for less important cases, to explore the defendant's position, to bring the dispute into the open and to the general attention of the community, or because his case was clearly structured in parish and age-group relationships. On the other hand, where support of his agnates was important or where his case was clearly structured in lineage relationships and norms, the plaintiff would tend to choose a moot.

6. *The foregoing principle 4 implies that the members of the society are structured into membership of overlapping groups, so that there is a plurality of frames of reference for perceiving the nature of situations of conflict and the roles of the disputing parties and other actors therein, as well as pressures by such groups upon the disputing parties to resort to and respect the principles of the mediation process.* It was said above that there should be a certain degree of choice among mediation procedures and flexibility and advantage in pursuing them. In the light of the emphasis upon agreement and the de-emphasis of sanctions in the dispute-settlement processes of the Arusha, it was imperative that some form of social control, if not force, be used to influence disputants toward settling their disputes and carrying out agreements for their settlement. This was found in the fact that no matter how the dispute was perceived, whether arising in the context of parish or lineage relationships, there were always social groups associated with the disputing parties who not only actively supported them in the resolution of their respective claims, but also, and importantly so, exerted pressures to move them towards settlement. A disputant could not afford to alienate his supporting groups and to place himself outside the reciprocal relationships which they provided. The supporting groups "can appeal to the value and the norms of group unity; they may deny him, or at least threaten to deny, the full privileges of membership either directly or by understood implication." Pressures upon disputing parties to settle their disputes consisted of

> appeals to past precedents, and to custom established by the ancestors; appeals to right behaviour, and especially right behaviour to close associates (near agnates, age-mates); threats of disapproval and ostracism, and promises of approval, fellowship and cordiality; threats to curtail rights and privileges and offers to maintain or even increase them; appeals, both emotional and practical, to the cause of group unity.

Not only was there the pressure of disapproval for failure to accept a reasonable proposal for settlement, but there was also promised praise and esteem for accepting the views of his associated groups as to an appropriate disposition of his case. Thus positive as well as negative pressures were exerted towards proper behavior by a party in the mediation process.

Another factor was that some of the participating groups were more distantly related to the disputants than others. They would, in such case, take a more objective view of the case. They would be ready to accept more impartial and less one-sided possibilities for settlement and argue the reasonableness of such proposals with both sides. Again, when the disputants resided a considerable distance from each other or they were distantly related to each other, group pressures played a lesser role in the outcome of the proceedings. There was a greater emphasis upon the ideal norm in the discussions, although the settlement was still one which had to be reached by agreement.

7. *The society should be so organized that its members belong to a number of overlapping groups, so as to lessen the tendency to perceive disputes in rigid terms and to diminish the likelihood of intergroup conflict developing in situations of interpersonal conflict.* This proposition is an implicate of proposition 6. As pointed out in the previous pages of this study,[13] interpersonal conflict is upon occasion tied in with conflict as to how a group shall constitute itself. Frequently, interpersonal conflict leads to the fission of a group into new and lesser groups. When the members of a society are organized into a number of complementary and overlapping groups, which are not perceived as incompatible with each other in function and character, stability is promoted. Its members are subject to crisscrossing pressures toward coherence. Interpersonal conflict is not so readily perceived to be tied in with the entire structure of the society. The multiplicity of loyalties, perceived as compatible, reduces the stress of value conflict in the members of opposing groups and thereby tends to promote cooperation and peaceful relations among groups.

8. *The parties to a dispute should have less power at their disposal than the other actors engaged in the mediation process.* This proposition is an implicate of proposition 6. Involvement in a dispute by the disputants or by the members of their associated groups having the closest relationships with them frequently reached the point that there was no ability on either side to accept a reasonable settlement. When this occurred, the Arusha always had the possibility, and generally used that possibility, of calling in more distantly related parties or "outsiders" to act in a more impartial capacity. Such persons could more readily perceive the reasonableness of a compromise for settlement and exert pressure upon both sides to accept it.

9. *The mediation process should be so organized that conflict can be readily bipolarized into two opposing groups having similar bases of power which are clearly defined. It should also be organized so as to define clearly the social boundaries of a situation of conflict.* The pairing process in Arusha society operated in the dispute-settlement

---

13. E.g., *supra* p. 77.

procedures to structure the group interests involved in a dispute into two opposing sets of power relations that tended to be fairly equal in strength. This, in and of itself, promoted the peaceful settlement of disputes. Little purpose would be served by a resort to violence when a stalemate would result. One finds here, in effect, a balance-of-power system built into the very web of the conflict-resolution system of the Arusha. The pairing process also defined the primary social and political units involved in the disputes.

10. *An informal, confidential, and intimate procedure should be provided to handle delicate or stressful situations of conflict.* The conclave was used in intra-group disputes and in situations generally where it was important to have an open, intimate atmosphere of freedom of expression, an absence of outside interruptions, and an ability to take particular positions and retract from them with greater ease than in a large public meeting. Conclaves were closely connected with the hearing of a dispute in the larger body of the parish assembly or the lineage moot. A breakdown of the larger meeting would lead to the face-to-face negotiation, intimacy, and pressures of the conclave to settle the difficult points. Or the breakdown of a conclave would lead to resort to the larger body to see whether a different frame of reference might bring success. After an agreement in general terms had been reached in the larger body, the matter would then be referred to the conclave to work out the details and to oversee the performance of the agreement of settlement.

11. *The mediation procedures should be so organized as to recognize and enable the handling of intra-group and inter-group conflict as tied in with situations of interpersonal conflict.* As noted above, the Arusha dispute-settlement procedures were articulated with their respective social and political groupings in a most unique and desirable way. It was possible for a dispute to be seen in more than one institutional setting and for it to be resolved by more than one dispute-settlement procedure. The point which is now emphasized is that whatever procedure was in fact selected and accepted by the persons concerned as appropriate for the purpose, that procedure had its own unique meaning in terms of social and political conflict within the society. If the parish assembly was the forum chosen, then the disputes were characterized in age-group rivalry. If the external moot was chosen, then inter-lineage conflict was the context within which the dispute was viewed. If the internal conclave or internal moot was chosen, then the conflicting interest groups within the social structure in question were still part of the frame of reference within which the dispute was perceived and handled. The pairing

process provided a means for the expression of the conflict between group interests and values involved in the dispute as resolution of the interpersonal conflict took place. The several social structures were divided into two parts to the extent necessary to enable each dispute to be resolved by a mechanism which brought into the open opposing interests within or between groups.

12. *The basic elements of fairness and adequacy of hearing, presentation of pertinent evidence, and search for fact consensus should exist.* The hearing of cases in Arusha dispute-settlement procedures gave each person qualified to speak and interested in speaking full opportunity to be heard. Witnesses were called and questioned. The proceeding took place with the commitment to investigate the facts to the point that further inquiry would not yield further certainty. The facts that were certain and those that were doubtful were made generally clear. Loquaciousness and prolonged tendency to discuss irrelevant matters by lesser actors were discouraged, while the principal actors were trained to avoid such behavior.

13. *There should be persons skilled in the performance of leading the mediation process, negotiating, and arriving at a settlement acceptable to both sides.* The principal actors in the dispute-settlement procedures, namely, the spokesmen and counsellors, were carefully selected and were well-trained in the performance of their roles. Only persons having suitable intelligence, personality, and temperament were chosen to occupy these offices. Means of training in the performance of their roles were provided prior to the time they assumed them, as, for example, in the age-group system.

Where groups were large, unwieldy, diverse in the drives of their members to press to a conclusion of the matter, and prone to stray from the central theme of the discussion, it was essential to have trained personnel skilled in the arts of negotiation, discussion, and reaching acceptable settlements. Arusha dispute-settlement procedures did have such personnel.

14. *There should be organized means of community support in inducing disputing parties to initiate or respond to the mediation process, carrying it forward to completion in a final settlement agreed to by both sides, and performing the agreed settlement. A disputing party should not be an isolated actor as he performs his role and tries to reach a favorable outcome of his case.* The above statement makes explicit as a separate proposition a point already developed (see 6 above). The supporting groups of disputing parties pressed them to resort to the settlement procedures, to continue to move toward a settlement after the procedure was started, and to

carry out a settlement when it was reached. A disputing party, more-over, did not have the arduous psychological task of being his own advocate.

15. *Sanctions should be available for, and should consistently be applied to, departures from those norms for behavior which are necessary to maintain the integrity and effectiveness of the mediation process.* A disputing party before a parish assembly could not be compelled to carry out its decision unless that decision was so unani-mously held in the assembly that his refusal angered the spokesmen of his age group and caused them to apply coercive measures, in-cluding a fine, to compel his performance. Usually no problem of enforcement of the settlement arose, because it was agreed to by both parties. As one Arusha counsellor put it: "We discuss and dis-cuss the matter (in dispute) and then we agree. When we agree, that is the end. What else is there to do?"

It was important to perform the agreed settlement immediately, either at the public meeting itself or at a conclave then fixed and held promptly. If this was not done, a new gathering or conclave would be necessary to go over the argument again, the same negotia-tions and pressures would have to be renewed, and another settle-ment would have to be reached and supervised.

Coercive measures and supernatural forces actuated through ritual were used to maintain the effectiveness of the mediation process it-self. They were not used as a means of punishment for the commis-sion of an offense or wrong. Wrongful action was recognized, means were established to repair the injury resulting from it, but, when compensation was obtained for the wrongdoing, there was no further interest in the matter.

There were ceremonies designed to support the agreement reached. When the final agreement of settlement was arrived at, both dis-puting parties provided beer for all assembled to drink. A major offender, whose responsibility was clear, might be required to pro-vide a commensal meal of meat as well. The act of sitting and drinking together on the part of the two disputing parties and their supporters marked the accord. It symbolized the elimination of con-flict and bad feeling between the parties.

An extremely strong pressure towards the settlement of disputes existed in the rule that all the participants in a dispute could not avail themselves of the mediation process until the prior dispute was fully settled. This rule extended to the spokesmen, counsellors, and notables of the supporting groups, as well as the members of such groups themselves. Denied access to such an important group process, pressure upon recalcitrant parties to abandon the positions creating the delay was strong indeed.

Within the group to which a disputing party belonged, physical force could be used and was used to compel performance of a settlement or attendance at an assembly or moot as principal or witness. However, such coercive measures were prohibited against members of a different group.

Proper conduct in assemblies or conclaves was sanctioned by the imposition of fines. These were directed against the disputants' making accusations against notables of failure to give proper support, imputations against the character of notables, and brawling or rowdy behavior or other misconduct interfering with orderly proceedings. The fines consisted of the offering of beer or an animal to be killed and eaten. The giving of the beer or food symbolized the begging of pardon by the party at fault for an offense to those he had offended. The act of consuming the fine marked their acceptance of his apology and the re-establishment of proper relations. The fine did not carry the character of punishment.

Appeals to supernatural intervention were used only in extreme circumstances which threatened the integrity of the mediation process or important group interests. When a party was so contumacious that his group's interests were threatened, a notable, usually a spokesman or counsellor, could curse him by invoking Engai, the high god, to send misfortune to him or his close relatives. This would be used, for example, in a case of a man who had long refused to accede to the reasonable demands of his agnates, reviled his relatives, and threatened self-help.

Oaths and ceremonies consisting of appeal to supernatural forces to bring illness or death to an offender were used when bad relations existed between parties who had made an agreement settling a dispute and such bad relations threatened to lead to conduct renewing the dispute and breaking the agreement. They were also used in cases involving breach of norms based on interests in land or marriage relations.[14]

Conclusion

Law and the legal process were most minimally developed among the Arusha. There was very little of a sanctioning process for viola-

---

14. Gulliver, *op. cit.*, Chaps. 9-11, quotations at pp. 241-242, 253, 182, 181, 183-184, 188, 193, 197, 178, 236-237, 275, 232.

tions of valued norms, except for the readiness of individuals to defend their honor and interests by fighting. The violence of such fighting was controlled by limiting it to the use of sticks. There was no belief in a supernatural process of retribution for wrongdoing, although supernatural power was invoked in the performance of ritual to preserve the welfare of the people as a whole. There was a high social value of harmony and peace in interpersonal relations. There was no third-party decision-making body; only a plurality of mediation procedures were available for the solution of interpersonal conflict. The existence of considerable tension as a result of this situation was evidenced in the periodic performance of ritual against witchcraft.

There was a logical interdependency of the above elements of their culture. The absence of an institutionalized sanctioning process for the violation of norms apparently led to the use of violence both as aggression and as a means of self-help, together with belief in witchcraft. Social control over violence was exerted by limiting it to the use of sticks. There was periodic resort to ritual to control witchcraft. Another consequence of the absence of an adequate system of social control was the development of a high social value on the preservation of peace and harmony in social relations. This value operated both to diminish resort to violence in individual conflict situations and to support the process of peaceful settlement of disputes.

With only the most rudimentary perception of law, in the sense of a system of legal norms supported by a sanctioning process, the Arusha were unable to develop the concept of an authoritative, third-party decision-making body. They instead developed the mediation process to a degree that capital and labor groups in national societies and states in international society might well envy and emulate today. Supernatural power and social pressures, together with the social premium on peace, compelled individual acceptance of mediation procedures as a means of dispute settlement. These procedures utilized agreement of the disputing parties as a means of ending conflict. Such agreements could be reached only peaceably through discussion and settlement. The value of a peaceful outcome was preferred over that of fair reparation for wrongful injury. The Arusha were satisfied with outcomes of their mediation procedures which would seem most unsatisfactory to a western mind, with its insistence upon respect for rights and their vigilant enforcement. The Arusha man had a high frequency of interpersonal contacts with his neighbors and relatives and a correspondingly high degree of attachment to peaceful relations with them. When disputes arose with persons not so closely situated or related, he tended to be more concerned with the preservation of norms and the due reparation of injuries flowing from their breach.

An Arusha man was supported in the dispute-settling procedures by the members of the relevant groups to which he belonged. These were identified by the characterization of the nature of the dispute, in terms of group relations, made by the disputing party in invoking the particular settlement procedure, e.g., age–group relations or lineage relations. Arusha society was so structured in overlapping memberships in groups identified by age and functional status, on the one hand, and lineage status, on the other, together with identifications made on the basis of geographical location, that a high degree of flexibility of choice in dispute–settlement procedures existed. Another all-pervasive element of structuring group relations was the pairing process that divided into two halves most of the significant social and political structures. This assisted in the dispute–settlement process by creating opposing sides for the handling of disputes. Indeed, the appearance in Arusha society of a dual structuring of kinship groups of similar but opposing groups at one level, which are united at a higher level—a form of social structure found in a number of West African societies—suggests that perhaps the most important function of such a structuring of a society is in providing a framework and procedure for handling conflict situations.

The mediation process was marked not only by the support given to a disputing party by his relevant groups but also by the pressures of such groups upon him to move toward an agreement settling the dispute and carrying out such agreement. The goal of the mediation process was the reaching and performance of the agreement for its settlement and not punishment of the wrongdoer. Sanctions were imposed on disputing parties as they departed from the minimal standards of conduct necessary to preserve the viability of the mediation process.

The plurality of mediation procedures has to be seen as a product of the plurality of social structures in which they took place. Arusha society was a pluralistic society, in which no single type of social structure handled all human affairs. Accomplishment of social, political, and legal functions was distributed among a variety of groups of kinship, age, and territorial character.

The experience of the Arusha points to a possible new model of an international society of peace. One of the currently held models of a world order of peace is a monolithic world government which would possess sufficient power of forceful coercion to prevent any one state or group of states to resort to war. The other is universal disarmament. The new model suggested by the Arusha would be a pluralistic world order, in which states would have overlapping memberships in a wide variety of international organizations and forms of international cooperation so that they would value peace more than war—at least to the extent of cutting down very markedly and in an increasing degree their resort to war. When the members of states come to value their participation in the life of world society as the Arusha valued relations with their neighbors, we may then come to change our perception of regional blocs, for example. Instead of viewing them as selfish, particularistic, and opposed to world consensus, they would be seen as support groups for disputing states in arriving at a peaceful settlement. Their representatives would take part in the settlement process. They would thereby foster the growth of mediation for the peaceful solution of international controversy, supplementing the action of international courts. A proliferation of mediation procedures, creating the possibility of choice among them by disputing parties, might well importantly promote the peaceful relations of states.

Chapter 15

The Nyakyusa

Geography and Economy

THE NYAKYUSA are a Bantu-speaking people living at the north end
of Lake Nyasa in a portion of the Great Rift valley. They numbered
about 235,000 around 1950. Their land is lush and beautiful, surrounded by mountains. Small lakes are found in the craters of old
volcanoes, beyond which green fields and pasture lands extend. Many
streams flow down the mountain slopes, for rainfall is very heavy.
The average rainfall in the valley is over 100 inches each year. The
dry season is short and almost disappears in the hills.

The people are skilled and industrious farmers, as well as keepers
of cattle. They grow a large variety of crops, including bananas,
beans, maize, sweet potatoes, and millet, with rice and coffee being
recent additions. They are very well fed and shortages or famines
rarely occur.

They were an isolated people, with high mountains surrounding
three sides of the country and Lake Nyasa to the south. Slave caravans passed them by.[1]

Values and Personality Traits

Women praised men "for sexual skill and attentiveness, for vigour
in hoeing and skill in housebuilding, and for kindness." Sexual ne-

1. M. Wilson, *Good Company: A Study of Nyakyusa Age-Villages* (London,
New York, Toronto, 1951), 1-8.

glect, laziness, impotence, and cruelty were reprobated and might cause a woman to leave her husband. Men admired women "for sexual skill, cleanliness, and beauty, for regular cooking and hard work, and for gentleness in speech and behavior."

The Nyakyusa were organized into age-villages consisting of men of roughly the same age living in the same community, together with their wives and children. This fact led to the development of social values based on the gratifications associated with such a mode of social organization, such as generosity in entertaining others, and maintenance of the system itself. The principal values of Nyakyusa society will be listed below.

"THE ENJOYMENT OF GOOD COMPANY." The organization of male village residents into age groups was a common feature of a number of East African peoples. The Nyakyusa were unique in that their villages were formed as a result of a group of boys or young men of much the same age joining together in a single settlement. All villages thus formed retained the quality of contemporaneity of the male heads of the constituent households. In this context, the Nyakyusa highly valued those aspects of life for which they had the term *ukwangala,* which meant "the enjoyment of good company." More specifically, it meant friendliness among adult males, expressed in eating, drinking, and talking together. It meant generosity, expressed in entertaining one's contemporaries not only upon formal, established occasions for feasts but also at other times. It meant generously extending help to one's neighbors and being obliging and sympathetic. It meant participation in such important neighborhood events and ceremonies as birth, marriage, and death.

WISDOM. Wisdom *(amahala)* was attained through experience developed as the result of companionship and mutual discussion. The quality of wisdom was shown in neighborliness, restraint, decorum, and respect for law.

DIGNITY. Dignity and impressiveness of manners and the possession of a well-designed, well-built home and surrounding shade trees were admired. The possession of a fine home and wealth, however, was not to be enjoyed selfishly. Their use must be hospitably extended to others, if their possessor was not to be accused of witchcraft. The emphasis on dignity was tempered by admiration of the qualities of cheerfulness, wittiness, and geniality.

DECENCY. The separation of sons from the homes of their fathers and mothers, as they formed their own villages at an early age, was accompanied by strong condemnation of any contact by a son with that part of his parents' life which involved their sexual activities.

He was expected to eat at home after he left it to live in the village of his age-mates. He was not, however, to sleep there and come in contact with his parents' intimate relations. There was also a severe taboo on personal contacts between fathers-in-law and their daughters-in-law.

DISPLAY OF SELF AND POSSESSIONS.   The Nyakyusa male liked to exhibit a strong, well-formed body, to show his physical strength and adroitness in dance, and to reveal a belligerent and truculent personality. He took pride in a well-constructed and well-ordered home. The Nyakyusa dwelling was unusually handsome in design and setting.

SUBMISSIVENESS IN WOMEN AND SUBSERVIENCE TO THE INTERESTS OF MALES.   Women occupied a very subordinant position. They were not expected to assert themselves but instead to show obedience and respect and to display a submissive manner. They were meekly to comply with the demands of their husbands. Wives were taken from the village of their parents at an early age to live in the age-village of their husband. Thus isolated and dominated, they were compelled to serve the interests of their husband and his age-mates. For example, the first wife to be taken to the age-village of young men was expected to cook for all who might desire food from her household. Competition among polygynous wives for status and favor in relations with their husband promoted their subservience to the interests of males.

EGALITARIANISM.   Group pressures were used to keep neighbors from getting either too far ahead of one another in wealth. Pride in possessions and esteem of others for generosity in sharing food and beer in feasts helped to make a man diligent and industrious. But one who was too energetic in the accumulation of wealth "overstepped" his neighbors. If one man's crop was conspicuously better than that of his neighbors, it was considered to have been achieved illegally at their expense by drawing fertility from their fields. It was important to keep in step with one's neighbors in tilling fields and burning fields at the same time.[2]

Religion

Nyakyusa tradition taught that they were a people to whose land a group of mythical founding heroes came. One of the heroes created

---

2. *Ibid.*, Chap. 4.

crops while another created both crops and people. The descendants of the people he created became the chiefs of th. Nyakyusa, who were, as a consequence, related to one another. These descendants were also believed to have brought fire, cattle, iron, and seed to the land. The persons of the chiefs and their heirs were thought to possess a creative, supernatural force. Ordinary men possessed the supernatural power of "breath-of-men," as explained below. This supernatural power of the members of a community held in check any tendency of chiefs to be arbitrary in the use of their authority. The "breath-of-men" would bring fever or paralysis in such circumstances to those in authority. The use of both farming and cattle herding as ways of life by the Nyakyusa was a product of the union of the two groups, that is, the newcomers and the existing inhabitants of the land.

The practice of living in age-villages was held to be the outcome of an episode in which a chief looked upon his daughter-in-law and took her and loved her. This so shocked men that ever thereafter sons built their homes and lived separately from their fathers so that the latter should never see their daughters-in-law.

The Nyakyusa had a practical, friendly outlook on life.

> Health, fertility, and amity between kinsmen are what they seek. . . . What men seek to know are the causes of misfortune—public and private —and the identity of witches. . . . Men are preoccupied with their relationships to other living men—their kinsmen, neighbours, and fellow office-holders—and with their dead fathers. They are not concerned with their relationship to Kyala [one of the two founding mythical heroes]. The rituals celebrated by kinsmen are to the shades not to any supreme God, and it is quarrelling between kinsmen that angers the shades and makes the celebration of certain rituals necessary. The communal rituals are directed toward heroes who are also forefathers, and it is quarreling between chiefs and priests or village headmen that disturbs the natural order and causes disease or failure of crops.

Chiefs performed rituals to cleanse the country of rats, wild pigs, and epidemics. They employed certain medicines to bring rain and to insure the fertility of the soil. From the chief and his medicines flowed good fortune for men, their families, crops, and success in war. When harmony prevailed between a chief and his village headmen, priests, and kinsmen, all would go well with the people; friction between them would lead to misfortune.

Medicines of great magical power were used to create in the chiefs spiritual power and the qualities of dignity, majesty, and the ability to inspire awe and fear, which were believed necessary for governing others. These medicines were also believed to install in the chiefs courage and ferocity in war, raiding for cattle, and protecting one's own cattle, as well as the ability to attract immigrants to the country. Medicines were also used to protect chiefs against the dangerous powers of the sacrificial sites which they used in rituals, to insure success in war, to aid in discovering witches and averting their evil power, to make their capitals grand, and to cause thieves to reveal themselves. Medicines were necessary to achieve authority, victory, and successful rule. The kind of medicine used and the strength of dosage employed varied with the office held and the character of the individual, whether chief or headman, vigorous personality or weak.

Medicines of magical powers were used for an extraordinary range of purposes. They were employed to reinforce the supernatural powers of chiefs, in the procedure of ceremonies, to promote private ends, such as success in love, litigation, or growing crops, to bring harm to others, to protect against the aggression of others, to cure illness, and to search out wrongdoers through the ordeal or other uses of magic to detect guilt.

Godfrey Wilson described the elements of Nyakyusa religion as follows:

> Religion enters continually into family life and helps to maintain wider kinship bonds also. The Nyakyusa religion falls, broadly, into three intimately related parts: the ancestor cult, witchcraft, and magic. Taken as a whole their religion, as they believe, secures for them many of the most important values of life—health, good crops, and success in various enterprises; it provides an intelligible explanation of death and misfortune by tracing them to the ill will either of the ancestral spirits or of living men acting through witchcraft or magic; in its rituals it resolves the emotion of fear and replaces it by hope and confidence; while the believed destructive action of the ancestors and of men is generally, though not entirely, linked with morality. The commonest explanation of misfortune is that some wrong done by the victim, or by his close kinsman, has provoked the spirits or his fellow men to anger.

The supernatural world, consisting of the ancestors, witches, the "breath-of-men," and medicines, provided means for supporting ideal and valued norms of behavior and sanctioning departures therefrom, as well as achieving personal ends.

Breaches of kinship obligations, such as lack of respect by a son for his father or failure to feed the children of a dead kinsman, were believed to lead to the anger of ancestral spirits visited in the form of sickness or misfortune. When a person became sick, a diviner would be consulted. The latter would suggest various possible causes for the illness in order that the true cause might be determined, that is, some failure to meet a kinship duty.[3]

The preservation of valued norms within the lineage, that is, obligations owed the ancestors and living members of the family, was the concern of the ancestors. They would bring illness and misfortune to members of the family who violated such obligations. Their vengeance could be invoked by a father praying to the ancestors and "muttering" aloud the circumstances of the offending behavior. Sometimes, without such invocation, a dead father would speak to his son as he slept and reproach him for wrong family behavior. Fear of consequent punishment would lead to reform or compliance with the violated norm, such as a failure to give cattle for a brother's marriage or to feed a mother.

Witches were persons possessed of magical power by virtue of the possession of pythons within the belly, whereby such persons could exert their will to bring evil or good to others. Witches were not concerned with family relations but rather with relations within the community. The failure of a rich man to entertain others generously, the achievement of an unusual amount of wealth, the performance of much greater work in the fields than one's neighbors, the excessive performance of household tasks by a wife, were held to excite the envy, anger, and retaliation of witches. Witches themselves were persons who were unpopular and exhibited unfavorable personality traits, such as undue pride and withdrawal from contacts with others.

There were witches who used their magical powers for the defense of those victimized by aggressive witchcraft. Such witches were termed "defenders." They were held to have only one python in their belly, whereas witches who used their power for evil purposes were believed to have more than one python in their belly. The village headman, the assistant headman, and other persons as well were "defenders."

The keeping of a grudge, the harboring of anger and resentment, was held to be the source of witchcraft. Witches were persons who kept such emotions bottled up within them. A headman described the process as follows: "The root of witchcraft is this—these are the quarrels that are pregnant with witchcraft. But if he lets it out and

---

3. M. Wilson, *Communal Rituals of the Nyakyusa* (London, New York, Toronto, 1959), Chaps. 2-4, 7-8, quotations at 68; G. Wilson, "An African Morality," *Africa*, IX (1936), 75; G. Wilson, "The Nyakyusa of South-Western Tanganyika," *Seven Tribes of British Central Africa*, eds. E. Colson and M. Gluckman (London, 1951, reprint 1961), quotations at 261, 262, 266-267.

tells me that I have wronged him in some way then the quarrel has no menace in it. It is when he lets nothing out and stays silent, though angry in his heart, that he comes in dreams to throttle me. That is the root of witchcraft." On the other hand, the symbolic act of blowing water from one's mouth expressed the expelling of anger, the confession of misdeeds, and repentance. Prayer was made by this symbolic act, followed by speaking with the spirits. The act also implied the extension of forgiveness to another.

The working of witchcraft upon its victims was typically expressed in the term that the witches were "throttling" him. Other terms were that they were "choking," "trampling," or "eating him inside." It should be noted that certain of these terms were also used to refer to sexual relations.

There could hardly be a clearer illustration of the psychology of repression and frustration.

When a man experienced illness or misfortune, either in himself or through a member of his family, and had doubt as to the cause or the identity of the witch, he would consult a diviner and confess all his sins or name all the persons suspected as witches. The diviner would then identify the source of the misfortune.

Accusations of witchcraft were tried before the chief by means of an ordeal which involved drinking a certain potion. Failure to vomit after drinking meant guilt of witchcraft.

The members of the village were believed to possess a supernatural power to punish the violation of approved and valued standards of conduct throughout the entire range of social behavior. The use of this power became institutionalized in a series of steps which represented a sanctioning process applied against any person guilty of wrongdoing. This sanctioning process was not conceived to be the function of a third party or some supernatural agency but was instead simply the joint action of the community itself employing supernatural power to visit punishment upon wrongdoers. The husband who mistreated his wife and the chief who abused his power over his people could equally be brought to justice and punished by the "breath-of-men." The village headman possessed this power to an unusual degree and led his people in the imposition of their sanction. He also brought it to bear upon chiefs who used their authority unjustly. The "breath-of-men," as a penalty, was manifested in the failure of crops, sterility of wives, and illness and death in the families of those who had incurred its application. Thus the Nyakyusa had a strong fear of their neighbors as a source of sanctions against breaches of valued norms of conduct.

There were several steps involved in the use of the power of the "breath-of-men." First, there was the public knowledge that someone in the village had signally and frequently failed to meet an obligation owed his relations or neighbors. Second, there was the invocation of punishment. This consisted of the neighbors "muttering" or "murmuring," that is, vocally condemning, the wrong conduct in question. Third, there was the experiencing of the punishment of the wrongdoer. Fourth, there was the due performance of the breached norm by the wrongdoer, such as the fair treatment of an abused wife, the showing of respect by a son to his father, or the performance of overly-delayed ritual ceremonies. Fifth, there was the commensal feast tendered the members of the age-village by the wrongdoer or by his father. At this feast, the sin which caused the penalty was openly discussed, its commission admitted by the wrongdoer, and the responsibility of bringing punishment for it was admitted by the neighbors. Finally, a medicine man would administer a medicine designed to bring about future correct conduct in the premises by the wrongdoer.[4]

The supernatural world of the Nyakyusa mirrored the conflicts and resultant tensions of the temporal world and provided means for their control. The abuse of authority of a chief and persistant violations of valued norms of conduct by individuals were controlled by man's own exercise of supernatural power in the form of the "breath-of-men." This sanctioning process was one which could be employed by a village community. It would seem to have arisen as a social necessity to control deviant behavior in a pluralistic society which highly emphasized age and territorial relationships as a means of organizing its action. Witches were believed to use their supernatural power to control departures from community standards of conduct. Their evil powers were subject to control by other witches possessed of a supernatural power to combat them. The identity of evil witches could also be discovered by resort to diviners. Persons suspected of witchcraft could have their guilt determined by supernatural means, in the form of the ordeal. Ancestral spirits sanctioned violations of valued norms occurring within the family group. The total process could well be described as a system for the supernatural control of conflict arising from abuse of power and violations of valued norms in community and interpersonal relationships.

---

4. *Ibid.*, Chap. 7, also pp. 109-121; M. Wilson, "Divine Kings and the 'Breath of Men'," *Frazer Lecture* (Cambridge, England, 1959); G. Wilson, "Introduction to Nyakyusa Law," *Africa*, X (1937), 16.

Social and Political Organization

KINSHIP RELATIONS

Kinship groups were means whereby the Nyakyusa individual satisfied his needs for a home, land, food, sexual relations, offspring, and religion. They also provided means for social control and dispute settlement. Yet provision for these needs through kinship groups did not take place in isolation from age groups and the chief. The Nyakyusa settled in age-group villages. The chief was an intermediary with the spiritual world.

A Nyakyusa man did not marry until after reaching about twenty-five years of age, while girls married ten years or more earlier. Girls were betrothed when very young and began to visit their future husband's homesteads at the age of eight or nine. They moved there permanently at puberty. While families were ideally polygynous, it was not until a man was forty-five years of age or older that he headed a polygynous family. A sampling of 3,000 men of eighteen years of age or over showed thirty-four per cent bachelors, thirty-seven per cent monogamists, and twenty-nine per cent polygynists. Since sons worked in their fathers' fields until they were married, the head of the compound family enjoyed considerable wealth.

In the polygynous family, each mother cooked for and ate separately with her own children. She provided food for her own sons, even after they left the household to live in a separate village with their age-mates. Usually the sons and their friends would take turns eating with their respective mothers.

A lineage of three generations determined the ownership and control of cattle, inheritance, and basis of ancestor worship. Marriages between descendants of a common great-grandparent were disapproved and between descendants of a common grandfather were impossible. Agnatic genealogies extended six to nine generations. Chief's lineages included as many as nineteen generations and lineages of commoners linked with those of chiefs were traced for a longer period than usual.

There was no myth of universal common descent of the dwellers in a chiefdom, but it was a fact that members of lineage found greater support and safety within the chiefdom in which their ancestors lived.

The husband and wife cooperated in cultivation. The husband hoed the land while the wife sowed, weeded, and reaped. Unmarried sons hoed with their fathers, sometimes limiting their work to the fields of their own mothers. Sons and their age-mates would help fathers in heavy building tasks. Sons also worked in the fields of their wives' parents, both after betrothal and marriage.

Cattle represented property in which the male members of a lineage spanning three generations had rights and interests. The devolution of cattle by way of inheritance was designed to keep the common herd intact, with the person exercising control over it subject to duties of providing cattle for various occasions such as marriage and death. The holder of the family cattle was responsible for providing cattle to enable the marriage of his sons and sons' sons. Reciprocal exchanges of cattle with relatives reinforced lineage ties.

Relationship between two lineages was created by the transfer of cattle in connection with marriage. It was thereafter marked by exchange gifts of food and by gifts of cows at burial ceremonies. Lineage groups joined in ritual performances at birth, marriage, death, and sickness or misfortune.

Children were held to have an obligation to their parents for their upbringing. A boy had a special obligation to recompense them for his marriage-cattle. A girl was expected to fulfill her obligation by marrying and not becoming divorced, so that her father acquired and kept the cattle representing her bridewealth. A son was expected to fulfill this obligation by hoeing his father's fields.[5]

Tensions arising in family conflicts were allowed release at a funeral or marriage feast, when a person was permitted to express his hostilities and resentments against others who had departed from valued norms of family behavior.

AGE-VILLAGES

The organization of all Nyakyusa villages was on the basis of a group of age-mates living in the same locality. From about six to ten or eleven years of age, boys slept in their parents' homes and tended the calves, but not the full-grown cattle, of their fathers. At ten or eleven years of age, a group of about a dozen boys would build small huts for themselves on land on one side of their parents' village provided for them by their fathers. As they grew older, they were joined by younger boys mostly from the same village until the older boys in the group reached sixteen to eighteen years of age. At

---

5. M. Wilson, "Nyakyusa Kinship," *African Systems of Kinship and Marriage,* eds. A. R. Radcliffe-Brown and D. Forde (London, New York, Toronto, 1950), 111.

this point, further admission to the new age-village was closed. When they reached puberty, they began to herd their fathers' cattle and to help him in hoeing his land. As each boy grew older, he would build a larger and more substantial hut for his own occupancy. It was to this hut he would bring his wife, at about age twenty-five. Until that time, he would sleep in his own age-village, but he worked with his father and ate his mother's food in her house.

As marriages took place, the age-village expanded. Houses were built bigger and farther apart. New fields were brought into cultivation and tilled by men and their wives.

Eight or ten years after marriages began to take plase in the age-village, when the young men began to reach the age of thirty-three or thirty-five, the fathers of the young men transferred to them the authority over the country in a ceremony called the "coming out." This entailed the creation of two new chiefdoms, each constituting four villages, one chiefdom headed by the first son of the old chief and the other by his second son. The headmen of the villages were chosen by the old men from the commoners on the basis of their membership in respected families, wealth, ability to judge cases, popularity, courage, and ability to lead in war. At the "coming out," one of the older men first "caught" or took hold of the commoner who was to be the headman of the senior village of the first son of the old chief. The leader of the senior village of the second son was next chosen. The headman of the next senior village of the first son was then selected. This process was repeated until all headmen of the eight villages were "caught."

The young men were settled in new age-villages and were given new land to cultivate. Often the old men would move a short distance to provide room for the young men. A series of events comprised the "coming out" ceremony. They were the public recognition of the new villages of young men and of the two new chiefs, the selection of the new headmen, the treatment of the young chiefs and headmen with medicines to make them dignified and powerful, a cattle raid, the establishment of the new villages on adequate land, and the marriage of the young chiefs.

Each of the two new chiefdoms had two "sides," in that half of the wives of each chief were drawn from one division, consisting of two villages, and half were drawn from the other division, also consisting of two villages. A chief's son from each of the two divisions eventually succeeded to control, as chief, of the division in which he was born. This would take place in the next "coming out" ceremony.

Each of the new chiefs exercised judicial authority in his land and led his people in war and funerals. Appeals in difficult cases could be taken to the old chief and his village headmen from the young chiefs and their village headmen.

Each village was in turn divided into sections under the leadership of assistant headmen, appointed by the headmen of the village. If a village was unusually large, it would often split into two substantially independent sections after the occurrence of the "coming out" ceremony. There were also two boys' divisions attached to each village of mature men.

It thus becomes apparent that the "pairing process" of the Arusha was duplicated in large measure among the Nyakyusa, with the latter having the unique distinction of the males living in age-villages throughout most of their lives. There was always a set of three age-villages and sometimes a set of four age-villages. First, the village of boys and young men not yet independent, second, that of mature men who had administrative and military functions, third, that of the late chief and his headmen having ritual functions, and, upon, occasion, a village of a fourth generation. Each age grade or generation covered a span of thirty to thirty-five years and each age-village comprised an age group embracing five to eight years. The occupants of the boys' and young men's village ranged from about ten to thirty-five years of age, those of the men's village ranged between thirty-five and sixty-five, and those of old men who had handed over their authority but possessed ritual functions, sixty-five and older.

The fact that Nyakyusa men lived with their age-mates from about age ten or eleven for the rest of their lives, coupled with the values placed upon companionship, neighborliness, and working, feasting, and conversing together, meant that family and kinship relations did not loom as large in their lives as they did in many African peoples. Indeed, the departure of sons from their homes to live in age-villages meant that Nyakyusa villages were not composed of people closely linked by common lineage ties.

Kinship groups were part of age groups living in an age-village together. Two age-villages combined into halves of a chiefdom, which was composed of four villages. Chiefdoms were created by the splitting up of a parent chiefdom at the "coming out" ceremony. Thus the Nyakyusa were organized into a plurality of groups characterized by the pairing process. The "coming out" ceremony provided a constitutional procedure for the release of tensions built up within groups as they lived together and expanded in size for about three or three and a half decades.

AUTHORITY OF CHIEFS

A chief, together with his great commoners, exercised authority in a number of religious, economic, and legal activities. He provided military leadership. Chiefdoms today vary in size from about 100 to 3,000 adult men.

In summary, the Nyakyusa were organized into a plurality of governing groups which operated to integrate them into an interdependent system or whole. Their political structure and recruitment to office combined elements of appointment to office through inheritance, as well as on the basis of ability. Chiefdoms were inherited by the sons of chiefs but village headmen were "caught" or selected by the old men from commoners on the basis, in general, of ability. The residents of each age-village had an unusually strong sense of unity from their "coming out" together, their contemporaneity, and emphasis on the values of companionship, neighborliness, and the like. Yet each generation was split at the "coming out" into two sections each led by a son of the old chief. Thus there were constitutional outlets for divisive tendencies within groups as they increased in number and diversity of alignments of membership.[6]

Law: Land and Inheritance

The village could be considered to be the ultimate owner of the land. The village headman, as representative and corporate head of the village, was the guardian of the land rights, controlled unused land, allotted land to newcomers, and settled land problems and disputes. Each man resident in the village had a right to a site for his house, a banana plot, and arable land. He also had a right to graze his cattle in the communal pastures.

A man enjoyed security in the use of his land; it was not subject to seizure or loss during his life in his age-village. When he left the village, he gave up his land. Nevertheless, his land was left idle in the hope that he would return, and his former neighbors would do all that they could to persuade him to return. If a man found that he was unable to cultivate all of his land, perhaps as a result of his sons leaving him to work their own land, he still had the power to refuse the village headman's request to give up any part of it.

New settlers were welcomed to the village. They were provided

6. Wilson, *Good Company*, 149-151; G. Wilson, "The Nyakyusa of South-Western Tanganyika," 282-283.

with a house site, sufficient land for cultivation, and helped with food until their first harvest.

Gulliver makes the following summary points concerning the land system:

i. Land was plentiful in relation to the people's needs and extensive areas were left untouched.

ii. Land was owned by the village as a group, acting under its own headman, who was the arbiter and the allocator of fields.

iii. Land was held in usufructory right only by a resident member of the village, and every resident had the right to a house and banana-grove site, to sufficient arable land and to the use of communal pastures and woodland.

iv. The individual's security of tenure was good, in so far as this was thought at all important.

v. The power of the chief was slight in land matters; he had no authority to allocate land.

vi. Other villages, whether of the same chiefdom or not, had no claim in, or authority over, a village's land and land affairs.

Inheritance was first through a man's full brothers or, failing such brothers, through half-brothers linked through their mothers. Only if such relatives were lacking, did his eldest son inherit and then only if he were of adult status.[7]

Law: Procedures of Dispute Settlement and Other Legal Procedures

Certain conflict situations arising between villages would lead to fighting in which spears were employed as weapons. These included the seduction of a wife by a member of another village, a cattle raid made by another village, or a boundary dispute.

The handling of disputes within villages usually involved the disputing parties asking a third person, whom they both respected and who was not involved in the dispute, to decide the matter. Disputes between kin were preferably submitted to a senior kinsman for decision but they were also taken to a respected neighbor for disposition. The third party listened to both sides and made his decision. It was not considered binding on the parties. They would carry it out only if they agreed with it. If the third party was unable to make a decision or his decision was not accepted by the parties and the

---

7. P. H. Gulliver, *Land Tenure and Social Change among the Nyakyusa*, East African Studies, No. 11 (Kampala, Uganda, 1958), 5-11, quotation at 10; R. de Z. Hall, "Nyakyusa Law from the Court Records," *African Studies*, II (1943), 153; Wilson, "Nyakyusa Kinship," 117-119.

dispute still continued, resort was then made to the village headman for decision. Finally, appeal could be made to the chief's court.

Individuals had the privilege of using forces in vindicating violations of certain approved norms. A father or one of his neighbors could beat a child for wrong behavior, a husband could beat his wife for misconduct, a father-in-law and his sons could beat a son-in-law who misused his wife, and a cuckolded husband and his brothers could torture and even kill his wife's lover. In case of murder, the kinsmen could kill the murderer or bring him before the chief, who imposed a fine which went to the injured relatives. A creditor could go armed, joined by one or two kinsmen, to collect a debt.

The disputes which were brought to third parties or the village headman for settlement concerned the ownership, destruction, or sale of property, including personal property, assault, insulting behavior, adultery, and violation of duties owed other members of the family.

In witchcraft cases, upon the occurrence of events which could be considered as attributable to witches, such as a sudden fall in the milk supply or a serious illness, a public meeting would first be held in which the possible witches were not named but were warned generally to stop their practices. If the condition still continued, the people discussed with the village headman their dreams about who might be responsible. The resulting list of those possibly guilty was read aloud in a meeting in the presence of some one who was a "defender," or person who used his witchcraft powers to defend against aggressive, evil witchcraft. When the "defender" failed to respond "yes" to a particular name, this identified the witch. The person thus charged could appeal to the ordeal to prove his innocence but, if he failed to vomit the potion administered to him, he was banished from the village. Often his cattle and crops were taken by the chief, who killed one or more of the cattle for "the innocent" to eat.

Banishment from the village was the usual penalty for witches, thieves, and adulterors, for each performed acts which brought or might bring harm to the village.

A formal procedure before witnesses of turning over cattle at the time of marriage took place, in order to lessen the likelihood of later disputes as to the facts of the transfer. When a stranger to the age-village was granted land, it was done by the village headman with the consent of the chief and after consultation with the members of the village. He was informed of any right of his neighbors relating to his land.[8]

---

8. Wilson, *Good Company*, Chap. 7; Wilson, "Nyakyusa Kinship," 135.

Conclusion

The Nyakyusa were a Bantu-speaking people living in a richly endowed land. Its setting was beautiful, surrounded by mountains on three sides with Lake Nyasa to the south, dotted with lakes, flowing streams, and having heavy rainfall. The homes of the Nyakyusa were architecturally striking and well-constructed. The people were both cultivators of land and herders of cattle.

They had a unique form of social and political organization that the cultural trait of age groups, often manifest in African societies, was expressed in the form of age-villages, in which men of closely contemporaneous ages lived most of their lives, from boyhood until death. This structure of society was accompanied by the social values of "good company" and admiration of a set of traits comprising wisdom, dignity, decency, pride in display of self and possessions, subservience of women, and egalitarianism.

It was Nyakyusa tradition that they were a product of the original inhabitants of their land who came to be led by an alien group of chiefs who traced their descent from mythical founding heroes who came from outside. Social and political organizations were formed principally at the age-village level. The headmen of such villages were selected from commoners at a "coming out" ceremony held every thirty-three or thirty-five years. This ceremony constituted new chiefdoms under new chiefs and created new age-villages upon new land under new headmen. The structure of authority and land holding under the old chief was then supplanted by a new structure of two new chiefs and their chiefdoms, consisting each of four age-villages. These four age-villages were in turn divided into divisions of two age-villages each. Certain sons of chiefs, born of wives drawn from each division, were marked to be new chiefs of each division at the next "coming out" ceremony.

The activity of witches was an important part of Nyakyusa life. Their power to bring sickness or misfortune to others could be directed to personal ends as aggressive witchcraft. On the other hand, "defenders" had the mystical power to protect persons against the evil use of witchcraft. The "breath-of-men," representing in effect the public opinion of a village brought to a focus by the mystical powers of the village headman, sanctioned breaches of both kinship and village norms. It also operated to keep in check the arbitrary exercise of authority by chiefs. Medicines of magical power were used for an extraordinary variety of purposes.

The "breath-of-men," as a sanction for wrongdoing, operated in a sequence of events in which men of the village "murmured" about the violation of an important norm of conduct, thereby invoking supernatural punishment of the wrongdoer, the sinner was punished by experiencing illness or misfortune, leading to his reformation and correct conduct. A commensal feast then took place, where the commission of the sin and the taking of steps to bring the penalty were openly acknowledged by the guilty person and his neighbors, respectively. Finally, a medicine designed to prevent the future occurrence of the offense was administered by a medicine man present at the meal.

Lineage groups were shallow, a group of three generations being the most important. Farming tasks were carried out on a basis of division of labor between the husband and his unmarried sons performing the heavy labor of hoeing, on the one hand, and the wives performing the labor of sowing, weeding, and harvesting, on the other hand. Cattle were used for food and payment of bridewealth. A family herd of cattle was the subject of rights and interest for the members of three generations. Inheritance was primarily patrilineal, though relationships with the mother were also important for this purpose.

Disputes were settled by the parties referring them to a senior relative or a respected neighbor for hearing and decision. His decision could be either accepted or rejected by the parties. If rejected and the dispute still continued, appeal could be successively made to the village headmen and the chief's court. Individuals were privileged to resort to force to protect their important rights when they were violated by others. War between villages occurred as a result, among other things, of lust for women and theft of property.

Part Seven

SUDAN

Chapter 16

The Nuer

Geography and Economy

THIS book began with a classic study of a segmentary society, that is, Fortes' study of the Tallensi of West Africa. It closes with Evans-Pritchard's classic study of another segmentary society, the Nuer of East Africa. The Nuer are found in the savanna and swamps of the Southern Sudan. They were an expanding people. At the beginning of the nineteenth century they were located to the west of the White Nile. At the close of the century they had extended eastward to Ethiopia and southward to the headwaters of the Bahr el Zeraf river. Their land in the north extended northeast of Sobat river and northwest of the Bahr el Ghazal, occupying both banks of these tributaries of the Nile. In 1940, they were said to number over 200,000. In 1954 they were estimated to number over 350,000. Together with their neighbors, the Dinka, at whose expense most of their expansion took place, they form a subdivision of the Nilotic group of peoples. The languages of the Nuer and the Dinka are closely related.

The Nuer countryside is characteristically an open plain growing high grasses and occasional thickets of acacia bush. The open grasslands extend into vast distances with almost no trees. There are also thick bush lands, sandy ridges, marshland, and large rivers.

Nuer villages were built upon mounds, ridges, or high land free from the flooding which takes place in much of the country in the rainy season. The homesteads, consisting of dwelling huts and a cattle byre, were not located close together. The Nuer valued neighbors but not near neighbors. The land immediately surrounding the homestead was cultivated and separated one homestead from another. When the land was exhausted, the Nuer family moved to a new home.

The Nuer lived at a subsistence level, with a simple diet of milk, milk foods, millet in the form of porridge and beer, maize, and meat. In the wet season, they were driven to the high ground of their permanent villages. This was the time when grain and meat became important in their diet. In the dry season, they were compelled to live in camps in the marshlands and on the banks of rivers. There they found grass for their cattle plentiful, and fish became an important food. They had no iron or stone, few specialized skills, and engaged very little in trade.

The Nuer were a cattle people. The care and use of cattle dominated their patterns of life. They loved their cattle, identified themselves with their cattle, sought to acquire cattle, and preserved them as their most highly prized possession. Cattle were the source of their bridewealth, the means for ritual sacrifice, and a source of food, though they were not kept to provide meat for regular food consumption. Cattle raids among the neighboring Dinka were an established means for acquiring cattle.

Cattle were held by families and were a nexus of rights, duties, and privileges among the members of the family. Men were preoccupied with cattle, not only in their care but in the orientation of their interests as well. They were vitally concerned with cattle, discussed matters concerning cattle, and even took names which referred to their favorite oxen as names for themselves.[1]

Religion

The Nuer believed that God was the creative spirit. He was located in the sky, but he also made his presence felt by man on earth. He was the guardian of the established norms of behavior in relations with others in that their breach would bring misfortune. A man who carried out his obligations to others, including his relations with the spiritual world, was in the right. As such, he was not visited by God with those punishments in the form of misfortunes which were suffered by persons guilty of fault in their relations with others.

---

1. E. E. Evans-Pritchard, *The Nuer: A Description of the Modes of Livelihood and Political Institutions of a Nilotic People* (Oxford, England, 1940), Chaps. 1, 2, pp. 3-4; P. P. Howell, *A Manual of Nuer Law* (London, New York, Toronto, 1954), 7-16.

When an individual experienced misfortune, he was led to a self-search to find some omission or wrong in relations with others for which he was responsible. Men in their prayers sought a condition of peace with God and a deliverance from the evils of life.

There were a number of spirits of the air, associated with sickness, rain, lightning, rivers, streams, and war. Occasionally men were possessed by the spirits. Such a person, after recovery from the seizure, possessed powers of healing, divination, and exorcism. A prophet was a person who had been seized by a spirit and was permanently filled with spiritual power. He performed sacrifices for individuals when they needed spiritual assistance, as in illness or making war. Individuals who died as a result of lightning or certain other causes might become spirits. Such a spirit frequently would acquire significance for the members of a particular lineage. Animals, plants, and objects might acquire significance as totems for social groups or individuals. Fetishes were employed for private ends.

God brought about the punishment of men for their faults but punishment was lessened when the breach of a norm was accidental or unintentional. Incest or the eating of human meat could take place without the offender actually knowing the nature of his act. While some slight misfortune could be expected to ensue in such a case, a serious one was not expected to occur as a result. A killing with a fishing spear imported less premeditation than a killing with a club, and the former entailed less compensation to be paid by the killer.

After death, the soul of a man continued to exist as a ghost. Because it then became near to God and could more readily invoke God's punishment, it could successfully appeal to God to cause vengeance (*cien*) to be taken upon others who had wronged it in its lifetime. The killing of a kinsman would cause his ghost to haunt his killer and bring eventual death to him. Any man who was wronged by another might, after death and as ghost, take vengeance on the wrongdoer. This sanctioning power of ghosts was manifested soon after death and arose from the fact that they recently became ghosts.

Duties owed others by virtue of their social status, such as the duties of a son to his father or mother or the duties owed a mother's uterine brother, members of an age set, the leopard-skin priest, and the man of the cattle, were sanctioned by the ability of the person to whom the duty was owed to curse those who owed such duties for their non-performance. A curse need not even be expressed. A "curse of the heart," the unspoken sentiment following a justified grievance, would be sufficient to bring harm to the wrongdoer.

Curses were imprecatory prayers to God. Blessings of God could also be brought to another by an older person spitting on the head of a younger or by a person simply thinking well of another.

Ultimately God was the arbiter and the sanctioning agent for all faults. The curse invoked God's power to punish. Ghostly vengeance for wrongs suffered when living was a product of the ghost's intercession with God. God in his own capacity as spirit would independently visit with disaster those who seriously neglected to conform to the standards of the society in displaying "meanness, disloyalty, dishonesty, slander, lack of deference to seniors, and so forth. . . . Nuer seem to regard moral faults as accumulating and creating a condition of the person predisposing him to disaster."

Sacrifice was made to God and not to ghosts. It was made to avert God's punishment for a known transgression in relations with others or to expiate an unknown wrong to others which had brought sickness or other misfortune. Sacrifice cast out present misfortune by acknowledging and expiating past wrong or prevented future misfortune by maintaining correct relations with the spiritual world. Sacrifice could be either personal, for the benefit of a particular person or persons, or it could be made for a collective purpose, for the benefit of a social group. Sacrifices of the former category were propitiatory or expiatory in character. They were made because of the commission of a fault or to avert or bring to an end a present misfortune. The latter were made in connection with, for example, *rites de passage,* including initiation, marriage, and death.

> The primary purpose of collective sacrifices, and also their main function, is to confirm, to establish, or to add strength to, a change in social status—boy to man, maiden to wife, living man to ghost—or a new relationship between social groups—the coming into being of a new age-set, the uniting of groups by ties of affinity, the ending of a blood-feud—by making God and the ghosts, who are directly concerned with the change taking place, witnesses of it.

Collective sacrifices involved the social structures of the society. They were made "on behalf of social segments, lineages, and age-sets, which are concerned as whole groups," and not merely individuals and happenstance collections of individuals. They "concerned relations within the social order and not relations between men and their natural environment."

Four steps marked the ceremony of sacrifice: presentation, consecration, invocation, and immolation. In the first step the animal was presented to God by staking the animal to the ground. Consecration took place by rubbing the back of the animal. The invocation was made by the person officiating, who stated the purpose of the sacrifice. This was to petition God for appropriate action, such as relief from sickness. In very formal sacrificial ceremonies, several invocations might be made and each speaker was obliged to reveal the grievances he held. The act of immolation was marked by a ceremonial killing of the animal. The cooking and eating of the animal, which then followed, was not a part of the rite of sacrifice, but it completed the ceremony and had social significance.

Sacrifice was designed to take away or avert evil or misfortune. The evil was considered to go into the earth with the blood of the animal. God "turns away" from the matter, he is "finished with a thing." By the sacrifice, God was considered to be placed in a situation of obligation or debt to the giver of the sacrifice. The sacrifice was a ransom which redeemed the giver from misfortune which would otherwise come to him. More fundamentally, the idea was that God had been wronged by some fault of an actor, who must perform a sacrifice in order to compensate or indemnify God for his wrongful act.

The Nuer emphasized the intent or purpose of the sacrifice. It was not a matter of emotion. There was little or no religious exaltation. Sacrifice was a matter of sincerity of purpose. In surrendering his cattle to God, as a sacrifice, the Nuer man was giving, in a sense, a part of himself, such was his identification with his cattle and the value he attached to them. His herd was maintained, among other things, for sacrificial needs. The act of consecration, the rubbing of ashes on the back of the victim, marked his identification with the victim and the transfer of his fault to the victim. Sacrifice expiated wrong, purified the guilty, and averted evil which would otherwise flow from the commission of wrong.

> Once again, this is an old problem. In trying to solve it we must recall that the purpose of Nuer piacular sacrifices is either to get rid of some present evil or to ward off some threatening evil, and also that the evil is very often connected with ideas of sin, fault, and error, and hence with feelings of guilt. The notions of elimination, expulsion, protection, purification, and propitiation and expiation cannot easily be separated out in these sacrifices, though in any particular sacrifice it may be possible to say that one or other notion is most in evidence. The sense of fault is, as we have noted, clearly expressed in the sacrificial rites, in the confession of grievances and resentments, which is a feature of some sacrifices, and also in the sacrificial invocations, which must state a true account of everything which has led up to the crisis. But it is most clearly and dramatically expressed by the common practice of all present placing ashes on the back of a beast and then either washing them off or slaughtering it. Nuer say that what they are doing is to place all evil in their hearts on to the back of the beast and that it then flows into the earth with the water or the blood. This is not

done in most piacular sacrifices, but in almost all such sacrifices someone places ashes on the victim's back on behalf of those for whom the sacrifice is being made; and Nuer say of the sacrifice that whatever evil has occasioned it is placed on the back of the victim and flows away with its blood into the earth. . . . They are asking God to take away the evil and that the evil may be ransomed or expiated or wiped out with the victim. It is clear, therefore, that the laying on of hands is not only a consecration and an identification but also a transference on to the victim of the evil which troubles the sacrificer, and which, as we have noted earlier, is in a sense Spirit itself. It is put on to the victim and departs with its life. The victim thus has the role of scapegoat. This does not mean that the victim is made responsible for the evil. There is no suggestion of *poena vicaria*. The ox is not punished in the place of the man but is a substitute for him in the sense of representing him. In the laying on of hands the ideas of consecration, identification, and transferrence seem to be blended in the representation of a substitute. If this is so, it would follow that what the sacrificer is doing is to identify himself with the victim within the meaning of the transferrence. In other words, he identifies that part of himself which is evil with the victim so that in its death that part may be eliminated and flow away in its blood.

The supernatural world was linked with procedures for the control of homicide, as well as other offenses, in the office of the leopard-skin priest. These priests were drawn from certain clans. One of their principal functions was to preserve kinship groups, where the killing of a member of one group by a member of another occurred. Any such killing created the risk that *nueer,* a form of death, would come to the killer and his kin and the kin of the dead man. This condition could be removed only by confession of the killing and performance of sacrifice by the leopard-skin priest before food or drink was taken by the slayer. The kin of the dead man and of the slayer were also under the threat of *nueer,* if either side should eat or drink with the other or from vessels which the other had used. This threat similarly could be removed only by sacrifice and the payment of cattle. The purpose of the payment was to compensate the kin for the loss of a member and to provide bridewealth for a bride who would become the symbolic wife of the ghost and the wife in fact of a brother of the deceased. It was her role to carry on the name of the deceased. The payment of such cattle as compensation had a different purpose from the payment of cattle used in the sacrifice.

The killing created the danger of a blood feud between the two kin groups. The slayer could receive a sanctuary from the leopard-skin priest until the risk of existence of a blood feud was removed by the payment of compensation at a stipulated rate. A man accused of killing could free himself from the charge by swearing an oath before the leopard-skin priest under penalty of death, if it should be false. The leopard-skin priest was a mediating agent between the two kin groups, acting as negotiator and mediator to the end that each side could insist on preserving its honor and yet move toward settlement. He performed the sacrifice which closed the blood feud and supervised the payment of compensation.

The leopard-skin priest performed the ceremony of sacrifice when close relations had committed incest. In less serious cases of incest, the head of the family or the guilty man himself performed the ceremony. The leopard-skin priest also acted as a mediator to bring about a settlement of other disputes.

The leopard-skin priest derived his spiritual power from his relation to the earth. The term leopard-skin priest had its origin in the leopard skin he wore over his shoulders as a symbol of office. A more usual title among the Nuer was priest of the earth. He was held to have a mystical tie with the earth. His curses had a special power because they could affect a man's crops and his welfare generally, since all acts were performed on the earth. He performed ritual in connection with seeding and preventing harm to the crops.

The man of the cattle was another hereditary and traditional holder of an office of a supernatural character whose primary function was to preserve the health and fertility of the cattle. He performed ritual to promote success in cattle raids. He determined when a new age-set should open and when it should close. He performed the sacrifices in connection with opening and closing age sets and he named the sets. He also performed fertility rituals for women.

The holder of another hereditary office had the function of blessing the water to the end of bringing plenty of fish and success in catching them.

Evans-Pritchard described the role of priests in Nuer religion with the statement that "the Nuer have priests who perform certain politico-religious functions but their religion is not intrinsically a priestly religion."

The Nuer consulted diviners and also believed in the existence of witches. The latter were thought to bring harm or even death to those who incurred their anger. They could be killed without the payment of compensation to their kin.[2]

---

2. E. E. Evans-Pritchard, *Nuer Religion* (Oxford, England, 1956), 193, 199, 280-281, 300. It should be noted that Evans-Pritchard reported that he "never observed the procedure" of the leopard-skin chief acting as mediator (p. 163).

Values and Personality Traits

Nuer society was marked by recognition of the independence and dignity of the individual. This was linked with a high degree of preference for individual freedom of action and for life within the circle of the family and the homestead. A man wanted neighbors, but they must not be close to his home. The Nuer were highly attached to their villages and even to the sections of the villages in which they had long lived. They were sensitive in matters concerning their honor. They were ready to take offense and quick to be insulted. When a man felt that he had been wronged, he immediately challenged the offender to a duel, since there was no established authority for settling disputes from whom he could obtain redress. Readiness to fight was his protection against aggression. Evans-Pritchard stated that he was informed by a Nuer that the following were causes of fighting: "a dispute about a cow; a cow or a goat eats a man's millet and he strikes it; a man strikes another's little son; pasturage rights; a man borrows an object, particularly a dance ornament, without asking its owner's permission." It will be noted that many of these instances reflect violation of norms that would be deemed appropriate for settlement by legal or quasi-legal processes in other societies.

Children were trained to handle their disputes by fighting. Skill in fighting was a valued and necessary quality. Courage was among the highest of virtues. Fighting between boys took place with spiked bracelets. Men of the same village fought with clubs. Men of different villages fought with spears. Blood feuds within a tribe were part of the procedure for obtaining reparation for violation of a norm.

The Nuer accepted no ruler or authority except within the kinship system. They were highly egalitarian and democratic. Wealth did not create deference by others, only envy. No one recognized superiority in another, although respect to elders was shown. Desired action by others was not elicited when it was communicated in the form of a command. A request for a favor or action had to be expressed in kinship terms in order to elicit a response. There was no duty to obey any authority if the result was against one's interests.

Other peoples were held in contempt. The submissiveness of other peoples to chiefly authority was a matter of astonishment. Strangers were treated with indifference. Yet the Nuer were kind and gentle to one another in misfortune and sickness. They accepted friendship, if it was offered on the basis of equality of status. Evans-Pritchard described the source of certain Nuer personality traits as follows:

> Nuer are most tenacious of their rights and possessions. They take easily but give with difficulty. This selfishness arises from their education and from the nature of kinship obligations. A child soon learns that to maintain his equality with his peers he must stand up for himself against any encroachment on his person and property. This means that he must always be prepared to fight, and his willingness and ability to do so are the only protection of his integrity as a free and independent person against the avarice and bullying of his kinsmen. They protect him against outsiders, but he must resist their demands on himself. The demands made on a man in the name of kinship are incessant and imperious and he resists them to the utmost.

Admired personality traits, the possession of which in an unusual degree elevated the holder to a position of esteem and influence, were generosity in the giving of cattle and in hospitality, wisdom and an even temper in acting as a third party in the settlement of disputes, ability to hold the group together, courage, and leadership in war. Leadership among the Nuer was embodied in "the desire and the ability to bind the people together; to mediate and to settle internal quarrels and disputes; to negotiate agreements with other tribes and peoples if they are to the advantage of the Nuer; to maintain good relations with neighbors; in fact, to check the process of fission which to the Nuer is highly undesirable." Leadership was derived from the ability to speak the will of the people. It was based on the power of persuasion, not dominance.

When a man rose to a position of leadership in a Nuer community he was called a bull. He was usually a member of the dominant clan or of an important, long-established lineage. He was generally the head of his family and master of his homestead or a hamlet. It was necessary for him to possess sufficient cattle to entertain generously and to attract followers. "Lineage, age, seniority in the family, many children, many alliances, wealth in cattle, prowess as a warrior, oratorical skill, character, and often ritual powers of some kind, all combine in producing an outstanding social personality who is regarded as head of a joint family of a cluster of cognatic kinsmen and affines, as a leader in village and camp, and a person of importance in the rather vague social sphere we call a district."[3]

---

3. E. E. Evans-Pritchard, *Kinship and Marriage Among the Nuer* (Oxford, England, 1951), 130; Evans-Pritchard, *The Nuer*, 150-152, 181-184, quotation at 184; Howell, *op. cit.*, pp. 31-34, quotation at p. 33.

Social and Political Organization

Evans-Pritchard pointed to the contextual significance of lineage relationships when he said: "A Nuer rarely talks about his lineage as distinct from his community, and in contrast to other lineages which form part of it, outside a ceremonial context. . . . Nuer think generally in terms of local divisions and of the relations between them, and an attempt to discover lineage affiliations *apart from their community relations, and outside a ceremonial context,* generally led to misunderstanding in the opening stages of an inquiry." (Italics supplied.) Lineage relationships had significance in territorial, political, ritual, and exogamic contexts. They were cues to appropriate action in that, given a particular type of cultural situation, a Nuer would adapt to it by identifying himself with the particular lineage group which was the proper instrument to handle the situation.

The word *cieng* illustrates the point. It could be said to mean "home," but there was no single referent for *cieng*. Its meaning shifted according to the situation in which it was used and the values which that situation brought to the fore. It was a term whereby a man identified himself with the relevant territorial group in a concrete situation. Thus *cieng* could mean the land of the Nuer, if he was away from it, or his tribe, tribal segment, village, or homestead, among others. He would identify himself with one of these in order to place himself meaningfully in the situation. He would tend to think of the particular group with which he identified himself as being opposed to another group of similar character or structure. *Cieng* could mean any one of a number of social groups depending upon the group values which were pertinent in the situation.

The smallest unit of social organization was the hut of a wife and her children, sometimes also occupied by her husband. The family group or polygynous family was the homestead of huts and a cattle byre. The family was the basic economic unit, which dwelled in the village in the rainy season and the cattle camp in the dry season.

Membership in the village community was identified on the basis of relationship to the dominant clan in the village. Ordinarily lineage relations were determined on the basis of agnatic ties. If none existed, then ties with the dominant lineage of the territory were found to exist on the basis of cognation or adoption. Everyone in the territory in question was conceived to be linked, either through the male or female lines, with a common ancestor.

Lineage ties structured action within villages or cattle camps as follows:

> A Nuer community, whether small or big, is not composed exclusively of members of a single lineage and their wives or, correspondingly, not all members of a lineage live in the same community. On the other hand, in any large village or camp there is represented an agnatic lineage of one or other order and into the growth of this lineage are grafted, through the tracing of descent through females, branches which are regarded in certain situations and in a certain sense as part of it and in other situations and in a different sense as not part of it. Other lines and persons are grafted into the lineage by adoption, but this can only happen to Dinka and other foreigners, not to men of true Nuer origin. Attached to the lineage, directly or indirectly, are also a considerable number of affines of diverse kinds.
>
> In their collective relations with other communities, and as seen collectively by the members of these communities, there is a fusion of the attached elements with the lineage. They are incorporated in it, and the resultant whole is spoken of as the *cieng* or *wec*, community, of the lineage, which is both its core and the symbol of its social identity as a unit in the tribal system.

Not merely the village community but the "whole society can be regarded as a network of strands of relationships which regulates relations between persons throughout Nuerland, or can be viewed as a set of relations between local groups in which these strands are ordered by the lineage system into corporate collectivities on the basis of territorial distribution."

The village functioned as an economic unit and as a political unit for fighting others and support in blood feuds. An aggregate of villages or camps, which had easy and frequent intercommunication and joined in dances, intermarrying, feuding, raiding, and camps, became a district of the tribe. A tribe was segmented into sections, each of which had "its distinctive name, its common sentiment, and its unique territory." Each segment was "crystallized around a lineage of the dominant clan of the tribe and the smaller the segment the closer the genealogical relationship between members of this clan fragment. Also the smaller the segment the more the age-set system determines behaviour and produces corporate action within it. . . . The members of any segment unite for war against adjacent segments of the same order and unite with these adjacent segments against larger sections." The segments of a tribe were of three orders, primary segments, which were divided into secondary segments, which were in turn divided into tertiary segments. The division usually followed the segmentation of the lineages of the dominant clan.

There were fifteen tribes. Each tribe had a name which referred to both its members and to the country it occupied. That country was vigilantly defended by its members and was economically self-sufficient throughout the year. The members of a tribe identified themselves with it and were strongly attached to it in sentiment. They considered themselves bound to unite in its defense and to join in raids on other tribes or upon the Dinka people. Killing of one member of a tribe by another member of the same tribe was considered to create an obligation to pay bloodwealth. This was not the case when a member of one tribe killed a member of another tribe. The obligation to pay compensation to other tribal members for torts other than homicide was also held to exist but was much less recognized in fact than the obligation to pay compensation for homicide.

Evans-Pritchard described the salient elements of a tribe as follows:

> A tribe has been defined by (1) a common and distinct name; (2) a common sentiment; (3) a common and distinct territory; (4) a moral obligation to unite in war; and (5) a moral obligation to settle feuds and other disputes by arbitration. To these five points can be added three further characteristics, which are discussed later: (6) a tribe is a segmented structure and there is opposition between its segments; (7) within each tribe there is a dominant clan and the relation between the lineage structure of this clan and the territorial system of the tribe is of great structural importance; (8) a tribe is a unit in a system of tribes; and (9) age-sets are organized tribally.

Organization of action of persons living in territories ranging from that of the village to the tribe was effectuated by associating each territorial unit with a dominant lineage. Evans-Pritchard stated this principle as follows:

> The association of the tribal system with a clan may thus be supposed to influence the form of the lineage structure. We may further emphasize the morphological consistency between the two structures. There are always more villages than tertiary segments in a tribe and more tertiary segments than secondary segments, and so on, so that, since each territorial unit is associated with a lineage, the narrowing of such units from the multitude of villages to the single unit of the tribe must be reflected in the conceptual structure of the lineage system, there being a multitude of minimal lineages, fewer minor lineages, and so forth, till the single unit of the clan is reached. If this suggestion is accepted it is evident that the lineages are in number and structural position strictly limited and controlled by the system of territorial segmentation.

A segmentary society is considered to be one which has no centralized locus of authority for organizing action to meet concrete situations. Actors instead adapt to situations by identifying their appropriate role in lineage terms and by performing such role. The
content of such role performance is largely determined by institutionalized patterns of behavior instead of commands emanating from
authority. This is not to say, however, that holders of authority do
not exist in segmentary societies. They do exist, but the source of
their authority is their position as elder, husband, or father in the
lineage group, on the one hand, or as possessor of spiritual power in
the capacity of priest or medicine man, on the other hand. Action in
general is organized on a kinship basis to handle particular situations, the appropriate kinship structure being determined by the
character of the situation. Herein lies the meaning of Evans-
Pritchard's statement that "the political system is an equilibrium
between opposed tendencies towards fission and fusion, between the
tendency of all groups to segment, and the tendency of all groups to
combine with segments of the same order . . . although any group
tends to split into opposed parts these groups must tend to fuse in
relation to other groups, since they form part of the segmentary system." The question always is: What group is the appropriate group
for dealing with the problem?

Evans-Pritchard depicted the various kinship groups, ranging from
the minimal to the maximal lineage, as reflecting a "structural system
of time-reckoning." The organization and interaction of social groups
was determined by their members having a shared identification with
a common ancestor. The more remote that ancestor in terms of
genealogical time or sets of generations, the greater the time-depth
of the group and the larger its size. Stated otherwise, the range of
membership in a kinship group was a product of the remoteness in
time of the common ancestor which it selected for its point of reference. Evans-Pritchard's concept of "structural distance" referred to
the distance between social groups expressed in terms of shared
values. For example, members of the same age-set were closer to one
another in shared values than different age-sets. A village was structurally closer to another village of the same tribe than it was to a
village of a different tribe, even though the latter might be located
territorially very near to it.

The qualities of personality and position which led to a man becoming a leader or a "bull" in a Nuer community were discussed
above under the topic of personality traits. A bull, in his role of head
of a family, took leadership in settling its affairs and deciding such

common problems as when to change camp. Within the village he occupied a position of influence but not of political authority. There was no headman or village council. Men who achieved prowess in war would bring followers to them when they led raids but they had no official status of commander.

The lineage and clan structures manifested in the family, the village, the district, the segments of the tribe, and finally the tribe, assumed political significance in situations where the realization of the values of one group came into conflict with those of another opposing group.

Evans-Pritchard pointed out that group solidarity was a product of the degree of contacts its members had with one another and that, consequently, smaller groups were more cohesive than larger groups. He also pointed out that opposition between groups did not increase in intensity as a factor of size of groups. He affirmed that integration in Nuer society was a product, in part, of the processes in which opposition between its elements came to the fore. It was not the external pressure of the Dinka which created integration among the Nuer. The Dinka were not aggressive against the Nuer, whereas the Nuer were aggressive against the Dinka. It would seem that "the maintenance of tribal structure must rather be attributed to opposition between its minor segments than to any outside pressure."

In order to appreciate the last statement, its background must be delineated. Opposition between minor segments typically appeared in the blood feud. The blood feud, in turn, was part of a total process whereby values were preserved when the killing of a member of one group by the member of another group took place. The Nuer were unique in the degree to which they relied upon self-help, as distinguished from the power of ancestral spirits, as a sanction against wrongs. Violent conflict or the threat thereof was an essential part of the sanctioning process applied to offenses, notably homicide. Seen in this light, the violence of the blood feud preserved, rather than destroyed, integration of the group. Without its use as a means of social control sanctioning violations of valued norms, the group would have not held together. Anarchy would have developed. Indeed, precisely this situation developed as one moved from the smaller groups to the larger groups of the tribe and found that the latter were less ready to use violence as a means of collecting compensation for intergroup homicide. It was reported that: "The larger the segment involved the greater the anarchy that prevails." When killings of members of a large tribal segment by those of another occurred "nothing is done to avenge them or to pay compensation for their deaths." The generalization may be advanced that whether a man saw himself as a member of a group for the purpose of realizing values depended on whether action *within* the group or action *by* the group against other groups was the instrument for value realization. In the latter situation, groups were perceived in opposition to one another.

The age-set system existed among the Nuer but lacked the significance it held in a number of other East African societies. It was principally important for defining the status of seniority, equality, and juniority among males, thereby indicating the appropriate behavior patterns of deference and respect from juniors to seniors and of joking, playing, eating, and working together. Age-mates were expected to extend hospitality to one another, to share their possessions, and to experience a feeling of mystical union with one another as a result of their common initiation into the age-set. Age-set membership was also important for indicating certain ritual behavior. It appeared that the age-set system "influences persons through a kinship idiom and on the patterns of kinship. The sets never act corporately, but they function locally between individuals and, in ceremonial situations, between small aggregates of persons who live near to one another, for a man only has frequent contacts with those members of his set and of other sets who live in his district." The age set did not have military significance, since men fought by villages and tribal sections. Kinship and local ties determined where a warrior fought in the ranks. The man of the cattle was responsible for opening and closing the initiation periods and fixing the period of years embraced in a set, which was usually four.[4]

War

Armed conflict took place between adjacent tribes of the Nuer, typically as a consequence of individual inter-tribal killings. Fighting among the Nuer was principally a means of protecting rights when they were violated. War with neighboring peoples, notably the Dinka but also the Anuak and certain other peoples, was waged primarily for cattle but also for individual captives. Raiding Dinka for cattle was one of the principal pastimes of Nuer men. Expansion of the Nuer into Dinka territory and absorption of Dinka captives into the Nuer lineage system were a part of the Nuer culture. Absorption of

---

4. Evans-Pritchard, *op. cit.*, quotations at pp. 203, 142, 122, 247-248, 147-149, 150, 157, 180-181, 259; Evans-Pritchard, *Kinship and Marriage*, 23, 147-148, 178.

Dinka captives was made relatively easy by the cultural affinity, language similarity, and sharing of common values of the two peoples.[5]

Law: Property

A tribe, a segment of a tribe, a lineage, and a family each had an exclusive relationship to its territory and a set of relationships in common in its territory. The land controlled by each group consisted of high land for permanent dwelling in the form of villages, hamlets, and homesteads and also for cultivation, land at a lower level for grazing in the early months of the dry season, and land in the marshes bordering on rivers and drainage channels for dwelling in camps, fishing, and grazing during the dry season. The land of each group was identified as originally belonging to a nuclear clan or lineage which was the original occupant. Other groups coming later to the territory attached themselves to a lineage by real or fictitious relationship, principally through intermarriage. Such groups linking themselves to the nuclear lineage through marriage were termed "sons of daughters," as opposed to descendants of the original settlers, who were "sons of bulls." Both groups, the descendants of the original lineage and those linked with them through later association, had exclusive control of an aggregate of dwellings, arable and grazing land, water and fishing rights, which was used throughout the year.

The land occupied as the homestead of each family was used until its fertility was exhausted, which occurred in a few years, since there were no crop rotations and cattle droppings were not employed as fertilizer. Ownership implied the right of a man and his family to use the land they cleared, to the exclusion of all others for so long as they wished, and the right to the products of the land and of their labor on it. The latter right was subject to the duty to feed kinsmen who had suffered loss through the weather or otherwise. Ownership of a herd of cattle was subject to duties owed sons and kinsmen in contributing to bridewealth upon marriage and to compensation payments for homicide.

Upon a man's death, his eldest son inherited his huts and cattle byre. His other sons had the right to continue to live in the homestead indefinitely, though they were expected to make new homes upon marriage, but they had no interest in any specific parts of their

5. Evans-Pritchard, *The Nuer*, 125-135.

father's land. Since land was plentiful, it was always possible for them to create new homesteads in open land. Usually a man would divide his cattle among his sons or brothers before his death. If not, the descent of a man's cattle to his eldest son was subject to the duty of the latter to provide cattle as bridewealth as his brothers married, each in order of his seniority. Inheritance in general was on patrilineal lines to a man's sons or, if none, to his brothers or his brothers' sons. Cattle which a wife held in her own right, for example, cattle inuring to her directly or indirectly as shares in bridewealth, went to her own sons and not to her father's family. Personal property, such as spears, shields, canoes, and the like, were divided by common agreement among a man's sons. Particularly cherished objects, such as a spear having a sacred meaning, could be indicated by a man before his death to go to his eldest son.

The practice of the Nuer to move their families and cattle for food, water, and grazing in the dry season was a limiting factor on the acquisition of personal possessions. Only a small amount of such property could be moved. Moreover, they engaged in little trade with other peoples. Articles requiring skill in manufacture, either of local or external source, were the subject of individual ownership and protected from theft. There was also ownership of spirit medicines.[6]

Law: Wrongs and Remedies

The processes of applying sanctions when violations of valued norms of behavior took place, the reparation of wrongs, and the settlement of disputes among the Nuer took place in a context of self-help, including the blood feud, kin and community pressures, and mediatory procedures for resolving conflict. The clustering of the relevant patterns of behavior reflected a number of principles:

1. There was a perception of conduct in terms of *cuong* (right) and *duer* (wrong). *Cuong* meant conduct to the performance of which a man was entitled as a right and which, if infringed upon or denied him by another, constituted a *duer* or wrong justifying resort to force by the injured party as a sanction.

2. A scale of compensation existed for a wide variety of injuries sustained as a result of wrongs, including homicide, personal injury, adultery, and seduction. The amounts stipulated took account of such matters as the intentional or accidental cause of the injury, the

---

6. *Ibid.*, Chap. 5.

remoteness in time of the event causing the injury, and the status of the person injured. They provided the basis from which the parties proceeded to negotiate any agreement for settlement.

A killing resulting from a fighting spear required a higher rate of compensation than one caused by other means, since the implication of premeditation or intent was clearer. Where more than one person was involved in the killing, all were held responsible but the one who struck the first blow had the greatest degree of responsibility. Failure to confess a killing promptly heightened the seriousness of the offense. On the other hand, death occurring as a result of an old wound or an accidental death meant reduced compensation. Killing in stealth or ambush was strongly reprobated, although it did not entail an increase in compensation. Smaller compensation was owing for the death of slaves or witches and no compensation was payable when the slaying of a witch took place in accordance with the will of the community.

Adultery required the payment of compensation to the woman's husband but not if he was impotent. Whether she was barren or prone to have illicit relations were circumstances affecting the payment of compensation.

There was a most detailed scale of payment of compensation for fractures of bones in different parts of the body and loss of eye or eyes.

3. The commission of a wrong would justify measures of self-help consisting of resort to force by the injured person, as well as support by his kinsmen in overcoming resistance against the use of force. It would also justify a man and his kinsmen in taking cattle by stealth from the herd of the family group of the wrongdoer. Whether substantial support of a man's cause would be forthcoming from his kinsmen would depend upon the degree to which he was in the right in the dispute. Aid would be denied if he was in the wrong. He would then experience the sanctions of loss of privileges as a member of his community, disapproval, and denial of respect and cooperation by his neighbors.

A man was quick to react against a wrong or insult by a duel with the person who had wronged or offended him. Such duels took place in accordance with prescribed rules. There was no authority for protection to whom he could turn; only his kinsmen would come to his assistance. There was no notion that spiritual punishment would eventually strike a wrongdoer. The readiness of a man and his kin to resort to arms in defense of their rights was their only protection in such situations.

4. The likelihood of the dispute-settlement process taking place and the eventual settlement of a dispute depended on the nearness of the disputing parties to one another as kin and neighbors, as well as the clarity of responsibility for the wrong. These factors determined the ability of a man to attract supporters who would aid him in enforcing his rights as the injured party or defending his rights as the party charged with wrongdoing.

5. Disputes between groups arising out of the killing of a member of one lineage group by that of another were settled by a process consisting of the following steps: (a) threat of or resort to violence (i.e., the blood feud) as a measure of self-help and vindication of honor by the aggrieved group, (b) intervention by the leopard-skin priest as a mediating agent using persuasion, the sanctity of his person, and the magical power of his office, including when necessary the threat of a curse, to influence the opposing groups to an agreement for settlement, (c) the reaching on a basis of unanimity of a negotiated settlement providing for the transfer of cattle in accordance with the applicable standard in the scale of compensation payments, which was usually modified as a result of the negotiation, (d) the performance of the agreed settlement, including the immediate transfer of a certain number of cattle and the completion of the transfer of the remaining cattle over a period of time, and (e) the performance of ritual with the leopard-skin priest, and the sacrifice of cattle, in the case of homicide, to appease the ghosts, to drive away death from the village into the bush, and to purify the kinsmen on both sides from uncleanness.

Blood feuds were most frequent and intense between small kinship groups but such feuds could not long endure within a village. The minimal lineages on both sides were the ones directly involved in the feud. Sometimes feuds would spread as a result of the network of kinship ties to bring in whole communities or even tribal sections against one another. The kinsmen of the slain man would try to kill the killer but they could also kill any of his close agnates as vengeance.

6. The role of a leopard-skin priest in the process of mediation and negotiation following a homicide was (a) to open discussion with the ("people of the man," that is, the people of the deceased, on behalf of the "people of the compensation," that is, the people of the killer, whereby the former could honorably profess to forego their claim to avenge the killing of a member of their group by resort to violence (it should be noted that, while a settlement of a homicide might prevent immediate violence between the groups, it did not neces-

sarily prevent all future violence between the groups as a result of the killing), (b) to act as a face-saving intermediary between the opposing groups in reaching the terms of settlement, and (c) to threaten spiritual sanctions, if necessary, in order to persuade the opposing groups, and particularly the people of the slain man, to arrive at an agreed settlement.

When a man killed another, he immediately went to the leopard-skin priest, who performed a ritual of purification. Until this was performed, the killer could not eat or drink. He also gave the leopard- skin priest a steer, ram, or male goat for sacrifice. The priest gave him sanctuary from vengeance until the final settlement.

After a lapse of time of several weeks, in order to permit tempers to cool, the priest would open negotiations with the people of the slain man. He would obtain their offer of settlement and communicate it to the people of the slayer. It was a point of honor to refuse settlement but pressure from the priest, including, if need be, the threat of a curse, pressure from more distant relatives of the slain man, together with the pressure of custom itself, would bring about the final agreed settlement, which usually was a compromise.

Evans-Pritchard noted the elements necessary for agreeing to a final settlement:

> The five important elements in a settlement of this kind by direct negotiation through a chief seem to be (1) the desire of the disputants to settle their dispute, (2) the sanctity of the chief's person and his traditional role of mediator, (3) full and free discussion leading to a high measure of agreement between all present, (4) the feeling that a man can give way to the chief and elders without loss of dignity where he would not have given way to his opponent, and (5) recognition by the losing party of the justice of the other side's case.

7. In wrongs other than homicide, the role of the leopard-skin priest was that of a mediator to whom both parties resorted as a matter of mutual consent.

8. Another sanction employed among the Nuer was the seizure of cattle, usually by stealth, by a person who considered that he was entitled to take them as a consequence of a debt owed him, including compensation for wrong which had been suffered but had not been necessarily previously agreed to be paid. If the seizure was regarded as one of right by the owner of the cattle, then no further action would be taken by the owner. If not, it would lead either to negotiations for the settlement of the dispute or to violence between the parties and their kin. The taking of cattle without some legal basis of justification was an act of war between the groups concerned.

9. Wrongs, other than homicide, included personal injury, defamation of character, adultery, sexual intercourse with concubines and unmarried girls, elopement and abduction, theft of cattle, and theft of other personal property.[7]

Conclusion

The Nuer were a segmentary society living in the savanna and swamps of the Southern Sudan. They were located at first on the west but expanded to the east of the White Nile. They were a migratory society moving in the dry season from permanent dwellings on higher land to lower land adjoining river banks and drainage channels, where fish became an important part of their diet. Otherwise, their food consisted mostly of milk, milk foods, meat, and grain foods from millet and maize. They were a pastoral, farming, and fishing people but their culture was most profoundly influenced by the fact that they were a cattle people.

Wisdom, generosity, hospitality, maturity, courage, skill in war, skill in persuasion, and an even temper in aiding others to settle their disputes, were admired personal qualities. Their possession was necessary in order for man to become a leader in Nuer society. The Nuer were a highly individualistic people, sensitive of their honor, convinced of their superiority over other peoples, quick to take offense, and ready to react with violence when they experienced wrongs at the hand of others.

There was little appearance of authoritative roles, save that of the father in the family, the successful warrior as the leader in war, and the leopard-skin priest. The last named commanded respect and a certain degree of acceptance of his authority in performing his role of bringing about a termination of blood feuds, though he was primarily a mediating agent. Action was organized on the basis of lineage membership. A person regarded himself as a member of his tribe, tribal section, clan, lineage, or family, dependent on whether the particular situation called for action by one or the other of these groups. His readiness to commit himself to any action involving the interests of others depended on the importance of the values involved. Only the value of the protection of life itself would cause him to ally himself with tribal action in war. Otherwise, his readiness to avenge with violence wrongs to others depended upon the nearness

---

7. *Ibid.*, pp. 150-176; Howell, *op. cit.*, pp. 22-34, 39-70, 155-177, 198-203, quotation at p. 164.

in kinship and residence of the killed or injured party. Integration of social groups in Nuer society depended on the degree to which the group was useful for realizing values by action within the group and action by the group against others. As social groups increased in size in terms of numbers, their members had an increasingly remote kinship ties and were, moreover, farther distant in terms of residence from one another. Interaction within such groups as a means of value realization was much less than in smaller groups closer in kinship relations and residence. It was the small group with whom he co-operated in many ways and which aided him in time of need. It was the small group that vindicated his rights through the blood feud and supported him in conflict with members of other groups.

Ordinarily lineage relationships were determined on the basis of agnatic ties. However, association with an older lineage was possible on the basis of cognation or adoption.

The age-set system appeared in Nuer society but was not used as a means for organizing action in war. It indicated the status of seniority, equality, and juniority and the patterns of behavior appropriate between males of different age sets or of the same age set, such as the deference and respect which juniors owed seniors.

War with adjacent peoples, principally the Dinka, armed conflict between tribes, and blood feuds between lineages were a part of the life of males. Raiding Dinka for cattle, captives, and territory was a familiar part of life, and many Dinka were absorbed into the Nuer in this manner. The Nuer were an expanding society.

Land was plentiful and land disputes were accordingly rare. Disputes over cattle were much more frequent. Each tribe, tribal segment, lineage, and family had its own territory within which, during the course of a year, it dwelled in its permanent homes or fishing camps, cultivated grains, grazed cattle, and fished. Personal property consisted of cattle, other livestock, and a small amount of personal possessions. A man's land, huts, and cattle byre descended to his eldest son. The cattle were held for the benefit of all sons for bride-wealth and also for the benefit of kin in payment of compensation for wrongs committed by such kin. A wife's own cattle descended to her sons.

The Nuer did not rely upon the spiritual world to punish wrong-doers for wrongs but instead used forceful measures of self-help. The readiness of a man or a lineage group to fight to defend rights from violation was the principal surety of respect for rights by others. There were clearly defined standards of rights and wrongs to the point that they were expressed in a scale of compensation payments of considerable detail and refinement.

Settlement of homicide took place in a series of steps, consisting of reaction against the wrongs by resort or threat of resort to violence in the form of the blood feud, reaching, through negotiation under the aegis of the leopard-skin priest, a settlement providing for the transfer of cattle to the family of the slain man and his kin in an amount derived from a standardized scale of compensation payments, the performance of the agreed settlement, and the performance of ritual and the sacrifice of cattle. The leopard-skin priest also occasionally acted as a mediator in the settlement of wrongs other than homicide. Another sanction applied by a party to whom a debt was owed, including compensation for an unremedied wrong, was the secret taking of cattle from the herd of the person who was considered to owe the debt.[8]

8. For a short description of the Nuer, see E. E. Evans-Pritchard, "The Nuer of the Southern Sudan," *African Political Systems*, ed. M. Fortes and E. E. Evans-Pritchard (London, first edition 1940, 1962 reprint), 272.

Part Eight

CONCLUSION

Chapter 17

Statement of Findings: Principles and Propositions

IT IS the purpose of this chapter to draw together the data contained in Chapters 4 to 16 and the appendices into a comprehensive set of principles and propositions. These represent the application of the inductive method to such data, setting forth the correlations to be found therein. With respect to the abstracts of the behavior of the seven tribal societies contained in Appendix B and cited below, the writer investigated the literature on them in precisely the same manner as all the other societies investigated. This procedure was carried out to the point that a chapter describing each such society was first written and used for the purpose of arriving at the statements set forth below. It was then rewritten in the form of an abstract which was incorporated into Appendix B. Among other reasons, this step was taken to avoid undue length. The bibliography at the end of each abstract will enable others to explore such societies in greater detail.

The principles and propositions below are distributed among six principal categories, namely, the supernatural world, structures of social action, types of societies and social relationships, conflict, control, and law. These basically reflect the fundamental categories of order, conflict, and control expressed in Chapter 1, with the first three relating primarily to order. Each statement is subjected to the following numbering system:

First numeral followed by a decimal point = principal category.
Second numeral followed by a decimal point = subdivision of principal category.

Third numeral followed by a decimal point = principle or proposition.

Each statement not only begins with a number as above described, but it also ends with one or more numbers. The latter refer to the numbers of chapters or the places in the appendices in which particular peoples are described. It should be understood that the statements characterize the behavior of the peoples identified as a group but do not always apply in their full entirety to each people in the group.

The reader should at this point recall the discussion of the methodology of this chapter, the reasons for its inclusion, and the limitations to which it is subject, made at pages 00 to 00 above. Particularly important is the point that the assertions made are limited to the data and are not advanced as statements of universal application.

The first principal category to be analyzed is that of the supernatural world. It should be appreciated that modern man's view of this world as one of extra-sensory perceptions was not that of tribal man. It was, for tribal man, a part of his world of reality.

1. Supernatural World

ORDER

1.1.1. Man's image of his supernatural world, consisting of its actors and instruments operating as a whole so as to realize his basic personality needs, is derived from his cognition of the temporal social order in which he lives and his position therein, and, as such, it reflects both the strengths and inadequacies of the structuring of his society. 4,5,6,7,8,9,10,11,12,13,15,16,App. B1,2,3,4,5,6,7.

1.1.2. Belief in supernatural power is manifested in a belief in a supreme god, gods, spirits, persons, and objects as instruments for bringing good or bad fortune. 4,5,7,8,9,10,11,12,13,14,15,16, App. B1,2,3,4,5,6,7.

1.1.3. Posts such as diviners, witches, sorcerers, witch doctors, and medicine men, together with fetishes or objects embodying supernatural power or performing the function of communicating with the supernatural world, are believed to be able to influence the impact of supernatural power upon human affairs and to influence its aid in attaining desired goals. Such goals include the averting or inflicting of misfortune. 4,5,6,7,8,9,10,11,12,13,14,15,16,App. B1,2,3,4,5,6,7.

1.1.4. Kinship structures of social action tend to develop an ancestor cult in which posts and shrines exist for communicating with and propitiating the ancestors and invoking their aid to bring good fortune and to avert misfortune. The ancestors are believed to perform a sanctioning process of visiting misfortune upon wrongdoers within the kinship group. 4,5,10,11,12,13,15,16,App. B2,3,6.

1.1.5. Agricultural society may develop the belief that the welfare of its people is linked with the supernatural power of the earth and the performance of ritual is essential to preserve a state of harmony with the earth. The set of beliefs associated with this belief is known as the earth cult. Aspects of this cult are the attribution to the earth of the power to bring good or bad fortune to the people in such matters as the fertility of the land in crops and the fertility of wives in offspring, together with the power to punish the people for failure to observe rituals and the principles of good behavior. Ritual performance may develop to the point that there is a post acting as intermediary with the earth. An earth cult is developed in varying degrees in different societies. 4,5,8; *cf.* 16 (leopard-skin priest).

1.1.6. Societies with a complex, hierarchical structure may develop a belief in a supreme being. 5,7,8,12,16,App. B6.

1.1.7. A kinship-structured society may develop a belief in a supreme god as well as ancestor spirits and witches. 12,13,14,App. B6.

1.1.8. Kingdoms which were both of an agricultural and a war-making nature may develop in varying degree a belief in a number of gods and spirits. Gods were functional in character, each concerned with a particular aspect of life, such as war, hunting, and fertility. Posts such as prophets, witches, and sorcerers were believed to be able to invoke and influence the supernatural power of spirits to attain desired ends, which were principally the infliction of deprivations upon others, sometimes as a sanctioning process. 10,App. B2,3.

1.1.9. A kinship-structured society, engaged from time to time in war and performing a number of pursuits, believed in many gods, each devoted to a particular social function and possessing a priest. 8,App. B1.

1.1.10. A kinship-structured society, which also possessed a hierarchical organization for war and dispute-settlement purposes, possessed a belief system consisting of belief in a supreme god and lesser gods and spirits, an earth cult, and an ancestor cult. The stool, as a symbol of office, also symbolized a linkage with the spiritual world. 5.

1.1.11. An urban society, which possessed a hierarchical authority structure under a king but was also a kinship-structured society, developed a belief system in the existence of a supreme god, the devil, the gods of divination, harvest, war, and numerous other gods, as well as an ancestor cult. 7.

1.1.12. Pluralistic societies sometimes developed a belief in a supreme god, lesser gods and spirits, an earth cult, and an ancestor cult. 8, *cf.* 15.

1.1.13. A pluralistic society developed a belief in a chief endowed with a wide range of supernatural powers to prosper the community in addition to his judicial functions and limited political functions. 15,App. B7.

1.1.14. A pluralistic, pastoral society, considerably organized on a segmentary basis, developed a ritual procedure of sacrifice of cattle and ensuing commensal meal of the meat to propitiate the supreme god in conflict situations of importance to social groups or to propitiate the supreme god because of individual wrongdoing. 16.

1.1.15. A pastoral society developed a belief in an office of a supernatural character, termed the man of cattle, who performed ritual to prosper the cattle herds, promote success in cattle raids, and enhance the fertility of women. 16.

1.1.16. A society which had a minimal social order had a correspondingly minimal conception of a supernatural order. Witches and witchcraft pervaded the life of the people and brought evil and misfortune. 9.

1.1.17. A kinship-structured society, which had failed to develop other types of structures of social action or offices or posts of authority for handling conflict situations and the conduct of war, developed a belief that persons in the society who possessed supernatural power had a secret organization of their own with officials possessing authority and rank. 9.

1.1.18. A kinship-structured society developed a belief in the demonic character of persons who were members of structurally distant kinship groups or were spatially distant. 11.

INDIVIDUAL PERSONALITY

1.2.1. The symbolism of the elements of the personality served to identify a person's position in the structures of social action in which he acted and his ties with the supernatural world. 5,7,9,App. B1.

1.2.2. Societies which are kinship-structured and possess a belief in the power of the supernatural world, notably in ancestral spirits, to affect human affairs, may develop a belief that the individual personality has some component which links it with the supernatural world. 4,5,7,8,9,11,12,13,App. B1,6.

1.2.3. In certain kinship-structured societies possessing an ancestor cult, the individual personality was believed to be composed of elements symbolically identifying the principal linkages of the individual with the supernatural and temporal world. 5,App. B1.

1.2.4. The belief in the personality element set forth in statement 1.2.2. above included the belief that such an element may possess a supernatural power to bring misfortune to others. 9.

1.2.5. A society, which was hierarchically organized under a king but was also kinship-structured, developed a concept of the individual personality as composed of a physical and mental body united in the heart, or "heart-soul," which in turn was linked with the supreme god. This divine aspect of the individual existed before birth, was subject to reincarnation, and determined his reward or punishment after death. 7.

1.2.6. In a matrilineal, kinship-structured society possessing an ancestor cult, the individual personality was believed to be comprised of elements symbolically identifying the linkages of the individual with his father, his mother and her blood line or clan, his ancestors, and the supernatural world. There was also a symbolic element which identified his distinctive personality or character and disappeared with his death. 5.

AUTHORITY

1.3.1. A post or office exercising temporal authority may be supported by a belief in its linkage with the supernatural world and ability to influence supernatural power to bring about desired outcomes in human affairs. 4,5,7,8,9,10,12,13,14,15,16,App. B1,2,3,4,5,7.

1.3.2. The possession of a post of authority and the exercise of authority by its occupant may be symbolized in one or more objects associated with the post. 5,8,10,16,App. B2,3.

1.3.3. In a society characterized by an extreme belief in the personal possession of supernatural power and its use for personal ends, including the achievement of positions of leadership and the bringing of misfortune to others, a belief developed in the existence of a supernatural means to control the abuse of such power. 9.

CONTROL: WITCHES AND WITCHCRAFT

1.4.1. Witches and the practice of witchcraft provide a means for releasing tensions arising out of interpersonal relations, including frustration and aggression. 4,5,9,11,13,15,16,App. B3,4,6.

1.4.2. Witches were perceived to possess evil power. 4,8,9,11,12,13, 14,15,16,App. B3,4,6,7.

1.4.3. Charges of using witchcraft operated as an instrument of social control. 4,8,9,11,13,15,App. B3,4,6.

1.4.4. Undue possession of supernatural power and abuse of such power by witches may be subject to control by supernatural means, such as medicine men, witchdoctors, "good" witches, diviners, objects, substances, and ritual performance. 8,9,12,14,15,16,App. B1,4.

CONTROL: THIRD-PARTY DECISION MAKING

1.5.1. A belief may develop in diviners and oracles as third-party decision-making agents in conflict situations involving the violation of valued norms. 8,11,13,15,App. B3.

CONTROL: SANCTIONING PROCESS

1.6.1. A belief may exist in supernatural power operating as a sanctioning process to punish those who violate valued norms. Such a belief is particularly characteristic of kinship structures of social action which typically lack a sanctioning process of a temporal nature. 4,5,8,9,10,11,12,13,15,16,App. B2,3,4,6.

1.6.2. The belief set forth in statement 1.6.1. may be manifested in the form of a belief in a supreme god who sanctioned departures by a social group from valued norms and in ancestral spirits who sanctioned violations of valued norms by individuals. 11,12,13.

1.6.3. The belief set forth in statement 1.6.1. above may be manifested in the form of a belief in a supreme god and ancestral spirits both operating as sanctioning agents. 16.

1.6.4. A pluralistic society, considerably relying upon the action of a segmentary structuring of social action and self-help as sanctioning processes, developed a belief in a supreme god operating as a sanctioning process, together with a minimal belief in ancestors acting as a sanctioning process. 16.

1.6.5. The same society developed a belief in supernatural power operating as a sanctioning process as a result of a ritual curse by an individual. 16.

1.6.6. A pluralistic society, organized in kinship, age, territorial, and, to a certain extent, organizational structures of social action, developed a belief in the supernatural power of a community to apply sanctions by invocation in the form of a ritual performance. 15.

1.6.7. A pluralistic society which had very little of a belief system concerning the supernatural world and of a sanctioning process (whether supernatural or temporal) for the commission of wrongs relied upon vigilant protection by an individual of his rights and upon mediation for the control of conflict. 13.

1.6.8. Certain kinship-structured societies in which there was no independently functioning sanctioning process within the kinship group, either of a supernatural character (e.g, ancestral spirits) or a temporal character (e.g., authority able to impose physical sanctions), developed a belief in the practice of witchcraft to an extreme degree in interpersonal relations within the kinship group, including the infliction of deprivations through witchcraft brought about by a person in order to punish another for a wrong suffered. 9,App. B4.

ISLAM AND AFRICA

1.7.1. Conversion to the faith of Islam is more readily made in nomadic, urban, or trading societies in which individualism is more emphasized than it is in the tightly-knit, agricultural, kinship-structured societies emphasizing the unity of the kinship group with the ancestors, the earth, and the gods and spirits. 6.

1.7.2. Acceptance of the Islamic faith took place in three stages: (1) acceptance of some aspects of Islam without displacing the traditional religious beliefs, (2) a dual system of religious beliefs, consisting of considerable acceptance of Islam yet retention of the indigenous beliefs, and (3) genuine acceptance of Islam and discarding of the older religious beliefs. 6.

2. Structures of Social Action

BASIC ASSUMPTIONS

It will be observed that the first set of statements made below are captioned by the letters of the alphabet instead of numerals. This is done for the reason that they represent basic assumptions, which are believed to be empirically valid independent of the data which are the subject matter of this study, but which are also consistent with or supported by the data.

A. A structure of social action will develop when its members possess, among other things, a common experience in a culture, including a common language, frames of reference, constructs, values, and priorities of values. They must also perceive and accept the structure of social action as an appropriate means for goal attainment, value realization, and control of conflict.

B. Tribal society exhibits the following types of structures of social action: (1) kinship, (2) territory, (3) age, (4) association, and (5) organization. Kinship structures are the most frequent form of structuring social action and persist as other types of structures of social action appear in a society. When a society is structured in two or more types of structures of social action, it is a pluralistic society.

C. The history of culture reflects a progression from kinship to organization as the principal modes of structuring social action in society. Such a progression takes place in a context of pluralistic structuring of social action in society.

D. Cultural change, representing innovations in the modes of adaptation by a society to its environment, can be comprehended by its members only in terms of its existing categories of perceptions, frames of reference, constructs, and knowledge. The constant challenge which cultural change presents to man is in developing the requisite cognitive understanding of the empirical characteristics of the changing world in which he lives.

E. Authority is appropriate for coordinating action and will be accepted by individuals for that purpose, among other things, in (1) situations of a fluid, unpredictable character in which qualities of leadership, personal ability, experience, and judgment on the part of the repository of authority can provide better adaptation than role performance or the unguided action of a person, (2) situations involving the making, selection, and performance of plans, and (3) situations in which the making of decisions settling conflict between persons or groups concerning the allocation of limited resources or the violation of valued norms will promote value realization.

F. Role relationships, other than the role relationship arising from the exercise of authority, are appropriate for coordinating action in a stable, predictable environment in which institutionalized patterns of behavior can effectively realize values.

G. Authority is supported by the contentment following goal attainment or value realization when it is perceived that this is brought about by the successful performance of function by authority. Thus it may be said that conflict supports authority as authority resolves conflict.

H. Authority is supported by its perceived ability to inflict deprivations in the form of a sanctioning process upon those who (1) contest or fail to conform to its exercise in the performance of its function or (2) violate the norms which it is the responsibility and function of authority to maintain.

I. When authority is regularly exercised for the performance of a specific function, as, for example, in dispute settlement or war-making, it tends to become lodged in a post or office which is filled on the basis of the ability of its occupant to perform its function.

J. The exercise of authority in a post or office for the performance of function in a variety of situations develops the perception or concept of jurisdiction or competence, that is, the relevance to, or the appropriateness of, the exercise of authority in a particular situation for carrying out the functions entrusted to such post or office.

KINSHIP STRUCTURES OF SOCIAL ACTION

2.1.1. This and the following statements through 2.1.23 concern the family: The family performs reproductive, economic, educational, and ritual functions. 4,5,6,7,8,9,10,11,12,13,14,15,16,App. B2,3,4,6.

2.1.2. The extended family has a unique and intimate relationship with the land it occupies which it has received from its ancestors and will pass on to succeeding generations, distributes among its members in accordance with their needs, and works to produce crops to satisfy present needs and to accumulate a surplus for future adversity. The land in question and the ideal of a harmonious relationship with such land are at times each identified by a language symbol. 4,5,8,9,App. B1.

2.1.3. In East Africa, the polygynous family tends to occupy the dominant social role of the extended family in West Africa. It is hypothesized that its appearance is somewhat correlated with cattle-keeping societies. Either form of family will, nevertheless, provide a source of males to tend the cattle herd and enable it to be kept in larger numbers than the monogamous or nuclear family. They also provide a larger number of warriors to acquire cattle by cattle raids and to defend against cattle raids. 10,12,13,14,15,16,App. B2,6.

2.1.4. Certain cattle-keeping societies found their most significant kinship group to be one comprising three generations. Such a group was important for the purpose of the ownership, care, and inheritance of cattle, together with, in varying degree, economic cooperation, handling of adversity, leadership, and war. 6,15 (nuclear polygynous families in a three-generation family structure).

2.1.5. Authority over the family, including dispute settlement, is usually exercised by the father or, in the event of his death, by another senior male member or by a brother of the father. 4,5,7,8,9, 11,12,13,14,15,16,App. B1,2,3,4,6.

2.1.6. In a matrilineal, kinship-structured society, the head of the household or elder was elected by the senior members of the group. 5.

2.1.7. In a matrilineal, kinship-structured society, the authority of the male head of a household may be diminished by the perception that his children belong to the clan of their mother. 5.

2.1.8. In a kinship-structured, urban society, the male head of the family, elected by its senior male members, occupied the post of authority, settled disputes, and was linked with the supernatural world as priest of the family god. App. B1.

2.1.9. A father's authority is supported by the power to inflict corporal punishment (4,10), supernatural power (4,5,8,9,11,12,13,15, 16, App. B6), and disposition of family resources (4).

2.1.10. Abuse of a father's authority may be controlled by denial of reciprocal services by the son or by supernatural power, 4,9.

2.1.11. The head of the family is also its ritual head and intermediary with the supernatural world. 4,5,6,7,8,11,12,13,15,16,App. B6.

2.1.12. Allocation of the resources of the family was made by its head on the broad principles that the land was to be allocated for use in accordance with need and that those who contributed to the needs of the household were entitled to a just share of their labor. 4.

2.1.13. In a polygynous family, each wife had her own allotment of land. 9,15,16.

2.1.14. In a kinship-structured, urban society, the wife carried out trading activities and possessed her own property. App. B1.

2.1.15. A husband valued sexual skill, industriousness and skill in the performance of tasks, and gentleness in his wife. 15.

2.1.16. A wife valued sexual skill, industriousness and skill in the performance of tasks, and kindness in her husband. 15.

2.1.17. In an agricultural society, a father had control over his son's labor, an over-right in his son's personal property, and the right to pawn or even sell his children. A son was allowed to have personal property and his own plot of land. Children were expected by their parents to show filial piety and respect and to perform their family duties. 4.

2.1.18. In a kingdom characterized by war-making and slave-owning, children were expected to show unquestioning obedience and humility to their father and were severely punished for their failure to do so. 10.

2.1.19. In a kingdom engaged in war-making, the relationship of the father to his children was stern and distant, while the children were expected to be deferential and submissive. App. B2,3.

2.1.20. In a kinship-structured society possessing age groups, the father's relationship with his children was gentle in style, while the children were expected to be respectful and obedient. 12.

2.1.21. The relationship between the mother and her children tends to be warmer and closer than between the father and the children. 12,App. B2,3.

2.1.22. Learning in the ways of the culture tends to be provided by the father to his sons and by the mother to her daughters. 4,App. B2,3.

2.1.23. In a polygynous family, a senior wife instructed and acted as a patroness for a junior wife upon occasion. 14.

2.1.24. Kinship groups embracing a greater sized structural span of generations than the extended family are employed for purposes of exogamy, ritual, dispute settlement, war, defense, and hospitality. The number of types of such groups found in a society, e.g., minimal, medial and maximal lineage groups, together with clans and tribes, is a function of the political, social, and other purposes which such groups are called upon to perform. 4,5,6,7,8,9,10,11,13,14,16,App. B1,2,3,4,5,6.

2.1.25. The proliferation of segments, or lineage groups having a wide variety of identifications of origins by way of descent, in a kinship society is a function of the need to find a basis for unity and cooperation among persons drawn from otherwise diverse kinship origins, notably in the settlement of interpersonal conflict, but also for other common purposes as well. 4,5,8,9,11,12,14,16,App. B4,6.

2.1.26. A society exhibiting kinship structures of social action may order such structures into a series of levels of similar but opposing kinship groups, with (1) the kinship groups in each level being identified by descent from a common ancestor of the same degree of remoteness or structural distance from the last-born generation and (2) each kinship group in the same level being perceived to be in opposition to the others yet successively united in more inclusive kinship groups at higher levels identified by common descent from an ancestor of an increasingly remote structural distance from the last-born generation. This dual structuring of kinship groups enables the performance of exogamic, political, dispute-settlement, and war functions. 4,5,7,8,9,14,16.

2.1.27. The dual structuring of social action noted in statement 2.1.26 may be utilized in territorial structures of social action. 15,16.

2.1.28. Posts or bodies exercising authority in kinship structures of social action tend to exhibit the following characteristics: (1) the father occupies the post of authority in the family, (2) the senior, most-structurally distant male progenitor of the family, usually termed an elder, or a group of such progenitors, usually termed the council of elders, typically become the repository of authority in kinship groups of a greater structural span than the family, (3) election or selection from the senior males of such more inclusive kinship groups will occasionally determine the occupancy of a post of authority, and (4) succession to the post of authority of the father in the family, upon his death, will tend to be vested in his eldest son or brother, though occasionally appointment to the occupancy of such a post may be made by a council of elders of the larger kinship group in which the family is embraced. 4,5,8,9,10,11,12,13,14,15,16,App. B2,3,4,6,7.

2.1.29. When authority is exercised in kinship structures of social action, abuse of authority may be controlled by informal measures, such as denial of reciprocal benefits. 4,App. B5.

2.1.30. Norms may develop in a society and become perceived and valued as an interdependent and cohesive whole, sometimes identified as such by a language symbol. 9,12,13 (*tiliet*).

2.1.31. A kinship-structured society will emphasize personal traits and values of parental duty, filial piety and respect, acceptance of parental authority, loyalty, amity, solidarity, cooperation, and harmony. The ideal male personality is a person of judgment, restraint, responsibility, and industriousness. 4,12,App. B3,4.

2.1.32. A kinship-structured society valued conformity, respect to others, and gentleness. It disapproved meanness, disloyalty, dishonesty, slander, and lack of respect by juniors to seniors. 16.

2.1.33. In the same society, qualities which were admired in a leader were generosity, wisdom, even temper, ability to hold a group together, ability to persuade others and to arrive at agreements with other peoples, neighborliness, character, courage, and prowess in war. Family connections, seniority, possession of numerous offspring, and ritual power were also important. 16.

2.1.34. In a kinship-structured society, the individual was perceived to possess meaning or significance as a result of his social relationships. 12.

2.1.35. Kinship groups are linked with the supernatural world and are supported by its power in the manner indicated in this and the following statements through 2.1.39: The head of each kinship group acts as its intermediary with the supernatural world, performs ritual to maintain good relations with the supernatural world and to bring about preferred outcomes of situations, and is supported by supernatural power in the exercise of his authority. 4,5,6,7,8,11,12,13,15, 16,App. 2,5,6.

2.1.36. Kinship structures of social action characteristically rely upon supernatural power to act as a sanctioning process. 4,5,8,9,11, 12,13,15,16,App. B3,6.

2.1.37. A society characterized by kinship structures developed a belief in a supreme god, who sanctioned departures by a social group from valued norms, and in individual ancestral spirits, who sanctioned individual violations of valued norms. 11,12,13.

2.1.38. When authority is lodged in posts identified in kinship terms, symbols appear which identify the linkage of the post with the supernatural world and the ability of the occupant of the post to invoke supernatural power to support his exercise of authority. 4,5,8.

2.1.39. Perception of the increasing territorial and structural distance of other groups, including kinship groups, by the members of a kinship group was linked with a perception of a corresponding increase in the demonic quality of such other groups. 11.

TERRITORIAL STRUCTURES OF SOCIAL ACTION

2.2.1. It is hypothesized that the high frequency of interaction among persons who identified one another in terms of their spatial relationship and not their kin relationship, who perceived one another as possessing personalities, and who valued one another for purposes of value realization, made it possible for tribal man to perceive himself and others as discrete individuals apart from their position in kinship groups. It also made it possible for him to perceive posts of authority in impersonal, non-kinship terms. See statement 2.6.1 below.

2.2.2. Territory becomes a basis for structuring social action in such forms as kingdoms, districts, towns, and villages, with authority exercised in such offices as kings, chiefs, and headmen. 6,7,10,13,15, 16,App. B1,2,3,4,5,7.

2.2.3. A territorial structure of social action of the size of a village or town enables the realization of the following values by its members: (1) action in interpersonal relations of an intimate, friendly nature, in addition to those of the family, (2) satisfaction of the personality need for belongingness, (3) economic cooperation, including provision of public lands and services, a reserve supply of available land for allocation for private use as needed, and an accumulation of crops to meet adversity, (4) added strength in war and defense, (5) provision of posts of authority for the realization of common values and dispute-settlement bodies, in addition to the traditional kinship structures and dispute-settlement bodies, (6) assimilation of strangers to enhance the power of the community, and (7) ritual, including the belief in the possession of supernatural power by those occupying posts of authority and their ability to use it as a means of attaining common goals. 6,7,8,13,15,16,App. B1,4,7.

2.2.4. Territorial structures of social action larger than a village enable the realization of the following values by their members: (1) strength in war and defense, (2) freedom and security in movement from place to place, (3) provision of land, slaves, and booty gained through war, (4) provision of an organizational authority structure, in addition to kinship groups for realization of common values, (5) ritual, including the belief in the possession of supernatural power by those occupying posts of authority and their ability to use it as a means of attaining common goals. 6,7,8,10,13,14,15,16,App. B2,3,7; *cf.* 11.

2.2.5. In territorial structures of action, notably in structures larger than a village, but also including villages, posts for the exercise of authority tend to assume the characteristics of an office. 6,7, 10,15,App. B1,2,3,5,7.

2.2.6. Kingdoms and chiefdoms are typical forms of territorial structures of social action. They assume a hierarchical structuring of authority in the appearance of offices which exercise authority over lesser portions of territory than the entire kingdom or chiefdom. 6,10,15,App. B2,3,7.

2.2.7. Authority over diverse groups in a particular territory is sometimes exercised through a dominant lineage group. 8,11,16,App. B2,4,5.

2.2.8. Authority over diverse groups in a particular territory is sometimes exercised through age groups. 12,13,14,15,App. B6.

2.2.9. Common membership in a kinship group, i.e., common descent from the same remote ancestor, may be used to create an authority structure for a cluster of local settlements or villages. 9,11.

2.2.10. The dual structuring of social action noted in statement 2.1.26, with respect to kinship structures of social action, may also appear in territorial structures of social action. 15,16.

2.2.11. The pattern of settlement in towns, consisting of a central town for defense, sometimes lesser settlements located nearby, outlying farm land near enough for working by day from the town or settlement, was highly useful for defense purposes. 7,App. B1.

2.2.12. Urban, trading societies emphasized the values of wealth, family, prestige, good fortune, success and political protection. Other values were rectitude, truth, and the keeping of covenants. 6,7.

Age Structures of Social Action (age groups)

2.3.1. Age groups are a means for performing a very wide variety of social functions. These include the inculcation of attitudes, morals, and values in *rites de passage,* companionship, entertainment, mutual protection, social power, and working together in performing political, military, legal, and other community functions. 8,12,13,15,16,App. B6,7.

2.3.2. The exercise of authority is not required for the realization of many of the values, such as companionship, towards which the action of an age group is directed, subject to the following exceptions: (1) authority is exercised by a person perceived to possess supernatural power in a *rite de passage,* notably in initiating membership into the first age group, such as the circumcision ceremony, (2) authority is exercised by a leader or group of leaders within an age group in performing such functions as war, dispute settlement, and public labor, and (3) authority is sometimes exercised by the members of a senior age grade over the next lower junior age grade. 8,12,13,15,16,App. B6.

2.3.3. Age groups perform political, military, social, and legal functions for the village. The senior age grade performs ritual and dispute-settlement functions, the middle age grade performs military and public functions, aids in the performance of political, legal, and ritual functions by the senior age grade, and sometimes acts to prevent the abuse of authority, while the junior age grade tends to perform executive functions and to act as police. 8,12,13,15,16,App. B6.

2.3.4. An age group possessed a code of regulations for the behavior of its members and sanctioned violations of such regulations. 8.

2.3.5. An age group emphasized the values of loyalty, devotion, and unselfishness. 12,16.

2.3.6. A pluralistic society, in which age groups were highly important, developed attachment to the values of friendliness, generosity, egalitarianism, enjoyment of occasions of mutual entertainment, pride in possessions, display of self, personal qualities of wisdom, dignity, and decency, together with submissiveness of women to male dominance and interests. 15.

2.3.7. Leadership qualities which were valued included intelligence, personality, reputation, success in affairs, and talent for war-making or settling disputes. 12,16.

2.3.8. The headman in a village organized on the basis of age groups was selected on the basis of his membership in a respected family, wealth, ability to decide disputes, popularity, and courage and leadership ability in war. 15.

ASSOCIATIONAL STRUCTURES OF SOCIAL ACTION

2.4.1. An association structure of social action enables the realization of specific values by its members, such as fishing, dancing, music, feasting, magic, and title holding. 8,App. B1, 7.

2.4.2. An associational structure of social action was transformed into an organization when its members subjected themselves to the exercise of authority by the occupant of an office to attain goals. App. B1.

ORGANIZATIONAL STRUCTURES OF SOCIAL ACTION

2.5.1. Hierarchical authority structures, including kingdoms and chiefdoms, possessing the power to inflict physical sanctions in support of the exercise of authority, tend to appear in war-making societies. 5,6,10,11,App. B2,3.

2.5.2. The ability of an occupant of a post or office to attain goals through the exercise of authority becomes a factor in his selection. 5,6,10,15,App. B1,3,5.

2.5.3. The selection of the occupant of the post of a king or a chief on the basis of his ability may also be subject to his family or kinship identification, for example his membership in a particular family, lineage, or clan. 6.7,10,15,App. B2,3,5.

2.5.4. A hierarchical structuring of authority in a society sometimes has the exercise of authority in posts or offices supported by a belief in the linkage of the holders of such posts or offices with the supernatural world and ability to influence the operation of supernatural power. 5,15,App. B2,3,5,7.

2.5.5. Symbols or objects may represent a post or office, the legitimacy of its occupancy, and the power, both supernatural and temporal, which supports the exercise of authority by the occupant of the post or office. 5,8,10.

2.5.6. A ceremony may develop for the installation of a person in the occupancy of the office of the king or other office of peak coordination in a society. The symbolic elements of such ceremony will identify and commit the holder of such office to the performance of its functions in accordance with their required standards of performance. 5,10,App. B3,5.

2.5.7. A kingdom and a chiefdom are maintained, among other things, (1) by a reciprocal flow of services between king or chief and subjects, (2) upon occasion, by payment of taxes or levies, from the subjects to the king and lesser holders of offices, and (3) by provision of public services and benefits from the king and such office holders to the subjects. 6,10,App. B2,3,5,7.

2.5.8. A kingdom devoted to the conduct of war and acquisition and use of slaves was maintained by the following principles, among others: (1) the king attracted support by the distribution of valued offices and largesse, (2) the king commanded respect through fear of brutal displays of his power, (3) administration, including appointment to and removal from office, was directed by the king in a manner designed to maintain power and to prevent the development of dissident centers of power, and (4) offices and procedures functioned to control the abuse of authority. 10.

2.5.9. A chiefdom, which was engaged in the expansion of its territory and upon occasion waged war, exhibited the principles of behavior set forth in statement 2.2.4., although not in the same manner and degree. App. B5.

2.5.10. An administration system in a kingdom was directed to providing labor, warriors, and taxes for the king and providing roads, a third-party decision making process, opportunities for personal advancement, and largesse to the subjects. 10.

2.5.11. When authority is exercised in an office, procedures and means appear for the control of abuse of authority, both of a supernatural and temporal character. Not the least of these is the practical need of a leader to retain the support and following of those under his authority as against competing opportunities available to them to move into other authority structures. 6,7,8,12,15,App. B1,2,3.

2.5.12. The authority structure of a kingdom was reinforced by the power to exclude a lawful holder of land from its continued use. While such a power might, upon occasion, be exercised arbitrarily, its proper exercise was deemed to be limited to situations where the holder had failed to perform obligations owed the state. 10,App. B2.

3. Types of Societies and Social Relationships

PLURALISTIC SOCIETIES

3.1.1. Reference is made to the hypothesis set forth in statement 2.2.1. Pluralistic societies enabled man to participate in diverse types of structures of social action and contexts other than purely kinship ones. It thereby became possible for a person to perceive himself and others as individuals possessing unique personalities apart from the group or groups to which they belonged.

3.1.2. In a pluralistic society, the family and sometimes larger lineage groups remain but political, military, social, legal, and religious functions are performed by a variety of social structures, bodies, officials, and posts. 5,6,7,8,10,12,13,14,15,16, App. B1,5,6,7.

3.1.3. As a consequence of its possession of a variety of types of structures of social action, a pluralistic society will exhibit a variety of types of posts and offices exercising authority. 5,6,7,8,10,12,13,14, 15,16,App. B1,5,6,7.

3.1.4. A variety of third-party decision-making bodies and procedures are available in pluralistic societies for the settlement of interpersonal conflict. 8,12,14,15,App. B7.

3.1.5. A society organized in kinship structures of social action will move toward one organized in organizational structures of social action as authoritative posts appear which (1) are filled on an appointive or elective basis and (2) are able to apply physical sanctions to support their exercise of authority. 5,App. B7.

3.1.6. In the course of the movement described in statement 2.6.5., a society may exhibit an order of an intermediate nature embodying kinship, territorial, and organizational structures of social action. App. B5,7.

3.1.7. A pluralistic society became an achieving society when it possessed a variety of skills, occupations, and opportunities for success and was characterized by competition and rivalry between individuals and groups. It had a number of ways to achieve influence, prestige, and esteem and a variety of social groups to be used as instruments of support in conflict situations. Influence and prestige could be attained through the use of clientage, titles, political power, social contacts in many and diverse groups, and the ability to organize farming activities and acquire the control of land. Leadership was acquired through knowledge of village and lineage history, wealth, ability to speak clearly and persuasively and to influence others. Honesty and kinship loyalty were valued traits. 8.

3.1.8. In a pluralistic society, persons of wealth could acquire titles and a certain degree of legitimate authority and power through acquiring membership in a title-holding association. 8.

3.1.9. An achieving society developed personality traits of initiative, shrewdness, leadership, skill in decision making, honesty, and loyalty. 8.

3.1.10. A pluralistic society, in which age groups were highly important, developed attachment to the values of friendliness, generosity, egalitarianism, enjoyment of occasions of mutual entertainment, pride in possessions, display of self, personal qualities of wisdom, dignity, and decency, together with submissiveness of women to male dominance and interests. 15.

3.1.11. A pluralistic society with almost no development of a sanctioning process, whether of a supernatural or temporal character, developed a personality trait of vigilance and use of violence in protecting one's honor and interests, together with a widespread and strongly held value in settling disputes peacefully, for which the mediation process was available. 14.

3.1.12. A pluralistic society, in which an independently functioning sanctioning process did not exist, except through the operation of the supernatural world, developed a personality trait of vigilance in the defense of one's honor and rights on the part of males and readiness to fight to punish violators of one's rights. 16.

3.1.13. In a pluralistic society embracing both kinship and age groups, the young learned the types of behavior which were socially appropriate and the importance of personal relations and of adherence to social obligations. 12,13,14.

3.1.14. In a pluralistic society structured in both kinship and age groups, an age group acted as a means for controlling the abuse of kinship authority. 8.

PASTORAL, CATTLE-KEEPING SOCIETIES

3.2.1. A very high priority was accorded to the value of preserving the cattle herd and techniques were developed for its preservation and growth. 6,13,15,16.

3.2.2. The sons in the family succeeded to the ownership of the family herd through its distribution upon the marriage of each son. 6.

3.2.3. The most significant kinship group was one comprising three generations. Such a group was important for the purpose of ownership, control, and inheritance of cattle, together with, in varying degree, economic cooperation, handling of adversity, leadership, and defense against attack. 6,15.

3.2.4. A balance was maintained between the size of its social units and the size of its herds. 6.

3.2.5. Its leaders tended to be selected on the basis of ability. 6,15.

3.2.6. An office of a supernatural character developed, termed the man of the cattle, who performed ritual to prosper the cattle herds, promote success in war for acquiring cattle, and enhance the fertility of women. 16.

3.2.7. Constitutive conflict manifested itself in fission in the dry season, when the dispersal of the herds for pasturage was necessary. 6.

3.2.8. A code of valued norms and admired virtues existed. These were linked with the keeping of cattle and included care, patience, fortitude, forethought, prudent planning, modesty, and reserve. 6.

3.2.9. The individual was deemed to feel shame in the belly, exercise patience and fortitude in the heart, and employ care and forethought in the head. 6.

3.2.10. The ultimate ownership and authority to control or grant the right of use of land was considered to lie in the people as a whole or in a territorial structure of social action. 13,15.

SLAVE-OWNING SOCIETIES

3.3.1. A society engaged in the acquisition and use of slaves was (1) organized on a large territory, (2) in the form of kingship and a hierarchy of officials, (3) possessed an established military force with an appointed commander, and (4) distributed rewards to office holders, of which the most important were fiefs worked by slaves. (5) Slaves were also distributed in such a manner as to promote attachment to and maintain the authority system. 7.

3.3.2. Where fidelity in the discharge of office was important, a slave might be appointed to fill it. 6.

3.3.3. A warring, slave-raiding society developed a protectorate or satellite territory, the people of which were utilized for providing a continuing supply of slaves and were protected against raiding by other groups. 6.

3.3.4. A society exposed to external attack and itself a slave-raiding and slave-owning society, lived in walled compounds, towns, and villages. The typical kinship group did not extend more than two generations back. A community was organized on the basis of possessing a common chief, a common religious head, and a common group of markets. 6.

DOMINANCE-SUBORDINATION RELATIONSHIP

3.4.1. In a society where a people small in numbers had achieved dominance over a much larger subordinate people, the former pastoralists and keepers of cattle and the latter agriculturalists, the dominant group was considered to be intelligent, astute, authoritarian, refined, courageous, and cruel, while the subordinate group was held to be less intelligent, industrious, strong, obedient, and crude in manners. Superiority and inferiority infused social relations. The young of the dominant group were indoctrinated in the virtues of self-control, trustworthiness, generosity, liberality to the poor, and courage in carrying out responsibilities. 6 (Tutsi-Ruanda).

3.4.2. In the same society, the dominant group controlled the political and administrative system, levied taxes, and were the exclusive owners of cattle. 6.

3.4.3. The same society was characterized by a considerable use of the clientage relationship. 6.

3.4.4. In the same society, a member of the dominant group, who will be termed the superior, was held to be intelligent, refined, astute, courageous, authoritarian, severe, master of self, trustworthy, and generous. A member of the subordinate group, who will be termed the inferior, was held to be industrious, strong, obedient, submissive, and crude in manners. The superior displayed arrogance and command, on the one hand, and protection and compassion, on the other hand, in his relations with the inferior. The inferior conformed to the superior's expectations and concealed distasteful matters. The superior had the power to intervene in the inferior's activities. 6.

3.4.5. In a highly authoritarian kingdom, personal relations with the king by his subjects were marked by abject humility, submission, and conformity to the king's character and mood. The society was characterized by attention to personal appearance and concern over the saving of face in personal relations. Valued personality traits were foresight, adaptability, shrewdness, and efficiency. 10.

3.4.6. Relationships between a political superior and his followers were marked by dignity, impassivity, and aloofness on the part of the superior, together with the extension of hospitality to his followers, and by complete acceptance of the superior's authority on the part of his followers. 10.

CLIENTAGE RELATIONSHIP

3.5.1. When persons possessing political or economic power perceived such power could be usefully employed in delegating its exercise to others for mutual benefit, they may assume with such others the role relationship known as patron and client, herein termed clientage. A strong motivating factor on the part of the client is the realization which it provided of the value of security in a society characterized by personal insecurity. 6.

3.5.2. A kingdom engaged in war as an instrument for gain may develop clientage relationships. 6,10.

3.5.3. As clientage becomes an established role relationship in a society, a formalized procedure may develop for initiating the relationship and formally committing the patron and client to the future performance of its essential norms. 10.

4. Conflict

WAR

4.1.1. This and the following statements through 4.1.5. concern war as an instrument for goal attainment and value realization. War may be conducted to acquire land, booty, such as cattle, or slaves.

It may also represent the response of defense against armed attack. 6,9,10,12,13,14,15,App. B2,3,5,7.

4.1.2. The following developments occur in war-making societies in varying degree: (1) those responsible for leadership in war occupy posts or offices which are filled on the basis of ability, even when kin affiliation is also a factor, (2) the conduct of war tends to become a central aspect of their political and economic life, (3) authority relationships tend to become marked by patterns of dominance and subordination, (4) sanctions of a physical nature support the exercise of authority and punish norm violation, and (5) the society tends to become attached to the values of achievement and the possession of wealth and power. 5,6,10,12,13,14,15,16,App. B1,2,3,5,7.

4.1.3. A post existed for the purpose of communicating with the supernatural world to determine whether a contemplated war would be successful or for influencing supernatural power to bring about success in war. 5,10,12,13,15,App. B1,7.

4.1.4. When the conduct of war became a central aspect of a society and importantly provided opportunities for a successful warrior to achieve economic rewards and a rise in social status and possession of power, a high degree of attachment developed in the society to the values of achievement and success in competition for advancement in social status and power. 10.

4.1.5. When the conduct of war became a central aspect of a society, its authority structure was utilized for tax collection for the benefit of occupants of the authority structure and for public benefits. 6,10,App. B2.

4.1.6. This and the following statements through 4.1.8. concern war as a sanctioning process. War, i.e., the use of force, between kinship groups performed the functions of (1) a sanctioning process for the commission of serious wrongs, such as the killing of members of one group by members of another, (2) the release of tension between groups as a result of (1) above, and (3) promoting harmony between kinship groups after the cessation of violence, to which end a ritual affirmation of unity took place. 4,8,9,12,15,16.

4.1.7. Social controls were employed to prevent the spread of war and resort to undue violence. 4,8,9,12,13,15,16,App. B4.

4.1.8. Covenants and treaties were employed in the settlement of war. 8,9.

Constitutive Conflict

4.2.1. Constitutive conflict will tend to appear in a group and disintegration will tend to take place therein when its members find that identification with and participation in the group fails to provide adequate value realization and goal attainment in comparison with constituting a new group or the availability of other groups for the desired purposes. 4,11,App. A.

4.2.2. When a kinship structure of social action is precariously constituted, constitutive conflict may be engendered by partisan attitudes expressed by the opposing constituent groups over the validity of the application of a particular norm to a conflict situation. Unless consensus over the conflict issue is achieved, the conflicting constituent groups will separate and form new groups which may or may not thereafter have friendly relations with the former parent group. 4,11,App. A.

4.2.3. It is hypothesized that the principle set forth in statement 4.2.2. may represent a principle in the action of all enduring groups, namely, the pulls of opposing positive and negative value realization resulting from continuing interaction by the members of the group may reach such a precarious equilibrium that a minor interpersonal conflict situation will engender a chain of reactions throughout the group representing constitutive conflict and resulting in the dissolution of the group.

4.2.4. A sequence of events in which constitutive conflict was frequently manifested in a society consisted in (1) acceptance of legitimate authority, (2) emerging conflicts of interest between constituent groups, (3) increasing seriousness of such conflict, (4) assertion of conflicting claims of the legitimacy of existing authority posts, (5) fission of the dissident constituent groups into new and independent groups, and (6) legitimation of their new status. 11.

4.2.5. Constitutive conflict frequently occurred in a society in a sequence of action involving (1) breach of an important norm in interpersonal relations, (2) spreading impact on such breach to the point that a crisis situation in immanent fission of a kinship group was presented, (3) use of conflict-settlement procedures, and (4) either reintegration or fission of the opposing kinship groups. App. A.

4.2.6. The structuring of kinship groups into opposing parts of a larger kinship unit forms a basis for indicating the line of fission in the event of constitutive conflict. In general, fission will tend to take place in a kinship group as the structural distance of their common ancestor increases. 4,6,8,9.

INTERPERSONAL CONFLICT

4.3.1. Interpersonal conflict involving situations of frustration arising from a failure by persons to perform an expected, institutionalized sequence of action may entail the non-performance of structural and behavioral norms.

4.3.2. The perception of a structural norm and the significance of its violation, as distinguished from a behavioral norm, rests in the circumstances that the former involves (1) norms the violation of which are perceived to impair the support provided by the super-natural world to the authority structuring of a society or (2) norms the maintenance of which are deemed highly important in the society as a whole, or, otherwise stated, norms which are linked with the bonds which are perceived to unite and maintain the social order. 5,8,9,11,12,13,15,16,App. B5,6,7.

4.3.3. Murder, incest, witchcraft, treason, ritual uncleanness, failure to respect posts of authority linked with the supernatural world, and persistent committing of serious offenses by an individual are almost universally regarded as violations of structural norms, while suicide, theft, and adultery have a lesser degree of frequency of recognition as violations of structural norms. 5,8,11,12,13,14,15,16, App. B6,7.

4.3.4. Violations of structural norms tend to be subject to severe physical sanctions, including death. Ostracism and banishment are sometimes employed. Punishment of such violations may also be believed to be a function of the supernatural world. 5,8,11,12,13,14, 15,16,App. B7.

4.3.5. Behavioral norms secure the enjoyment of value realization by an individual in action involving his person, property, and valued interpersonal relations. Behavioral norms are involved in such disputes as assault, defamation, theft, and interference with the enjoyment of property and the marriage relationship. Behavioral norms are reinforced by a variety of sanctioning processes, including the infliction of deprivations by supernatural and temporal power and the exaction of reparation. 7,8,9,12,15,16,App. B2, 7.

4.3.6. The securing through law of the expectations involved in the performance of contracts appears in an urban, trading society. 7.

4.3.7. The principle of *pacta sunt servanda* may also appear in the making of treaties terminating war which is employed as a sanctioning process between kinship groups structurally distant from one another. 8,9.

5. Control

5.1.1. The absence in a society of adequate processes of control of a temporal character conduces to the appearance of tension and hostility among its members and supernatural or symbolic processes of control, such as rituals of rebellion, witchcraft, and supernatural sanctioning processes. 4,5,8,9,10,11,12,13,15,App. B2,3,4,6.

5.1.2. Charges of practicing witchcraft and resort to witchcraft operate as an instrument of social control. 4,8,9,App. B3,4.

5.1.3. Control of tensions arising from continuing conflict situations may take place in the form of "rituals of rebellion," such as periodic occasions for indulging in license and promiscuity, together with expressions of condemnation, hostility, resentment, ridicule, taunting, and jesting. 4,11,15.

5.1.4. Control of constitutive conflict may take place through periodic rituals and ceremonies emphasizing in symbolic form the goal and value of harmony in the kinship group. 4.

5.1.5. The reintegration process is particularly applicable to situations likely to involve constitutive conflict. 4,App. B4.

6. Law

BASIC ASSUMPTIONS

A. A society has law, in the sense of legal norms, when it has valued norms the violation of which subjects the violator to a sanctioning process. A society has law, in the sense of a legal process or a legal system, when violations of legal norms are determined by a third-party decision-making body.

B. Norms not involving the application of a sanctioning process but instead defining the creation, nature, and termination of interests in, or statuses which individuals have with respect to, objects in the form of land, things, and persons (property, and marriage), including the transfer of interests in land and things (property), are necessary for determining the circumstances in which legal norms will secure the expectations of value realization, which persons have in their relations with such objects, from interference by others.

C. It is necessary for the emergence in a society of a third-party decision-making body for the settlement of disputes concerning the violation of legal norms that there shall be a common sharing of values and the priority of values with respect to such norms. The common sharing in the priority of values embodied in legal norms is necessary to enable the decision-making body to make effective choice in the selection of the applicable legal norm in a conflict situation involving competing legal norms.

LEGAL NORMS: DEFINITIONS

6.1.1. A legal norm supports a valued social norm by subjecting a person who fails to perform it to a sanctioning process.

6.1.2. Legal norms comprise structural norms and behavioral norms, as defined in statements 4.3.1. to 4.3.5.

THIRD-PARTY DECISION-MAKING BODIES

6.2.1. The composition of a third-party decision-making body is determined by the possession by its members of (1) impartiality and wisdom, flowing from seniority in age and from the social and structural distance of its members from the disputing parties, (2) authority, inhering in the occupancy of a post or office perceived to be of an authoritative character, and (3) power, inhering in the ability (a) to inflict deprivations by supernatural or temporal means upon those who flout its authority and (b) to impose sanctions through either supernatural or temporal means upon wrongdoers. The principle of representation of the social groups which are subject to its jurisdiction also determines its composition. 4,5,6,7,8,9,10, 12,13,14,15,App. B1,2,4,6,7.

6.2.2. The composition of third-party decision-making or dispute-settlement bodies falls into the following types or variations thereof: (1) kinship tribunals, (2) territorial tribunals, (3) office tribunals (i.e., tribunals based on the possession of an office or a leadership post), and (4) *ad hoc* decision-making bodies called into being for the settlement of a particular dispute. 4,5,6,7,8,9,10,12,13,14,15,16,App. B1,2,3,4,6,7.

6.2.3. The degree to which a third-party decision-making body will possess authority (i.e., the power to make binding decisions) is influenced by its perceived ability to apply supernatural or temporal power. Where such ability is lacking, dispute-settlement procedures will tend to require the consent of the disputing parties to a settlement or to become a mediation process. 12,14,16,App. B3,4,7.

6.2.4. The jurisdiction of a third-party decision-making or dispute settlement body over persons comprehends all persons within its constituent kinship or other social groups or its territory. 4,5,6,7,8, 10,12,13,14,15,App. B1,2,3,4,6,7.

6.2.5. The jurisdiction of a third-party decision-making body over subject matter is influenced by the structural distance of its members from the persons subject to its jurisdiction. The greater the structural distance the more likely its jurisdiction will be confined to important offenses and appeals from third-party decision-making bodies which are closer in structural relationship to the persons subject to their jurisdiction. 7,8,10,12,15,16,App. B2,6,7.

6.2.6. The segmentary structuring of kinship groups in a society into successive series of units, with each series of units being identified by common descent from an increasingly remote common ancestor and each unit in a series perceived to be in opposition to the others but united in a unit in the succeeding series, has the function, in the control of conflict, of indicating (1) the social groups which come into conflict as a result of interpersonal conflict and thereby to set the stage for the successive appearance of plaintiff and defendant in the dispute-settlement process), (2) common membership in a larger social group, which provides the basis for the goal of achieving harmony through resolution of the conflict, (3) the appropriate third-party decision-making body and procedure for dispute settlement, and (4) the path of cleavage in the event of fission as an outcome of constitutive conflict. 4,5,8,14,16.

6.2.7. Disputes arising between members of different kinship or territorial groups are settled by resort to a third-party decision-making or dispute-settlement body. In kinship groups, this body is typically the council of elders, the representative quality of which determines its jurisdiction over persons. 5,7,8,9,12,13,14,15,16,App. B4,6,7.

6.2.8. Disputes between members of a small kinship group, notably the family, are settled within the group by its head. 5,7,8,9,10,11, 12,13,14,15,16,App. B4,6.

6.2.9. Decision by third parties of disputes between members of different kinship groups sometimes requires agreement of such members in order for the decision to be effectuated in action. 15.

6.2.10. Inasmuch as territorial structures of social action are the principal modes for the exercise of authority in a kingdom or chiefdom, its decision-making or dispute-settlement bodies perform their function within such structures of social action. 6,7,10,15,16,App. B2,7.

6.2.11. A kingdom or chiefdom exhibits a hierarchy of courts, ranging from those of the king or chief to those of lesser posts of authority and finally to the village, with the higher courts having jurisdiction over important cases and acting as courts of appeal. 6,7,10,15,App. B2,7.

6.2.12. In a kingdom having control over considerable territory, the legal system exhibited the following principles: (1) local courts decided minor cases while important violations of law were reserved for the central courts at the capital, (2) the king was responsible for the correction of abuse of political or administrative power but would often fail to carry out this responsibility because of considerations of political power, (3) fief-holders decided cases involving magic, land, and abuse of authority of chiefs who were under their authority. 6.

6.2.13. As a society becomes pluralistic in character and marked by diverse types of posts and personnel exercising authority and influencing action, its decision-making or dispute-settlement bodies tend to be drawn from all such types of social structures, posts, and personnel. 8,12,13,14,15,16,App. B6,7.

6.2.14. In a pluralistic society organized in both kinship and age groups, a senior member of an age group may act as a third-party decision maker in disputes. 8,12,13,14,15.

6.2.15. In certain pluralistic societies, there were a variety of third-party decision-making bodies available to disputing parties for the purpose of indicating a solution of their conflict but not necessarily rendering a final, binding decision. There was, however, no appeal from a tribunal possessing supernatural support for its exercise of authority. 8,App. B7.

6.2.16. Action of a third-party decision-making body having a linkage with the supernatural world may sometimes be invoked by consent of the parties expressed in the form of an oath. 5,App. B1.

6.2.17. Action of a third-party decision-making body may sometimes be invoked by paying the judges a fee. Further payments of fees sometimes may be demanded until the close of a case. Such a mode of involving action is particularly evident in pluralistic societies. 7,9,10,12.

6.2.18. A third-party decision-making body, which was perceived to have no supernatural power but instead relied on temporal power and was composed of persons holding office who were accustomed to the receipt of tribute, exacted onerous fees for performing its function and accepted bribes. 10.

6.2.19. Certain pluralistic societies, with little development of a sanctioning process either of a supernatural or temporal character, relied upon mediation for dispute settlement. 14,16.

6.2.20. The successful performance of mediation as a dispute-settlement procedure requires a high degree of attachment by the members of the society to the value of peace and harmony in social relations, as well as a highly developed technique in the use of the mediation process. 13,14,16.

6.2.21. No mediation process can successfully take place unless it is performed in a social setting where the actors have a substantial consensus on norms for behavior and priorities of the values embodied in such norms, together with some form of social or supernatural pressure to move the disputing parties toward the acceptance of peace instead of conflict as a continuing social relationship. 14,16.

6.2.22. No mediation process can successfully take place unaffected by the perception of the participants of the degree of fault of each of the disputing parties. 14,16.

6.2.23. The individual acknowledgement of fault and the public perception of the likelihood of fault, even though not outwardly communicated, influenced acceptance of the outcome of a mediation process. 13,14,16.

6.2.24. Supernatural means, such as the use of the diviner, the ordeal, and the oath, are sometimes employed to determine the identity of norm violators. Supernatural means are also used to insure the giving of true testimony by witnesses. There is a tendency to use supernatural means for the above purposes in trials involving violations of structural norms. 8,9,10,11,12,13,15,App. B4,6.

6.2.25. Oracles and diviners may act as third-party decision-making agents in conflict situations involving the violation of valued norms in order to determine the identity of a person who has committed a wrong or an offense. 8,11,App. B3.

6.2.26. A supernatural decision-making and sanctioning process for offenses committed within a kinship group developed in the following sequence of events: (1) commission of the offense, (2) secret invocation by an elder of punishment of the offender by the ancestors, (3) experiencing of misfortune by the offender, (4) publication of the prior invocation by the elder before a diviner and validation of the act of invocation by the diviner, and (5) performance of a sacrifice, commensal meal and ritual of purification, and process of reintegration by the parties involved and their kinsmen. 11.

SANCTIONING PROCESS: RETRIBUTION

6.3.1. The process of the institutionalized application of deprivations upon violators of valued norms, which may be termed the sanctioning process, may be applied by temporal or spiritual actors or both. 4,5,6,7,8,9,11,12,14,15,App. B1,2,3,4,5,6,7.

6.3.2. The reliance of a society upon physical sanctions (e.g., beating or other infliction of pain, killing) to support authority and norm-observance is influenced by the degree to which the society exhibits the following elements, among others: (1) structures of social action other than kinship structures, (2) members who are perceived in other than kinship terms, (3) posts or offices not identified in kinship terms, (4) kinship structures displaying structural distance from offenders, and (5) war-making as a part of its culture. 4,5,6,7,8, 10,12,13,15,16,App. B1,2,6,7.

6.3.3. The extent of use and severity of physical sanctions in a society is influenced by (1) the degree to which it has moved away from primarily a kinship-structured society toward a pluralistic society, (2) the degree to which authority is vested in office, and (3) the degree to which it is a war-making society. 5,6,7,12,13,15,16,App. B1,6,7.

6.3.4. Societies which relied upon the application of physical sanctions tended to rely upon severe physical sanctions to support respect for and the exercise of authority. 5,App. B7.

6.3.5. When a society has a warrior group or a junior age group, they will tend to be relied upon to support the authority of third-party decision-making bodies and to apply physical sanctions. 8,12, 13,App. B6.

6.3.6. A regularized procedure of killing between kinships groups, which are structurally distant from one another, acts as a sanctioning process for such inter-group offenses as murder. 4,10,12,15,16.

6.3.7. Measures of self-help, including the blood feud, tend to be subject to procedural rules designed to limit the retribution or reparation which is exacted so that it is proportionate to the injury suffered. 12,16.

6.3.8. Measures of self-help directed to inflicting violence upon the group to which a wrongdoer belongs may be subject to procedural rules designed to control the weapons employed so that less dangerous weapons are used for less serious offenses. 16.

6.3.9. A pluralistic society, considerably organized on a segmentary basis, which had a relatively minor perception of ancestors performing a sanctioning process, believed in a supreme god performing a sanctioning process and resorted to self-help by the individual and the blood feud by the kinship group to sanction wrongs to the individual and inter-group killings, respectively. 16.

6.3.10. A pluralistic society organized in kinship, age, and territorial structures of social action developed a sanctioning process in which a group of males who were of the wife's lineage imposed physical sanctions upon her husband for violation of his marriage obligations and a group of males who were of the husband's lineage imposed physical sanctions upon third parties who aided the wife in the violation of her marriage obligations. 15.

6.3.11. The sanctioning process may take place through a belief in supernatural power punishing violators of valued norms. The principal agents for this purpose are the supreme god, the ancestor spirits, the earth, and witches. 4,5,8,9,10,11,12,13,15,App. B2,3,4,6.

6.3.12. The belief set forth in statement 6.3.11. sometimes takes the form of a belief in a supreme god sanctioning departures by a social group from valued norms and ancestral spirits sanctioning violations of valued norms by individuals. 11,12,13.

6.3.13. A pluralistic society, considerably reflecting a segmentary structuring of social action and relying upon self-help as a sanctioning process, developed a belief in a supreme god acting as a sanctioning agent, together with a minimal belief in ancestors acting as sanctioning agents. 16.

6.3.14. The same society developed a belief in the supernatural power of an individual to visit misfortune upon others through a supernatural sanctioning process the application of which was invoked by a ritual act in the form of a curse. 16.

6.3.15. A pluralistic society, organized in kinship, age, territorial, and, to a certain extent, organizational structures of social action, developed a belief in the ability of a community to invoke supernatural power to apply sanctions. 15.

6.3.16. The same society developed a ritual procedure of sacrifice of cattle and ensuing commensal meal of its meat to expiate wrongdoing and to avert supernatural sanctions therefor. 15.

6.3.17. The absence of an adequate sanctioning process in a society will conduce to the appearance of tension and hostility among its members to an unusual degree. 9,App. B4.

6.3.18. A kinship-structured society, in which there was no independently-functioning sanctioning process within the kinship group, either of a supernatural character (e.g., ancestral spirits) or a temporal character (e.g., authority able to impose physical sanctions), developed a belief in the practice of witchcraft to an extreme degree in interpersonal relations within the kinship group, including the infliction of deprivations through witchcraft brought about by a person in order to punish another for a wrong suffered at his hands. 9,App. B4.

6.3.19. Societies which relied upon the supernatural sanctioning process tended to rely upon curses to support the authority of a decision-making body and the ordeal to ascertain guilt and to insure the giving of true testimony by witnesses. 5,12,15,App. B6.

6.3.20. A pluralistic society, which had almost no sanctioning process for the violation of valued norms, believed supernatural power influenced community welfare. Ritual and physical sanctions were employed to punish failures to respect its dispute-settlement procedures and persistent violation of its important norms. App. B7.

6.3.21. A secret society, the members of which assumed masks or symbols of ancestral spirits, performed a sanctioning process for cases of adultery and witchcraft. Other secret societies operated to maintain law and social order. 8.

SANCTIONING PROCESS: REPARATION

6.4.1. The appearance of reparation in the form of compensation for wrong suffered is a product of the possession by a society of substantial, measurable units of wealth, such as livestock. 12,13,16, App. B6.

6.4.2. The reparation of injuries through compensation may develop to the point that tables of compensation are employed, which take account of the nature of the injury and degree of fault involved. 12,16,App. B6.

6.4.3. War, as a sanctioning process for inter-group offenses, may sometimes be terminated by the payment of compensation by the group responsible for the injury. 8,12.

REINTEGRATION PROCESS

6.5.1. The reintegration process refers to the sequence of acts symbolizing the restoration of harmony between disputing parties and the groups of which they are members. It takes place in a variety of forms, ranging from a token sharing of food to a highly developed ritual. 7,12,14,16,App. B3,4,5.

6.5.2. In societies in which amicable interpersonal relations are valued highly, the sanctioning process of exacting compensation for wrongdoing is coupled with the wrongdoer paying compensation in the form of animals consumed as meat in a commensal meal in which the injured party and the wrongdoer join, together with their supporters. Ritual purification will usually follow such a meal. 11,12, 14, 16,App. B4.

6.5.3. Periodic rituals and ceremonies emphasizing in symbolic form the value of harmony in the social group increase attachment to that value and tend to reduce constitutive conflict. They also serve to reestablish stability after the termination of a conflict situation. 4,14,16,App. A.

LAND LAW
BASIC ASSUMPTIONS

A. Land law consists of legal norms relating to the use of land. These deal with situations involving the organic relationship of a social group and its members to the land for sustenance and gain. The most important social group for this purpose is the family. Land law delineates rights of access to land, rights to the use of land, rights for the transfer or pledge of land, and rights to the inheritance of land. The interests in land which land law defines are protected from interference with their enjoyment by legal norms.

B. Disputes concerning land arise as a consequence of its scarcity, which is a product of density of settlement or the labor involved in reclaiming land from its virgin state and placing it in condition for economic use.

GENERAL RULES

6.6.1. The exclusive right to use land for an indefinite period is acquired by (1) placing open, unclaimed land in a cultivable condition and using it or (2) grant of the right to use land from a person or group authorized to do so. Such a right is subject to inheritance. 5,7,8,13,14,15,16,App. B6.

6.6.2. When a person clears or reclaims land from its virgin state, he enjoys a preferred position in his right to use it. 7,8.

6.6.3. The ultimate ownership or control of land and the power to allocate the use of land inheres in a social group. 4,5,7,8,9,10,12, 13,15,16,App. B1,2,3,4,6,7.

6.6.4. A certain post of authority in a social group controls the allocation and use of land. This tends to be an office in a territorial structure of social action and the head of a kinship group for lineage land. Each such post has its particular sphere of competence. Abandoned land reverts to the social group for re-allocation. The head of the social group can either grant, or exercise or veto over the grant by others, of the right to use land to strangers. 7,8,9,10,11,15,App. B2,3,4,6,7.

6.6.5. Membership in a social group by a man implies the right to use of such land as he needs. 4,5,7,8,9,10,12,15,16,App. B1,2,4,6,7.

6.6.6. A right to use land for an indefinite period can usually be acquired by a stranger only through acquiring membership in the social group which has the power to grant such right. 7,9,10,15,16, App. B2,4,7.

6.6.7. The relationship of the extended or polygynous family to the land which it has received from its ancestors and which it will pass on to its succeeding generations is unique in the effectiveness of use of such land for gratifying personal needs, providing security against drought and adversity, and in the norm that it is not to be alienated. 4,5,9,10,12,13,15,16,App. B1,6,7.

6.6.8. Succession to the use of land remains within the family by descent, usually to the sons and otherwise to the brothers of its holder. In a polygynous family, land allotted to wives will tend to remain theirs after death of their husband. 12,13,15,16,App. B4,6,7.

6.6.9. The alienation of land is usually not possible under the rules of land law but the transfer, pledge, mortgage, or lease of it to another under limited, specified conditions is sometimes possible in varying degree. 5,8,9,13,App. B6,7.

6.6.10. Security of tenure in land is subject to the principle of effective use, that is, a person or social group holding an exclusive right to use land retains that right only so long as the land is used or, at least, not abandoned. When land ceases to be used or is abandoned, it reverts to the social group controlling its use for re-allotment. 7,8,9,10,13,App. B1,2,3,4,6,7.

6.6.11. A system of land law under community control allocated land on the basis of land devoted to community or public needs, land available for grant for private use, and land for use by lineage groups. Land in the last category was held subject to limited public rights, such as the right to hunt, to collect firewood, and to pass over it for access to water. 7,13.

6.6.12. The authority structure of a kingdom may be reinforced by a power in the king to exclude a lawful holder of land from its continued use. While such power could, upon occasion, be exercised arbitrarily, its proper exercise was deemed to be limited to situations where the holder had failed to perform obligations owed the state. 10,App. B3.

Rules when Land Supply is Plentiful

6.6.13. Each resident of the community is entitled to have a home site, land for tilling and other types of use, and use of public or community land. 8,13,15,App. B6, 7.

6.6.14. The transferability of land and admission to the social group is relatively easy of accomplishment. 8,15,App. B6.

6.6.15. In a pastoral society, the ultimate ownership or authority to control or grant the right of use of land is considered to be in the people as a whole or in a territorial structure of social action. 13,15.

6.6.16. The interest of a community in retaining a land holder as a member thereof extended to the point that he could prevent the re-allotment of his land by the village after he had ceased to use it or even after he had left the village. 15.

RULES WHEN LAND SUPPLY IS LIMITED

6.6.17. The social group controlling the use of land acquires increased power to insure the effectiveness of its use. 7,App. B2.

6.6.18. A formal procedure may develop to evidence an intent by a holder of land that it is not to be deemed abandoned by virtue of its non-use. Unless such procedure is followed, non-use will cause land to be available for re-allotment to persons other than the last person to use it. App. B2.

6.6.19. Interests of different types of use in the same land are recognized and land may be held subject to performance of obligations owed to public authorities, such as the king or a chief. 7,10, App. B2.

6.6.20. As density of settlement increases, the amount of land subject to the disposition of the social group diminishes, and the amount of land under individual use and control by small lineage groups increases, together with the power to transfer its use to others, although the consent of the social group to a transfer to a stranger may be necessary. 8,9.

6.6.21. When density of land settlement reaches the point of a tightly-knit, urban community, the individuation of land control may lead to the right to alienate land without community consent. 7.

6.6.22. Rules insure the right of an individual to the use of his land in accordance with his needs. The rules of succession to land are framed to this end. 8,9.

6.6.23. As interests in and users of land multiply, rules render more precise the rights, duties, and privileges involved in such interests and users. 7.

6.6.24. Leases, and particularly short-term leases, are employed to promote land use without loss of the underlying right to use such land. 8.

6.6.25. Land is held for public use, such as sacred groves, meeting places, roads, and paths. 12.

6.6.26. The community has the power to acquire land for public use. 8.

6.6.27. A special land tribunal or a post concerned with the settlement of land use disputes may exist. 8,12.

6.6.28. Specific land areas are devoted to particular types of economic use, such as house land, farm land, grazing land, and outlying land. 8,13.

6.6.29. A stranger may acquire a right to use land by establishing his residence in the community and assimilation into some kinship group. 7,8,9.

6.6.30. Consent of the community is required when land is allotted to a stranger. 5,8.

6.6.31. A pledge of land may upon occasion be transformed into a right to use. 8.

6.6.32. The sanction which a family may apply when it is denied needed land by the community is that of leaving the community. 9.

6.6.33. A society developed a process of acquiring land through war conducted by the particular kinship group which was short of land against another structurally distant kinship group or a group which had no kinship ties but which were spatially near to the kinship group in need of land. 9.

RULES OF A PASTORAL, CATTLE-KEEPING SOCIETY

6.6.34. Except for land in cultivation, land is used and classified into different categories of use so as to promote opportunity for grazing to the utmost extent. 13,15,App. B6,7.

6.6.35. The ultimate ownership and authority to control or grant the right of use of land is considered to lie in the people as a whole or in a territorial structure of action. 13,15.

6.6.36. A man could acquire the right to use for an indefinite period the land next to his dwelling, provided that he cultivated the land and continued so to employ it. 13.

6.6.37. The sale of land was not possible. 13,App. B7.

RULES OF A KINGDOM WITH A BUREAUCRATIC STRUCTURE OF CHIEFS AND OFFICIALS

6.6.38. Land was granted by the holders of offices and was held by the tenants subject to the condition that they supply goods and services to the king and other office holders. 10,App. B2,3.

6.6.39. Land was held as an incident of the holding of office and for the benefit of the incumbent, with no right to the benefits flowing from its control when he ceased to occupy his office. 5,10.

6.6.40. Ordinarily a person using land had the right to continue to use it until he abandoned it. 10.

6.6.41. When the use of land was granted by the holder of an office, any holder of such office had the power to terminate the right to use such land, but this was held to be properly exercised only as a sanction for the non-performance of duties owed the office holder and not to be exercised against tenants who had a long period of tenure and were still using the land. 10,App. B3.

Chapter 18

Modern Implications

1. KINSHIP structures of social action and territorial structures of social action at the village level represent a framework for living in which man can effectively realize the values of intimate, high-frequency interactions with others. It is believed that there is a need in modern society for the provision of the opportunity to realize the values incident to neighborliness. It is believed that modern man needs the support and encouragement of others close to him, such as kin and neighbors, in his confrontation with the extreme psychological pressures of modern society.

2. Tribal society insisted upon the value of harmony in interpersonal relations in kinship groups. It held that it was more important to settle disputes than it was to vindicate rights. On the other hand, modern society has become increasingly centered upon the maintenance of rights and increasingly less concerned with the performance of obligations. Assuredly there is a need for a better balance or ranking in the priority of these values in modern society. There is a need in both national and international society for the value of harmony to supplement the value of insistence upon rights.

3. As tribal man today moves into the world of the nation-state and the industrial corporation, his culture fails to provide him with the learning to perceive the nature of that world and a value system which would enable him to adapt to it successfully. Similarly, as modern man of the nation-state and the industrial corporation moves into the world society of today, his culture fails to provide him with the learning to perceive the nature of that world and with a value system which would enable him to adapt to it successfully.

As a consequence of the foregoing trends, modern man is turning to a world of symbolism, just as tribal man turned to a symbolic supernatural world, to help him to understand his temporal world and overcome the problems which it presents. This is not, however, the symbolism of religion. Synthetic symbols of political leaders are created by the arts of mass communication employing the media of mass communication. The creation and use of political symbols supplant the rigors of intellectually grasping, on an empirical basis, the nature of the world with which modern man is confronted, perceiving the nature of the problems which it creates, and reaching solutions for those problems. The aggressive impulses which the frustrations of the day bring to modern man are vented symbolically in the drama of the stage, movies, and television. Literature becomes a literature of fantasy and a realization in the world of imagination of the values of release of tension in violence and sex which have become so central to modern man. Even his wars become means for the attainment of symbolic goals. He fights wars under the illusion that he thereby brings an end to all wars or to all aggression. The resources which he employs to preparing for war and waging war would go far toward eliminating the causes of war and enhancing the opportunity to live the good life.

4. One problem which tribal man faces in molding his framework for living into one which will be viable in the modern world is his value attachment to small kinship and territorial groups, notably his family and his village, and his lack of attachment to large groups with whose members he has little personal contact. It will be necessary to increase radically the priority of his value attachment to such modern structures of social action as the state and the industrial corporation. The African state is composed of diverse peoples and tribes. The larger the territory which it embraces, the greater will be the difficulty of creating a viable state because of the greater number of such peoples and tribes. The political solution of adopting a federal union is not likely to be effective because it only symbolically solves the problem. It merely holds up the goal of political unity without demonstrating the value importance of that goal in concrete ways in the lives of individuals. The most effective way of creating value attachment to the African state by its citizens is to follow the development strategy of promoting growth at the village level, as set forth in statement 10 below.

5. Notwithstanding the political difficulties of maintaining effective control as the territory of an African state expands, as set forth in statement 4 above, there is a built-in propensity to expand and to

resort to war for this purpose. This lies in the distribution of peoples and tribes within the territorial boundaries of today's African states. These are a product of the happenstances of history and imperial, colonial rivalries and many times do not accomodate the territorial location of such groups. When the members of a new African state perceive that members of one of the tribes in their territory are found in the territory of another African state, they will be regarded as political captives to be given their freedom under the citizenship and control of the new state in question. Each of the two states in question will adopt the same perspective of the situation. War will likely ensue as a means of solving the resulting conflict situation.

6. Tribal man's inability to perceive an individual as intrinsically possessing dignity and worth and entitled to respect, except when he is a member of the same kinship or other group to which there is a strong common attachment, must be supplanted by the perception of members of the modern nation-state that the individual in that context, at least, possesses such dignity and worth and is entitled to respect.

7. It is similarly true that no viable structure of social action embracing all the peoples of the world and no final solution for the problem of war can be reached until all such peoples share the perception of the dignity and worth of the individual and his personal right to respect.

8. The concept of the role which was so useful in clarifying the interrelationships of social behavior and law in this study would be most useful in bringing the rules of modern law closer to the needs of technological, industrial, organizational society. As the specificity of tasks has increased in modern societies, so has its role relationships. Many of such role relationships are embodied in vast corporate organizations which are in turn engaged in role performance which was formerly that of the individual entrepreneur, such as the provision of goods and such services as transportation and communication. Modern law often focuses upon issues of individual responsibility for deviant role performance and ignores the fact that such performance takes place in an organizational structure of social action. By insistence upon perspectives of action and norm creation in individualistic terms, such as negligence and fault, it ignores the fact the organizational performance of social roles must equally conform to standards and norms resulting in effective performance of function. Liability in such cases should be determined on the basis of whether there has been a departure by the organization itself from socially requisite standards of behavior in the performance of

its role. Moreover, such generalized, abstract legal standards of performance as reasonableness, due care, and fiduciary obligation should be rendered more precise by factual analysis and norm-definition and norm-application in terms of role performance.[1]

9. Another problem facing tribal man today is the complex of values, attitudes, perceptions, and tensions which is centered in his preference for the value which has been termed egalitarianism in the above pages. It is believed that this value is a combination of the positive and negative values of conformity, envy, fear, and resentment. It is also a manifestation of both direct and displaced aggression against the rich, the powerful, and those who surpass their neighbors in achievement. It is a product of the close interpersonal relationships of village life. The demand which it embodies that all shall conform to a common denominator of work and achieving the economic rewards of work must be eliminated and supplanted by the values of an achieving society if the African state is to possess the culture of modern, technological, industrial society.

10. The value of egalitarianism discussed in statement 9 above is but one consequence of village life which is for tribal man his most significant structure of social action beyond his family. The creation of a viable African state demands that the nature of village life must be transformed. Given a scarcity of resources available to such a state, both in terms of its own resources and those extended to it by international aid, the strategy of development should emphasize development at the village level on a broad front. The progress which such an approach would yield, in terms of value realization and growth in individual personality of the members of the state, would make the state a much better framework for living than emphasis on industrial and military development. Unfortunately, the latter approach seems to be the one which is more appealing to the centers of political power and, accordingly, to the political leaders of the emerging African states. Yet a government which vigorously pursued a policy of village development would establish a strong, enduring political base. Such a policy would be the most significant step which could be taken to create a sense of identification with and attachment to the state, which is the very foundation of nationality and the nation-state. It may also be observed, in this connection, that the concept of pacification at the village level, including village development, represents the only realistic, enduring solution of the problem of civil or constitutive conflict in Viet Nam.

---

1. See K. S. Carlston, "Psychological and Sociological Aspects of the Judicial and Arbitration Processes," *International Arbitration: Liber Amicorum for Martin Domke,* ed. P. Sanders (The Hague, 1967), 44.

11. The persistence of the cultural perception of tribal man that war is an ordinary, necessary, and desirable form of intergroup relationships and mode of attaining goals will tend to create a way of war instead of a way of peace among the new African states. This propensity to war will be strengthened by tribal man's perception of the nature of the individual noted in statement 6 and his attachment to the goal and value described in statement 5 above.

12. The first of the basic assumptions, with which the statement of findings concerning structures of social action was approached (page 389 above), was that the members of such structures must possess a common experience in a common culture and must perceive and accept the structure as an appropriate means for goal attainment, value realization, and control of conflict. It is believed that this assumption is also valid in its application to the creation of structures of social action in world society. One consequence of this fact is that the growth of a stable world order and of law for that order will be more rapidly and effectively attained by greater emphasis on international regional cooperation and development. The development of international river basins on the model of the Tennessee Valley Authority in the United States, common markets, and regional planning for economic development are some of the modes of such development.

13. It was noted in statement 6.1.19. of Chapter 17 above that, where there is a minimal development of a sanctioning process to support legal norms, a mediation process may appear and develop to great refinement. The possibilities of the mediation process in the settlement of international disputes should be vigorously pursued.

Appendix A

A brilliant description of constitutive conflict was made by V. W. Turner in his concept of the "social drama," as exemplified in the Ndembu of Northern Rhodesia.[1]

The Ndembu were highly mobile. Fission of groups from established villages frequently took place, as well as movement of individuals among villages. The ancestor cult among the Ndembu was "associated with the bush, its dangers and blessings, with the transcience of settlement, with the hazards of life, and with the mobile human group itself rather than its specific habitation." Ndembu ritual emphasized links of likeness and temporary association of a non-lineage character. There was often a high degree of tension in the village and resulting cleavage created "a completely new unit," which soon had left only "a vague sense of common maternal descent" with the parent village.

The Ndembu were a hunting people, as well as tillers of the land. This fact, and the necessity of protection from slave raiders, led to a pattern of settlement in villages, which were more often small than large. The men of a village were united by blood ties of common matrilineal descent, while their wives came from different localities and kinship groups. Marriage, in other words, was virilocal. The possession of common kinship supported cooperation among the men.

Nevertheless, men needed women for their personal and corporate survival. The individual man owed his care and nurture to a woman, his own mother. Similarly, the group of male villagers needed their sisters to ensure the survival of their village as a social entity. To bring them back into the village entailed the male group's coming into conflict with

1. V. W. Turner, *Schism and Continuity in African Society* (Manchester, England, 1957), 173-175, 76-77, 79, 237-238, 95, 116, 138, 148, 157, 178, 122-126, 290, 303, 91-92, 161-162, 328, 330-331.

other men. So that the very exclusion of female kin from villages in order that male kin might live together provided the principal source of conflict and unrest among Ndembu men as a whole.

There was a built-in tendency to tension and resultant fission within the village when the third generation after its founding was reached.

When a village contains only two generations of hut-owners it may be regarded as a bilateral extended family. But when three generations of adult hut-owners form its members, incipient cleavage along lineage lines becomes detectable. If a headman has two fertile sisters each has become the founder of a lineage. The principle of the unity of the matricentric family comes into conflict with the unity of the matri-lineage, and each matricentric family or *alliance of matricentric families with a common grandmother* is a potential source of village cleavage and the potential starting-point of a new residential unit. . . . It may be that the original sibling-group which founded the group has been reduced in numbers by death. *In any case its authority is continually threatened within the village by the maturation of the junior adjacent generation, the leading men of which are eager to obtain the headmanship.* (Italics supplied.)

The total pattern of composition of a village was described as follows:

The Ndembu village, then, in its social composition represents at once a veiled struggle between the two powerful principles of *familial* and *lineal* organization, and an attempt to reconcile these by a set of compromise formations between their modes of social control. In the course of the struggle these principles mutually inhibit one another, so that lineages remain shallow and extended families break up or lose their membership through the pull of matrilineal affiliation. The struggle is itself a manifestation of the deeper opposition between male and female in Ndembu society. Each village represents an attempt to estab-lish a patriarchal settlement in the teeth of basic matrilineal descent. But the male kin who reside together with their wives and families are themselves interrelated by matrilineal ties which persist, while ties with their children which interlink them in co-residence are more tenuous and friable, snapping with the divorce of their wives, with the marriage of their daughters, and with the frequent defection of sons to their own matrilineal kin on attaining maturity. On a village genealogy the line of descent, the spine of village continuity, is through women whose brothers are marginal to it. But in any given village at any specific point of time the line is broken or in rare cases even invisible. For the resi-dential core of a village consists of men linked to one another through women, most of whom may be absent at any one time, or who are already dead. In the course of events, however, nearly every village contains some female members of its nuclear matrilineage, who have returned to it after divorce or widowhood, or reside there in cross-cousin or grandparent-grandchild marriage, or whose husbands live uxorilocally. These women betray by their presence the fundamentally matrilineal character of the local unit.

Such a society may be said to be prone to tension and conflict and, indeed, conflict frequently occurred. Yet this was a special type of conflict. A breach of some valued social norm often led to constitutive conflict. It expanded throughout the village and brought into the open a latent tendency to conflict among different lineages. Such conflict was concerned with the fundamental question of how the group should constitute itself over time. It concerned the principles and values which its social order should reflect. Six conflict situations generally falling into this pattern, which Turner termed "social dramas," were described.

SOCIAL DRAMA I. Sandombu killed an animal and failed to give to the headman of his village, who also happened to be Sandombu's uncle, the share of the animal that was the headman's due by custom. A bitter dispute between the two ensued in which Sandombu uttered some words which could be understood to mean that he was going to invoke sorcery against his uncle. A few days later the uncle fell ill and died.

Sandombu was denied succession to the headmanship in favor of a certain Mukanza. The reason for this was professed by the village members to be that he caused the death of the previous headman by sorcery. Turner reported that the more important and underlying reason for his failure to succeed to the post arose from the fact that his appointment would violate certain fundamental norms and values of the village.

SOCIAL DRAMA II. Sandombu beat his wife without, it was felt by many villagers, justification. When others intervened, he reacted with anger and reviled all those who were present. The next day his mother suddenly died, and he was expelled from the village for having caused her death by sorcery. After a year, he was allowed to return in penitence and perform ritual purification when a divination revealed that another had caused her death. The breach of the norm against wife beating which initiated the conflict quickly expanded to entail the issue of succession to headmanship and interlineage rivalry, with the final result that Sandombu was formally denied the office of headman.

SOCIAL DRAMA III. A public calamity consisting of an epidemic of malaria struck a village. This touched off a search for the cause, which was held to fall in one of two categories, either certain members of the group were sorcerers possessing and exercising evil powers against other kin or the group was being punished by ancestor spirits for having neglected them or violated norms of kinship. The final outcome was the common acceptance of the explanation that a certain ancestor spirit was the cause of the misfortune because his relatives had neglected to care for him properly in his lifetime. If proper care were now given such ancestors, the headman of the group, Mukanza, who was ill, would become well and further misfortune would be averted. Before such a solution was finally adopted, however, the blame for the illness was tentatively placed on one Kasonda, in considerable measure because his guilt would serve the interest of a certain lineage which was in conflict with another. Kasonda, in turn, responded by shifting the responsibility to a wronged ancestor. This idea was generally accepted, thereby promoting village solidarity and preventing further cleavage of the two conflicting lineages.

SOCIAL DRAMA IV. A young bride died, and the death was attributed to the witchcraft of an old woman. Belief in her sorcery arose because she was partly of foreign origin and had conducted herself in certain ways opposed to the standards of the community. Sandombu, who was trying to build up a following of dependents with a view to an eventual headmanship, invited her to live on his farm. She did this and brought her daughter and her daughter's child with her, thereby increasing the matrilineal side of his group, a matter which was important in the event of future cleavage.

SOCIAL DRAMA V. At a celebration, Sandombu's wife, who was a daughter of Mukanza, the headman, accused him of giving away beer to ingratiate himself with people so that he could become headman, instead of buying needed cloth for clothes. He tried to beat her, but she ran off to her father's home. Sandombu went to Mukanza's hut to reclaim his wife. Mukanza had been told by his daughter, in the meantime, that Sandombu had been boasting that he was in fact senior in position to Mukanza. Mukanza commanded Sandombu to take back his wife, but Sandombu refused and charged both his wife and her mother, Mukanza's wife, with witchcraft. The next day Sandombu took back his wife but was told to appear before the village to explain his conduct. A representative spokesman said that the matter should be kept within the village and should not spread farther. He told Sandombu that he should make redress first to his wife, in the form of giving her some new cloth, and second to her mother, in the form of a cash payment. Sandombu refused. Later he

was successful in certain slander litigation and used some of the recovery to perform the indicated redress. Sandombu's success in the
litigation, which affected the interlineage rivalry present in the
village, enhanced his esteem in the village, and his final making of
the indicated redress restored momentary stability in the village. It
should be noted that Sandombu's enhanced position in the village
was in large part a product of the then current status of the conflicting lineages and the rising importance of one of them.

SOCIAL DRAMA VI. This episode occurred considerably prior to the
time of the above and involved a period of several years in which
fission of the village took place. The village was then full of tension,
and constant bickering occurred. There was no recognized headman,
and there were a number of contestants for this post, with their
respective followings. When the conflict had the outcome of a certain
Kahali establishing his headmanship, two leading contestants and a
considerable part of their followers left the village and established
their own settlements elsewhere. One of these groups was composed
of distant matrilineal relatives of the Mukanza group while the other
occupied the status of slaves, which status the British authorities
were attempting to outlaw. In other words, both groups were considerably alien to the established constituency of the village. Nevertheless, one of the seceding groups thereafter established friendly
relations with the parent village.

The first comment to be made upon the above episodes is to note
the fact that the higher degree of tension and conflict among the
Ndembu, as compared with the Tallensi, was accompanied by a
much higher degree of utilization of witchcraft in the social system.
There may be some degree of correlation between the two phenomena when conflict and tension in primitive society are not re-
lieved by other processes of social control.

Turner raised the fundamental question of what aspects of the
above disputes were appropriate to settlement by jural or legal
mechanisms and what were appropriate to ritual settlement. His
discussion of this question utilized Social Drama II by way of illustration. It is valuable in clarifying the meaning of that which is legal,
as distinguished from that which is political. It is accordingly quoted
in some detail:

> Is there any way in which we may distinguish between the implicit
> aims and functions of these different modes of redressing and adjusting
> conflict—jural and ritual? It would seem, at the present stage of anthro-
> pological enquiry, that *jural machinery is employed when conflict be-*
> *tween persons and groups is couched in terms of an appeal by both*

contesting parties to a common norm, or, when norms conflict, to a common frame of values which organize a society's norms into a hierarchy. Thus, when Sandombu spoke angrily to his relatives, they all accepted a common norm governing social intercourse—namely, that no person should curse another by raising a powerful ghost. In other words, human beings who were members of a single society had an interest in one another's welfare and should not wish one another dead. In Ndembu society the wish is thought often to be father to the deed; in fact, when it is publicly expressed, it is stated by custom to have the mystical power to do the deed. Thus, Sandombu argued that he had not cursed but had only reviled, while his relatives held that he had not reviled but had cursed. Both sought to justify their actions in terms of the common norm that cursing is anti-social and immoral. The corresponding jural situation where two norms come into conflict but are hierarchically organized is exemplified in the history of Sandombu's marriage. Although Sandombu treated Zuliyana abominably in Ndembu eyes, beating her without cause, no divorce action was undertaken by her relatives. A norm of Ndembu society is that relatives should protect a married woman from an unjust husband. But the unjust treatment must continue for a long time and be exceptionally severe before they intervene to end the marriage. The norm that marriages should remain unbroken supervenes over the norm that relatives may at times offer sanctuary to an ill-treated wife. In this case Sandombu's beating of Zuliyana did not bring jural mechanisms into action although it might well have done so if Zuliyana had refused to go on living with her husband. (Italics supplied.)

On the other hand, ritual mechanisms are invoked when it is felt that the fundamental norms of society themselves are threatened or challenged, not by a single individual but by the social group which operates by means of adherence to them. It is not that persons or groups phrase their disagreements in terms of a common norm to which all parties basically conform, but that hostility comes to be felt by all concerned against the constraints imposed by the norms themselves. *Rebellion develops against the very way the social system is ordered,* and a challenge is made to the established moral order, with its norms and their evaluative framework. I venture to suggest that every time a norm is broken by one individual, a temptation is experienced by every other individual in the group to do likewise. Breaches represent constant temptations to the members of the group to rebel against norms critically connected with the unity and persistence of the group. These tendencies to come into conflict with the norms must be purged of their socially disruptive quality if the group is to remain integrated. Ritual is the social mechanism by which a group is purged of the anarchic and disruptive impulses which threatened its crucial norms and values. These impulses are present in the majority of its members and come dangerously near to overt expression if there has been a long series of quarrels between its members. (Italics supplied.)

But this temptation to rebel and even revolt, may also be fed by constant disputes between individuals and factions, *which in fact manifest deeper conflicts between different social processes.* . . . (Italics supplied.)

On this view of society, norms and their supporting values can only *appear* to be consistent, since they must cover the presence of contradictions within the structure itself. The contrary processes are likely each to be stated in norms. Hence situations must arise where the norms which determine the course of action to be taken cannot be clearly and consciously affirmed for the acceptance of all parties, since each can claim some support from customary values. It is here that intrigue may become rife and disruptive. In Ndembu society, based as it is on close interpersonal ties, it is also at this stage that ill-feeling becomes charged with the malevolent, mystical power of witchcraft and sorcery. Ill-feeling is not merely immoral: it is charged with the danger of disease, death and other misfortunes to one's fellows.

Here judicial decision can condemn one or more of the disputants, but it cannot always relieve the quarrels so as to preserve the threatened relationship. . . .

Hence, it seems to me, after a major crisis produced by these conflicts of process, rituals are employed to affirm that reconciliation has been achieved. These rituals may even be employed after a judicial decision appears to have settled rights and wrongs, when in fact the cause of dispute is beyond settlement. And finally, when all attempts to preserve existing relationships have failed, final breaches, often provoked by witchcraft charges, are confirmed by rituals which restate the norms as consistent and enduring, even though new relationships have been established. *Those who disputed bitterly for headmanship within a village, may become helpful relatives when they reside in two different villages which appear to conform to the Ndembu ideal.* (Italics supplied.)

Turner suggests that:

Judicial mechanisms tend to be invoked to redress conflict, where the conflict is overt, and these judicial mechanisms involve rational investigation into the motives and behaviour of the contending parties. Ritual mechanisms tend to be utilized where conflict is at a deeper level.

But conflict was at a "deeper level," not because it involved the spiritual world as such, but rather because it involved the spiritual world as a symbol for and means of control of deep-seated and widespread conflict within a society concerning its structure as an embodiment and expression of its basic values.

Ritual in Ndembu society was concerned with the affirmation and preservation of its basic values and institutions. Turner stated in this connection:

Most Ndembu rituals tacitly recognize the instability of villages and of the relations between villages, but posit the ultimate unity of all Ndembu in a single moral community. The instability of kinship and political relations is recognized in the fact that the dominant social element in the composition of ritual assemblies is not a kinship group but an association of adepts who belong to many kinship groups. Also, the dominant symbols in the cluster of symbolic objects and activities associated with each ritual do not reflect or express major aspects of the social structure, but rather the values which all Ndembu possess in common, such as, for example, the fertility of women, crops and animals, huntsmanship, health, and the power of the ancestors to bestow or withhold such benefits. The ultimate unity of all Ndembu is expressed in the composition of ritual assemblies.

He later added:

Thus the *unity* of all Ndembu is only perceived in situations arising out of the *breach* of *specific* relations, usually couched in terms of kinship. A society continually threatened with disintegration is continually performing reintegrative ritual. Ritual among Ndembu does not express the kinship and political structure as in a firmly organized society; rather it compensates for their deficiencies in a labile society.

It is now possible to state the elements or "processional form" of Turner's "social drama." He said:

After a while I began to detect a pattern in these eruptions of conflict: I noticed phases in their development which seemed to follow one another in a more or less regular sequence. These eruptions, which I call "social dramas," have "processional form." I have provisionally divided the social process which constitutes the social drama into four major phases:

(1) Breach of regular norm-governed social relations occurs between persons or groups within the same system of social relations. Such a breach is signalized by the public breach or non-fulfillment of some crucial norm regulating the intercourse of the parties.

(2) Following breach of regular social relations, a phase of mounting crisis supervenes, during which, unless the conflict can be sealed off quickly within a limited area of social interaction, there is a tendency for the breach to widen and extend until it becomes co-extensive with some dominant cleavage in the widest set of relevant social relations to which the conflicting parties belong. The phase of crisis exposes the pattern of current factional struggle within the relevant social group, be it village, neighborhood or chiefdom; and beneath it there becomes visible the less plastic, more durable, but nevertheless gradually changing basic social structure, made up of relations which are constant and consistent.

(3) In order to limit the spread of breach certain adjustive and redressive mechanisms, informal or formal, are speedily brought into operation by leading members of the relevant social groups. These mechanisms vary in character with such factors as the depth and social significance of the breach, the social inclusiveness of the crisis, the nature of the social group within which the breach took place and the degree of its autonomy with reference to wider systems of social relations. They may range from personal advice and informal arbitration, to formal juridical and legal machinery, and, to resolve certain kinds of crisis, to the performance of public ritual.

(4) The final phase I have distinguished consists either in the reintegration of the disturbed social group or in the social recognition of irreparable breach between the contesting parties.

In short, the *processional form* of the social drama may be formulated as (1) breach; (2) crisis; (3) redressive action; (4) re-integration or recognition of schism. . . . Implicit in the notion of reintegration is the concept of social equilibrium. This concept involves the view that a social system is made up of interrelated units, of persons and groups, whose interests are somehow maintained in balance; and further, that when disturbance occurs, readjustments are made which have the effect of restoring the balance. But it is necessary to remember that after disturbance has occurred and readjustments have been made, there may have taken place profound modifications in the internal relations of the group. The new equilibrium is seldom a replica of the old. The interests of certain persons and groups may have gained at the expense of those of others. Certain relations between persons and groups have increased in intensity while others may have diminished. Others again may have been completely ruptured while new relationships have come into being. A social system is in dynamic movement through space and time, in some way analogous to an organic system in that it exhibits growth and decay, in fact the process of metabolism. In one aspect, the social drama is a process which reveals realignments of social relations at critical points of structural maturation or decay; in another, it may be regarded as a trial of strength between conflicting interest in which persons or groups try to manipulate to their own advantage the actually existing network of social relations, both structural and contingent, within the system. Thus the social drama may represent either the natural, inherent development of a given social system through space-time at a distinct phase, at a critical point of maturation, or the deliberate attempts by some of its members to accelerate or retard that development. It may be either an index or a vehicle of change. In most cases both aspects are present.

Turner summarized his study in part as follows:

My spatial unit of study has been the village, my unit of time the social drama. I have tried to marry the general to the particular by analyzing a series of social dramas in the history of a single village. That village's membership was organized by the structural principles isolated during the synchronic study of a number of villages. But these principles were there interrelated in a unique way. In the social dramas I have tried to show how in specific situations certain principles came into conflict, and how attempts were made to maintain the unity of the disturbed group despite such conflict. Three main types of conflict became visible in the course of the social dramas: (1) conflict between principles of organization, receiving behavioural expression as choice between conflicting loyalties; (2) conflict between individuals or cliques for power, prestige or wealth; and (3) conflict within individual psyches between selfish and social drives. . . . In ritual the ideal unity of the disturbed social unit in question is counterpoised against its real internal divisions, which arise from situationally incompatible rules of custom. Ritual sometimes restores the unity of a village torn by structural cleavages . . . but if schism is irremediable ritual *restates in what are usually emotionally charged circumstances the highest common values of Ndembu society.* (Italics supplied.)

Ritual and fission, among the Ndembu, appeared to be the means for dealing with situations in which three different kinds of conflict converge. The first is interpersonal conflict concerning the application of norms. The second is the conflict of politics concerning the person who shall be headman and the groups which shall be influential in determining the direction of the affairs of the society. The third is constitutive conflict concerning the very bases upon which the society shall constitute itself for the indefinite future, that is, the nature of the order which it shall assume and the basic values which it shall reflect.

Appendix B

1. The Gã.

A people settled in towns in the coastal region of Ghana. They pursued trading, farming, and fishing. There were a number of groups organized to perform the functions of music, dance, and fishing, as well as war. There were numerous courts. Offenses were subject to sanctions, if they affected important interests or if their adjudication took place before an important court. Many injuries escaped the imposition of sanctions. Responsibility for offenses tended to lie in the family of the offending person. M. J. Field, *Religion and Medicine of the Gã People* (London, 1937, 1961); M. J. Field, *Social Organization of the Gã People* (London, 1940); M. Manoukian, "Akan and Ga Adangme Peoples of the Gold Coast," Ethnographic Survey of Africa, Western Africa, ed. D. Forde (London, 1950) Part I, 66-104; A. B. Quartey Papofio, "The Native Tribunals of the Akras of the Gold Coast," *Journal of the African Society*, X (1911), 320, 434, XI (1911), 75.

2. The Soga.

The Soga are located in Uganda, northeast of Lake Victoria and east of the Nile River, with Lake Kyoga on the north. They were an agricultural society, socially structured in kinship groups and politically structured into states headed by kings who governed with a hierarchical authority structure. The mechanism of king, princes, chiefs, and village headmen carried out military, tax-gathering, and judicial functions. D. E. Apter, *The Political Kingdom in Uganda* (Princeton, 1961); L. A. Fallers, *Bantu Bureaucracy* (Cambridge, 1956); A. L. Fallers [sic], "The Politics of Landholding in Busoga," *Economic Development and Cultural Change*, III (1955) 260; L. A.

436   Social Theory and African Tribal Organization

Fallers, "Changing Customary Law in Busoga District of Uganda," *Journal of African Administration*, VIII (1956), 139; M. C. Fallers, "The Eastern Lacustrine Bantu (Ganda, Soga)," *Ethnographic Survey of Africa*, ed. D. Forde (London, 1940), Part XI, 40.

3. The Nyoro.

The Nyoro are found in Uganda in a region to the east of Lake Albert and to the south and west of the Victoria Nile. They were farmers and once possessed great cattle herds. They were another of the Bantu kingdoms lying in the territory between the lakes of Albert, Tanganyika, and Victoria bearing the most resemblance to the Ganda. Control of interpersonal conflict was handled not only by adjudication in village tribunals but also by procedures of divining and sorcery. Settlement of disputes in the neighborhood had the purpose of restoring good relations rather than imposing punishment for fault. J. Beattie, *Bunyoro: An African Kingdom* (New York, 1960); J. Beattie, "Sorcery in Bunyoro," Witchcraft and Sorcery in East Africa, eds. J. Middleton and E. H. Winter (New York, 1963), 27; J. H. M. Beattie, "Informal Judicial Activity in Bunyoro," *Journal of African Administration*, IX (1957), 188; J. H. M. Beattie, "Neighborliness in Bunyoro," *Man*, LIX (1959), 83; J. H. M. Beattie, "Nyoro Kingship," *Africa*, XXVII (1957), 317; J. H. M. Beattie, "Rituals of Nyoro Kingship," *Africa*, XXIX (1959), 134; J. H. M. Beattie, "The Kibanja System of Land Tenure in Bunyoro, Uganda," *Journal of African Administration*, VI (1954), 18.

4. The Amba.

The Amba live in the westernmost portion of Uganda in the Western Rift valley. They were agriculturists. The village was the largest group and was perceived to have at its core a maximal lineage. Disputes were settled either within the family by the father, who was its governing figure, or by the male members of the village in a moot. The suffering of misfortune through witchcraft or the spirits of the ancestors was viewed to be the consequence of a person's misdeeds. E. H. Winter, *Bwamba: A Structural-Functional Analysis of a Patrilineal Society* (Cambridge, 1956); E. H. Winter, *Bwamba Economy*, East African Studies No. 5 (Kampala, Uganda, and London, 1955), 1-16; E. Winter, "The Aboriginal Political Structure of Bwamba," *Tribes Without Rulers*, eds. J. Middleton and E. Tait (London, 1958), 136; E. Winter, "The Enemy Within: Amba Witchcraft and Sociological Theory," *Witchcraft and Sorcery in Africa*, eds. J. Middleton and E. H. Winter (New York, 1963), 277.

5. *The Alur.*

The Alur occupy a territory in Uganda to the south of the Lugbara people and extending westward for seventy to eighty miles from the Albert Nile and the western shore of Lake Albert. They had an agricultural economy.

The Alur society provided a unique form of structuring social action. It was intermediate between the kinship group and the organization as structures of social action. It also embodied aspects of territorial groupings. It exhibited a hierarchical structure of authority in its territorial structuring of social action. Chiefs and chieflets were drawn from a chiefly lineage. They exercised authority over diverse peoples in their respective territorial jurisdictions. Control of supernatural power supported their exercise of authority. A lineage unit had a corporate and territorial aspect. Authority and law were supported by a sanctioning process of a physical nature. Abuse of authority was in some measure controlled. The chiefdom provided its subjects with greater opportunities for value realization than those offered by competing political and social orders. The subjects supported their receipt of a flow of material benefits from the chief by a counter-flow to him of tribute and services.

The salient aspects of the Alur political organization were as follows:

1. The sharing of a common metaphysical outlook.

2. The assumption of an unquestioned right to rule on the part of those occupying positions of authority and the display of a limited degree of brutal power in the performance of their roles, coupled with the perception by their followers that they possessed an ability to rule.

3. The offering to other peoples of the opportunity to join the society and thereby obtain an improved means for realizing their values.

4. The selection of persons to occupy lesser offices on a basis of their capacity to perform those offices satisfactorily from the standpoint of value realization.

5. The provision of effective means to control the abuse of authority and to escape from situations of abuse of authority.

6. The shared recognition of a common identity and idea of public order reinforced by ritual performance and perceived linkage of the holders of authority with the supernatural world.

7. Possession by those holding authority of sufficient force to maintain their authority in the face of challenge by dissidents.

8. Tolerance of local autonomy by the holders of ultimate authority, coupled with the ability and will to maintain local order and to do so in a manner not likely to cause further disruptions to arise.

A. W. Southall, *Alur Society: A Study in the Processes and Types of Domination* (Cambridge, 1956).

6. The Kamba.

The Kamba live in Kenya on the eastern slopes of the Kikuyu highlands. They were an agricultural people who also possessed considerable livestock, including cattle. Social and political action was structured through the extended family and district units composed of extended families. Age sets determined the warrior and elder groups. A senior council of elders was the administrative and judicial body. Oaths and ordeals were relied upon to establish truth in litigation procedure. A fixed scale of compensation for homicide, injury, adultery, and theft existed. Ritual killing for death by witchcraft and repeated theft was practiced. The basic concerns of the legal system were the protection of the group from witches and incorrigible thieves and the restoration of relations impaired by wrongdoing through the payment of compensation. K. G. Lindblom, *The Kamba in British East Africa* (Upsala, 1916); D. J. Penwill, *Kamba Customary Law* (London, 1951); J. Middleton, "The Central Tribes of the North-Eastern Bantu," *Ethnographic Survey of Africa*, ed. D. Forde, Part V, 72-95.

7. The Sukuma.

The Sukuma live in Tanzania to the south of Lake Victoria. They were agriculturists. About half of them owned cattle. They were organized into a pluralistic society exhibiting aspects of kinship, territorial, age, and associational structures of social action. They were also organized under a chief, with his appointed officials and traditional council of elders. The parish assembly and the council of parish elders were the principal repositories of political power but the chief, the parish headman, and the great commoner also exercised certain political functions. There were three judicial bodies, the chief's court, the headman's court, and the council of parish elders. There was a marked tendency to organize into voluntary associations, consisting of secret societies and dance societies. There was an agricultural association under the control of an official known as the great commoner. Control of the abuse of power by a chief existed through the practice of emigration to another chiefdom, together with the respect for tradition imposed upon him by his elders.

Physical coercion, including imposition of the death penalty, was used to insure respect for the holders of political and judicial offices and to secure the proper performance of these functions. An unusual community sanction existed in the practice of ostracism of those who had failed to observe basic norms important for the preservation of common community interests. While the penalty of ostracism could be lifted by the payment of a small expiatory fine, a recalcitrant offender who failed to mend his ways could be expelled from the community by decision of the parish assembly. H. Cory, *The Indigenous Political System of the Sukuma and Provisions for Political Reform,* East African Studies, No. 2 (Nairobi, 1954); H. Cory, *Sukuma Law and Custom* (London, New York, Toronto, 1953); H. Cory, *The Ntemi: Traditional Rites of a Sukuma Chief in Tanganyika* (London, 1951); B. J. Hartley, *Land Tenure in Usukuma,* Tanganyika Notes and Records, No. 5 (Dar es Salaam, 1938), 17.

Bibliography

Books

Abraham, P. *The Mind of Africa*. Chicago, Toronto, London, 1962.

Abraham, R. C. *The Tiv People*. 2d ed.; London, 1940.

Ajisafe, A. K. *The Laws and Customs of the Yoruba People*. Lagos, 1946.

Allport, F. H. *Theories of Perception and the Concept of Structure*. New York, London, 1955.

Anderson, J. N. D. *Islamic Law in the Modern World*. New York, 1959.

Apter, D. E. *The Political Kingdom in Uganda*. Princeton, 1961.

Arnold, M. B. *Emotion and Personality*, II. New York, 1960.

Ashby, W. R. *Design for a Brain*. New York, 1952.

Beattie, J. *Bunyoro: An African Kingdom*. New York, 1960.

Bentsi-Enchill, K. *Ghana Land Law: An Exposition, Analysis, and Critique*. London, 1964.

Berkowitz, L. *Aggression: A Social Psychological Analysis*. New York, 1962.

Bohannan, P. *Justice and Judgment among the Tiv*. London, New York, Toronto, 1957.

——— (ed.). *Law and Warfare: Studies in the Anthropology of Conflict*. New York, 1967.

———. *Tiv Farm and Settlement*. ("Colonial Research Studies," No. 15.) London, 1954.

———. *Social Anthropology*. New York, 1963.

Busia, K. A. *The Position of the Chief in the Modern Political System of the Ashanti*. London, New York, Toronto, 1951.

Buss, A. H. *The Psychology of Aggression*. New York, London, 1961.

Cagnolo, C. *The Akikiyu: Their Customs, Traditions, and Folklore*. Nyeri, Kenya, 1933.

Carlston, K. S. *Law and Organization in World Society*. Urbana, 1962.

———. *Law and Structures of Social Action*. London, New York, 1956.

Chubb, L. T. *Ibo Land Tenure*. Ibadan, 1961.

Coker, G. B. A. *Family Property among the Yorubas*. 2d ed.; London, Lagos, 1966.

Cory, H. *The Indigenous Political System of the Sukuma and Provisions for Political Reform*. ("East African Studies," No. 2.) Nairobi, 1954.

———. *The Ntemi: Traditional Rites of a Sukuma Chief in Tanganyika.* London, 1951.

———. *Sukuma Law and Custom.* London, New York, Toronto, 1953.

Coser, L. *The Functions of Social Conflict.* Glencoe, Ill., 1956.

Danquah, J. B. *Akan Laws and Customs.* London, 1928.

Dollard, J. *et al. Frustration and Aggression.* New Haven, 1939.

Downes, R. M. *The Tiv Tribe.* Kaduna, Nigeria, 1933.

Durkheim, E. *The Elementary Forms of the Religious Life: A Study in Religious Sociology.* New York, 1954 [?]

East, R. M. *Akiga's Story.* London, 1939.

Edelman, M. *The Symbolic Uses of Politics.* Urbana, 1964.

Eisenstadt, S. N. *From Generation to Generation.* Glencoe, Ill., London, 1954.

Elias, T. O. *Groundwork of Nigerian Law.* London, 1954.

———. *Nigerian Law and Custom.* 3 ed.; London, 1954.

———. *The Nature of African Customary Law.* Manchester, 1956.

Evans-Pritchard, E. E. *Kinship and Marriage Among the Nuer.* Oxford, England, 1951.

———. *The Nuer: A Description of the Modes of Livelihood and Political Institutions of a Nilotic People.* Oxford, England, 1940

———. *Nuer Religion.* Oxford, England, 1956.

———. *Witches, Oracles, and Magic Among the Azande.* Oxford, 1937, reprint 1950.

Fallers, L. A. *Bantu Bureaucracy.* Cambridge, 1956.

Festinger, L. *A Theory of Cognitive Dissonance.* Evanston, Ill. and White Plains, N. Y., 1957.

Field, M. J. *Religion and Medicine of the Gã People.* London, 1937, 1961.

———. *Social Organization of the Gã People.* London, 1940.

Forde, C. D. (ed.). *African Worlds: Studies in the Cosmological Ideas and Social Values of African Peoples.* London, 1954.

Frazer, J. G. *The Golden Bough: A Study in Magic and Religion.* 12 vols. 3rd ed.; London, 1911–15.

Freud, S. *The Ego and the Id.* London, 1927.

———. *The Future of an Illusion.* New York, 1957.

———. *New Introductory Lectures on Psychoanalysis.* New York, 1933.

———. *Totem and Taboo: Some Points of Agreement between the Mental Lives of Savages and Neurotics.* Translated by J. Strachey. New York, 1952.

Fyzee, A. A. A. *Outlines of Muhammedan Law.* 2nd ed.; London, 1955.

Gerth, H. and C. W. Mills. *Character and Social Structure: The Psychology of Social Institutions.* New York, 1953, edition of 1964.

Gluckman, M. *Custom and Conflict in Africa.* Glencoe, Ill., 1955.

———. *The Ideas in Barotse Jurisprudence.* New Haven, London, 1965.

———. *The Judicial Process among the Barotse of Northern Rhodesia.* Glencoe, Ill., 1955.

———. *Order and Rebellion in Tribal Africa.* New York, 1963.

———. *Politics, Law, and Ritual in Tribal Society.* Chicago, 1965.

Goebel, J., Jr. *Cases and Materials on the Development of Legal Institutions.* Brattleboro, Vermont, 1946.

Green, M. M. *Ibo Village Affairs.* London, 1947.

————. *Land Tenure in an Ibo Village* ("Monographs on Social Anthropology," No. 6.). London, 1941.

Greenberg, J. *The Influence of Islam on a Sudanese Religion* ("Monographs of the American Ethnological Society," No. 10.). New York, 1946, p. 1.

Gulliver, P. H. *Social Control in an African Society, A Study of the Arusha: Agricultural Masai of Northern Tanganyika.* London, 1963.

Hall, C. S. and G. Lindzey. *Theories of Personality.* New York, 1957.

Hassan, Malam and Malam Shuaibu. *A Chronicle of Abuja.* Translated by F. Heath. Abadan, 1952.

Haydon, E. S. *Law and Justice in Buganda.* London, 1960.

Herskovits, M. J. *Man and His Works: The Science of Cultural Anthropology.* New York, 1948.

Hobley, C. W. *Bantu Beliefs and Magic.* Rev. ed.; London, 1938.

Hodgkin, T. *Nigerian Perspectives: An Historical Anthology.* London, Ibadan, Accra, 1960.

Hoebel, E. A. *The Law of Primitive Man.* Cambridge, Mass., 1954.

Hogben, S. J. *The Mohammadan Emirates of Nigeria.* London, 1930.

Honigmann, J. J. *Culture and Personality.* New York, 1954.

Hopen, C. E. *The Pastoral Fulbe Family in Gwandu.* London, Ibadan, Accra, 1958.

Howell, P. P. *A Manual of Nuer Law.* London, New York, Toronto, 1954.

Huntingford, G. W. B. *The Nandi of Kenya: Tribal Control in a Pastoral Society.* London, 1953.

————. *Nandi Work and Culture.* London: H.M.S.O., 1950.

Idowu, E. B. *Olódùmaré: God in Yoruba Belief.* London, 1962.

Irstam, T. *The King of Ganda: Studies in the Institutions of Sacral Kinship in Africa.* ("Ethnographical Museum of Sweden, Stockholm, New Series," Pub. No. 8.) Lund, Sweden, 1944.

Kagwa, A. *The Customs of the Baganda,* ed. M. M. Edel. Translated by E. B. Kalibala. New York, 1934.

Kardiner, A. *The Psychological Frontiers of Society.* New York, 1945.

Kenyatta, J. *Facing Mount Kenya: The Tribal Life of the Gikuyu.* London, 1953, first printing, 1938.

Khadduri, M. and H. J. Liebesny. *Law in the Middle East.* Washington, D.C., 1955.

Kluckhohn, C., H. A. Murray, and D. M. Schneider (eds.). *Personality in Nature, Society, and Culture.* 2nd ed.; New York, 1953.

Lambert, H. E. *Kikuyu Social and Political Institutions.* London, New York, Toronto, 1956.

Leach, E. R. *Political Systems of Highland Burma.* London, 1954.

Levine, R. A. *Dreams and Deeds: Achievement and Motivation in Nigeria.* Chicago, London, 1966.

Lewin, K. *A Dynamic Theory of Personality: Selected Papers.* New York, London, 1935.

Lewin, K. *Resolving Social Conflicts.* New York, 1948.

Lewis, C. I. *An Analysis of Knowledge and Valuation.* La Salle, Ill., 1947.

Lindblom, K. G. *The Kamba in British East Africa.* Upsala, 1916.

Linton, R. *The Cultural Background of Personality.* New York, 1945.

————. *The Study of Man: An Introduction.* New York, London, 1936.

Llewellyn, K. and E. A. Hoebel. *The Cheyenne Way: Conflict and Case Law in Primitive Jurisprudence.* Norman, Okla., 1941.

Lloyd, P. C. *Yoruba Land Law.* London, New York, Abadan, 1962.

Lowie, R. H. *Primitive Religion.* New York, 1924.

———. *Social Organization.* New York, 1948.

Lucas, J. O. *The Religion of the Yorubas.* Lagos, 1948.

L. Mair. *Primitive Government.* Baltimore, 1962.

Mair, L. P. *An African People in the Twentieth Century.* London, 1934.

Malinowski, B. *Crime and Custom in Savage Society.* London, 1926.

———. *Magic, Science and Religion.* Glencoe, Ill., 1948, reprint New York.

———. *A Scientific Theory of Culture and Other Essays.* Chapel Hill, N.C., 1944.

Maquet, J. J. *The Premise of Inequality: A Study of Political Relations in a Central African Kingdom.* London, Ibadan, Accra, 1961.

Maslow, A. H. *Motivation and Personality.* New York, 1954.

May, R. (ed.). *Existential Psychology.* New York, 1961.

Meek, C. K. *Law and Authority in a Nigerian Tribe.* London, New York, Toronto, 1937.

Meyerowitz, E. L. R. *The Sacred State of the Akan.* London, 1951.

Middleton, J. *Lugbara Religion: Ritual and Authority Among an East African People.* London, 1960.

Middleton, J. and D. Tait (eds.). *Tribes Without Rulers: Studies in African Segmentary Systems.* London, 1958.

Mill, J. S. *On Bentham and Coleridge.* New York, 1951.

Miller, G. A., E. Galanter, and K. H. Pribram. *Plans and the Structure of Behavior.* New York, 1960.

Mowrer, O. H. *Learning Theory and the Symbolic Processes.* New York, 1960.

Nadel, S. F. *A Black Byzantium.* London, New York, Toronto, 1942.

———. *Foundations of Social Anthropology.* Glencoe, Ill., 1958.

———. *The Nuba: An Anthropological Study of the Hill Tribes in Kordofan.* Oxford, 1947.

———. *The Theory of Social Structure.* Glencoe, Ill., 1957.

Newakamna, O. *The Customary Laws of Succession in Eastern Nigeria.* London, Lagos, 1966.

Norbeck, E. *Religion in Primitive Society.* New York, 1961.

Obi, S. N. C. *The Ibo Law of Property.* London, 1963.

Ogden, C. K. and I. A. Richards. *The Meaning of Meaning.* 8 ed.; New York, London, 1956.

Ollennu, N. A. *Principles of Customary Land Law in Ghana.* London, 1962.

Ortega y Gassett, J. *Concord and Liberty.* New York, 1946.

Osgood, C. E. *Method and Theory in Experimental Psychology.* New York, 1953.

Ottenberg, S. and P. Ottenberg (eds.). *Culture and Societies of Africa.* New York, 1960.

Parsons, T. *The Social System.* Glencoe, Ill., 1951.

Parsons, T. and E. A. Shils. *Toward a General Theory of Action.* Cambridge, Mass., 1951.

Parsons, T. and N. J. Smelser. *Economy and Society: A Study in the Integration of Economic and Social Theory.* Glencoe, Ill., 1956.

Penwill, D. J. *Kamba Customary Law*. London, 1951.

Pound, R. and T. F. Plunkett. *Readings on the History and System of the Common Law*. 3 ed.; Rochester, N.Y., 1927.

Prins, A. H. J. *East African Age-Class Systems*. Groningen, Djakarta, 1953.

Prosser, W. L. *Handbook of the Law of Torts*. 3 ed.; St. Paul, 1964.

Radcliffe-Brown, A. R. *Structure and Function in Primitive Society*. London, 1952.

———. *Taboo*. Cambridge, England, 1939.

Radcliffe-Brown, A. R. and C. D. Forde (eds.). *African Systems of Kinship and Marriage*. London, 1950.

Rahim, A. *The Principles of Muhammedan Jurisprudence*. London, Madras, 1911.

Rattray, R. S. *Ashanti*. London, 1923, 1955.

———. *Ashanti Law and Constitution*. London, 1929, 1956.

———. *Religion and Art in Ashanti*. London, 1927, 1954.

Routledge, W. S. and K. Routledge. *With a Pre-historic People: The Akikiyu of East Africa*. London, 1910.

Redfield, R. *The Primitive World and its Transformations*. Ithaca, 1953.

Rheinstein, M. *Max Weber on Law in Economy and Society*. Cambridge, 1964.

Roscoe, J. *The Baganda: An Account of their Native Customs and Beliefs*. London, 1911.

Ross, E. A. *The Principles of Sociology*. New York, 1920.

Ruitenbeek, H. M. (ed.). *Psychoanalysis and Existential Philosophy*. New York, 1962.

Sargent, S. S. and M. W. Smith (eds.). *Culture and Personality*. New York, 1949.

Schacht, J. *Origins of Muhammedan Jurisprudence*. Oxford, 1950.

Schapera, I. *Government and Politics in Tribal Societies*. London, 1956.

———. *A Handbook of Tswana Law and Custom*. 2 ed.; London, New York, Cape Town, 1955.

Selznick, P. *Leadership in Administration: A Sociological Interpretation*. Evanston, Ill. and White Plains, N.Y., 1957.

Simpson, G. *Conflict and Community*. New York, 1937.

Sinnott, E. W. *Biology of the Spirit*. New York, 1955.

Smith, M. G. *The Economy of Hausa Communities of Zaria*. London, 1955.

———. *Government in Zazzau*. London, New York, Toronto, 1960.

Snell, G. S. *Nandi Customary Law*. London, 1954.

Southall, A. W. *Alur Society: A Study in the Processes and Types of Domination*. Cambridge, England, 1956.

Southwold, M. *Bureaucracy and Chiefship in Buganda*. ("East African Studies," No. 14.) London, 1961.

Spencer, P. *The Samburu: A Study of Gerontocracy in a Nomadic Tribe*. Berkeley, Los Angeles, 1965.

Stenning, D. J. *Savannah Nomads*. London, Ibadan, Accra, 1959.

Sullivan, H. S. *Fusion of Psychiatry and Social Science*. New York, 1964.

Swanson, G. *The Birth of the Gods: The Origin of Primitive Beliefs*. Ann Arbor, 1960.

Thomas, N. W. *Anthropological Report on the Ibo-Speaking Peoples of Nigeria*. London, 1913 and 1914.

Trimingham, J. S. *A History of Islam in West Africa.* London, Glasgow, New York, 1962.

Turner, V. W. *Schism and Continuity in African Society.* Manchester, England, 1957.

Turney-High, H. H. *Primitive War: Its Practice and Concepts.* Columbia, S.C., 1949.

Tylor, E. B. *Primitive Culture.* 2 vols. 2 ed.; London, 1873.

Van Gennep, A. *The Rites of Passage.* Translated by M. B. Vizedom and C. L. Caffee. London, 1960.

Vesey-Fitzgerald, S. *Muhammedan Law.* London, 1931.

Vaihinger, H. *The Philosophy of "As If."* London, New York, 1924.

Wallace, A. F. C. *Culture and Personality.* New York, 1961.

Watt, W. M. *Islam and the Integration of Society.* London, 1961.

Weber, M. *The Sociology of Religion.* Translated by T. Parsons. Boston, 1963.

———. *The Theory of Social and Economic Organization.* Translated by A. M. Henderson and T. Parsons. New York, 1947.

Wheelis, A. *The Quest for Identity.* New York, 1958.

Wiener, N. *Cybernetics.* New York, 1948.

Williams, J. A. (ed.). *Islam.* New York, 1961.

Wilson, G. W. and M. Wilson. *The Analysis of Social Change.* Cambridge, England, 1945.

———. *Good Company: A Study of Nyakyusa Age-Villages.* London, New York, Toronto, 1951.

Winter, E. H. *Bwamba: A Structural-Functional Analysis of a Patrilinear Society.* Cambridge, England, 1956.

Articles

Ajayi, F. A. "The Future of Customary Law in Nigeria." *The Future of Customary Law in Africa.* Leiden: Afrika-Instuut, 1956, p. 42.

Anderson, J. N. D. "Customary Law and Islamic Law in British African Territories." *The Future of Customary Law in Africa.* Leiden: Afrika-Instuut, 1956, p. 70.

Asante, S. K. B. "Interests in Land in the Customary Law of Ghana—A New Appraisal," *Yale Law Journal,* LXXIV (1965), 848.

Baxter, P. T. W., and Butt, A. "The Azande and Related Peoples of the Anglo-Egyptian Sudan and Belgian Congo," *Ethnographic Survey of Africa* (Part IX), ed. D. Forde. London, 1953, p. 119.

Beattie, J. "Sorcery in Bunyoro," *Witchcraft and Sorcery in East Africa,* eds. J. Middleton and E. H. Winter. New York, 1963, p. 27.

Beattie, J. H. M. "Checks on the Abuse of Political Power in Some African States," *Sociologus,* IX (1959), No. 2.

———. "Informal Judicial Activity in Bunyoro," *Journal of African Administration,* IX (1957), 188.

———. "The Kinbanja System of Land Tenure in Bunyoro, Uganda," *ibid.,* VI (1954), 18.

———. "Neighborliness in Bunyoro," *Man,* LIX (1959), 83.

————. "Nyoro Kingship," *Africa,* XXVII (1957), 317.
————. "Rituals of Nyoro Kingship," *ibid.,* XXIX (1959), 134.
Beech, M. "Kikuyu System of Land Tenure," *Journal of the African Society,* XVII (1917–1918), 46, 136.
Berkowitz, L. and J. A. Green. "The Stimulus Qualities of the Scapegoat," *Journal of Abnormal and Social Psychology,* LXIV (1962), 298.
Bienenfeld, R. "Prolegemena to a Psychoanalysis of Law and Justice, Part II—Analysis," *California Law Review,* LIV (1965), 1254.
Biobaku, S. O. "An Historical Sketch of Egba Traditional Authorities," *Africa,* XXII (1952), 35.
Bohannan, L. 'A Genealogical Charter," *Africa,* XXII (1952), 301.
————. "Political Aspects of Tiv Social Organization," *Tribes Without Rulers: Studies in African Segmentary Systems,* eds. J. Middleton and D. Tait. London, 1958, p. 33.
Bohannan, L. and P. Bohannan. "The Tiv of Central Nigeria," *Ethnographic Survey of Africa* (Western Africa, Part VIII), ed. D. Forde. London, 1953.
Bohannan, P. "The Differing Realms of Law," *American Anthropologist,* LXVII² (1965), No. 6., p. 33.
————. "The Migration and Expansion of the Tiv," *Africa,* XXIV (1954), 2.
Brown, P. "Patterns of Authority in West Africa," *Africa,* XXI (1951), 261.
Bruner, J. S. "On Perceptual Readiness," *Readings in Perception,* eds. D. C. Beardslee and M. Wertheimer. Princeton, 1958, p. 686.
Buchanan, K. "The Northern Region of Nigeria: The Geographical Background of its Political Quality," *The Geographical Review,* XLIII (1953), 451.
Busia, K. A. "The Ashanti," *African Worlds,* ed. D. Forde. London, New York, Toronto, 1954, p. 190.
Carlston, K. S. "International Administrative Law: A Venture in Legal Theory," *Journal of Public Law,* VIII (1959), 329.
————. "Psychological and Sociological Aspects of the Judicial and Arbitration Processes," *International Arbitration: Liber Amicorum for Martin Domke,* ed. P. Sanders. The Hague, 1967.
————. "Theory of the Arbitration Process," *Law and Contemporary Problems,* XVII (1952), 631.
Dundas, C. "Native Laws of Some Bantu Tribes of East Africa," *Journal of the Royal Anthropological Institute,* LI (1921), 217.
————. "The Organization and Laws of Some Bantu Tribes of East Africa," *ibid.,* XLV (1915), 234.
Easton, D. "Political Anthropology," *Biennial Review of Anthropology,* ed. B. J. Siegel. Stanford, Calif., 1959, p. 210.
Evans-Pritchard, E. E. "The Morphology and Function of Magic: A Comparative Study of the Trobriand and Zandi Ritual and Spells," *American Anthropologist,* XXXI (1929), 618.
————. "The Nuer of the Southern Sudan," *African Political Systems,* eds. M. Fortes and E. E. Evans-Pritchard. 1 ed. London, 1940, 1962 reprint, p. 272.
————. "The Political Structure of the Nandi-Speaking Peoples of Kenya," *Africa,* XIII (1940), 250.

Fallers, L. A. "Changing Customary Law in Busoga District of Uganda," *Journal of African Administration,* VIII (1956), 139.

――――. "The Politics of Landholding in Busoga," *Economic Development and Cultural Change,* III (1955), 260.

Fallers, L. A. *et al.* "Social Stratification in Traditional Buganda," *The King's Men: Leadership and Status in Buganda on the Eve of Independence,* ed. L. A. Fallers. London, New York, Nairobi, 1964, p. 64.

Fallers, M. C., "The Eastern Lacustrine Bantu (Ganda, Soga)," *Ethnographic Survey of Africa.* (Part XI), ed. D. Forde. London, 1960, p. 40.

Feshbach, S. "The Stimulating Versus Cathartic Effects of Vicarious Aggression Activity," *Journal of Abnormal and Social Psychology,* LXIII (1961), 381.

Forde, C. D., "The Cultural Map of West Africa: Successive Adaptations to Tropical Forest and Grasslands," *Transactions of the New York Academy of Sciences,* Ser. 2, XV (1953), 206.

Forde, D. "The Context of Belief: A Consideration of Fetishism Among the Yako," *Frazer Lecture.* Liverpool, 1958, p. 21.

――――. "The Integration of Anthropological Studies," *Journal of the Royal Anthropological Institute,* LXXVIII (1948), 8.

Forde, D. "Justice and Judgment among the Southern Ibo under Colonial Rule," *African Law: Adaptation and Development,* eds. H. Kuper and L. Kuper. Berkeley, Los Angeles, 1965, p. 79.

――――. "The Yoruba-Speaking Peoples of South-Western Nigeria," *Ethnographic Survey of Africa* (Western Africa, Part IV), ed. D. Forde. London, 1951, p. 1.

Forde, D., and G. I. Jones. "The Ibo and the Ibibio-Speaking Peoples of South-Eastern Nigeria," *Ethnographic Survey of Africa* (Part III), ed. D. Forde. London, New York, Toronto, 1950, p. 25.

Fortes, M. "Human Ecology in West Africa," *African Affairs,* XLIV (1945), No. 174, p. 27.

――――. "Ritual and Office in Tribal Society," *Essays on the Ritual of Social Relations,* ed. M. Gluckman. Manchester, 1962, p. 53.

――――. "The 'Submerged Descent Line' in Ashanti," *Studies in Kinship and Marriage* ("Royal Anthropological Institute Occasional Papers," No. 6), ed. I. Shapera. London, 1963, p. 58.

Frenkel-Brunswik, E. F. "Personality Theory and Perception," *Perception: An Approach to Personality,* eds. R. R. Blake and G. V. Ramsey. New York, 1951, p. 356.

Fried, J. "The Relation of Ideal Norms to Actual Behavior in Tarahumara Society," *Southwestern Journal of Anthropology,* IX (1953), 286.

Geertz, C. "The Impact of the Concept of Culture on the Concept of Man," *Bulletin of the Atomic Scientists,* XXII (1966), No. 4, p. 2.

Gluckman, M. "African Jurisprudence," *Advancement of Science,* XVIII (1962), 439.

――――. "Les Rites de Passage," *Essays on the Ritual of Social Relations,* ed. M. Gluckman. Manchester, 1962, p. 1.

――――. "Rituals of Rebellion in South-East Africa," *Frazer Lecture,* 1952. Manchester, 1952.

Goss, A. E., and G. J. Wischner. "Vicarious Trial and Error and Related Behavior," *Psychological Bulletin,* LIII (1956), 35.

Greenberg, J. "Islam and Clan Organization among the Hausa," *Southwestern Journal of Anthropology*, III (1947), 193.

Gulliver, P. H. "Anthropology," *The African World: A Survey of Social Research*, ed. R. Lystad. New York, Washington, London, 1965, p. 57.

———. "Land Tenure and Social Change among the Nyakyusa," *East African Studies, No. 11.* Kampala, Uganda, 1958.

———. "Structural Dichotomy and Jural Processes Among the Arusha of Northern Tanganyika," *Africa*, XXXI (1961), 19.

Hall, R. de Z. "Nyakyusa Law from the Court Records," *African Studies*, II (1943), 153.

Hartley, B. J. "Land Tenure in Usukuma," *Tanganyika Notes and Records, No. 5,* Dar es Salaam, 1938, p. 17.

Henderson, R. H. "Onitsha Ibo Kinship Terminology: A Formal Analysis and its Functional Applications," *Southwestern Journal of Anthropology*, XXIII (1967), 15.

Hoebel, E. A. "Three Studies in African Law," *Stanford Law Review*, XIII (1961), No. 2, p. 418.

Horton, R. "A Definition of Religion and Its Uses," *Journal of the Royal Anthropological Institute*, XC (1960), 201.

———. "Destiny and the Unconscious in West Africa," *Africa*, XXXI (1961), No. 1, p. 110.

Horton, W. R. G. "God, Man, and the Land in a Northern Ibo Village Group," *Africa*, XXVI (1956), 17.

Huntingford, G. W. B. "Nandi Witchcraft," *Witchcraft and Sorcery in East Africa*, eds. J. Middleton and E. H. Winter. New York, 1963, p. 175.

———. "The Southern Nilo-Hamites," *Ethnographic Survey of Africa* (Part VIII), ed. D. Forde. London, 1953, p. 23.

Janis, I. L. "Motivational Factors in the Resolution of Decisional Conflicts," *Nebraska Symposium on Motivation, 1959,* ed. M. R. Jones. Lincoln, 1959, p. 198.

Jeffreys, M. D. W. "Law among the Nuer," *African Studies*, XVI (1957), 115.

Jones, G. I. "Ibo Age Organization with Special Reference to the Cross-River and North-Eastern Ibo," *Journal of the Royal Anthropological Institute*, XLII (1962), 191.

———. "Ibo Land Tenure," *Africa*, XIX (1949), 309.

Kenyatta, J. "Kikuyu Religion, Ancestor-Worship, and Sacrificial Practices," *Africa*, X (1937), 308.

Kluckhohn, C. "Navaho Witchcraft," *Papers of the Peabody Museum of Archaeology and Ethnology, Harvard University*, XXII (1944). No. 2, p. 51.

Kuper, H. and L. Kuper (eds.). "Introduction," *African Law: Adaptation and Development.* Berkeley, Los Angeles, 1965, p. 3.

Lloyd, P. C. "Agnatic and Cognatic Descent among the Yoruba." *Journal of the Royal Anthropological Institute, I* ([New Series] 1966), 484.

———. "Sacred Kingship and Government Among the Yoruba," *Africa*, XXX (1960), 221.

———. "The Traditional Political System of the Yoruba," *Southwestern Journal of Anthropology*, X (1954), 365.

———. "The Yoruba Lineage," *Africa*, XXV (1955), 234.

Low, D. A. "Religion and Society in Buganda, 1875–1900," *East African Studies, No. 8.* Kampala, Uganda, 1956.

Lowie, R. H. "Hidatsa Men's Societies," *Anthropological Papers of the American Museum of Natural History*, XI (1916), 225.

———. "Military Societies of the Crow Indians," *ibid.*, p. 147.

Mair, L. P. "Baganda Land Tenure," *Africa*, XI (1933), 187.

Malinowski, B. "Culture," *Encyclopedia of the Social Sciences*, IV. New York, 1931, p. 621.

———. "A New Instrument for the Interpretation of Law—Especially Primitive," *Yale Law Journal*, LI (1942), 1237.

Manoukian, M. "Akan and Ga-Adamgme Peoples of the Gold Coast," *Ethnographic Survey of Africa* (Western Africa, Part I), ed. D. Forde. London, 1950, p. 9.

Maslow, A. H. "A Dynamic Theory of Human Motivation," *Understanding Human Motivation*, eds. C. L. Stacey and M. F. de Martino. Cleveland, 1958, p. 26.

Matson, J. N. "Judicial Process in the Gold Coast," *International and Comparative Law Quarterly*, II (1953), 58.

McConnell, R. E. "Notes on the Lugwari Tribe of Central Africa," *Journal of the Royal Anthropological Institute*, LV (1925), 439.

McNeil, E. B. "Psychology and Aggression," *Journal of Conflict Resolution*, III (1959), 195.

Middleton, J. "The Central Tribes of the North-Eastern Bantu," *Ethnographic Survey of Africa* (Part V), ed. D. Forde. London, 1953, p. 11.

———. "The Concept of 'Bewitching' in Lugbara," *Africa*, XXV (1955), 252.

———. "The Political System of the Lugbara of the Nile-Congo Divide," *Tribes Without Rulers: Studies in African Segmentary Systems*, eds. J. Middleton and D. Tait. London, 1958, p. 203.

———. "Some Social Aspects of Lugbara Myth," *Africa*, XXIV (1954), 189.

———. "Witchcraft and Sorcery in Lugbara," *Witchcraft and Sorcery in East Africa*, eds. J. Middleton and E. H. Winter. New York, 1963, p. 257.

Middleton, J. and E. H. Winter (eds.). "Introduction," *Witchcraft and Sorcery in East Africa*. New York, 1963.

Miller, N. E. "Experimental Studies of Conflict," *Personality and the Behavioral Disorders*, ed. J. McV. Hunt. New York, 1944, p. 431.

P. Morton-Williams. "An Outline of the Cosmology and Cult Organization of the Oyo Yoruba," *Africa*, XXXIV (1964), 243.

———. "The Yoruba Ogboni Cult in Oyo," *ibid.*, XXX (1960), 362.

———. "Yoruba Responses to the Fear of Death," *ibid.*, p. 34.

Mukwaya, A. B. "Land Tenure in Buganda: Present Day Tendencies," *East African Studies, No. 1.* Kampala, Uganda, 1953.

Nadel, S. F. "The Kede: A Riverain State in Northern Nigeria," *African Political Systems*, eds. M. Fortes and E. E. Evans-Pritchard. London, New York, Toronto, 1940, pp. 165, 177.

———. "Witchcraft in Four African Societies: An Essay in Comparison," *American Anthropologist*, LIV (1952), 18.

Nader, L. "The Anthropological Study of Law," *American Anthropologist*, LXVII[2] (1965), No. 6, p. 3.

Norbeck, E. "African Rituals of Conflict," *American Anthropologist*, LXV (1963), 1254.

Opler, M. "Themes as Dynamic Forces in Culture," *American Journal of Sociology*, LI (1945), 198.

Opler, M. E. "An Interpretation of Ambivalence in Two American Indian Tribes," *Journal of Social Psychology*, VII (1936), 82.

Osgood, C. E. "Cognitive Dynamics in the Conduct of Human Affairs," *Public Opinion Quarterly*, XXIV (1960), 341.

Ottenberg, S. "Ibo Receptivity to Change," *Continuity and Change in African Culture*, eds. W. R. Bascom and M. J. Herskovits. Chicago, 1959, p. 130.

————. "Inheritance and Succession in Afikpo," *Studies in the Laws of Succession in Nigeria*, ed. J. D. M. Jerrett. London, 1965, p. 33.

————. "The System of Authority of the Afikpo Ibo in Southeastern Nigeria." Ph.D. Thesis, Northwestern, 1957.

Parsons, T. "The Theoretical Development of the Sociology of Religion," *Essays in Sociological Theory Pure and Applied*. Glencoe, Ill., 1949, p. 52.

Partridge, C. "Native Law and Custom in Egbaland," *Journal of the African Society*, X (1911), 422.

Pastore, N. "The Role of Arbitrariness in the Frustration-Aggression Hypothesis," *Journal of Abnormal and Social Psychology*, XLVII (1952), 728.

Peristiany, J. G. "Law," *Institutions of Primitive Society*, eds. E. E. Evans-Pritchard *et al*. Glencoe, Ill., 1956.

Phillips, A. "The Future of Customary Law in Africa," *Journal of African Administration*, VII (1955), No. 4, p. 151.

Pospisil, L. "Kapauku Papuans and their Law," *Yale University Publications in Anthropology*, 1958, No. 54, p. 248.

Provinse, J. H. "The Underlying Sanctions of Plains Indian Culture," *Social Anthropology of North American Tribes*, ed. F. Eggan. 2 ed.; Chicago, 1955, p. 341.

Quartey-Papafio, A. B. "The Native Tribunals of the Akras of the Gold Coast," *Journal of the African Society*, X (1911), 320, 434, XI (1911), 75.

Radcliffe-Brown, A. R. "Preface," *African Political Systems*, eds. M. Fortes and E. E. Evans-Pritchard. London, New York, Toronto. 1940, xiv.

Ramponi, E. "Religion and Divination of the Logbara Tribe of North-Uganda," *Anthropos*, XXXII (1937), 571, 849.

Richards, A. I. "Authority Patterns in Traditional Buganda," *The King's Men: Leadership and Status in Buganda on the Eve of Independence*, ed. L. A. Fallers. London, New York, Nairobi, 1964, p. 256.

————. "Social Mechanisms for the Transfer of Political Rights in Some African Tribes," *Essays on the Ritual of Social Relations*, ed. M. Gluckman. Manchester, 1962, p. 175.

————. "Traditional Values and Current Political Behavior," *The King's Men: Leadership and Status in Buganda on the Eve of Independence*, ed. L. A. Fallers. London, New York, Nairobi, 1964, p. 294.

Sahlins, M. O. "The Segmentary Lineage: An Organization of Predatory Expansion," *American Anthropologist*, LXIII (1961), 322.

Sapir, E. "Symbolism," *Encyclopedia of the Social Sciences*, XIV. New York, 1934, p. 492.

Schapera, I. "Malinowski's Theories of Law," *Man and Culture*, ed. R. Firth. London, 1957, p. 139.

――――. "Some Comments on Comparative Method in Social Anthropology," *American Anthropologist,* IV (1953), 352.

Schwab, W. B. "Kinship and Lineage among the Yoruba," *Africa,* XXV (1955), 352.

Shepardson, M. "Navajo Ways in Government," *Memoir 96, American Anthropological Association,* LXV² (June, 1963), No. 3.

Singer, M. "Summary of Comments and Discussion," *American Anthropologist,* XV (1953), 364.

Smith, M. G. "Exchange and Marketing among the Hausa," *Markets in Africa,* eds. P. Bohannan and G. Dalton. Chicago, 1962, p. 299.

――――. "Hausa Inheritance and Succession," *Studies in the Laws of Succession in Nigeria,* ed. J. D. M. Jerrett. London, 1965, p. 230.

――――. "On Segmentary Lineage Systems," *Journal of the Royal Anthropological Institute,* LXXXVI² (1956), 39.

――――. "The Sociological Framework of Law," *African Law: Adaptation and Development,* eds. H. Kuper and L. Kuper. Berkeley, Los Angeles, 1965, p. 24.

Southwold, M. "Leadership, Authority and the Village Community," *The King's Men: Leadership and Status in Buganda on the Eve of Independence,* ed. L. A. Fallers. New York, London, Nairobi, 1964, p. 210.

Spiro, M. E. "Ghosts, Ifaluk, and Teleological Functionalism," *American Anthropologist,* LIV (1952), 497.

Spiro, M. E. and R. G. D'Andrade. "A Cross-Cultural Study of Some Supernatural Beliefs," *American Anthropologist,* LX (1958), 456.

Stein, M. I. "Creativity and Culture," *Journal of Psychology,* XXXVI (1953), 311.

Stenning, D. J. "Transhumance, Migratory Drift, Migration, Patterns of Pastoral Fulani Nomadism," *Journal of the Royal Anthropological Institute,* LXXXVII (1957), 57.

Tanner, R. E. S. "Law Enforcement by Communal Action in Sukumaland, Tanganyika Territory," *Journal of African Administration,* VII (1955), 159.

Tate, H. R. "The Native Law of the Southern Gikuyu of East Africa," *Journal of the African Society,* IX (1909–1910), 233.

Thorndike, E. I. "The Law of Effect," *American Journal of Psychology,* XXXIX (1927), 212.

Turner, V. W. "Symbols in Ndembu Ritual," *Closed Systems and Open Minds: The Limits of Naivety in Social Anthropology,* ed. M. Gluckman. Chicago, 1964, p. 20.

Wilson, G. "An African Morality," *Africa,* IX (1936), 75.

――――. "Introduction to Nyakusa Law," *ibid.,* X (1937), 16.

――――. "The Nyakyusa of South-Western Tanganyika," *Seven Tribes of British Central Africa,* eds. E. Colson and M. Gluckman. London, 1951, reprint 1961, p. 253.

Wilson, M. "Divine Kings and the 'Breath of Men,'" *Frazer Lecture,* 1952. Cambridge, England, 1959.

――――. "Nyakyusa Kinship," *African Systems of Kinship and Marriage,* eds. A. R. Radcliffe-Brown and D. Forde. London, New York, Toronto, 1950, p. 111.

Wilson, M. H., "Witch Beliefs and Social Structure," *American Journal of Sociology*, LVI (1951), 307.

Winter, E. "The Aboriginal Political Structure of Bwamba," *Tribes Without Rulers*, eds. J. Middleton and E. Tait. London, 1958, p. 136.

————. "The Enemy Within: Amba Witchcraft and Sociological Theory," *Witchcraft and Sorcery in East Africa*, eds. J. Middleton and E. H. Winter. New York, 1963, p. 277.

Winter, E. H. "Bwamba Economy," *East African Studies No. 5*. Kampala, Uganda, and London, 1955.

Index